MANAGING TWENTYFIRST CENTURY ORGANISATION

MANAGING TWENTYFIRST CENTURY ORGANISATION

S. G. BHANUSHALI

Himalaya Publishing House

MUMBAI • NEW DELHI • NAGPUR • BENGALURU • HYDERABAD • CHENNAI • PUNE
LUCKNOW • AHMEDABAD • ERNAKULAM • BHUBANESWAR • INDORE • KOLKATA • GUWAHATI

First Edition : 2006
Reprint : 2011

Published by : Mrs. Meena Pandey
for **HIMALAYA PUBLISHING HOUSE PVT. LTD.,**
"Ramdoot", Dr. Bhalerao Marg, Girgaon, **Mumbai - 400 004.**
Phones: 2386 01 70/2386 38 63, Fax: 022-2387 71 78
Email: himpub@vsnl.com
Website: www.himpub.com

Branch Offices:

New Delhi : "Pooja Apartments", 4-B, Murari Lal Street, Ansari Road, Darya Ganj, **New Delhi - 110 002.** Phone: 23270392, 23278631 Fax: 011-23256286

Nagpur : Kundanlal Chandak Industrial Estate, Ghat Road, **Nagpur - 440 018.** Phone: 2738731, 3296733 Telefax : 0712-2721215

Bengaluru : No. 16/1 (Old 12/1), 1st Floor, Next to Hotel Highlands, Madhava Nagar, Race Course Road, **Bengaluru - 560 001.** Phone : 22281541, 22385461, Telefax: 080-22286611

Hyderabad : No. 3-4-184, Lingampally, Besides Raghavendra Swamy Matham, Kachiguda, **Hyderabad - 500 027.** Phone: 040-27560041, 27550139, Mobile:- 09848130433 Telefax: 040-27560041

Chennai : No. 85/50, Bazullah Road, T. Nagar, **Chennai - 600 017.** Phone: 044-28344020, 32463737, 42124860

Pune : No. 527, "Laksha" Apartment, First Floor, Mehunpura, Shaniwarpeth, (Near Prabhat Theatre), **Pune - 411 030.** Phone: 020-24496323/24496333/32326733

Lucknow : Jai Baba Bhawan, Near Manas Complex, Church Road, Aliganj, **Lucknow - 226 024.** Phone: 0522-2339329, 9305302158, 9415349385

Ahmedabad : No. 114, "SHAIL", 1st Floor, Opp. Madhu Sudan House, C.G.Road, Navrang Pura, **Ahmedabad – 380 009.** Phone: 079-26560126, Mobiles: 09327324149,09314679413

Ernakulam : No. 39/104 A, Lakshmi Apartment, Karikkamuri Cross Rd., Ernakulam, **Cochin – 682011**, Kerala. Phone: 0484-2378012, 2378016, Mob.: 09344199799

Bhubaneswar : 5 Station Square, **Bhubaneswar (Orissa) - 751 001.** Mobile: 9861046007, E-mail:- orissa@himpub.com

Indore : Kesardeep Avenue Extension, 73, Narayan Bagh.Flat No. 302, IIIrd Floor, Near Humpty Dumpty School, Narayan Bagh, **Indore (M.P.) 452 007** Mobile: 09301386468

Kolkata : 108/4, Beliaghata, Main Road, Near ID Hospital, Opp. SBI Bank **Kolkata - 700 010.** Mobile: 09910440956, E-mail:- nkmitra@himpub.com

Guwahati : House No. 15, Behind Prajjyotish College, Near Sharma Printing Press, P.O. Bharalumukh, Guwahati - 781009 (Assam) Mobile: 07439040301; 07439040302

Printed by : Shri Krishna offset Press Delhi-93

PREFACE

Every human activity needs to be bound by an organisation. Organisation provides its constituents, base for their objectives, space for their role and support for their activities. The objectives, vision, mission of the organisation are related to the social milieu in which it functions. Naturally they are to undergo a change as the social relevance of the organisation changes and as the society itself changes. A number of all encompassing changes have taken place in the world milieu from the end of the Second World War. Political, social, economic and technological changes that have taken place have demanded organisational changes. In response to such expectations, people function has come in importance in relation to production, process and finance functions. This is true of business organisation as of all types of organisations. Changes in focal function require matching changes in organisational structure and management perspective. Good and sizable literature has been published on different aspects of organisational structure and management activity that is required to meet the demands and challenges of the world environment. However, there is hardly any comprehensive book encompassing all aspects of organisation and management activities that need to be evolved to meet the changing circumstances of 21st century. This book is an effort in that direction.

Technological changes, especially in the fields of production, process, distribution and information have changed the very context in which an organisation functions. These changes have necessitated upgradation of organisational structure and management style. New organisation and management that is required to address 21st century world environment must be synchronised with the organisational form and management style that is necessary to reap the advantages of the technological developments.

Both these types of changes have altered the inner strength of people from work power to knowledge power and the business organisations have become 'knowledge organisations', 'intelligent organisations'. Naturally, the organisational structure needs to be tuned to empower the 'employee-associates' working in the organisation. Management style has to acquire acumen to develop knowledge power that it needs to discharge its duties and make all efforts to utilise this knowledge fully and effectively. There should remain no positive or negative knowledge gaps in the organisation. This is very necessary to acquire competitive advantage and develop core competence. It is the first function of the management to enrich 'intellectual capital' of the organisation, so that world-class defect free products can be turned out to meet customer criteria. As a result, the management has to organise its employee force into 'teams' wherein communication of ideas, technologies, experiences result into synergic effect to make the product better every time and each time. The management must exercise its leadership to make these teams function most fruitfully.

Management is a social function. As it draws resources from the society, it is its obligation to satisfy all sections of the society. It can discharge this obligation by making its activities purposeful, target-oriented and transparent. It should treat all stakeholders equally and equitably

All these aspects need to be crystallised in the management of 21st century intelligent organisation. I have endeavoured to make all these aspects to be correlated and comprehensive to develop a new management paradigm to be identified as ' Managing 21st Century Organisation'.

Writing such a book is beyond the capacity of an individual. Many individuals and organisations have to cooperate in this endeavour in such a way that they become a cohesive team. I am grateful to the staff of Gayton Library and Civic Centre Library, Harrow, London for making available reference material that made the foundation of this book. I have drawn heavily from the writings of various authors. It is true that once the thinkers express their thoughts, they become the thoughts of the society. Even then it is our duty to express our obligations to them. I have expressed my debt to them at appropriate places.

My whole family has been involved for about two and half years in crafting this book. They have borne with me all moments of hard work, anxiety and patience. My appreciation of the intellect, endurance and patience of my sons Sandeep, Sachin and Sanjay and daughter-in-law, Deepa is beyond expression. I would be failing in my duties if I do not express my feeling of gratefulness towards them. The book would not have been in the present presentable form without their analytical insight and frank comments. My daughters-in-law and grand children have contributed in many ways. The book would not have been completed without their wholehearted involvement and encouragement. My wife, Smita has provided me much needed moral support and restraint so that the book can be through without impairing my health at this advanced age. It is needless to say; all the shortcomings and failings are mine. I request the students, teachers and readers to make constructive suggestions and comments to make the arguments this book more valuable and correct.

I thank wholeheartedly Ms. Meena Pandey and Shri K.N. Pandey of Himalaya Publishing House for publishing the book in such a short time.

— S.G. BHANUSHALI

CONTENTS

1 Development of the Concept of Management 1-32

2 Total Quality Management 33-70

3 Supply Chain Management 71-113

4 Six Sigma Management 114-143

5 Benchmarking 144-163

6 Relationship Marketing 164-190

7 Knowledge Management 191-209

8 Intellectual Capital 210-248

9 Core Competence 249-272

10 Corporate Governance 273-298

11 We will Manage This Way 299-321

LIST OF TABLES

1.1 Groups of Management Theories and Their Exponents (3)
2.1 Deming prize Winning Indian Companies (38)
2.2 Deming's, Juran's and Crosby's Steps for Quality and Management (39)
2.3 Seven Tools of Quality Improvement (42)
2.4 Goals for Different Stakeholders (50)
2.5 Quality Functional Deployment (51)
3.1 Delivery Time Measurement (79)
3.2 Weighted Average for Supplier Delivery Assessment (80)
3.3 Weighted Average for Supplier Defect Rate Assessment (80)
3.4 Quality Measurement (81)
3.5 Defect Rate and Delivery Time (82)
3.6 Performance of Supplier According to Four Latest Records (83)
5.1 Benefits of Benchmarking to the Organisation (146)
5.2 Key Success Factors of a Product (148)
5.3 Members of Benchmarking Team, Their Skills and Experience (152)
5.4 Financial Data of Partner Organisation (158)
5.5 Actual versus Target Performance Matrix (160)
6.1 Components of 4ps (167)
6.2 Dimensions of Service Quality (171)
6.3 Properties of Commercial Relationships (175)
6.4 Transaction Marketing and Relationship Marketing (181)
7.1 Knowledge Gap and Solutions (195)
7.2 Four Step Methods of Managing Knowledge (199)
8.1 Intellectual Capital and Its Components (211)
8.2 Values of Organisations (219)
8.3 Relationship between Value Creation and Value Extraction (220)
10.1 Theoretical Perspectives of Board Role on Corporate Governance (282)
11.1 Value System for Business Organisation (305)
11.2 Organisation Leadership (306)

LIST OF FIGURES

1.1 Basic Human Needs (16)
1.2 Basic Human Needs (17)
1.3 Basic Human Needs (18)
1.4 Basic Human Needs (18)
1.5 Basic Human Needs (18)
1.6 Porter's Five Process Model (25)
2.1 Taguchi Loss Function (36)
2.2 The Deming Cycle (39)
2.3 Transition to Quality Culture in an Organisation (44)
2.4 Transition from Traditional to TQM Organisation (48)
A) Traditional Vertical Organisation (48)
B) Horizontal Organisation (48)
C) TQM Organisation (48)
2.5 The Quality Circle (54)
2.6 Fishbone Diagram (62)
2.7 Pareto Diagram Exhibiting Defects in Bolts (63)
2.8 Flow Chart of Turning Process (64)
2.9 Flow Chart of Streamlined Turning Process (65)
2.10 Gantt Chart- Programming Activities (65)
2.11 Tally Chart and Histogram Exhibiting Car Delivery (66)
3.1 Flow Chart of the Department at the Middle of Production Process in the Division (76)
3.2 Flow Chart of Various Departments in a Division (76)
3.3 Supply Chain Map of an Organisation (77)
3.4 Supplier Monitoring System (79)
3.5 Fuzzy Set of Delivery Days (80)
3.6 Fuzzy Set of Defect Rate (82)
3.7 Weighted Average of Delivery Time (Adoption of Fuzzy Logic) (83)
3.8 Weighted Average of Defect Rate (Adoption of Fuzzy logic) (83)
3.9 Efficient Consumer Response Alliance Model (92)
3.10 An Enterprise Resource Planning System (99)
3.11 An Enterprise Application Integration (110)

3.12 The Generic Value Chain Model (112)
4.1 Distribution in Terms of Standard Deviation (116)
4.2 Taguchi Loss Function (117)
4.3 Pareto Chart Showing Proportion of Causes Leading to Failure (126)
4.4 Histogram Exhibiting Levels of Success (127)
4.5 Cycle Time Target and Achievement (127)
4.6 Areas of Success and Failure (Gantt Chart) (129)
4.7 Organisation of Six Sigma Project Team (132)
5.1 Process Flow in a Pharmaceutical Organisation (154)
6.1 Customer Relationship Life Cycle (179)
6.2 The Customer Grid (187)
6.3 The Sales Grid (188)
6.4 Total Relationship Marketing and Fuzzy Logic (189)
7.1 Transformation of Data, Information and Knowledge (193)
7.2 Process of Knowledge Transformation (194)
7.3 The Generic Value Chain (198)
7.4 Spaces of Knowledge Mapping (203)
7.5 Map Exhibiting Different Divisions and Their Relationship In an Organisation (204)
7.6 Knowledge Nodes and Interrelationship Between Them (205)
8.1 Chain Describing Creation of Value from Intellectual Capital (217)
8.2 Value Creation and Value Extraction (224)
8.3 Radar Chart (247)
9.1 Corporation Tree (253)
9.2 Linkage Between Explicit and Tacit Knowledge and Core Competence (260)

1 Development of the Concept of Management

New production methods introduced in several industries in 18th century dramatically altered functioning of these industries. In 1689 Thomas Sowery created a steam engine to pump water from mines. Thomas Newcomen developed a new version by 1712. James Watt and his partner Matthew Boultton made significant improvements, allowing steam engine to be used in many industrial settings including railroads and steamboats. These new methods included different machines, fresh sources of power and energy and novel forms of organising business and labour. For the first time technical and scientific knowledge was applied to business on a large scale. This growth was enabled by a variety of factors, technological and scientific progress, and improved management, expanding market due to large population, rising incomes and better transport and communication. Firms began to co-ordinate production and marketing across many business units.

Such technological and organisational developments improved productivity of production system in a great way. As an outcome of Industrial Revolution, industrial large scale organisations functioning continually twenty-four hours came into existence in capitalist economy. Naturally, a need was felt to decentralize the system of taking decisions and implementing them so that the large-scale business units can be managed efficiently. A new labour power capable of taking decisions and implementing them efficiently arose during this period. This labour power is management. Management as a new functional discipline was born to satisfy the need of running these large-scale organisations. Managers capable of taking logical decisions on the basis of information, knowledge and practical experience were found to be necessary to run such large business organisations. There was probably no room left for *ad-hoc* decisions. These organisations manifested themselves as joint stock companies. Management of such corporate bodies had to perform variety of functions – namely – (1) to identify and define objectives of business organisation, (2) to plan the policy to achieve these objectives, (3) to charter the process to organise programs and strategies for implementing this policy, (4) to organise all resources that are necessary to implement these programs and to achieve maximum utilization of these resources, (5) to monitor their achievements, and (6) to satisfy all the stakeholders who have contributed and subscribed to this business organisation. Managers introduced a number of practices and tricks to achieve these functions skillfully.

Management practices that were articulated to run these organisations came to be crystalised as theories of management. Management is a social and normative science; the managers do not function as outlined in management theories, but management theories generalize and theorise the various practices of managing organisations successfully practiced by prominent managers. Most of the large-scale industrial organisations came to be spread in capitalist economies, that is why management theories have been developed in capitalist economies. America and European countries have most of the management theories developed there. These business organisations have developed on principles of capitalist economies. That is why, we find that management theories are based on two assumptions; namely maximisation of profit and strike a balance in the relationship between power holding and authority holding factors that have collaborated in production process. Freedom of management theories was limited because of the organisational practices that tried to strengthen the basic framework of capitalist economy. These theories advocate strategies to achieve the above objectives of the joint stock organisations, while encircling in this limited orbit, even references to the political environment in which these organisations were functioning were totally ignored.

Management theories lay emphasis on such aspects that top-level management alone can understand, accept and think necessary to implement. This makes management theories addressed to only top-level management. It has never been considered that it is equally important that middle level and lower level management need to understand and learn these principles.

As in case of any theory in a social science, management theory must possess following five characteristic features to be worthy of a theory. These characteristic features are-

(1) Such a theory must be dealing with the problems of management of that time period.

(2) It must possess that substance to attract attention of concerned people and of general public.

(3) It must meet the needs of those business organisations and personal needs of managers to whom the theory is addressed.

(4) It must exhibit such distinguishing features that managers would realize that it can solve their problems.

(5) The theory must be capable of being presented by persons either through discussions, discourses, seminars, articles or through audio and/or audio-visual tapes in such a way that it would attract the attention of the people.

Any theory that can stand following five tests alone is accepted as a principle. These five tests are – (1) it must meet the needs of managers, (2) people must derive benefits from the concepts of the theory, (3) it must be true through time, (4) it must be capable of being promoted among business world, and (5) it must be capable of holding the organisation in its form.

A theory in the science of management, as of any accepted theory in any science, must be based on causal relationship as needed by inductive and deductive reasoning. Theory means systematic explanation. Theory is a supposition or a system of ideas explaining something, especially based on general principles. A theory is a structure that describes the working and interpretations of the various aspects of some phenomenon. Theory building involves observation of certain phenomenon over a reasonable long period by drawing representative sample to make generalization, which can be later on extrapolated, to specific situations faced by managers. In that sense management theory is nothing but generalization of good or bad experiences, generalization of cause and effect relationship, generalization of policies, strategies and problems to context. Prof. Sampat Singh has identified three models of education prevalent in the field of management. They are – (1) Professional's model, (2) Pragmatist's model, and (3) Humanist's model. It must be full of knowledge that is relatively applicable to various situations. Its assumptions, principles and systems must be such that they are helpful to managers in explaining and analyzing causal factors of any business situation. It must posses the strength that we should be able to forecast the outcome of our alternative actions.

The six theories that have been accepted till now are: (1) Bureaucratic theory of management, (2) Scientific theory of management, (3) Administrative theory of management, (4) Human relations theory of management, (5) Neo-human relations theory of management, and (6) Guru theory of management. All these theories are related to organisational management in capitalist system. These theories are based on certain assumptions and certain models of organisational structure and organisational technology. They are based on general understanding of how should the management be or should be in an organisation. It is necessary that if a theory is to be accepted, it must have utility rather than being correct. The information in respect of thinkers expounding these theories is presented in Table 1.1.

Table 1.1
Groups of management Theories and Their Exponents

Groups of management theories	*Main exponents of these theories*
Bureaucratic Theory	P. Blou, H. Brown, M. Krozier, E. Jakuson, Max Waber, Michaels, Thompson
Scientific Theory	Fredrick W. Taylor, Henry Gant, Frankand Lilian Gilbrath
Administrative Theory	Chester Bernard, Henry Fayol, M.P. Follet, J.D. Muni, M.P. Sloan, Herbert A. Simon
Human Relations Theory	T.N. Whitehead, E. Mayo, C.A. Brown, F.J. Rothlisberger, W.J. Dickson, George Hamons
Neo-Human Relations Theory	Chris Argyris, W.G. Bennis, R. Blake, J. Mautons, Fredrick Herzberg, R. Likert, Douglas McGregor, Abraham Maslow, E.H. Shane, D.C. McClelland, Paul Hersey, Kenneth Blankchart
Guru Theory	Peter Drucker, Tom Peters, Michael Porter, R.M. Canter, Lee Iacocca, K. Blanchart, Philip Kotler, Gary Hamel, Henry Mintzberg, M. Mucormac.

Discussion of these six management theories will enlighten us on the process of management in 20th century and enable us to discuss what should be the nature of strategies managing business organisation in the 21st century.

Bureaucratic Theory of Management

The logical correlation in the behaviour of people while social changes take place in capitalist system, plays an important role in developing a system of management. An action or an organisation system is logical if its objectives can be known easily from that action or organisational system. In such a situation people believe that the directive and the person giving the directive has the same element of divinity and has sole legal authority to give directive. People obey such directives. The organisational system so created is called bureaucracy. Concepts of legality, justice and authority are the foundation of this theory. Max Weber's theory pronounces that, in this stable and forecastable future rational bureaucratic organisation, we find that there is a long line of hierarchy, there is a network of rules, all things are looked objectively, there are full-time officers, there is a system of concentrating on the way of life and to distinguish between public behaviour and private behaviour. Bureaucracy is the most logical and rational structure of large organisations. Bureaucracies are founded on legal and rational authority that is based on law, rules and procedures. Positional authority of a superior over a subordinate stems from legal authority. Charismatic authority stems from personal qualities of an individual. Efficiency in bureaucracy comes from – (1) clearly defined and specialized functions, (2) use of legal authority, (3) hierarchical form, (4) written rules and procedures, (5) technically trained bureaucrats, (6) appointment to position based on technical expertise, (7) promotion based on competence, and 8) clearly defined career path. We find that there is a stable social and organisational framework based on particular functions and roles even if the organisation goes on becoming more complex in the modern system. As a result, we come to know that managers still believe in the Weberian bureaucratic theory of management.

Scientific Theory of Management

This is the second set of theories to explain the techniques to improve the productivity of physical labourers to the maximum extent and to enable them to concentrate their attention on factory work. These theories are of such nature that they cannot be practiced in pure form. Even then it must be admitted that they proved in the twentieth century as to how the framework of work can be conceptualised. Principles of scientific management are practised to a great extent even today. We find that in organisations or factories, scientific theory of management is implemented on shop floor where physical production is done and bureaucratic theory of management is practised in administrative department.

Fredrick W. Taylor wrote a book 'Principles of Scientific Management' (1911). He made hundreds of experiments and found that most of the jobs are done inefficiently and cause loss of labour, money and time. Labourers were performing jobs at the direction of the supervisor, which had no reason or rhyme. He wrote, 'The old fashioned dictator does not exist under scientific management. The man at the head of the business under scientific management is governed by rules and laws which have been developed through hundreds of experiments just as much as workman is, and the standards developed are equitable'.

According to him the objectives of scientific management are – (1) the development of a science for each element of a man's work and replace the rule of thumb methods, (2) the scientific selection, training and development of workers instead of allowing them to choose their own tasks and train them as best as they could, (3) the development of hearty co-operation between workers and management to ensure that work would be carried out in accordance with scientifically devised procedures, (4) the division of work between workers and the management is almost on the basis of equal shares, each group taking over the work for which it is best fitted, instead of former condition in which responsibility largely rested with the workers.

Based on these principles and proved on the basis of his experiments Taylor developed techniques of accurately measuring the time required and movements done by a worker in doing a job. He prepared methods to measure time required for each job and reduce it to minimum extent. He also found out method to study movements done by a worker while performing a job and reducing them to minimum so as to save his labour. For that, he selected the jobs done by labourer, divided them into small and simple parts and scientifically proved how time and movements can be saved by following measures developed by him; so their performance can be maximised and productivity can be improved. He based his theory on a unit of time. He believed that the principle of maximising efficiency of labourers can be achieved by pointing out the loss the nation suffers on account of inefficiency and scientific management alone can remove it. Science of management based on specifically decided laws, principles and rules is the true science. That is why he advocated an approach to industrial management that is developed by following certain objective techniques. He explained the importance of deciding to which industrial organisations this theory of management can be applied because organisational systems need to have acquired certain characteristic features. These features are –(1) there must be clear delineation of authority, (2) responsibility of each employee must be clearly demarcated, (3) planning should be separated from operations. Management should plan and organise the work by differentiating physical work from intellectual work, (4) management must have instituted incentive scheme for workers, (5) management should not interfere into day-to-day work of the employees. This he named 'management of exception', (6) every employee should be given specific task and he must be fully trained for that task. Labourers should embody these skills and actually put them into effect. As a result everybody would know what management expects from him, what is his responsibility and what incentives is he to get for doing work diligently and honestly. This improves the relation between management and labourers. All workers will become efficient in their work because they have mastered the skill and thereby achieve work of highest order.

Henry Gantt developed 'Gantt Chart' (Please refer to figure 2.10) which is used for scheduling multiple overlapping tasks over a time period. He focused on motivational schemes, emphasising the greater effectiveness of rewards for good works rather than penalties for poor work. He developed a pay incentive system with a guaranteed minimum wage and bonus system for people on fixed wages. He focused on importance of qualities of leadership and management skills in building effective industrial organisation.

Frank and Lillian Gilbreth developed a method by focusing on identifying elemental motions in work, the way these motions were combined to form methods of operation and basic time each motion took. They believed that it was possible to design work methods whcse time could be estimated in advance, rather than relying on observation-based time studies. Frank Gilbreth actually filmed physical labour movement. Study of such a film enables the manager to break down a job into its component parts and streamline the process. The Gilbreths believed that there was 'one best way' to perform an operation. However, this 'one best way' could be replaced when a better way was discovered. Gilbreth, on the basis of his research developed two concepts — motion study and time study. He defined motion study as dividing work into most fundamental elements possible, studying these elements separately and in relation to another and from these studied elements, when timed, methods can be developed to reduce waste to the minimum. The time study is defined as a searching scientific analysis of methods and equipments used or planned in doing a piece of work, development in practical detail of the best way of doing it and determination of time required. The Gilbreths developed symbols of operator charts to represent various elements of task such as search, select, grasp, transport, hold and others. This graphical symbol chart was named 'THREBLIG' — Gilbreth spelt backward.

Scientific management is based on following four principles –

(1) Scientific methods should be developed for each part of the work and they should be followed in place of *ad-hoc* methods of decision-making.

(2) An objective method should be developed for selecting labourers and it should be implemented. They should be thoroughly trained. Their abilities should be fully developed. And these methods should be practised in place of workers deciding their own method of work and preferring a system of training of their own choice.

(3) Management should treat workers well and behave with them in spirit of co-operation so that they would do every task on scientific basis developed for doing the work.

(4) Work and responsibility should be distributed equally and in a balanced manner between management and workers.

Taylor's views of motivation of workers have had a profound influence through the century until the present day. He believed that man is a rational human being and would make economic choices based on degree of monetary reward. This led him to devise payment systems that closely related the kind of effort he sought with level of rewards offered.

Taylor's impact has been so great that people still believe in his principles. He developed a concept of work design, work measurement, production control and other functions, that completely changed the nature of industry. Before the introduction of scientific management departments such as work-study, personnel, maintenance and quality control did not exist. Scientific management is also known as 'classical organisational theory' of management. Focus of this theory is on the structure of organisation, as a result scientific management theory led to evolution of bureaucratic structure.

Administrative Theory of Management

This set of theory concentrates on specialisation and hierarchy system that is necessary to reach the efficiency of business organisation to the highest level. These theories are founded on four principal principles, namely – (1) division of labour – every work should be divided in manageable tasks and should be done by a group of labourers specialised in doing this task. This improves quality of work, saves time, money and tools, (2) representation according to work and functional process – every worker should be part of a group to perform the work in which he is specialised. Thus, he would represent that group of workers, (3) organisational structure – The organisation should consist of hierarchy of authorities wherein every level of management has specific task to perform. The lower level of employees in the hierarchy should work as per the directions and orders received from higher level management, (4) scope of control-supervisors and managers above that level have a specific authority and that determines the span of control. Higher authorities have wider span of control. Some authors add a few more principle like discipline, integration of authority, unidirectional directives, remuneration, subjugation of individual interest in relation to public interests, centralization and feeling of co-operation, togetherness are these principles.

Henri Fayol emphasised, in his theory, importance of the manager and the functions of management. He is known as the father of modern management. He developed a framework for studying management. He prescribed five functions of management, namely, plan, organise, command, co-ordinate and control. His fourteen principles of management included — (1) division of work, (2) authority and responsibility, (3) discipline, (4) unity of command, (5) unity of direction, (6) subordination of individual interests to general interests, (7) remuneration of personnel, (8) centralization, (9) scalar chain, (10) order, (11) equity, (12) stability of tenure of personnel, (13) initiative, and (14) *espirit de corps* (union is strength).

Mary Parker Follett developed a theory according to which the organisation tries to satisfy (a) the universal goal, (b) the universal principle, and (c) the law of situation. The universal goal of an organisation is an integration of individual effort into a synergic whole. The universal principle is a circular or reciprocal response emphasising feed back to the sender. This is the concept of two-way communication. Law of situation emphasises that there is no one best way to do anything, but that all depends upon the situation.

Henri Fayol argued that 'solution of any problem depends upon identifying causal factors creating that problem and developing a system in which such causal factors will not crop up in certain circumstances. An efficient framework of rational thinking of management is developed out of such system'.

The thought advocated by this theory is widely criticized because it creates a long chain of hierarchy and control. Even then we find that the system in which the business organisations of today are structured is based on the principles outlined in these theories. Administrative system seems to exist even today to keep managers and officers under control. Fully integrated business organisations of today are framed on this model. Major limitation of these theories is that, the scope of authority of every individual being limited, a long hierarchy of authority needs to be created.

Chester Barnard developed the concepts of strategic planning and acceptance theory of authority. Strategic planning is the formulation of major plans or strategies, which guide the organisation in pursuit of major objectives. He argued that top executives have to perform three functions – (1) establish and maintain an effective communication system, (2) hire and retain effective personnel, and (3) motivate these personnel. Acceptance theory of authority states that managers only have as much authority as employees allow them to have. The acceptance theory of authority suggests that authority flows downward but depends upon acceptance by the subordinates. The acceptance of authority depends upon four conditions. They are – (1) employees must understand what the managers want them to do, (2) employees must be able to comply with the directive, (3) employees must think that the directive is in keeping with organisational objectives, and (4) employees must think that the directive is not contrary to their personal goals. Every employee has a zone of indifference or a range within which each individual would willingly accept orders without consciously questioning authority. It is up to the organisation to broaden each employee's zone of indifference so that manager's orders would be obeyed.

Herbert A. Simon developed 'A Behavioral Model of Rational Choice'. He argued that corporations try to earn just 'enough profit' and therefrom derive 'enough satisfaction'. Business organisations decide level of our expectations considering their needs, vigour, resources and urgency to earn satisfaction. Then they compare their success or failure, accomplished things with the level of expectations decided by them. Organisations are satisfied if performance stands to the level of expectations. However, the organisation analyses in this situation that the level of expectations fixed by it was not low and revise whether a correct stock has been taken of situational performance. If actual performance is greater than expectations, the organisation objectively analyses its success and evaluates the quality of its performance. If actual performance falls short of expectations then the organisation undertakes a program of improving quality of the source of information as well as the quality of information, capabilities and processes.

Human Relations Theory of Management

This group of theories is promulgated to humanise relations in various sections of society without obstructing the free business. It is necessary from social and economic point of view that there must be free competitive atmosphere between business organisations. But, having disputing and quarrelling relations between business organisations is socially and economically harmful to the society. The objective of human relations theory of management is like that of scientific theory, namely, to control groups of labourers and integrate their behaviour with that of the organisation. The idea of preaching or advising labour class to establish human relations is given importance in these theories. As these theories emphasise establishing relations with labourers, there is no need to reorganise the structure of the organisation. What is important is to change the strategies adopted by management.

Human relations theory is evolved out of research project that examined relation between production and atmosphere at work place. It was revealed that productivity of labourers improves if cordial relations are established with labourers and supervision is reduced. Essence of this theory can be expressed in following six points.

(1) It is necessary to concentrate our attention on people and relations with them rather than emphasising technical and economic factors in management.

(2) People behave in a particular way in organised situation.

(3) To induce, to initiate people is an important part in human relations.

(4) It is necessary to induce the whole group of labourers to create co-operation and co-ordination among the members of that group. Unless this is done no work can be realized from them.

(5) Both the individual and organisational objectives can be simultaneously satisfied by creating cordial human relations.

(6) Both, individuals and business organisations try to achieve maximum out of minimum inputs. That is, they try to achieve maximum efficiency.

T.N. Whitehead, Elton Mayo and George Homans under the leadership of Fritz Roethlisberger developed a theory of human relations. Mayo developed the concept of Hawthorne effect trying to find out the bias that occurs when people know that they are being studied. Hawthorne studies are significant because they demonstrated the important influence of human factors on worker's productivity. There were four major phases to the Hawthorne studies – (1) the illumination experiment, (2) the relay assembly group experiments, (3) the interviewing program, and (4) the bank wiring group studies. The intent of these studies was to determine the effect of working conditions on productivity.

(1) The illumination experiments tried to determine whether lighting would lead to increased productivity. Whether the worker group produced more when lights were turned up or down. It was discovered that this increased productivity was the result of the attention received by the group.

(2) The relay assembly group workers, worked in a special, separate area, were given breaks and had the freedom to talk. The group was continuously observed by supervisors. The supervisor consulted them prior to any change. However, the result was inconclusive.

(3) The interviewing program was conducted to find out whether productivity of workers who complained frequently about production had their complaints as a symptom of some underlying problem on the job, at the home or in person's part.

(4) The bank wiring group studies were thoroughly analysed. Increase in productivity was attributed to group dynamics. The conclusion of the Hawthorne studies was that there was no cause and effect relationship between working conditions and productivity. Worker's attitude was found to be important in determining his productivity. But the studies proved that attention to workers increases productivity.

Attention to develop human relations was given out of the necessity of attracting minds of labourers so that they would integrate with the objectives of the business organisation. If we can create familial atmosphere in the business organisation without disturbing the authoritative hierarchy and specialization, then we can bring under control labourers behaving in a different way than expected by the management. If authority is exercised under the pretext of showing parental care for the labourers then they respond positively to the actions of the management.

Informal groups in business organisation are so eager to establish relations with somebody, that they are ready to compromise with any group that shows social bondage with them. That means, it is easier to hold labourers psychologically. Such informal groups hold individuals and organisation hold informal groups. This system of providing psychological security to the workers was welcome by both, the managers and the labourers alike. Informal work groups have greater influence on productivity than the formal organisational structure. This theory seems to have substantiated only one side of truth, even then there is some truth in what this theory preaches. If management treats labourers kindly and skillfully, then workers, having hidden desire to have relations with somebody, can be made to co-operate in the production activity. This amply clarifies that there is positive relationship between good and cordial relations and productivity of labourers. If labourers are treated positively, if they are shown they are cared for; the improvement in human relations improves productivity.

Discontent among workers is the outcome of bad management. Human relations were stretched because the contact between top management and labourers was lost. This happened because the organisation of business units became huge and complex, specialisation went on increasing and technical development increased specialisation. Uncomfortable human relations increased the cost of production and there was an urgent need to reduce the same. All these factors made maintaining cordial human relations more acceptable to the management.

Social theories of management increased expectations of people from such theories. Improved human relations reduced the importance of trade unions. Productivity increased because conflict was replaced by co-operation. As the need of all employees of psychological satisfaction was fulfilled the very causes of conflict were done away with. Atmosphere in the organisation became conducive to increase production and productivity and improve quality.

Neo-Human Relations Theory of Management

Effect of these theories was found to be intense on managements in Europe and the USA. These theories are practised in the form of evaluation of performance of employees and consultation with them, training them as frequently as possible. Employees expect new opportunities in their work and they want to develop on the basis of that. If management functions in this way, employees will develop positive attitude towards work and would participate in achievement of the objectives of the organisation. Workers should be given an opportunity to do responsible and meaningful work. This is the basic foundation of neo-human relations theory of management.

Chris Argyris argued that following bureaucratic or pyramidal values lead to poor, shallow and mistrustful relationships. Bureaucratic values do not permit natural and free expression of feelings; such relationships are phony, non-authentic and result in decreased interpersonal competence. Without interpersonal competence or a 'psychologically safe' environment the organisation becomes a breeding ground for mistrust, inter-group conflict, rigidity and so on. This leads to decrease in organistional success in problem solving. On the other hand, if humanistic or democratic values are adhered to in an organisation, trusting, authentic relationships will develop in the organisation. This will improve interpersonal competence, inter-group co-operation, flexibility and increase organisational effectiveness. It is the environment in which people are treated like human beings, both organisational members and the organisation itself are given an opportunity to develop to the fullest potential and there is an attempt to make work more exciting and challenging.

In adhering to humanistic or democratic values we treat human beings as a person with a complex set of needs, all of which are important in his work and in his life. These humanistic or democratic values, as described by Chris Argyris are —

(1) The important human relationships are not only those related to achieving the organisation's objectives but those related to maintaining the organisation's internal systems and adapting to the environment as well.

(2) Human relationship increases effectiveness as all the relevant human behaviour (rational and interpersonal) becomes conscious, discussable and controllable.

(3) In addition to direction, controls and rewards and penalties, human relationships are most effectively influenced through authentic relationships, internal commitment, psychological success and the process confirmation.

Thus, Chris Argyris argues that it is necessary to adopt humanistic approach in behaving with labourers. Specialization and hierarchy should be reduced to the minimum. Management should behave as it talks and fulfill the promises so that labourers develop trust and relationship. There should be more emphasis on rewarding the performance than punishing failures. Management theory of achieving oneness with organisational objectives argue that organisation must create an atmosphere that will enable people to develop themselves into empowered personality. The structure of organisation must be such that needs of individual development and needs of productivity of organisation will remain co-ordinated with each other. The same thought is at the core of the neo-human relations theory of management.

Fredrick Herzberg contributed to neo-human relations concept by developing two theories of motivation. One is hygiene theory and the second is motivation theory.

Hygiene theory of motivation includes job environment. Hygiene factors include – (1) the company, (2) policies and administration of the company, (3) the kind of supervision under which labourers perform their jobs, (4) interpersonal relations, (5) working conditions, (6) salary, (7) status, and (8) security. Herzberg argues that these factors do not lead to higher level of motivation. But without these factors labourers remain dissatisfied and therefore it is difficult to motivate them. The second part of the Herzberg's motivation theory involves what people actually do on the job. The motivators are – (1) achievement, (2) recognition, (3) growth and advancement, and (4) interest in job. These factors result from internal generators in employees. If we have to achieve objectives of the organisation, hygiene approach and motivation approach must be done simultaneously. It is necessary that you treat the people as best as you can so they have minimum dissatisfaction. Treat people in such a way so that they get achievement, recognition for achievement, interest and responsibility and they can grow and advance in their work.

Working environment affects individuals and groups differently. Good working environment provides an individual at least sufficient for his basic needs, adequate security; it provides him an identity, provides him comradeship, freedom from boredom and interest during his working life. Working environment gives an individual self-fulfillment because of creating interest in job and job satisfaction and most importantly adores his status.

Good working environment boosts the morale of the group, helps the group to achieve objectives set by the organisation, and helps to develop adequate co-operation among members of the group. It motivates the group to do its best, maintain good human relations in the organisation and improves relations between management and trade union.

Thus, Fredrick Herzberg argued in his theory that healthy attitude affects performance of workers positively. Work empowerment helps to motivate the workers. Both these factors are of equal importance. Managers find this theory attractive because this technique of improving productivity can be effectively implemented even in existing organisational system. These principles were incorporated in the programs implemented in many countries to improve the quality of life of the labourers.

David C. McClelland concluded on the basis of findings of his research that the need for achievement (n-ach in short) is a distinct human motive. The motive of need for achievement can be isolated and assessed in any group. People set moderately difficult but potentially achievable goals. In biology this is known as 'overload principle'. Achievement motivated people are always more concerned with personal achievement than with the rewards for success. They get satisfaction from solving difficult problem. They have gambler's itch. They regard monetary reward as a means to assess their progress and compare their achievement with other people.

On the basis of these results of his research he developed training programs for business people to increase their achievement motivation. In the same way workers can be motivated to achieve goals that are little far away but are not unachievable. Achievement motivated people are the backbone of the organisation. However, such people should not have high need for affiliation ('n-affi' in short) because such people need support of others and cannot take decisions independently. Therefore, such managers need to be trained in human skills and patience for being effective managers.

McClelland's concept of achievement motivation is related to Herzberg's motivation hygiene theory. People with high achievement motivation tend to be interested in the motivators (the job itself).

Dr. Rensis Likert conducted a research on human behaviour within organisations and examined different types of leadership styles. On the basis of this study he asserted that maintaining good labour relations and high productivity, optimum utilisation of resources enables the organisation to earn maximum profits. The form of organisation that makes maximum use of its human capacity has highly effective work groups linked together in an overlapping pattern by other similarly effective groups.

He has identified four management styles.

These are –

(1) *Exploitation – Authoritative System* – In this management system decisions are imposed on subordinates, motivation is characterized by threats, high level of management have great responsibilities but lower levels have virtually none; there is little communication and no joint teamwork.

(2) *The Benevolent – Authoritative System* – In this management system leadership is condescending form of master-servant trust. Motivation is achieved by rewards. Managerial personnel carry responsibility but lower level management has no responsibility. There is little communication and little teamwork in the organisation.

(3) *The Consultative System* – Supervisors are the leaders in this management system. Supervisors have substantial but not complete trust in their subordinates. People are motivated by granting rewards: labourers are involved to some extent. High proportion of personnel, especially those at higher levels shoulder the responsibility of achieving organisation goals. There is some vertical as well as horizontal communication. The organisation has moderate amount of teamwork.

(4) *The Participative Group System* – This type of organisation is the optimum solution of maintaining cordial labour relations. Supervisors are the leaders. They have complete confidence in their subordinates. People are granted economic rewards based on goals that have been set in participation. Personnel at all levels carry and fulfill the responsibility of achieving organisational goals. There is good and meaningful communication. There is substantial amount of co-operative teamwork.

Rensis Likert recommended this fourth type of organisation as ideal. This is the profit-oriented organisation and it has concerns for human beings. All organisations should adopt this system. Changing organisational structure from its present state to ideal is bound to be painful and long-winded. But this exercise is necessary if organisation wants to achieve maximum rewards. If the organisational structure is to be transferred into a labour friendly structure, four features of effective management need to be put into practice. They are – (1) The organisation should discard old system of rewards and threats and instead institute modern principles and techniques to foster motivation to work. (2) Employees should be seen as people having their own needs, desires and values and their self worth must be maintained and enhanced. (3) The organisational structure should be tightly knit. Highly effective groups of employees committed to achieving objectives of the organisation should be built, and (4) Supportive relationships characterized by mutual respect should be developed within each group.

The participative groups should have at their centre work groups. The dynamics of these work groups should be highlighted by easy interaction between members of groups playing their respective roles and the members must have skilled leadership qualities. Such work groups must have a long history of existence so that they have well established, relaxed working relationship. Members of the work group need to have high degree of mutual trust so that they are loyal to each other and to the group. The norms, values and goals of the work group should be an expression of the values and needs of the members. All the work groups in the organisation should keep goals of each group in harmony with the goals of each other. Likert calls this function of members of work groups 'lingkingpin'.

Likert's theory is commonly known as 'system four' theory. It is democratic in nature. His each successive model of management, which are outlined in foregoing paragraphs, is an improvement on earlier model. Individuals working in companies must be organised in groups and they must be included in the official structure of organisational decision making system. These groups are to be so integrated with each other that labourers become members of more than one group at a time. These groups having become overlapped, there would emerge 'linking up' between these groups and their individual members. There is a positive correlation between the mental inclination of workers and their performance (As we will discuss later the present systems of total quality management, six sigma management, supply chain management, bench marking and total relationship marketing advocate formation of teams with overlapping memberships). This theory emphasises the point that groups of labourers, their interrelationship and practical importance of profit and loss are positively correlated. Likert developed a technique of measuring the status of the business organisation on the basis of inducement, communication, interaction, taking decision, fixing objectives, control and performance. This was done because mental situation of labourers is reflected in these factors.

Managers on the strength of their leadership can improve productivity of labourers by inducing people working under them. Managerial leadership can create feeling among people working in the organisation that interaction and friendly relations among all are helpful in improving productivity. That means, interaction and friendly relations enhance and maintain importance of labourers. Naturally, the measures and methods of psychological empowering of workers would be different in each of the above-discussed four categories of organisations.

The theory of 'Managerial Grid' developed by Robert Blake and Jane Moutone is based on the 'Leadership' theory of Rensis Likert. 'Ability' and 'Capacity to enter any field' are the two leadership factors considered in this theory. 'Direction given to workers' and 'direction given to production' are the two aspects of leadership. The characteristic feature of this theory is to bring these two concepts together. Management style depends upon these two aspects and it is understanding managerial class, people working under them, and colleagues and expression of these understandings in behaviour while working. This theory argues, that manager is an ideal who commands confidence of people working under him, who takes care of their interests, welfare and development but at the same time uses resources in such a way as to achieve maximum utilization and productivity. This management style enables the organisation and people to achieve both the things simultaneously, namely, to register success in life and to improve productivity as well as profitability.

Paul Hersey and Kenneth Blanchard in their theory of 'Situational Leadership' argue that effective leadership is the leadership system that is very easily acquired in a given situation. Managerial behaviour has two aspects, his behaviour about work and his behaviour about interrelationship. He should not develop one-way communication of directing persons to do work. He should endeavour to develop two-way communication by establishing inter-relationship. He should hear junior's thoughts, extend social and psychological support and give them mental power. This theory has given importance to achieve intellectual as well as mental maturity by enabling people to show desire to improve their behaviour. Maturity of individuals may be different with reference to different works.

Douglas McGreggor propagated theories 'X' and 'Y'. The first is the theory of 'X' assumptions. McGreggor argued that, generally people do not like to work; their attitude is to avert work. People should be coerced, should be controlled, should to be directed and if required must be shown fear of punishment so as to achieve the objectives of the organisation. Generally people try to avoid responsibility, their ambitions are limited; but most importantly they need security and direction about work. That is why managers rely more on granting awards, promises, threats and coercive methods. Managers implementing such string measures are known as 'X' managers. The theory expounding soft measures as described by McGreggor is 'Y' theory. This theory propagates that labourers can be induced to do work by measures to mend their mind and establishing communication with them. If managers can provide to the workers satisfaction from their work, workers would acquire knowledge of inherent features of the work and the production will increase. To create an atmosphere in the organisation to enable the workers to satisfy their own expectation is the function of the management.

Abraham Maslow has described five types of needs that are basic to the human being. They are— (1) Physiological needs, (2) Safety needs, (3) Love, (4) Esteem, and (5) Self-actualisation or self-fulfillment. He arranged them in a series of different levels or in order of importance. Behaviour of an individual is usually determined by his strongest need. Manager should have understanding about the needs that are commonly most important to people. There seems to be hierarchy into which human being arranges his needs. To begin with his physiological needs like food, clothing, shelter are most important and other needs have lesser strength of need. (Figure 1.1)

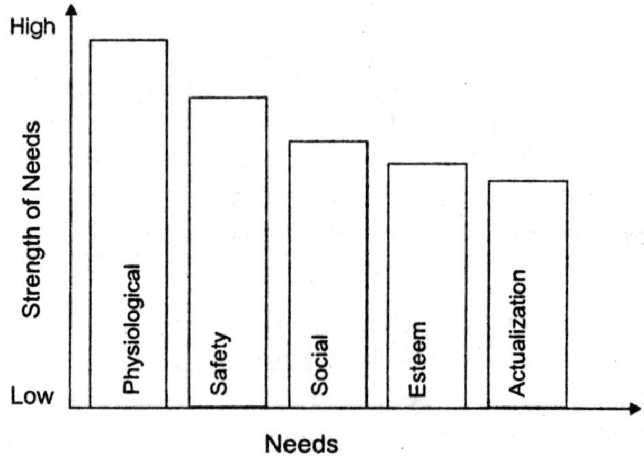

Figure 1.1
Basic Human Needs (1)

When physiological needs are satisfied safety needs become more important (Fig.1.2), then social needs become more important reducing the intensity of the earlier, physiological and safety needs. Most important needs of that time motivate and dominate the behaviour of the individual. When social needs are satisfied, people have a need for high evaluation of themselves that is firmly based in reality-recognition and respect from others. Satisfaction of these esteem needs produces feelings of self-confidence, prestige, power and control. People begin to feel that they are useful and have some effect on environment. When self-esteem need begins to be adequately satisfied self-actualization needs become more pre- potent.

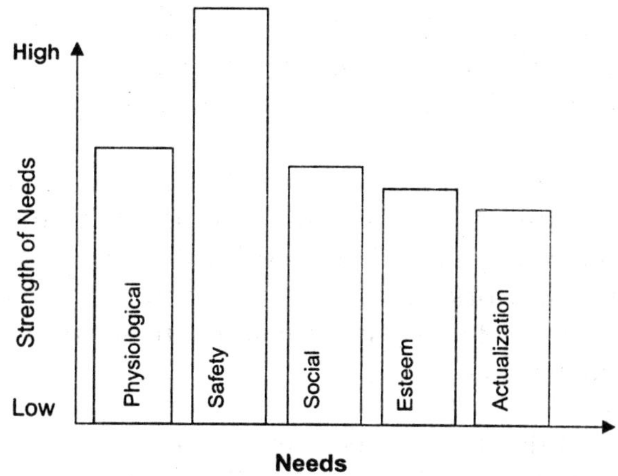

Figure 1.2
Basic Human Needs (2)

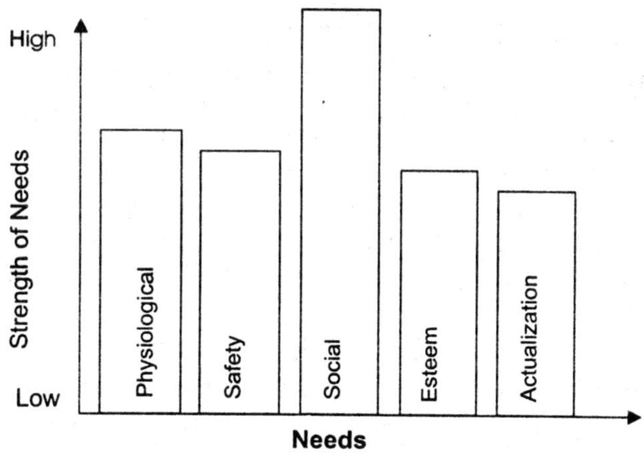

Figure 1.3
Basic Human Needs (3)

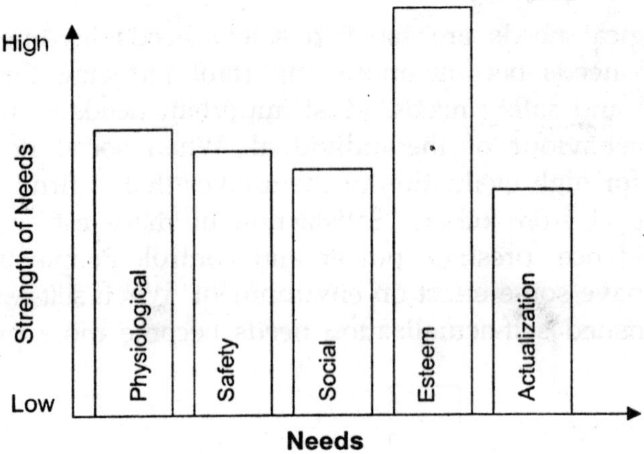

Figure 1.4
Basic Human Needs (4)

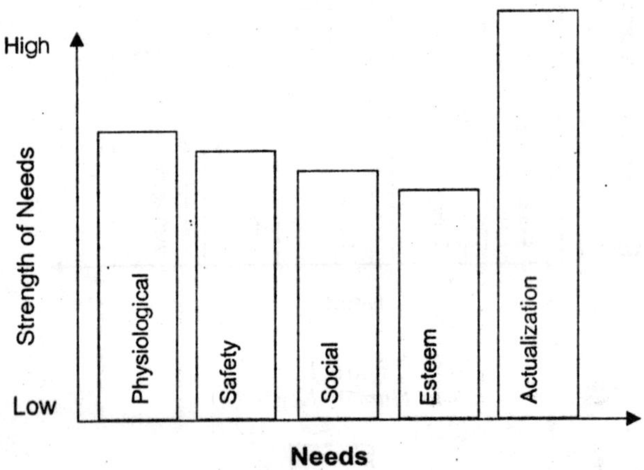

Figure 1.5
Basic Human Needs (5)

It is important to note that each level need, need not be fully satisfied to make successive need stronger. Self-actualisation is the need to maximize one's potential; self-actualisation is the desire to become what one is capable of becoming. Individuals satisfy these needs in different ways. Some people can be characterized as having satisfied to a large extent the physiological, safety, social needs and their behaviour tends to be dominated by esteem and self-actualisation activities. This tends to become more characterized if standards of living and levels of education continue to rise. Formerly management tried to satisfy earlier order needs of employees. However, in present situation they have to pay more attention to satisfy higher level needs for self esteem and self-actualisation.

The attitudinal structure of labourers can be modified to the extent the management can control the atmosphere surrounding the groups of labourers. Proportion of labour absenteeism and labour turnover can be reduced if their needs for self-esteem and self-actualisation are attended to the maximum extent. Labourers can be made to react the way management wants them to react by creating particular type of atmosphere. Therefore, what type of atmosphere around workers we need to create depends upon what type of attitudinal behaviour we want from them. That means, the theory gives us alternatives of choice. This theory is considered, therefore, to be important in the group of neo-human relations theories of management.

The neo-human relations theories of management put forth expectations that are not likely to be fully realised either from the side of management or from the side of employees. Even then, it must be admitted that these theories reckoned the needs of the people of getting status, acceptance and choice. These theories advocated that productivity of labourers can be improved by understanding the urge of the labourers to develop their capability fully and put it to use. They need to get satisfaction by utilizing this capability to achieve appropriate but challenging goals of the firms. These theories tried to improve productivity by introducing institutional developments. Redistribution of resources, availability of means of production, granting rewards and treating labourers as human beings were the four means suggested by these theories to bring attitudinal change and improve productivity.

These eight theories emphasized on bringing harmony between expectations of the employees and objectives of the business firms. This approach to management impressed many and the atmosphere in the organisation began to turn cordial and performance improved. Major message of these theories is that, managers should become more reliable, improve their capacity of developing mutual relations and change their values. Then appropriate and positive changes will take place in the organisation and workers will respond positively. The necessity of organisational development as expected in the neo-human relations theory of management was felt because a number of technological and social changes had taken place. Behavioural changes discussed in explaining various theories were the beginning of organisational changes. This has resulted into fundamental changes in organisational values.

Eight theories belonging to neo-human relations theories of management presented by Chris Argyis, Fredrick Herzberg, D. C. McClelland, Rensis Likert, Robert Blake and Jane Moutone, Paul Hersey and Keneth Blankchart, Douglas McGreggor and Abraham Maslow are discussed in foregoing paragraphs. These theories seem to have emphasized various aspects of human relations. They are — (a) Inducing people to work more and better, (b) Empowering and strengthening their attitude, (c) Improving performance on the strength of leadership qualities, (d) Commanding confidence of people on the basis of improved management style, and (e) Integrating employees to improve their maturity. These are all psychological aspects of human behaviour. This contribution of psychology to the theory of management is significant. 'Guru theories' emphasising choice of customers and competition in the market were developed in the latter years. However, human relation is the foundation on which these theories rest. It is the next step in the theories based on neo-human relations. Though no management theories have been propagated in post 1990s period, the new concepts developed during this period are based on the human relations.

Stephen Landen in his book 'Fish Tales' published in 2002 has advocated strongly some principles of management. We must consider the work we do as important. Any work that we do must be important from our point of view. People respect our work only if we consider it to be important. This is the first principle presented by Stephen Landen. His second principle states; respect about our work is exhibited in the way we perform our work. We feel interested in our work only if we put all our skill at stake. Then only we do that work whole-heartedly. He has given emphasis on doing the work joyfully. We must feel interested in our work, then only we feel it easy and we derive joy out of it. This is his third principle. The fourth principle advocated by him is making others day joyful and rememberable. We must give pleasure through our behaviour, our attitude to our customers, employees and labourers; we derive satisfaction out of this. We must involve ourselves fully, in our work; we must commit ourselves to it. Then we have strong hold on our work. Faith and being one with the work takes individual to the highest peak of success and honour. Competitiveness of the organisation in the market improves if management implements these principles in its organisation. This discourse is the new incarnation of psycho-analysis presented in the neo-human relations theories of management.

School of 'Guru' Theories of Management

Thinking in management theories seems to have developed radically since 1980s. School of 'Guru theories of management' focuses its attention on the concept of 'competing with other business organisations'. To meet the 'choice of customer' is the objective of business organisation. This directive principle is based on five assumptions. These assumptions are — (1) It is not possible to plan innovation, because we do not know on which factors does it depend? However, it is known that innovation takes shape out of many a 'experiments' done by employees. (2) We work with certain emotions in our mind. We involve ourselves in work. (3) Better and effective co-ordination can be achieved in the organisation with the help of value system and culture rather than with rules and directives. (4) Innovations are done on inducement of the customer. (5) Attitude of management towards production and behaviour with employees depends upon how much is the organisation customer oriented. All these five points are incorporated in different nature and in different proportions in 'Guru' theories of management.

'Guru' theories prescribe the type of business system that has to be developed to compete successfully in the selected market segment. 'Guru' theories state seven factors upon which success of management depends. They are – (1) Innovation should be considered as most important and maximum attention should be provided to innovate either new products or new methods of producing goods. (2) Emphasis should be given on 'team work'. Organisation of overlapping teams increases communication, co-operation and commitment among the employees. (3) Employees should be educated in new concepts, better methods and should be trained in new skills and techniques. Knowledge is power and therefore education and training empowers employees. (4) Workers should be induced to do their jobs wholeheartedly. Management should develop cordial relations with employees. This achieves greater involvement of employees in the working of the company. (5) Employees should be given freedom to take decisions in their areas of authority. As a result there would remain a few authorities in the firm. (6) Organisation should be de-layered by reducing and merging hierarchical ladder. (7) Rules and regulations should be reduced to the minimum. Breaking of bureaucracy improves fluidity in the organisation and reduces rigidity.

Authors propagating 'Guru' theories are categorized in three groups. These groups are – (1) Academic gurus are the professors in management educational institutions and authors of books, articles. They are associated with such management educational institutions. They write on new concepts of management. (2) Consulting gurus are the authors writing independently on concepts of management and giving consultation to business organisations on various aspects of management. (3) Hero gurus are the successful past and present executive officers working in multinational corporations. They have written biographical or autobiographical accounts of the various gimmicks and tricks they used in shaping strategies and policies that have become successful. The authoritative persons in Sikh and Hindu religions propagating and spreading religious principles are addressed as 'GURUS'. Directives given by them carry importance of a 'gospel'. We find such gurus in every aspect of our life. In the same way we find authorities establishing principles and spreading them in every section of business. They are management gurus. They are practical illustration of 'Production sector guru', 'Quality maintenance guru', 'Guru in financial sector'. They are the persons who discover implicit knowledge and secrets of business; they propagate and spread these principles. In 1980s managers were in need of more direction and new concepts to make management more effective. At that time 'Guru theories of management' came into propagation. In one way concepts of 'Guru theories' are related to the concepts of neo-human relations theories of management. The concepts established in 'Guru theories' are the next step to concepts preached in neo-human relations theories of management. However, 'Guru theories' have divorced from the impact of intellectual thoughts of neo-human relations theories of management. Commitment of workers to jobs, readiness to shoulder responsibility, creativity of employees, attitude to give more importance to people, time management are the principles expounded in the school of 'Guru theories' of management. More emphasis should be given on improving workmanship and quality so that labourers and employees would not leave the organisation. That will improve productivity of employees and their involvement in work.

These 'Gurus' assure managers of the strategic knowledge that will make them successful in this uncertain atmosphere. These 'Gurus' take perceptive view of changing atmosphere and that is why they can preach the principles that make managers successful.

School of Academic Guru Theories of Management

Academic Gurus are thinkers who while teaching and doing research work in educational institutions, develop own concepts on some aspects of management and popularize them. Developing new and newer strategies and plans for business have remained to be common thread in the 'Guru' theories. Peter Drucker observed 30 years ago that a company's first task is to create customers. The aim of marketing is to know and understand the customer so well that the product or service fits him and sells itself. Ideally, marketing should result in a customer who is ready to buy. All that should be needed then is to make the product or service available. Peter Drucker pointed out that it is more important to 'do the right thing' (effectiveness) than to 'do things right' (efficiency). But to be successful one has to excel at both. Further, he considers that business managers must be leaders. Leadership is not some mysterious blend of charisma and luck. Rather leadership commonly arises from a commitment to serve others rather than self. Effectiveness grows out of quest for doing the best. Managers must continually look at a wider context and explore the larger problem. He argues that we must focus on our strengths to make ourselves effective, then weaknesses are irrelevant. We must manage the time well. Peter Drucker argues that continuity of the big business enterprises is vital. Our society will not tolerate and cannot afford to see, such wealth producing resources jeopardised through lack of competent successors to today's management.

This discussion of Peter Drucker's thoughts on management gives us a kaleidoscopic view of how the emphasis in approach towards management has come to change. For him customer satisfaction, effective and efficient production process, management leadership, its strengths and continuity of succession of competent managers are most important things in the theory of management. We find continuity of his thought on succession of managers in Tom Peter's idea.

Philip Kotler argues that companies need to become customer focused. He being a strategic marketer has always suggested strong and fortified marketing strategies. He suggests that with a view to avoid duplication of our product, a producer must always give more importance to maintaining high quality of his products and/or services and must guard strongly the unique characteristic features of his product and/or service. If such quality is maintained, customer is satisfied and he insists on the same product. Producers should take every opportunity to ascribe intrinsic superiority to the product by giving a brand name to his product and/or service. Companies must have a long-term vision as to how and in which direction should the company develop. It must make every effort to turn this vision into reality. The first step in turning this vision into reality is to undertake an audit of current marketing function and process. The objective of the marketing audit is to assess effectiveness of a company's marketing function and process and provide recommendations for improvement. Marketing audit considers articulate defining the role of marketing; co-operation between marketing and other functional areas, gathering good and useful information and using it effectively. The processes like market planning, development of new product must be conceived and implemented rightly. All employees in the company must have fully understood marketing concepts and they must bring into practice what they have learnt. Such marketing audit is done by conducting in-depth interviews with company executives, managers and other stakeholders like customers. On the basis of such information collected marketing audit recommends initiative to make the organisation more responsive to the clients and customers it wishes to serve.

Philip Kotler recommends that all strategies and tactics must be integrated in a marketing plan that can be effectively executed by the marketing organisation. A sound marketing plan starts with an analysis of external and internal trends, a well developed segmentation scheme, meaningful positioning and a carefully crafted set of marketing tactics.

Gary Hamel visualizes that we have reached the end of incrementalism and only those companies that are capable of creating industry revolutions will prosper in the economy. His message is innovate or die, revolt or fail. He advises companies to be active because it is necessary to change before it is too late. He advocates 'business concept innovation' meaning that wealth-creating champions have unique capabilities, unique assets, unique value positions and unique market positioning abilities. They have the capacity to re-conceive existing business models in ways that create new value for customers, rude surprises for competitors and new wealth for investors. Simple product or marketing innovation will not do in the age of revolution. Radical invention, radical differentiation must be done if one is to survive.

Henry Mintzberg argues that the managers do not work according to the system developed by scientific analyst but by his implicit knowledge. The principle, that organisation should work for the objectives fixed by management, developed by Keneth Blanchart became most popular during the post Second World War period and is still holding fast in the minds of the managers. This principle seems to be incorporated in the employee performance evaluation scheme. It appears that intellectuals have developed theories as to how management must change to reap the benefits of changing times.

School of Consulting 'Guru' Theories of Management

Thinkers propagating new concepts in respect of business through own writings and acting, as consultants on that basis in business organisations are included in this category. They do very deep, penetrating and fundamental analysis of situations, atmosphere in business organisations, industries and markets and on the basis of that analysis theorise as to how these organisations should be managed. These consultants possess the skill and knowledge of forecasting how things will take shape in future, how changes will take place and possess knack to present them in an attractive and convincing manner. Business enterprise is a growing society and it has legal authority to discharge its own rights. This right can be transferred to some extent to the employees by empowering them to take decisions. These employees are a self-governed society in the business firm. Peter Drucker argues that every organisation possesses a manager that is a dynamic factor, providing soul to the organisation. Management is a fundamental and effective concept in all civilizations and four walls of the organisation do not bind its role. He states that every manager has to perform two functions. His first function is to create something synergic and huge by bringing various divisions together in the organisation. His second function is to strike balance between his decisions and acts in such a way that immediate and distant needs of the society can be satisfied. Peter Drucker put forth a new concept of 'Knowledge Worker' in 1963 and forecast that in future, business organisations will become knowledge organisations. This is coming true today.

Robert Blake and Jane Moutone prepared a formula to measure 'the proportion of performance of managers' and tried to measure success of individual managers. Concern about people and devotion to work were the two factors measured on nine-point scale and a net like diagram was prepared. The performance of managers in respect of these two factors was plotted on this diagram. Then it was realized that manager obtaining five-five point position on both these parameters could maintain the performance of the organisation at expected level by getting adequate work done from labourers. Terence Deal and Allen Kennedy maintain that management is a political game. They argue that managers, who can play such a move in the complexity of organisation by employing unwritten rules of life and win, are the successful managers. They play the strategy of pressurizing people working under them and get maximum work from them. W. E. Deming has given fourteen principles of successful management. His argument is that to make our organisation competitive, the quality of the product and services that we provide must be the highest. For that, all people including management must be imparted training of production technique, communication and information technology so that 'zero defect' products can be turned out. We must develop such a structure of the organisation that quality of everything in the company would improve.

Michael Porter propagates that competitive advantage can be secured by a business organisation by improving management of people and improving the structure of business organisation. Porter emphasized on making better use of human resources. Business organisations attain the highest status by effectively managing human resources. His concept of competitive advantage has come to be known as 'five forces model'. It involves relationship between competitors within the industry, potential competitors, suppliers and, buyers. The model is exhibited in figure 1.6. This provides solutions to any problem that he faces. While each industry involves all these factors, the relational strengths vary. Business insight of the management uses input from the user to create a unique model of the industry. Then thousands of 'rules' are applied to evaluate hundreds of marketing and business concepts as they relate to the user's unique circumstances. Manager with business insight fully implements the SWOT approach to analyse the strengths and weaknesses of his business. This analysis of marketing and business concepts and conclusions of SWOT analysis provide the organisation with a set of solutions. Strategy is key to corporate success. Improving operations in short term, growing business, gaining market positions and improving products and positioning them in the market are the major strategies of today because companies are locating where they can achieve cost effectiveness. The process of international specialization within the value chain is likely to continue. There is clustering of outsourcing, because cluster becomes a more efficient economic structure than a stand-alone company.

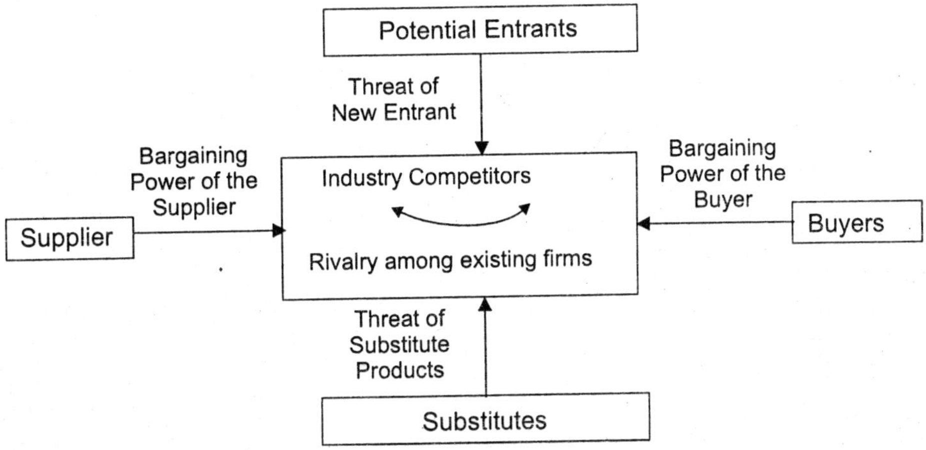

Figure 1.6
Porter's Five Forces Model

While discussing Indian business conditions, he observed that corporations once thought that more the expansion more would be the profits. So they expanded; but this resulted into production of one type of goods; stocks piled up, prices declined and losses were incurred. Now companies try to maintain their distinguishing feature in products and services and they try to create customers for their products. This gives choice to the customers and open competition develops; markets develop. Infosys and Wipro are the best examples of this. Indian companies should give up low cost mentality and learn to upgrade their skills from acquired companies. Indian companies should compete on skills and service delivery – a broader set of parameters than price. Acquisition should enable Indian MNCs to move to a different strategic focus. Indian companies should not over-invest because acquisitions can be done at lower cost. If the progress, status of the company is to be evaluated along with increase in sales and share in the market, return on invested capital must be gauged. If revenue is increasing without increase in return on invested capital then that may be detrimental to the growth of the company. Ranbaxy finds a different way like reverse engineering for itself and earns profit much more than others. Employees in such companies bring new ideas, innovate and find solutions to problems that crop up. Companies should not imitate others, that does not last long.

Today technology is developing fast as a result a product may be imitated before it comes to the market. To avoid that many companies change their policies often. That is also dangerous. We need today in a fast changing economy, long-term policy concentrating on particular aspects of business. Then only the companies may succeed. Now geographical clusters of industries are developing — California and

Bangalore are the clusters of software industry, Mumbai is the cradle of entertainment industry. Such clusters should develop infrastructure facilities of world standard. They should develop trained personnel. This is necessary. Industry should first satisfy consumers in its own country and then only should cater for the markets in other countries. Successful industries identify what product is suitable to their policy. They think of 'trade of strategies'. It means companies should keep themselves away from those things that bring success easily. This is most emotional challenge but it must be accepted. To turn back to traditional thinking, routine processes and the same product is the key to success.

Tom Peters finds that the year 2010 will be the 'Tipping Point' when companies will begin to feel leadership gap in their organisations. With so many boomer executives leaving the workplace the next sixty years will be critical in developing their replacement. Thus, leadership development is a matter of great concern today. Companies have to run courses to develop leaders. They must be taught trust, performance, strategy vision, values, credibility, commitment and organisational alignment. Tom Peters argues that we must co-ordinate leadership development with the leadership challenge. He has developed ' WOW Project' an innovative approach to the human side of project management that helps inspire teams and individuals.

School of Hero 'Guru' Theories of Management

Managers publishing the concepts and policies they implemented successfully while working, as chief executive officers are the hero managers. They believe that if other managers implement the tricks and policies that they had implemented would become successful. Their thoughts are learnt from experiences and are time tested. Their thoughts become authoritative because of the success they achieved. The nature of their writings is biographical or autobiographical. A manager has to perform following six functions, namely — administration and management, planning, implementation of decisions, initiatiation of people to work, get adjusted with circumstances and right choice of alternatives. Problem solving is the nature of their work. This theory of administrative management is founded on the unanimity of opinions of all. Labourers come to work with an expectation to get maximum wages. To plan the work, to get that work done and to disburse labourers' wages are the functions of managers. That means if labourers work more, they receive extra reward for that. If management does its work perfectly then maximum will be produced out of labour of workers and profits will increase. This theory emphasises that it is very important to create co-operation among different constituents of an organisation resulting in a balance between them for the interest of the whole organisation. Role of management is to develop organisational structure having least hierarchy and maximum elasticity, to allow empowered workers to take decisions by themselves, to think at global level by going beyond horizon where there are no national boundaries. This theory also gives stress on utilising natural knowledge that the individual possesses. It also puts emphasis on psychological and religious empowerment of workers. Analysis of these theories indicates that they have turned their focus from hard points like earning profits, improving productivity, to soft points like to add to the knowledge of workers, to develop their personality. It seems that there is an increasing trend on commercialising knowledge.

We have come to concentrate more on relationships between two systems rather than discussing dual character of the system as producers of goods and consumers of goods. There seems to be more discussion going on, on the relationship between creators of knowledge and users of knowledge. The thought that knowledge is not ultimate objective, it is a means to an end, is getting rooted.

M. Macramé on the basis of his extensive experience gives a management message—listen carefully what others say, review the first impression you have about a person and use it as and when needed what you have learnt about it. Speak with him in restrain, behave with him keeping a distance, observe him cautiously, and speak least with him. In this way try to understand the person who is either your colleague or junior and use this knowledge after you have full grasp of him to get work done from him.

Lee Iacocca, Chief Executive of Ford Motors and Daimler Chrysler Motor Company, argues that evaluate the work of your juniors every quarter and on the basis of that instruct them occasionally to improve their system of taking decisions, Managers should induce workers to work more. Juniors should be warned not to shift responsibility on others. Juniors should develop self-respect and enlighten themselves about the role they have to play in the new incarnation.

Lee Iacocca argues that leadership is demonstrated by words and actions. The effective leader is one who possesses excellent communication skills through the use of language. The power of language must be used to make things happen, to coalesce people and purpose for the ultimate good of the organisation. An effective leader must employ some control over individuals in the corporation. Iacocca empowered employees, boosted their moral and helped employees generate a sense of meaning in their work. Leader must have ability to spurt out the facts, not to be afraid of what they depicted and do the best. He made his employees believe in themselves. He states 'it is the job of the leaders to set the rules and enforce the rules and most important, when the rules do not work any more to change the rules.' The goal of the company must be realistic and if there is need to change, a change should be made. To become an effective leader he must take the risk. In communicating process, the delivery of speech should be loud, clear and get the right point. This is important because a good leader must be dominating, mentally and physically. While communicating, language skills are very important; they parallel listening skills that are also very important.

Discussion of these six groups of management theories brings out a few important points. Management is a social science; it is normative. People do not practise what management theories state, but management theories crystalise and generalise what people practise. Management theories do not prescribe a set of rules but direct as to what people should normally do if they have to succeed. In reality we find many a managers and leaders have succeeded even after defying the norms and directives of these management theories.

A review of these six groups of management theories reveals as to how the management practices have moved from product, organisation, and organisational structure, quality of the product to human aspect of production organisation. The attention to human aspects was in the first instance on customer satisfaction, then on customer delight, satisfaction of all stakeholders—all the aspects that were external to the organisation. Then the attention turned on to internal human aspects namely, management, leaders, employees—their empowerment for the betterment of the organisation.

The theme of the book is 'Management of 21st Century Intelligent Corporation.' Present business world is close and complex. It is so close that it is difficult to do anything without others in the business world knowing it. It is so complex that one has to take into consideration so many varied independent and interdependent factors while taking decisions. Technology is so fast changing that there is always a fear of a product becoming absolete as soon as it comes into the market. Business intelligence has developed into a new discipline. They provide perception of dynamic conditions in the environment. They also provide reasoning to interpret perceptions, solve problems, draw inferences and determine actions. Internet search agents such as Google, Alta Vista and Infoseak are level one-search engines providing basic information. Web Watcher known as semi-intelligent or software agents maintain user's profiles and notify the users whenever relevant information is found. They are level two agents. Diff Agents (CMU), Letizia (MIT) commonly known as learning or truly intelligent agents provide specially targetted information. They are level three agents. There are scheduling agents, search agents, report agents, presentation agents, navigation agents and role playing agents that do all types of jobs for the corporations. All big corporations employ all these agents not only to know what others are doing but what others intend to do. That is why management in such a complex business world itself is a very complex task. Management, thus has to do more work in managing business world than managing it's company. The whole corporate world of the new millennium is characterised by ever changing topography, both on the manufacturing as well as on the management front.

Technologies in manufacturing and in support systems are changing fast. Communication and information technology, have standardised as many components as possible so as to fit them into various products and various models. They have the developed common platform for sharing information and have developed ability to convert information into knowledge. They have taken all steps to educate, train and empower the people including suppliers and customers. They have developed themselves into what Philip Kotler calls 'The Stochastic Competitors 'who do not exhibit a predictable reaction pattern. As a result the Intelligent Corporations create a real time knowledge environment in which various functions and individuals can react efficiently in order to accept any challenge the corporation faces. As a result the corporations have become capable of absorbing new ideas quickly, they have the ability to adopt to new circumstances, ability to solve problems efficiently, mobilise appropriate resources and they have accumulated adequate experience what can be called as knowledge base. Corporations of 21st century are intelligent in the sense that they can do anything and everything quickly so as to save time, they can accept and face any challenges, they can create knowledge quickly and they are very adaptable, adaptable to new situations and new procedures. So they are the corporations that are able to react quickly to continuously changing circumstances successfully, face problems and challenges they have never anticipated. They are capable of transforming themselves in accordance with newly created circumstances. The ultimate benefit of such high Intelligent Quotient acquired by corporation is the satisfaction of the customer, surpassing even their expectations and maximisation of return on investment. Such intelligent corporations are going to dominate new millennium.

FUZZY LOGIC IN MANAGEMENT

In this complex world things are so complicated that they cannot be categorised as right or wrong. Between these two Aristotelian binary extremities there are a number of gray shades. That is why many a theories of management founded on the premises of these extremities do not provide solutions to the real problems in the world. Traditional western approaches to the world of management are based on the assumption that this is a right decision as opposed to wrong one. This does not fit in reality because most of the decisions are in gray area; they are neither wrong nor right. Most of the managers follow one path not because it is theorised in the science of management but because those who have taken that decision, that path, have become successful, are proved to be right. This uncertainty in market makes the world fuzzy, and therefore we would have to introduce this fuzzy factor in discussing managerial problems.

Loffi Zedeh first introduced fuzzy thinking. Jan Lukaseiwicz in 1920s developed multivalue logic. He argued that the binary thinking on which many a thoughts, theories in social sciences are founded is a crude simplification of inordinate complex world. This simplification is distorting simplification. Thus, we have to take a realistic view that most of the managerial decisions are relatively right or relatively wrong. Loffi Zedeh developed on this basis the principle of fuzzy sets a theory. The theory argues that there are a number of probabilities that are members of the set. They are equally right or wrong. This ill-defined situation needs to be discussed in managerial literature. This approach is successfully incorporated in the field of engineering and electronics and fuzzy phenomena are quite intelligently resolved. In engineering multiple attributes decision-making methods are used to deal with ill-defined or fuzzy situations.

Multi-stage decision making or fuzzy decision-making can be used to arrive at a set of alternatives that are available to the manager and with the help of arithmetic manipulation most appropriate decision can be arrived at. In business Process

Reengineering or in Total Quality Management approach our endeavour is to go as close as possible to the customer to discover what he really wants. Customer wants many a products with different facilities embedded in them. The question, which of the facilities is most wanted, can be answered with the help of fuzzy logic approach. This can be a positive step to channelise customer choice. Fuzzy logic can be used to find out what combination of characteristic features does the buyers expect from a product.

I have tried to discuss in this book the sets of membership in places wherever possible.

CHAPTER SCHEME

With a view to discuss how would the intelligent corporation be managed in 21st century, I have planned the layout of the book carefully by beginning with a survey of management theories. 1 have emphasised in this overview how has the point of discussion in these theories moved from production to persons. I have also stated the characteristic features of 21st century corporations and have introduced the concept of fuzzy logic as it can be applied in the science of management.

In second chapter I have discussed the concept, theory and practice of Total Quality Management. My focus is on explaining how it is necessary to make our company a quality company in and out to attain competitive advantage with a view to delight the customer.

Supply of goods, services, information and ideas must be kept uninterrupted and flow smoothly so as to maintain quality and keep the cost lowest. Third chapter is devoted to discuss the planning and implementing chain of supply from origin of raw material through to the end consumer. An effort is made to discuss the role and functions of information and information technology in improving efficiency and effectiveness of the supply chain.

Producing the goods and providing the services right first time with zero defect is the key to attaining total quality. This is discussed in the fourth chapter on Six Sigma Management. Methods of selecting Green Belt, Black Belt, Master Black Belt, Champions, and curricula for training them are discussed meticulously with almost all details.

Ideal for improving products, processes and delivery time need to be found out either from within the company or without. Benchmarking is the methodology used to search such an ideal. This is discussed in chapter five. Much effort is taken to analyse various facets of benchmarking so as to help managers to make their company best in the class.

If the corporation is to be made a quality corporation marketing concepts, products, services and ideas must be of equal quality as that of the products produced by the company. Sixth chapter takes a review of theories of transactional marketing and develops the concept of relationship marketing so that the customer can be bound to the company life time.

In chapters 2nd to 6th I have with a purpose discussed the methods of preparing the organisation so as to make it a structure suitable to initiate the program of TQM or SCM or Six Sigma, Bench Marking and Relationship Marketing. I have discussed at length the implementation of these programs, their monitoring and evaluation. All these programs can be successfully and effectively completed only if the corporation has well educated, rigorously trained, devoted and committed workforce. That is why I have devoted a full section in each of these chapters to training of the workforce. Present situation demands that all roles need to be performed by teams organised with specific objective. I have discussed formation, constitution of teams and roles they are expected to play and functions they are expected to perform. I have introduced fuzzy logic methodology in two chapters, as to how suppliers are to be selected in a supply chain and as to how salespersons and buyers can choose win-win situation in transaction of goods and services.

Chapter seven discusses creation, storage, transmission and sharing of knowledge. The world has come to realise that non-financial assets like knowledge are more valuable and value realising than financial and physical assets. With a view to make 21st century corporation, knowledge company, learning company, its management has to make deliberate efforts to increase the stock of knowledge in the company and make it flow through the organisation rather than hold it.

Eighth chapter is a step further in management of knowledge. Human capital, structural capital and customer capital make intellectual capital that the corporation has. Many companies in India have begun to measure the intellectual capital they have and publish it in annual reports. I have tried to develop a comprehensive, extensive and pragmatic model for measuring intellectual capital that the organisation has.

For a long time companies were evaluated on the basis of their performance, specifically financial performance measured on the basis of liquidity group of ratios, solvency group of ratios, efficiency and profitability group of ratios. However, in present world of intense competition and uncertainty companies are being evaluated on the basis of their performance in future which hinges upon knowledge the corporation has and intellectual capital it commands. Therefore, management of 21st century, intelligent corporation has to pay considerable attention to build up knowledge base of the company and intellectual capital it commands.

Competitive edge of a corporation depends upon identification of its core activities, nurturing of the core sector and extending it in all possible directions. Shedding of non-core activities is as important as strengthening and extending core activities. Every corporation has to make deliberate and concerted efforts to build its core competence so that it can squarely stand the challenges posed by complex world economy of the present century. Ninth chapter deals with this phenomenon.

Tenth chapter in this book is devoted to making the corporate body open, receptive, responsive and proactive in its management so that all stakeholders can be satisfied. Corporate governance is the topic of this chapter. I have tried to discuss in brief the theory of corporate governance and rights, duties and responsibilities of various partners in the corporate body. I have taken a brief review of measures taken in India to improve the quality of corporate governance.

Final and concluding eleventh chapter is devoted to summarise the discussion done in earlier ten chapters. It discusses the way a corporation needs to be managed in the 21st century. Developments of leadership, of individual and of the organisation are basic to the development of an organisation. It is accepted that all managers in the corporations and all organisations cannot achieve that coveted status of leadership. However, every manager and every organisation must make sincere efforts to at least march in that direction. With the spread of education, information and understanding customers have begun to expect goods of their choice that deliver maximum value at minimum price. So, organisations are obliged to customise production. Employees have also acquired knowledge and skills. They know what they desire from jobs they perform, they also know their strengths and employability. Therefore, they want work environment that gives them joy from the job they perform. Thus, the managements are obliged to workamise work places. In the concluding section of the chapter, I have discussed management in its various aspects that summarises the discussion of the entire book. After all it is our moral duty and social responsibility to organise economic activities for the betterment of the humanity.

❑ ❑ ❑

2 Total Quality Management

With the close of the Second World War, a number of changes have taken place in the corporate world as well in the government's attitude towards business. Japanese and German business houses emerged as tough competitors to the western-manufacturing corporations. Especially Japan has surpassed many a countries in developing and adopting new technology, dovetailing with innovative management initiatives and matching organisational forms. After Second World War Japanese industries adopted 'scrap and build' policy. Japanese companies used to consult each other and work together. They used to co-operate on technological development and share market information for the benefit of each other. While they used to interact with each other they did practice intense rivalry with each other. Second World War caused massive destruction of population, created shortage of labour force. Wages rose rapidly. Japanese firms were obliged to introduce automation by putting robots to work. They introduced CNC machines linked to computer aided engineering system, programmable logic controllers, automatic tool changers, laser optical systems, multi-layer fabrics, aluminum alloys, light emitting diodes, electrical control system, semi conductors[1] etc. At the same time they were aggressive in upgradation of human resources by introducing in-company rigorous training programs that focused on development of specific skills in fields relevant to the industry. Managers were required to pass tests to advance to the next level. Japanese industries were at ease in adopting parts of other cultures very quickly. Japanese corporations replace products frequently by introducing newer and better models. They responded very quickly to market demand and developed micro-segments of the world market through numerous product varieties.

Japanese industries have developed decentralised management style based on team structure in every activity. Members of each team are multi-skilled. Intensive, rigorous continuous training is given to each employee. Feeling of shame on not achieving required standard of performance, spirit of dedication and lifetime commitment fructified the new structure adopted by Japanese companies, making them symbol of 'JIDOKA' the quality principle. Japanese corporations have been able to penetrate deep into markets of all countries, through innovative characteristics of their products, low costs resulting from batch wise, customised production and aggressive marketing strategies. Their concept of market has come to be limited by the boundaries of earth.

Over the period of time this corporate culture has spread over to most of the countries of the world. Japanese firms had a perfect background prepared for the launch of quality program. W. Edwards Deming, who had been advocating 'quality' in products manufactured in industries, developed the concept of 'Total Quality Management'.

William E. Conway defines quality as 'the development' manufacture, administration and distribution of consistent low-cost products and services that customers want and need'. Quality is also defined as fully satisfying the agreed customer requirements at the lowest price. Quality is a way of managing, it is not a technical activity. W.E. Deming defines quality as predictable degree of uniformity dependability at low costs and suited to the market. Philip Crosby defined quality as conformance of requirements, not just goodness. Thus, quality is consistent, uniform standard product without any variance, produced at low cost and conforming to the agreed requirements of the customer.

David A. Ganin has stated that there are five principal approaches to defining quality. They are (1) *Transcendent approach* – It is not possible to define quality, it is known when the product is seen. Advertisement promotes transcendent approach when it says that supermarket 'where shopping is a pleasure'. *(2) Product based approach* – Durability and reliability, confidence in product defines quality. *(3) User based approach* – Consumer says that he likes the product because it possesses the qualities that he expects of a product, *(4) Manufacturing based approach* – Products conform to the requirements of the producer, and *(5) Value based approach* - Price of the product is acceptable as related to the quality of the product perceived by the consumer.[2]

Approaches to Quality

There are three broad approaches to quality –

(1) Quality Control Approach: It is the last minute checking of goods and services to remove any defects before the final customer receives the product. Inspecting the product after it is ready is definitely a good system but it is a poor system of ensuring quality because what we are doing is measuring performance of inspection and sorting process. It involves additional cost, the cost of examiner, the cost of time involved in inspection, the waste of rejection and probably of remachining the product. Moreover, delivery is delayed which may cause inconvenience to the buyer and may result into defection of buyer. This method is not practiced any more.

(2) Quality Assurance Approach: It is a method of reviewing the whole process of production to find a way of delivering quality every time. If anything is found to have gone wrong in the customer – supplier chain; the first step is to find out what has gone wrong in the process, why has it gone wrong. The second step is to prepare documents writing the procedures that are necessary to assure quality or zero defect product. The third step is to follow the procedure strictly so that the company reaches a particular acceptable level of quality. But, it means that 'acceptable level of quality' is not the best quality because there is always a room for improving quality. Acceptable quality level is a faulty concept because it implies that a level of failure is acceptable. It is always better to prevent error. It is also likely that the customer may be satisfied today with the quality of the product, but over a period of time his expectations will increase because other companies may be offeıing either better quality products may be at a little higher price or same quality product at a little lower price. It calls for a system that enables organisation to keep the customer satisfied with the quality of the product all the time.

(3) Total Quality Management Approach: It is an approach of developing whole organisation in such a way that it not only meets the expectations of the customers but exceeds it. The whole system in the organisation is so geared that the quality of the product or service from the very raw material to the point of delivery is maintained and every effort is made to improve the quality successively and continuously. Quality of product depends upon materials, machines, men, motivation, money, modem information methods, mounting product requirements and markets. Quality is the characteristic feature of the product or service that meets customer needs. Quality is composed of many separate elements depending upon the product or the service. These elements are specification, conformance, and reliability, cost (value) and delivery. To produce a genuine quality product or service, quality must be built in at the very start and must be maintained at every stage. The design of the product must be such that there would be no scope to make mistake. This approach of managing quality is called TOTAL because it encompasses everything the company does, all its processes and all its employees at every level in the company all the time. The word total is added to send the message that all processes, systems at all level of management and employees must be concerned with quality. Quality is everybody's business. Mohamed Zaire defines total quality management as 'a positive attempt by the organisation concerned to improve structural, infrastructural, attitudinal, behavioural and methodological ways of delivering to the end customer, with emphasis on consistence, improvements in quality, competitive enhancement, all with the aim of satisfying or delighting the end customer. Total quality management is not a separate initiative supporting business as usual, but it is the business itself'.[3]

Gilinni Taguchi looks to the concept of quality from quite a different angle. He defines quality as 'the loss a product causes to society after being shipped, other than losses caused by intrinsic functions. Individual buyer and society expects particular intrinsic characteristic of the product or the service, any variation in this characteristic is poor quality that causes loss to the society. Gilinni Taguchi with the help of concept 'Quality loss function' has qualified his definition of quality.[4] When there is any variation in the process or in the product, loss is caused to the society.

Figure 2.1
Taguchi Loss Function

In figure 2.1 loss is measured along vertical axis and on horizontal axis is measured the target to be achieved. 'Taguchi Loss Function' is a parabola wherein the lowest point represents the minimal loss in monetary terms caused to the society. This may happen due to heavy weight of the product, over-designing of the product, product being of larger size or less efficient, requiring frequent repairs, regular maintenance etc. Taguchi was of the opinion that quality of the product can be achieved by designing the product from the beginning in such a way that it will require no inspection. Taguchi method for design and experiment is a tool to reduce the inherent variety in product or process. It combines engineering and statistics to directly address the process variability problem. With a view to improve quality and reduce cost Taguchi has introduced the practice of product and process engineering so that the interfering factors can be identified and removed. Lower Specification Limit and Upper Specification Limit (LSL and USL) are the tolerance limits within which the problems of designing and processing the product can be defined. The lowest point of the parabola is the customer quality standard. Variation lesser than these tolerance limits alone would enable us to achieve quality of highest level. Problems of designing and processing are of two types: controllable problems are those, which can be addressed by improving, or inventing new process for producing the product. Uncontrollable factors are those which are inherent in the product itself. That means Taguchi concentrates on improving process to improve quality of the product. Taguchi recommends that the design process of producing product can be developed through three stages so as to achieve the desired quality

(1) Systems Design: Functions that the product is expected to perform are determined and a prototype of the product conforming with those functions is built.

(2) Parameter Design: The factors that affect the performance of the product are identified. They are classified into controllable and uncontrollable. Then various experiments are made so as to fix the combination of controllable and uncontrollable factors so the product is improved to the target level.

(3) Tolerance Design: If the product so processed through parameter design does not achieve the target quality then experiments are made by using improved grades of raw material, better machines, developing new process so that we achieve the target level of the quality.

I have discussed so far, how the Japanese corporations in the post Second World War period, were in readiness to welcome the concept of quality management and practice it. This they had to do under the pressure of demand situation, innovative initiative, organisational culture and devoted as well as empowered employees, availability of new technology and latter on exacting demand of consumers. Thereupon I have discussed various definitions and concepts of quality, quality management and total quality management. Total quality is not a destination, it is hardly a program or project, it is a corporate philosophy adopted to satisfy, delight the customer by delivering him goods and services that are yet in his dreams. Total quality management is a blanket concept encompassing various facets, different activities that make the management of quality in total. These facts, activities include benchmarking, supply chain management, six sigma management, total relationship marketing, knowledge management, intellectual capital management, core competence and corporate governance all in one. Implementation and practice of these eight components make TOTAL QUALITY. Each of these components can be independently practiced but introduction of all these aspects has a synergic effect. While writing this book, though these aspects of total quality management are discussed in separate chapters, it is only because of the fear of making the theme of the book complex beyond comprehension. Reader will find a strong thread of thought moving through all this discussion leading to management of World Corporation of 21st century.

One more point must be made clear before embarking upon discussion of practicing total quality management in a corporation, that the multinational corporations that are standing today as an hallmark of image and reputation have practiced and are practicing various components of total quality management as suitable and necessary for their organisation. Total quality management is an integration of all functions and practiced within an organisation. Xerox Corporation, Shell, Rover, Motorola, Hewlett Packard, IBM, Fujitsu, Sony, Honda, Toyota, Maruti Udyog Limited, Wipro Technologies Ltd., Hero Honda are a few of them. It will be evidently clear that they have captured competitive advantage because they have focused on CUSTOMER SATISFACTION and have changed, as the situation demanded. This had to be done because of either changing economic and business scenario or changing demands of the customers. The very fact that, total quality management is practiced for such a long time, it has come to stay as an integral part of the business. Many of the ideas on which total quality management is based will change and become more important than today. The concept of quality will become more crucial and many faceted. New approaches to qualify will emerge, as we will move on the path of attaining higher perfection in customer delight.

W.E. Deming popularised the concept of quality first through his writing and then Quality Approach by developing a system to integrate efforts to develop, maintain and improve quality by organising various groups in the organisation. Deming suggested that with a view to achieve high level of excellence, quality must be maintained at each and every stage of processing the product. The product must have uniformity and it must be dependable in its performance. In his opinion, as quality of the product improves, cost of production gets reduced. This will enable us to improve the quality further. We can capture greater share of the market and this will increase the jobs, as we are required to produce more. In the long run our capacity to survive in the market will improve. These consecutive actions are known as 'Deming Chain Reaction'. This discussion draws us to an important conclusion: workers are responsible for causing variation in quality. Therefore, we must concentrate on improving process to achieve the required quality.

Considering the importance of quality of product and service and W. Edward Deming's contribution to the concept, Japanese Government instituted Deming Prize in 1951. It is a matter of pride that as many as ten Indian Companies have been awarded Deming Prize as listed in Table 2.1.

Table 2.1
Deming Prize Winning Indian Companies

Year of Award	*Companies that have Won Deming Prize*
2001	Sundaram Brake Linings Ltd.
2002	T.V.S. Motor Company Ltd.
2002	Hi-Tech Carbon (GMPD) Ltd.
2002	Sanden Corporation
2002	Sundaram-Clayton Ltd. Brakes Division
2003	Birla Cellousic Kharah- A Unit of Grasim Industries
2003	Brakes India Ltd. Foundry Division
2003	Mahindra and Mahindra- Farm Equipment Sector
2003	Rane Brake Linings Ltd.
2003	Sona Kayo Steering Systems Ltd.

Deming has put forth a very simple method of solving problems. This is popularly known as Deming Cycle. It is exhibited in figure 2.2, where it is shown that as soon as we face a problem, we take an action to identify the cause and nature of the problem. Then we prepare a plan to find a solution to solve the problem. Deming has developed a theory of management, based on scientific and statistical principles in which people remain the least predictable and they are the most important part in maintaining quality. He has listed fourteen steps of management for T.Q.M. (These are given in Table 2.2).

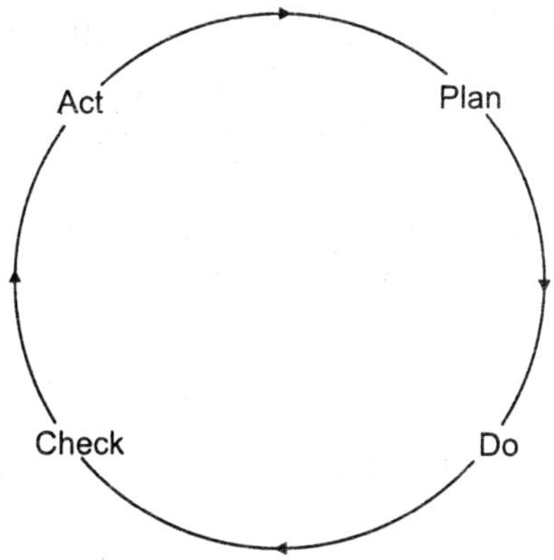

Figure 2.2 : The Deming Cycle

J. M. Juran, going one step further to Deming, added one more dimension to the concept of quality by introducing the managerial dimension of planning, organising and controlling T.Q.M. He focused the responsibility on management to achieve quality. He stated that management has to set up goals in clear terms. In his opinion quality of a product is FITNESS FOR USE in terms of design, conformance, availability, safety and field use. Customer's point of view is incorporated in his concept of quality. Deming concentrated on down-to-top management and worker's pride, but Juran focused on top-to-down management and on technical methods and workers' satisfaction and pride. He has enlisted ten steps for improvement of quality. (These are given in Table 2.2.) According to J. M. Juran quality must also be achieved in communication, management commitment and people.

In terms of Philips B. Crosby, quality is 'ZERO DEFECT.' The process of quality improvement is based on following absolute factors. They are – (1) Quality is not the goodness of the commodity; it is conformance to the requirements of the customer. (2) We can achieve quality by preventing defects from the beginning of the process of planning. Postproduction appraisal is 'quality control' which may require additional costs. (3) 'Zero defects' should be the standard of performance. (4) Price that we have to pay for non-conformance is the only measurement as to how have we performed. P.B. Crosby has stated fourteen steps for attaining quality. (These are given in Table 2.2).

Table 2.2
Deming, Juran and Crosby's Steps for Quality and Management

	Deming's 14 Points for Management	*Crosby's 14 Steps to Quality*	*Juran's 10 Steps to Quality Improvement*
(1)	Create constancy for the purpose of improvement of product and service. Allocate resources to provide for long-term needs with a view to become competitive.	Make it clear that management is committed to quality.	Build awareness for the quality and an opportunity for improvement.

(2)	Adopt the new philosophy. We are in a new economic age. We can no longer live with mistakes and defects.	Form quality improvement teams with senior representatives from each department.	Set goals for improvement.
(3)	Eliminate dependence on mass inspection. Quality must be built in the product. Quality must be the foundation on which the organisation is based.	Determine where current and potential problem lie.	Organise to achieve goals.
(4)	Eliminate awarding business based on price alone. Instead minimise total cost. Move toward a single supplier for any one item, on a long term relationship on loyalty and trust.	Evaluate cost of quality and explain its use as a management tool.	Provide training.
(5)	Improve constantly and forever the system of production and service and decreasing cost.	Raise the quality awareness and personal concern to all employees.	Carry out projects to solve problems.
(6)	Institute training on job.	Take actions to correct problems identified through previous steps.	Report progress.
(7)	Institute leadership. The aim of supervision would be to help people and machines do a better job.	Establish committees for zero defect program.	Give recognition.
(8)	Drive out fear; create a climate in which every one may work effectively for the company.	Train supervisors to carry out their part of quality improvement program.	Communicate results.
(9)	Break down barriers between departments. People in all departments must work as a team to tackle problems encountered with product or service.	Hold a 'zero defect day' to let all employees realise that there has been a change.	Keep score.
(10)	Eliminate slogans, exhortations and targets for the workforce asking for zero defect and new levels of production.	Encourage individuals to establish improvement goals themselves and their groups.	Maintain momentum.
(11)	Eliminate quotas. Eliminate management by numbers and numerical goals.	Encourage employees to communicate to management the obstacles they face in attaining their improvement goals.	
(12)	Eliminate barriers to pride of workmanship. Abolish merit rating and management by objectives.	Recognise and appreciate those who participate.	

(13)	Institute a vigorous program of education and self-improvement. Workers should be educated to use tools and techniques of quality.	Establish quality councils to communicate on regular basis.	
(14)	Take action to accomplish transformation. The transformation is everybody's job.	Do it all over again to emphasise that the quality improvement program never ends.	

The three gurus of TQM fix responsibility to achieve and maintain quality on the management. Education as regards concept of quality, its objective, measures to implement quality should be imparted to all people working at all levels in the organisation. Manufacturing design must also be so systemed that it achieves quality from the beginning to the end. 'Do it right the first time' is the mantra of TQM.

TQM is the integration of all functions and processes within an organisation to achieve continuous improvement in the quality of the product or the service. Corporate culture of quality, information systems, process controls, human resources programs, the factors that are known as corporate infrastructure are the basic components of TQM.[5] The objective of introducing TQM in an organisation is to achieve customer satisfaction. While quality improvement is a concept that addresses to the needs not only of the customers but also of all the stakeholders namely – employees, suppliers, owners, distributors and local communities. Quality improvement is the philosophy that everybody in the community has to adopt. The culture of the community will be so enriched that all in the community shoulder the responsibility of the success of society's endeavour crystallised in the form of organisation. In the process of quality improvement ethically all have attitude of integrity, honesty and respect for every individual. Organisation has to provide support to the community activities. The organisation in practicing quality improvement, beginning from itself would treat all employees fairly, offer career break facilities to child caring female workers with a chance to join the job back. The organisation would employ, if required, train and employ local people in large numbers. It would treat suppliers, contractors as partners and deal with them in such a way that both are benefited. It would design the production process so as to reduce solid waste and reduce pollution.

The organisation would construct social overheads as community halls, dispensary, hospital, school building, and library so that the organisation as well as the community enjoys the 'planning gain'. In the concept of quality improvement is enshrined responsibility of everyone to act in such a way to make organisation successful. This concept is named as 'intrapreneurship'. Individuals working in an organisation want much more than the pay packet. They need to have a partnership, an intrapreneurship in the organisation. So they derive psychological satisfaction of having built up an organisation with positive outlook. It is agreed that all people in the community and in the organisation cannot and should not become intrapreneurs.

Those who show the leadership qualities, possess expertise, interpersonal skills have a full opportunity to empower themselves by means of education and training. That way quality improvement has a simpler but challenging route. One has to change himself, his own behaviour. People have to put a good deal of effort in examining and developing their own attitude and behaviour. This will automatically influence other people in the organisation to imbibe these attitudinal traits in themselves. The process of implementing the concept of quality improvement can be charted like this. In the first place people must be ready to change. There would be some people in the organisation that have been awaiting a program of change. We call them as 'early adopters'. As there are some 'early adopters' in the organisation; there are also some employees in the organisation whose behaviour becomes irritating for their colleagues, superiors and for the organisation. They are usually categorised as 'problem employees' and are avoided by all. However, this attitude towards them aggravates the problem rather than solving it. 'Problem employees' are of two types. Some become so because of their negative attitude towards everything including themselves. Their approach can be changed by finding out their psychological mindset and can be counselled to turn their attitude from negative to positive. Some people become 'problem employees' because they lack the skill the job demands they are put into. Their problem can be resolved by transferring them to the job, they prefer and like. Earlier these 'problem employees' are identified and their problems resolved, better it is for the organisation. Once their style, attitude and expertise are tuned they can address the masses, for all can share a change exhibiting the benefits they have received. 'Early adopters' or such leaders can employ various approaches – flexible, inflexible, democratic, authoritative – appropriate for the purpose and should choose the right time to inculcate these qualities among the masses. Once the people in the organisation have readied to change, the tools and techniques of TQM can be more easily implemented to achieve the objective of customer satisfaction, customer delight. Larry Reynolds states that 'none of the ideas of quality improvement is new, ethical concerns stakeholder theory; the concepts of intrapreneurship all have long pedigrees. What is new is to combine them with some tools and techniques of TQM to produce a 'coherent approach' to developing organisations.[6] TQM provides guidance as to how in the face of pressure to deliver desired results in a complex situation the tools and techniques can be used. But the ethical and moral base that is required to stand in such a situation is provided by the concept of quality improvement. Thus, quality improvement is the body of knowledge that forms the basis for TQM. Zaire has suggested seven tools of quality improvement. They are given and described in Table 2.3.

Table 2.3
Seven Tools of Quality Improvement

	Name of the Tool	*Description*
(1)	The Relations Diagram Method	Used to relate complex cause and effect relationship.
(2)	KJM Method Affinity Diagram	Gives some order of verbal data by collation into similar categories so that it can be systematically analysed.

(3)	The Systematic Diagram	Helps effective planning so that objectives are achieved. It does this by showing the sequencing and interrelationships so that resulting actions are error free.
(4)	The Matrix Diagram Method	Helps clarify problems through multidimensional thinking. It studies the relationships between elements by showing the strength and weakness factors' influence, thus helping understanding the problem.
(5)	Matrix Data Analysis	Requires complex mathematical skills. Relies on systematic organisation and presentation of data so that relationships can be examined.
(6)	Process Design Program Chart (PDPC)	Helps select the best process for obtaining the desired results. It not only evaluates existing progress but also looks at alternatives through newly gained knowledge; so it is a dynamic approach.
(7)	The Arrow Diagram Method	Helps establish the most suitable daily plan for a project and also controls its progress. Uses arrows to define all tasks required for project, taking into account timing for each task.

Source: Zaire Mohamed, *Benchmarking for the Best Project.* p. 22 (Table 1.7)

Another concept that is akin to TQM must be discussed here. Prof. Kaoni Ishikawa developed in 1962 the concept of 'Quality Circle'.[7] The objective of 'Quality Circles' is to encourage workers themselves to find ways to improve processes. Quality circles try to develop initiative culture. Through the establishment of 'Quality Circles' workers become far more involved in the building process. Workers should take upon themselves the responsibility of improving quality. Quality has to be part of consciousness of the workers. The quality circle is a group of employees consisting of five to twelve volunteers. They work under the same supervisors. They, under the leadership of the same supervisors meet regularly, informally in normal working time and identify, analyse and solve problems related to their work. The supervisor functions as a facilitator and he must be trained to perform this function. With this type of impersonal and in-depth discussion, Prof. Ishikawa tried to fuse American best practices like flow line production techniques and traditional European craftsmanship with Japanese practices of teamwork. In a way he tried to bring craftsmanship back to groups rather than individuals. Prof. Ishikawa states that 'Quality circles' must be allotted adequate time for their suggestions to fructify. Results of suggestions made and implemented by 'Quality Circles' do not come immediately. Automobile producers accept and implement suggestions made by 'Quality circles' that save as small time as 0.6 seconds in production process. The results take little longer time to come but their effects are long lasting and beneficial.

It has been argued that TQM cannot be successfully implemented unless the organisation has a culture that backs up and facilitates change in the attitude and behaviour of the management, employees and the suppliers. Let us see, in this context, what organisational culture means. R. H. Kilman and his associates define culture as the pattern of shared beliefs and values that provide the members of an organisation, the rules of behaviour or accepted norms for conducting operations. It is the philosophies, ideologies, values, assumptions, beliefs, and expectations, attitudes and norms that knit an organisation together and are shared by the employees.[8] Unless organisational culture supports the strategy, quality improvement is not possible. According to P. B. Crosby, quality is the result of a carefully constructed culture; it has to be the fabric of the organisation. Successful organisations have a central culture around which the company revolves.[9] The organisation must plan, organise and control every activity seriously considering commitment to quality as the core culture. Culture can be imbibed through behaviour, experience as well as symbols. Prof. Kaoni Ishikawa has developed a fishbone diagram to exhibit transition of an organisation to quality culture.

Total Quality Transition

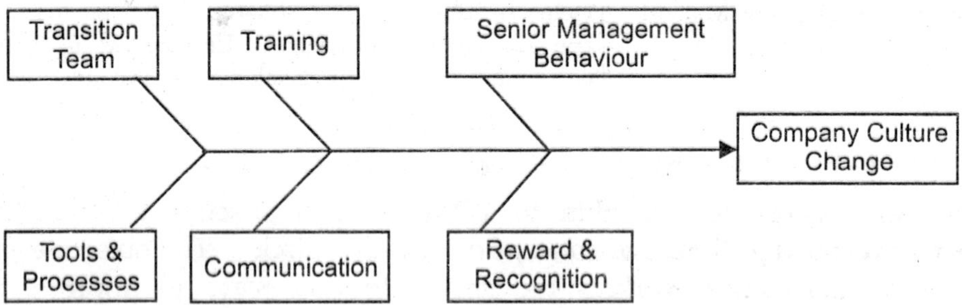

Figure 2.3
Transition To a Quality Culture in an Organisation

The organisation embarking upon TQM program must adopt a strategy that backs up the organisational goal of customer satisfaction. Some argue the other way also. They state that, the goals of the organisation must match its strategy. Whichever way we argue, it is certain that there must be coherence between strategy of the organisation and goals it cherishes to achieve. Corporate strategy is the pattern of decisions in a company that (1) determines, shapes and reveals its objectives, purposes and goals, (2) produces the principal policies and plans for achieving these goals, and (3) defines the business the company intends to be in, the kind of economic and human organisation it intends to be and the nature of economic and non-economic contribution it intends to make to its shareholders, employees, customers and communities. According to Michael Porter, competitive strategy is a broad formula for a business what it is going to compete, what its goal should be and what policies will be needed to carry out these goals. Business policies are guidelines for action and decision making that facilitates the attainment of objectives. Policies delineate its strategies fairly well. Thus, an organisation intending to introduce TQM program must examine its strategies and if found not in line with the requisites of TQM should restate them and thereupon reunite the policy statement in the light of restated strategy. Many a TQM projects fail because they are not focused on achieving customer critical criteria by inclusion of quality improvement programs like six sigma

Total quality management is a continuous process to be carried on for all the time to come so that total quality management itself becomes business. TQM is concerned with continuous improvement in performance. This should be an unending process. Doing gradual, unending improvement, doing 'little things' better, setting and achieving higher standards is called 'KAIZEN'. The message of Kaizen strategy is that not a single day should go by without some kind of improvement being made somewhere in the company. TQM is so integrated in the organisation that it becomes the philosophy of the organisation. It must be remembered that TQM or for that purpose achieving higher and higher quality successively – Kaizen – is not the objective, it is a means, a road to achieve the objective of customer delight. Sultan Kermaly defines TQM as – (1) Achieving total quality through gaining everyone's commitment and involvement. (2) Improvement of the quality of the organisation's products and services for the customer. (3) Customer oriented continuous improvement process. (4) Quality is conformance to the requirement. (5) Fitness for use. So continuous improvement in the performance of the product is at the core of TQM.[10]

It has been argued that TQM cannot be implemented successfully in all organisations. Organisational climate must be conducive and helpful to introduce TQM. TQM is essentially a management philosophy, therefore its success depends upon the trust and belief that management commands in the organisation. Trust in management depends upon three factors. (1) *An acceptance of the concept of management* – employees, suppliers, customers, government and the community should accept that it is necessary to have management to run the organisation smoothly and it has right to control the affairs of the organisation. (2) *The integrity of the management* – It is not enough that all accept the principle of management. The management and the managers must function, must act with integrity. They must exhibit high ethical standards in the sense that managers must always act as role models. They must do what they speak. Even a small lapse from this path may shake the belief in the integrity of the managers. Integrity is always hundred per cent, not even one per cent less. If there is integrity, there is or there is not. One must be able to walk his talk. (3) *Competence of managers* – Managers must be skilled and efficient in discharging their duties. They must be effective in their communication. They must keep the promises they make. This is essential because that guides, helps customers to make choices. Informed choices give better satisfaction. There must not be unjustifiable inequalities among the managers and the staff. Managers should be provided privileges that should be and appear to be justifiable. Managers must be able to address and solve all the problems put forth by the staff. They must be facilitators and removers of barriers. They must possess integrity, honesty and skills to do all functions. There are four types of skills –

(1) *Analytical skills:* They are trained in observing facts, situations and analyse the problems so as to find root cause of the problem. Good analytical thinking involves an ability to understand the significance of both the small details and the total situation.

(2) *Ability to create, readiness to change:* Managers must have the creative vision. This ability depends on a large extent on the experience, exposure of the

managers and their ability to learn, absorb and utilise the lessons to charge the imagination, innovativeness of their teammates.

(3) *Interpersonal skills:* Persons working as managers must have developed good ability to listen to the thoughts and expressions of others. They must be inquisitive to question readily so as to receive a meaningful feedback. Based on this information managers must be able to tell, persuade, negotiate ably and patiently with team fellows. Such discussion must result into facilitating the process of problem solving. These skills are crucial to the implementation of change that management desires to make so as to initiate TQM.

(4) *Ability to manage their own development:* Managers must develop themselves so that they can develop others. This can be done by understanding and committing fully to the philosophy of TQM. Unless the managers themselves are sure about the utility and success of TQM, they cannot convince others to commit to the philosophy of TQM. They must learn about various tools, measures and processes of TQM. Whenever an organisation has a sequence of activities directed towards a defined end result, it has a business process, which can be analysed and improved by TQM techniques.

Preparing Organisation for TQM

An organisation is obliged to introduce change either under the pressure of competition or under the thrust of customers' demand or suppliers' requirements. Shareholders may also insist on a change in the organisation so as to improve earnings and bottom line. Once it is agreed and accepted that the organisation needs to change, it must be decided which philosophy, which program should be adopted for effecting such a change and what should be the nature of change. Many an organisations appoint a team of people from itself while some seek consultation of specialised firms. The advice being to adopt Total Quality Management, the organisation begins to discard its old system of controls and checks. Larry Reynolds states that implementing TQM involves massive amount of personal and organisational change. He argues people are ready to change if –

(1) *There is external threat:* Changing nature and intensity of commercial competition or of government laws organisation may find it necessary to change. A number of mergers and acquisitions have taken place because of globalisation of market. The coming of cheap Chinese goods, joint ventures with foreign companies, incoming of foreign companies, reduction in customs tariffs, WTO agreement, TRIPS, TRIMS have created threat to Indian industry, service sector and agriculture. In 1985 with liberalisation policy adopted by the Government of India, companies began to reorganise themselves by concentrating on core sector so as to improve core competence, by introducing flat/horizontal organisational structure, by mergers and acquisitions, by reducing man power that is by becoming slim etc. They had to reorganise to reach quality.

(2) *Dissatisfied people:* If employees as well as shareholders are dissatisfied with existing policies and strategies then the organisation is obliged to introduce change. If the staff is unhappy with the working conditions, pay, job satisfaction or the quality of service conditions, then the company has to change. It is also quite likely that external pressure may create internal dissatisfaction.

(3) *Inspiring vision:* If the leader of the organisation or the top management is providing a vision inspiring people to change their attitude, culture and behaviour, then the organisation has to change. However, the visionary must be able to create clear picture as to what such a change will lead to. Dadi Seth provided such vision to Hindustan Lever Limited.

(4) *Knowledge of practical steps:* If people in the organisation have understanding as to which steps are to be first taken for betterment of the organisation then it is not necessary to map out the whole route from present situation to destination.

As a result of such attitudinal change among the people of the company, people co-operate and comply voluntarily to make quality the watchword. This change from control to commitment needs radical change in the organisational setup as well as in attitude and behaviour of the management, suppliers, shareholders and the community. Employees will be required to manage themselves to achieve common goals. As we will discuss in the chapter on 'knowledge management' all the people in the organisation will consider each other – manager and employees alike — equal and share knowledge rather than holding it as they used to do under old system of management based on principles of POEM. As a part of preparation for TQM the layers in the organisation will be reduced to the minimum so that the organisation can elicit greater employee commitment through shared decision making. The management should empower people so as to improve their morale and encourage genuine involvement in decision-making. This enhances company's image and assures company's viability in an uncertain world.

The organisation function of management involves developing a structure by bringing together many aspects and elements of business into a structured organisation. With a view to prepare for initiating total quality program positions of each group of persons are defined. The span of control is extended so as to make the organisation flatter. So that the structure of the organisation is based on cross-functional bias promoting flexibility. Such streamlined structure enables the organisation to focus resources on a particular TQM project. Information technology also had a radical impact on evolution of such a structure. More importantly, such de-layered organisation had to be transited into TQM organisation, inverting the organisational pyramid, so that the consumer is at the top of the organisation. Top management has to function as a facilitator, a coach, and an integrator, whose job is to remove the barriers that prevent subordinates from doing their jobs. The same role is to be performed by middle and functional management. The transition of traditional hierarchical structure of organisation (part A of the figure 2.4) is shown to change into de-layered organisation (part B of figure 2.4) and finally turning into TQM organisation (part C of the figure 2.4) in figure 2.4.

Transition from Traditional to TQM Organisation

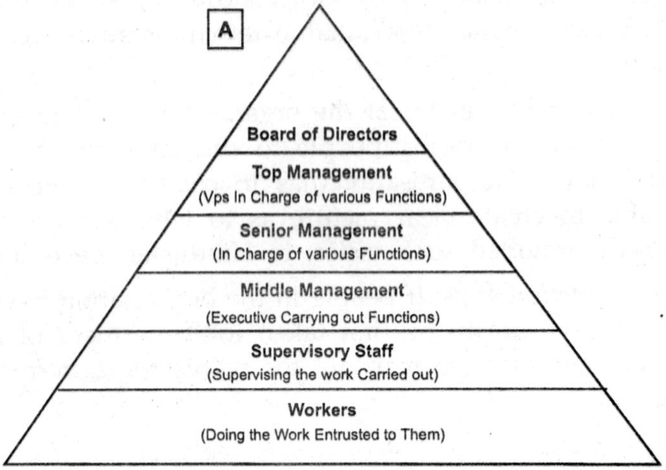

Traditional Vertical Organisation

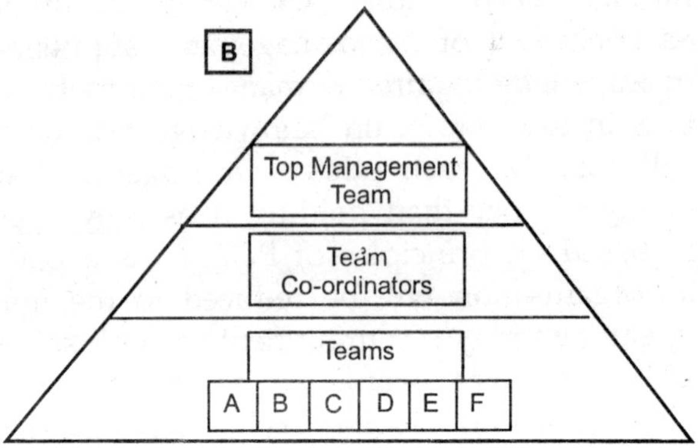

Horizontal Organisation

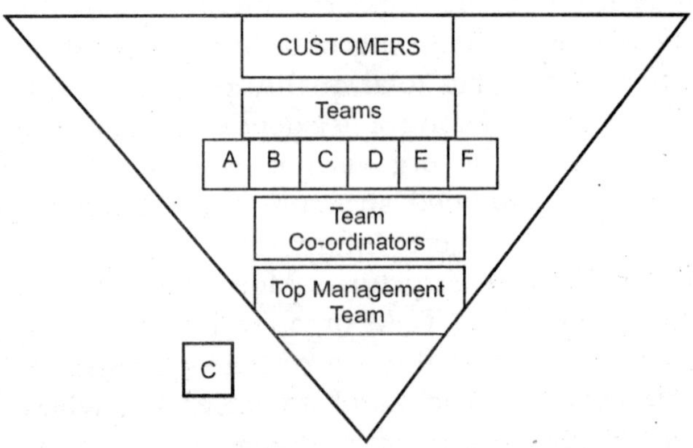

Figure 2.4
TQM Organisation

At all levels management must be conscious that they are role models for total quality. All people in the organisation ought to know what the customer requirements are and how best they can be met. TQM is not just an awareness of quality. It demands the implementation of a totally new system, the generic name of which is the 'Quality Delivery Process'. In such a system, it is ensured that everyone works on those activities that are most important for the success of the business. Company management should have firm conviction in quality and its improvement. Top management should make them individually and severally responsible for quality and gain commitment and involvement from their staff. There must be conviction and commitment throughout the organisation. Quest for quality depends upon conviction and commitment of employees and their behaviour towards colleagues and customers. Quality Company lives for customers. Each member of the organisation, in this system, endeavours to improve the quality of the work delivered to the customer – internal customer and the last person who receives the work. People inculcate the habit of doing it right at the first time. In such a system people harness the combined skills, ideas, experiences of the work group members to improve the business continuously through teamwork.

So, in preparing the organisation for TQM, the corporation has to benchmark the processes, functions to be perfected, to delayer it's structure. Managers and workers should work together by sharing experiences and knowledge. All focus their activities to meet customer requirements with commitment to 'Quality Delivery Process'.

BEGINNING TQM – THE RIGHT WAY

TQM is an approach to developing organisation so that it not only meets customer expectations but actually exceeds them. Success of TQM depends very much upon how it is implemented. To begin with, the organisation sets up the goals that it intends to attain. The goals that it should set up need to be benchmarked, internally as well as externally. Company should set up realistic goals; they must be stated in clear terms. To speak in terms of six-sigma project, 'the rate of rejection should be reduced to 3 pieces per million pieces within five year period' or 'We should capture 22 per cent of market share within next four years' should be the way to state goals. That means a time limit should also be set for achieving goals. This is to be achieved as conviction. As a part of this goal, yearly, half yearly, quarterly goals should be fixed; so that actual achievement can be compared with cherished goals. Goals specified for different stakeholders and evidence of their success can be exhibited as given in Table 2.4.[11]

Table 2.4
Goals Set for Different Stakeholders

	Stakeholder	*Goal*		*Evidence of Success*
(1)	Clients	Satisfaction	(1)	Bill paid on time.
			(2)	Reduce billing adjustment by 70 per cent.
			(3)	Improve accounts receivable days outstanding by 30 per cent.
			(4)	Increase referrals by 200 per cent.
			(5)	Increase client retention by 50 per cent.
			(6)	Increase score to 90 per cent on satisfaction survey.
(2)	Employees	Satisfaction	(1)	Decrease turnover rate to 7 per cent.
			(2)	Reduce rate of absenteeism to 10 per cent.
			(3)	Satisfaction survey score to be increased by 50 per cent.
(3)	Owners	Growth, Profit and Recognition.	(1)	Increase number of clients by 20 per cent and revenue per client by 200 per cent within 5 years.
			(2)	Increase earnings per share by 200 per cent.
			(3)	Get accreditation on ISO 9000.

Once goals are set, it is very essential that they are made known to concerned groups of people and a periodical review taken.

Having fixed the goals the corporation has to translate them into a strategy statement. Strategies set a broad formula as to how the business is going to attain these goals. It also mentions what policies would be needed to carry out these goals. Strategy statement declares principal plans required to be prepared for attaining the goals. This can take the form of a vision/mission statement as shown below.

Vision Statement of Larsen and Toubro Ltd.
L&T shall be a professionally managed Indian multinational, committed to total customer satisfaction and enhancing shareholder value. L&T-ites shall be innovative, entrepreneurial and empowered team constantly creating value and attaining global benchmarks. L&T shall foster a culture of caring, trust and continuous learning while meeting expectations of employees, stakeholders and society.

Vision Statement of Asian Paints (India) Ltd.
Asian Paints aims to become one of the top five Decorative Coating Companies worldwide by leveraging its expertise in the higher growth emerging markets. Simultaneously, the company intends to build long term value in the industrial coating business through alliances with established global partners. Our marketing strategy is — going where the consumer is.

Mission Statement of Hero Honda
We at Hero Honda are continuously striving for synergy between technology, systems and human resources to provide products and services that meet the quality, performance and price aspirations of our customers. While doing so, we maintain the highest standard of ethics and social responsibilities, constantly innovate products and processes and develop teams that keep the momentum going to take the company to excellence in the new millennium.

It is exhibited in figure 2.4 that de-layering the organisation, management and employees are grouped into different teams. One of the characteristic features of these teams is to be that the members are drawn from different areas possessing interdisciplinary, interdepartmental and inter-functional skills. Formation of such teams enables the corporation to configurate various sciences and technologies to develop and deliver a product that might not have even peeped into the dreams of customers. 'May Bake' car of Mercedes Benz, Mobile camera phone are just an examples. These teams are known as 'TOOLS OF TQM' because they are the means, they are the arms through which TQM is implemented.

TOOLS OF TQM

Total quality will not crop up automatically or autonomously. It is to be consciously, deliberately and effectively implemented. Success of TQM depends upon prioritising our goals correctly, planning for the process of introducing quality right from first cliff into the supply chain and executing the plan to the letter and spirit of the strategy and corporate mission. Teams are indispensable aspect of TQM because it is an integration of all functions and processes within an organisation in order to achieve continuous improvement of quality of goods and services. TQM is based on a number of ideas. It means thinking about quality in terms of all functions of the enterprise and is a start- to- finish process that integrates inter-related functions, sciences and technologies at all levels. TQM is a systems approach. Quality and productivity are two sides of the same coin. If quality is improved, productivity is improved and if productivity is improved quality is. Cost is reduced. Theoretical knowledge of engineers and practical experience of workers, both are essential for progress. This is possible only if workers are organised into teams with engineers as leaders. The shared decision making process facilitates change and has a synergic effect. Teamwork creates what Prof. Okuda calls as 'synergic partnership' where total output is greater than the output of individuals functioning. The idea of synergy is most important in teamwork, where the whole is greater than the sum of parts. Idea of teamwork is to promote collaboration, consensus, creative conflict and team winning. Various teams, circles, audits, groups, deployment are the tools of implementing quality.

Prof. Yaji Akao and Shigero Mizuno required that consumers' needs must be taken into consideration by designers to maximise consumer delight. They called this tool as 'Quality Functional Deployment'.

Table 2.5
Quality Functional Deployment

Customer's Need for 'X'	*Attributes of Product 'X'*				
	1	2	3	4	5
A	0	0	0	3	0
B	5	3	2	5	5
C	5	2	2	3	3
D	2	1	2	0	5
E	1	5	1	0	0

The Product Attributes are numbered as —

1	-	Colour of the product
2	-	Size of the product
3	-	Shape of the product
4	-	Smell of the product
5	-	Usefulness of the product

Information collected from the surveys, market research and conferences tells that —

Number 5	–	indicates strong correlation
Number 1	–	indicates weak correlation
Number 0	–	indicates no correlation.

Numbers in Table 2.5 explain that there is very strong correlation between colour, smell and usefulness of the product B needed by the customer. Therefore, designers must incarnate these attributes of the product when the product is conceived.

We discuss the tools of TQM in pages that follow –

(1) Quality Improvement Team

This team consists of representatives from various departments in the organisation. Their functions are to identify and eliminate wastes and wasteful practices. This team pays attention to the two major components – content and process. Content concerns are about the task or the subject of quality improvement projects to which the groups turn their attention. Process issues have to deal with how the group is working – how decisions are reached, how leadership is handled, how people inter-relate with each other, how conflicts and competitions are dealt with, group morale and so on. Quality improvement team has to deal with both the content and process aspects of components of production. Managers, as leaders of the quality improvement team, analyse group behaviour, with regard to involvement, influence, style of influence, decision-making, task functions, maintenance functions, group atmosphere, membership feelings and establishing group norms. They do so with a view to maintain and foster the team. Quality improveme t team members get together at fixed time to resolve particular quality problem.

There are a number of advantages in approaching the problem of quality improvement through a team. One of the strengths of using teams for TQM is that they can combine the mutually exclusive individual qualities that are needed for running the business today. A team can encompass the full range of characteristics needed for effective work. People in the team usually have more commitment to decision they were involved in making than to a decision taken by someone else. However, it is likely that, closer co-operation within each team may spark more antagonism and rivalry between teams. Effective work and good co-operation between teams is essential for the success of the TQM. Team leader must have creative ability to converge both these aspects to the benefit of the organisation. It depends upon the culture of the organisation whether the leader would have to use coercive ways of using authority or democratic approach to build commitment, involvement and loyalty among the members of the team. Team leader must be absolutely sure about the destination but flexible about exact route to get there. The organisation can form as many Quality Improvement Teams as are necessary to achieve highest quality to delight the customer. Probably the number of Quality Improvement Teams will depend upon various aspects of quality, that are benchmarked from different best in the class and the number of partners in the supply chain whose active co-operation and participation are necessary to achieve that standard quality.

(2) Quality Circles

Prof. Ishikawa developed in 1962 the concept of 'Quality Circles'. A quality circle consists of a small group of five to twelve employees normally working together for the same supervisors on similar or identical tasks. But the job of each worker is different. They meet regularly during work time under the leadership of supervisor but on voluntary basis. Their functions are to identify problems, analyse them and find out solutions. That means the objective of organising Quality Circles is to encourage workers/employees to find ways to improve processes. In some cases the workers themselves can implement these solutions immediately. In other cases the solutions are presented to the management for their approval. Quality Circles call for high-level skills of organising, running and collaborative problem solving, which are difficult to find. Most of the solutions put forth by Quality Circles lead to reduction in cycle time. To be successful, Quality Circles must be allotted adequate time. Suggestions put forth by Quality Circles may not lead to immediate results, but though delivered late their effects are long lasting. Leaders of Quality Circles i.e. managers must act as facilitators and they must be adequately trained to discharge this function effectively. It is difficult to muster full support of management in organising and functioning of Quality Circles because many managers feel that these circles give off time to gripe about the company, while some feel that they are encroachment on their authority. Even it is difficult to muster support of trade unions, because unions feel that Quality Circles are another form of managerial control. Moreover, unions are afraid that suggestions of Quality Circles if accepted and implemented may lead to lay-off of many employees because that may reduce cycle time. Such an antagonism from both quarters may lower the morale of the members of Quality Circle.

Figure 2.5
The Quality Circle

Task teams are a modification of Quality Circles. Task teams can exist at any level; a goal is given to them. In Quality Circles members are free to choose the problem they wish to solve. Self-managing work teams are an extension of Quality Circles, with a difference that members of self-managing work teams are empowered to exercise control over their jobs and optimise efficiency and effectiveness of total process. Members of self-managing work teams perform all tasks, complete entire job, setting up work schedules and making assignments to individual team members.

(3) Work Group

The issue identified by Quality Improvement Team for improvement of quality either by using better raw materials, better content of the product or by improving the process of producing a product, by improving delivery time are given as projects to the work group. The project team or Work Group 'owns' that project. The Work Group comprises of a manager and the staff that works under him or rather reports to him. The Work Group Manager is the leader of the team. The project team or Work Group continues to work together either till that problem is solved or the project is completed so as to satisfy the customer with the product. The Work Group determines the requirements of the customer. Members of Work Group discuss with the customer, customers or representatives of the customers, if they are many and assess the needs of the customer. Then they design the product in such a way that it is capable of delivering the quality required by the customer. Every Work Group is expected to work at least on one improvement project at a time.

If the organisation has decided to benchmark a particular process or processes from particular organisation the designated members of the Work Group study the process in our own company, collect adequate data and information about the process (es) of benchmarked company, discuss with the representatives of the benchmarked company the process (es), products to be improved and find out shortfalls in our own process (es) or product(s). Then it undertakes the measures that are found necessary to achieve target quality. If found necessary, representatives of the Work Group visit the plants of the benchmarked company. In completing their task the Project Team may be required to train its members or employees, recruit new employees and induct them into our culture, ethic, beliefs and most importantly to the project. The personnel aspect of the task of the Project Team being much important and requiring detailed discussion is attempted separately in this chapter. Equally so, the Project Team requires information, data from various sources; they are required to communicate to various people at various levels on a number of topics. Success of the program of improving quality depends upon information because it enables the Work Group or Project Team to plan and implement on sound foundation. It is also necessary that the Project Team receive continuous feedback as to how much have we achieved against the target that was fixed. Feedback is also necessary to judge whether the work done by the Project Team is on right track or not. So, information collection, transmission and dissemination being very important are dealt with separately in this chapter.

(4) Departmental Purpose Audits

A team of five to seven members working in the same department but performing different jobs is grouped. Head of the department, engineer, supervising them is the leader of the group. This team prepares a list of the tasks that workers in the department perform. The team then identifies at least five tasks that need to be reviewed. These five tasks are prioritised according to need for development and improvement. Suppliers providing spares, components are contacted and a series of discussions are held with them as to specifications of new design, quality of the material and process. It is found out as to what help and facilities would these suppliers require and what can they offer. Maruti Udyog Limited (MUL) undertook such a task on extensive and intensive scale in their supply chain to classify suppliers into various grades according to the tool-room they possessed, skills of employees they engaged, expertise of the engineers they had. In some promising cases representatives of the Maruti Udyog Limited helped these dealers in updating their tool-rooms etc. and in achieving the quality that the MUL expected from these class 'A' dealers.

(5) Quality Function Deployment

Quality Function Deployment helps us to meet customer requirements consistently, confidently, economically and competitively. The QFD has to perform the functions of changing the work culture of the employees; it tries to change the attitude of the people and processes through which they interact. The purpose of organising QFD is to put the responsibility of achieving quality on the shoulders of a team rather than on an individual. This improves the quality by doing the things right first time. Thus, costs are reduced. Wastes are eliminated and lead-time is reduced. So QFD is a technique of meeting all the requirements of the consumer right from increasing breadth of the product line to consistency of product quality with reduced price. The QFD tries to optimise condition of each employee so that customer's requirements can be satisfied. Customers and partners are brought together so they try to achieve the same aspirations. QFD thus endeavour to improve quality of goods continuously. An organisation may constitute a number of QFD teams so as to achieve multifunctional contributions.

SIX STEPS IN TOTAL QUALITY MANAGEMENT PROCESS

Putting the same scenario in functional form we state that there are SIX STEPS in total Quality Management Process.

FIRST STEP: The organisation has to understand a need for change. Past accomplishments do not ensure future success. Therefore, either because of external threat or internal satisfaction, peoples' vision as to how things could be done better is blurred. If people have a knowledge of first practical step, then change will be not only necessary but inevitable.

SECOND STEP: Considering the cry for a change, the organisation takes a quality initiative, for formulating clear vision as to where the company wishes to reach. Such a vision statement is a document of desired state that states in this process of change how do we reach the destination safe. So under the circumstances faced by the company the organisation would enlist the quality principles that are feasible and suitable.

THIRD STEP: The organisation takes to build up a strong infrastructure to integrate vision into business strategy. In the first instance a quality management department is set-up under the responsibility of one senior executive. Under this department all senior managers are grouped together so that they can be initiated to the quality imperatives. However, each senior manager is given freedom as to how the quality initiative is to be implemented in the division. Such decentralisation of implementation of quality initiative brings required flexibility into the program.

FOURTH STEP: The senior managers introduce the quality management program to the employees. Employees are trained as to what they are supposed to do to implement the quality program. Such training program begins from senior most level running it down in the organisation making managers as the focal point of the program. The managers are inducted to the concept of overall quality, company goals and follow up sessions pertaining to more specific and individual functions are organised. The nature of the training course may vary in divisions considering the difference in jobs performed in each division

FIFTH STEP: After completion of training the managers and team members begin to implement various facets of improving quality of process and the product. If required they are given counselling and coaching to improve their performance. Implementing the quality improvement program is very difficult because it requires rigorous effort to cast old success model and embrace a new one wherein day in and day out new things are to be done practically.

Managers have to record success or otherwise at each step so as to find out where we are going, how far are we going in relation to where we had planned to go, how far had we decided to go at each level. Managers have to appraise top management of this progress with recommendation for recognition of success stories. Honouring champions at lunches, at receptions can be encouraging.

SIXTH STEP: The organisation assesses its own record to find out whether they are on the right path, whether they are in the right direction. This is to be done regularly because quality improvement is a never ending process. The organisation evaluates the market, the customer needs and work processes. In the light of this evaluation the organisation would have to make suitable changes in the goals, strategies, plans and implementation of quality program.

TRAINING FOR TQM

Intensive and rigorous training sessions are arranged to acquaint everybody in the organisation with the concept of quality and make him achieve attitudinal change to welcome Total Quality Management program. Everybody is trained in interpersonal relationship behaviour, process of TQM, functions to be performed, and role to be played in making team work a success.

Persons selected for TQM program must possess abilities to think in new perspective in addition to performing their jobs efficiently. They must possess the attitudinal soundness and flexibility, firm ethical values, ability to analyse things. They should have a balanced personality, sharp problem solving ability in quality environment, ability to perform the qualitative work needed. They must be conversant with quantitative techniques. These persons should possess ability to work comfortably in different group settings. Human resource management, people function, in an organisation that has taken up TQM program must become a process of the function itself so that it promotes labour-management co-operation. This may help the organisation to increase and broaden employee responsibilities. With this set of employees the organisation schedules a training program. People should be drawn off 'utility mindset'. "Utility mindset' is the strong belief in the method of doing a work of being the only method. The management must make employees aware of the fact that there are various alternative methods of doing a work and some of them are better and they must be adopted and such new methods must be conceived and innovated.

In the first instance an orientation program is conducted for executive management. They are made familiar with the philosophy of TQM, role of executive management in initiating and carrying out TQM program. They are given an understanding of the responsibilities of this group of participants in providing positive and active support in running TQM program through. The group members are acquainted with consideration of long-term investment for the success of TQM program; exercising strategic and operational planning.

Then after, a training program is organised for persons belonging to middle management and supervising cadres. They are given a thorough understanding of

TQM philosophy, role that they are required to play in implementing TQM program. They are given a thorough training in organising and leading team from whom the task of quality improvement is to be taken. They are taught inter-personal communication skills, behavioural skills, skills of developing co-operation and coherence between members of the team drawn from various functional areas. They are given full understanding of paying attention to environmental issues. Member participants of this group have to spend more time and labour on learning tools and techniques of TQM. For example, they must be able to visualise the needs and requirements of customers; crystallise them into a plan to innovate processes so as to reduce cycle time, improve quality of the product, improve delivery time etc.

In the third instance, a training program is organised for technical and professional staff participating in TQM process. In this course, as in earlier two courses participants are given good understanding of TQM philosophy. They are trained to identify problems that can be taken up as tasks to improve quality of the product or of the service. Then the trainees are given grounding in skills required to solve problems. They are made familiar with using quantitative techniques measuring the progress of TQM program. These techniques are classified into five categories and are explained in brief below –

(a) Sales Basis: In this category ratios measuring growth in sales as compared to different parameters are calculated

(1) Sales per employee $= \dfrac{\text{Number of units sold}}{\text{Number of employees}}$

(2) Units sold per employee $= \dfrac{\text{Number of units sold}}{\text{Number of employees}}$

(3) Net sales per employee $= \dfrac{\text{Value of sales in rupees}}{\text{Value of total cost of employees}}$

These ratios may be calculated on monthly or quarterly basis and compared with the value of earlier ratio so as to assess the change.

(b) Value added basis: We would like to evaluate whether the contribution of the production process had increased over the period or not.

(1) Value added per employee =

$$\frac{\text{Value of sales in rupees} - \text{value of raw material etc.}}{\text{Number of employees}}$$

(2) Net value addition $= \dfrac{\text{Value of sales in rupees} - \text{value of raw material}}{\text{Value of total cost of employees}}$

(c) Inventory utilisation basis: We would like to assess whether we have improved utilisation of resources.

(1) Monthly inventory turnover $= \dfrac{\text{Monthly MCOs}}{\text{Average monthly inventory}}$

(2) Quarterly inventory turnover $= \dfrac{\text{Quarterly MCOs}}{\text{Average quarterly inventory}}$

(3) Annual inventory turnover = $\dfrac{\text{Annual MCOs}}{\text{Average annual inventory}}$

Where MCOs – manufacturing cost of sales.

(d) Product quality basis: It is an effort to find out whether the quality of the product has improved in the eyes of the customer or not.

(1) Defect rate – defects per million units produced.

(e) Financial measure basis: We would like to evaluate the contribution of TQM program to the financial strength of the company.

(1) Value added = Value of sales in rupees – cost of raw materials and parts purchased.

(2) Return on value added (ROVA) = $\dfrac{\text{Net profit before tax}}{\text{Value added in rupees}}$

(3) Earning rate = $\dfrac{\text{Ordinary profit}}{\text{Total assets}}$

(4) Value added labour productivity = $\dfrac{\text{Value added in rupees}}{\text{Number of employees}}$

(5) Growth rate = Growth of sales over level five years ago

$= \dfrac{\text{Value of sales in current year}}{\text{Value of sales five years ago}}$

This group is also trained in measuring success of TQM with the help of various graphical tools like – Fish Bone chart, Growth chart, Tally chart and histogram, BS 5750. (These charts are explained separately as tools of recording progress and success of TQM.) They are taught interpretation of expression put forth by these charts.

When these three training programs are being conducted a program is organised to train the trainers who will act as TQM facilitators. The group of participants will organise refresher courses for updating knowledge and skills of individuals, teams and newly recruited employees. The resource persons who conduct training for trainers and refresher courses are either hired teams of specialist organisations or are persons who have successfully participated in earlier TQM program in this or in other organisation.

It is important to note here that financial, infrastructural facilities and time required to be put into this training program should not be considered as expenditure but as investment. No compromise on any account should be done because that will be a compromise with quality drives, the main mission of TQM.

INFORMATION IN TQM

Information is crucial enabler in benchmarking, supply chain management, six-sigma management, and knowledge management as well to the Total Quality Management. Information systems serve as key to the success of organisation in quest of quality. In TQM program the need for change, the message of mission and policy, the goals of the organisation must reach in crystal clear words to all stakeholders – investors, employees, suppliers, management and customers. Various teams organised to identify, scrutinise the requirements of customers would have to reach this information to all employees in the organisation. There must be coherence in the efforts taken by different teams so as to avoid duplication of efforts and going off the tracks. That can be done with the help of communication of information. And for all this, organisation must have quality information system. The requirements of the company as regards components of products outsourced must reach the suppliers and their assurance must be at hand in the company. This also needs communication of information. Designing such an information system allows the TQM program to function efficiently, effectively and smoothly. In the effort to improve quality rigor of production process is enhanced and that rigor must be matched by the intense quality of information system. Information is critical to all functions, and all functions need to be integrated by information. Thus, an organisation launching TQM program needs integrated information system to record, store, and disseminate requirements of customers and to reach the specifications of that requirement to all the employees. Information system transmits efforts done at various levels, in various teams to reach the quality of the product to the need of the customer. Such system provides facilities of two-way communication with the supplier. This is one part information plays in carrying out and in the success of TQM.

Progress of TQM needs to be recorded at every step so as to be on the right track, to be at the right time. This is usually done by employing a number of statistical and graphical tools. These tools are performance indicators, Fish bone charts, Gantt charts, Tally charts and histograms, statistical process control, just in time — are the major tools. Use of these sophisticated tools need, on one hand, feeding accurate, timely and latest data and on the other hand, ability to analyse and draw conclusions therefrom and to reach them to the concerned people as immediately as possible. This would not be possible without an integrated information system. Processing data with the help of these tools is possible only if we have had at hand the best information technology wherein we feed the data to the computer, issue them necessary commands and get output that is objective, accurate, reliable and readily usable. This is second part played by information system and information technology in TQM.

Information systems incorporate the process of reengineering so that the TQM program can be run in a better way. Activities of engineering, manufacturing, marketing and support operations when integrated are known as process of reengineering. Such a system helps decision-making at the board level. The output of the statistical and graphical tools provides much-needed base on which strategy is formulated. Both the employees and the customers generate information. This also forms the basis of making decisions. In 21st century, where the nature of competition is changing fast, it is necessary that the management is provided with all required information to enable it to formulate strategy and implement the same.

It is necessary to integrate both these informations. Integration of processes and information can proceed as follows. – (1) Identify the market segment in which the company wants to compete. (2) Use data collected and analyse it to define the customer requirements in the chosen segment. (3) Translate these requirements into major design parameters to develop, produce, deliver and service the product that meets the customer requirements. (4) Complement the primary processes with support activities such as planning, finance, accountancy, management information system, personnel etc. (5) Sub-divide the organisation design parameters into the processes that are necessary to achieve quality differentiation. (6) Design the information requirements necessary to manage each process and integrate all processes horizontally. All these aspects of information help the organisation to position its status in the industry and market.

Customer values high the supplier who provides or delivers right information quickly. In engineering industry information systems helps to cut the cost effectively. Information systems help to reduce response time to the requirements of customers of FMCGs. In this market segment needs, tastes, fashions, likes and dislikes of customers change very frequently. If the organisation has to capture competitive advantage it has to respond as quickly as possible, either by introducing new products or new improved models of existing products.

The discussion presented in this section highlights imperative needs of having a well developed, closely integrated, function oriented information system and information technology. We will discuss in chapters on Benchmarking, Supply Chain Management, Six Sigma Management and Knowledge Management how a functional, well-integrated information system is a prerequisite for introduction and success of these concepts. And more importantly these concepts being an integral part of Total Quality Management importance of information system and information technology needs no further qualification.

TOOLS OF RECORDING AND MEASURING PROGRESS AND SUCCESS OF TQM

The goals of TQM are determined considering the requirements, perceptions and needs of consumers and the capacity of the organisation to enhance its resources, technical know-how and intellectual capital the company has. The management charts the schedule of time frame and proportion of the goal to be achieved in each time schedule so that the quality destination can be reached on time. Any deviation from the right path or slow down in the rate of attaining quality must be known on time so that appropriate measures can be taken to set the program on right path and time lost can be recovered. It also becomes necessary to appraise the progress made and maintained by supplier in the direction of achieving quality target. And all this needs to be done accurately, scientifically and quickly. That is why the organisation employs a number of statistical and graphical tools to record the progress and measure the success on the path of achieving desired quality. The tools are explained in a sequential form of finding root cause of quality of the product being less than desired to delivery of quality to the customer.

(1) Fish Bone Chart

This tool is also referred to as 'Ishikawa diagram'. A Co-operative Society producing milk and milk products found that the polythene bags in which milk was packed were giving way in between transit and the printed information was splitting. As a result milk bags of this co-operative society were being mixed with milk bags of other private sector milk-supplying organisation or were rejected by consumers as being unidentifiable and therefore unreliable. The Quality Improvement Team undertook the task of finding out the causes of such a problem. The findings of the study are presented in the form of a chart so that the processes or parts of processes that are a cause of the problem can be identified and action to remove the causal factors can be decided and implemented. This can easily be expressed in a geometrical diagrammatic form as exhibited in Figure 2.6.

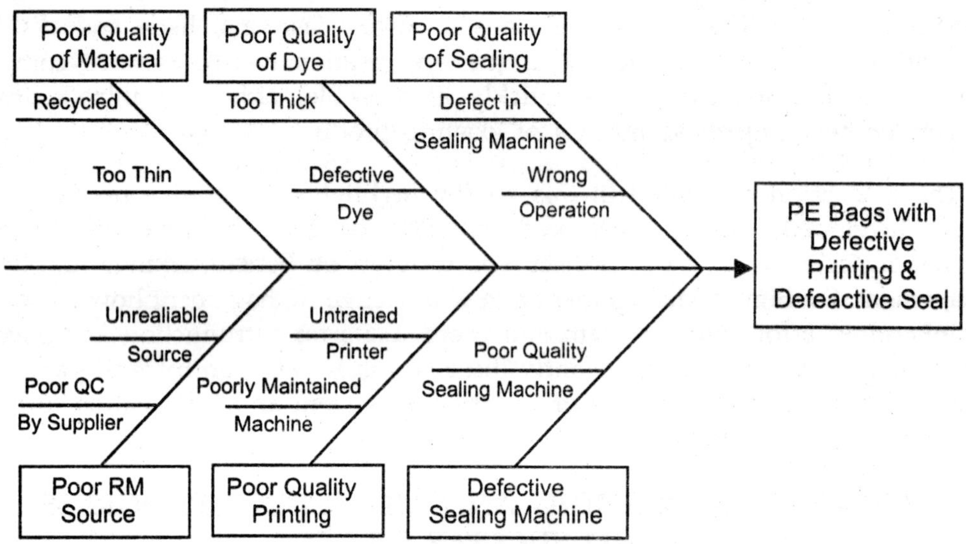

Figure 2.6
Fishbone Diagram

Thus, poor quality of printing of polythene milk bags was attributed to eight causes and breaking seal of polythene milk bags was ascribed to four causes. Having done this preliminary work the Quality Improvement Team identified that printing ink used for printing on polythene milk bags was inappropriate for such type of work and thus getting the right type of ink and using it for printing on polythene milk bags was the solution found. Secondly, it was found that the seal of all polythene milk bags did not break in transit. This was ascribed to negligence and lack of proper skill on the part of the operator. Therefore, a decision was taken to depute operators of these machines to receive rigorous training in respect of running the sealing machine properly and attentively. After completion of the training program, when these operators were put to work, the problem was fully resolved.

So with the help of fishbone diagram the Quality Improvement Team could achieve the quality target.

(2) Pareto Analysis

As we have seen in a very simplified form how twelve factors were identified with the help of Fishbone diagram as causes of poor quality of printing and of seal on polythene milk bags. In reality, there may be multiple of problems of poor quality caused by hundreds of factors. Each of the customers may be complaining about different type of shortcoming in the quality of the product. Pareto analysis offers a simple but powerful tool for separating significant factors from a mass of data. Wilfredo Pareto observed that eighty per cent problems are caused by twenty per cent factors listed. This observation is known as 'Pareto Principle'. The proportion may marginally change to 70 per cent and 30 per cent or so but the principle remains that many problems are caused by few factors. The effort of correcting all problems is not worth because many factors may be insignificant and may be nullified if major causal factors are remedied. Thus, identifying major factors causing quality problems and resolving them may be a major adjustment in improving the situation. It is revealed from the analysis done on the basis of Fishbone diagram that out of twelve probable causes of inferior quality of polythene milk bag, the Quality Improvement Team could single out only two factors as the cause of the problem.

Vikas Fasteners found the rate of rejection of the bolts supplied by them had gone much higher. Quality Improvement Team was asked to study the problem and take appropriate measures to improve the quality of bolts. Fish bone diagram analysis identified five defects – They were (1) Threads of bolts were defective, (2) Bolts had damaged heads as a result a spanner did not fit in, (3) Threads of bolts were broken, (4) Bolts had short shaft, (5) Some of the shafts were bent, (6) Others. They prepared a Pareto chart as given in Figure 2.7.

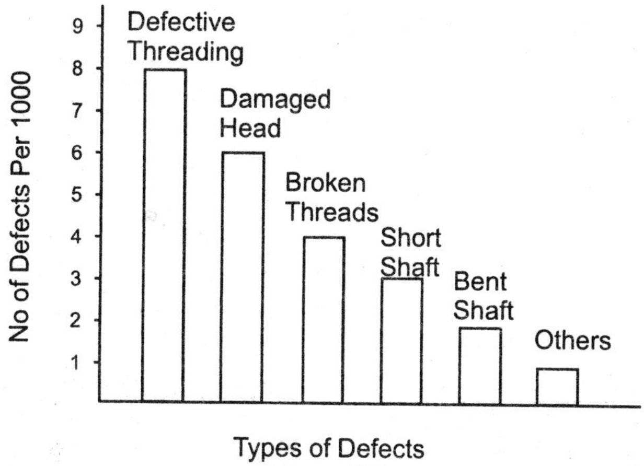

Figure 2.7
Pareto Diagram Exhibiting Defects in Bolts

It is revealed that first cause had resulted in thirty-three per cent of the rejection, second twenty five per cent, third sixteen per cent, fourth twelve per cent, fifth eight and half per cent and the sixth five per cent. Thus, first three causes were responsible for seventy five per cent rejection. Thus, the Quality Improvement Team took three decisions – (1) To purchase better quality polished iron bars for making bolts. (2) Bolt cutting and threading machines should be replaced. (3) Operators working on threading machine should be given intensive training.

(3) Flow Charts

They show how successive stages in process are laid out on the shop floor. To begin with we draw a diagram exhibiting the existing flow of work process from the start to the end. This enables us to identify the areas of waste that may reduce the quality of the product or service and increase cycle time of the product or service. Having identified the problem areas, we can take measures to avoid those links in the flow chart and thereby reduce cycle time, improve quality and make up the delivery schedule.

To explain the point we take an illustration of an ancillary engineering unit outsourcing turning of a component of automobile engine. The present work flow lay out enables us to draw a flow chart as given in Figure 2.8

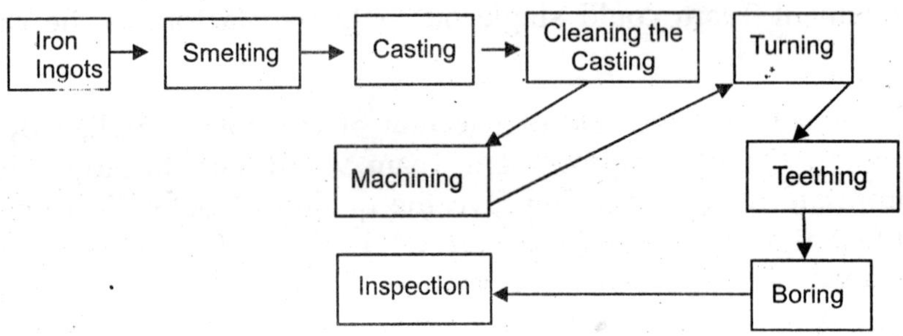

Figure 2.8
Flow Chart of a Turning Process

The flow-chart in Figure 2.8 exhibits a faulty lay out of machines causing unwanted extra movement of product in process causing lengthy product cycle, extra movement of workers, additional cost and then delayed delivery. This problem can be remedied by streamlining the layout of machines and reducing machine time by installing CNC lathe linked CAD system, which can perform functions of four machines. The cost of such machines is bound to increase capital investment. But space saved, labour time saved, reduced cycle time would improve bottom line. More importantly machines, especially computer-connected machines have built in quality. This will save more than the capital invested. This will change the flow diagram as shown in figure 2.9. By taking care of choosing better quality iron ingots and following standard assured method of smelting metal in the furnace and using better moulds, the quality of the product is so insured that the step of inspecting the product can be altogether dropped.

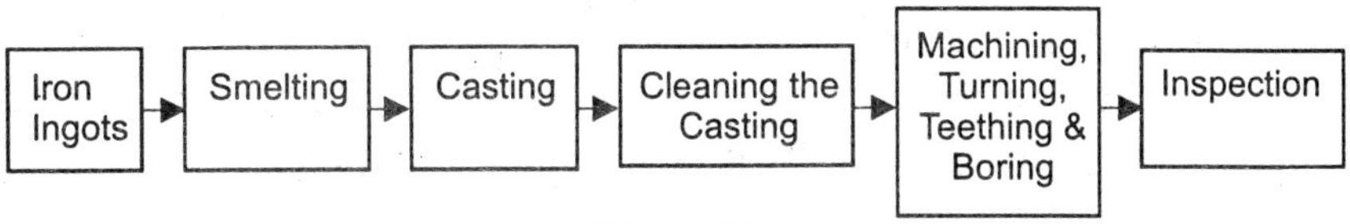

Figure 2.9
Flow Chart Of Streamlined Turning Process

So, by identifying the areas of waste, by installing machines imbibing state of art technology and by improving machine layout, we have been successful in reducing the production process from earlier nine stages to present six stages

(4) Gantt Chart

In some production or service units all the stages in activity do not take equal time. In some cases activities are to be sequentially followed as a result successive activity cannot be started unless earlier activity (activities) is (are) completed. In organisations where activities can be concurrently run, activity that takes longer time is to be started earlier and the activity that takes shorter time is to be started latter. Programming of such activities can be illustrated with the help of Gantt chart. Figure 2.10 exhibits the case.

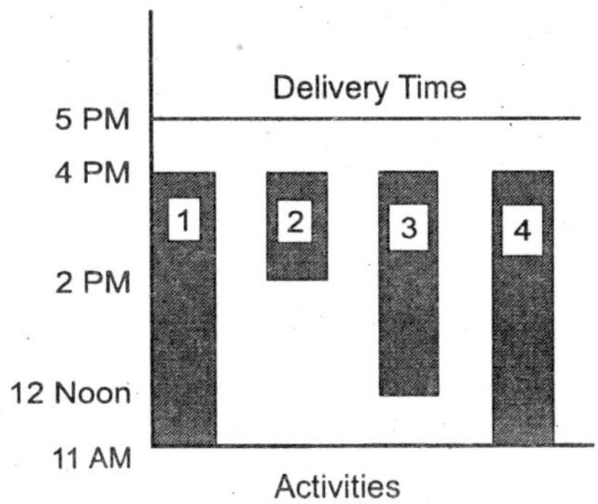

Figure 2.10
Gantt Chart – Programming Activities

We have accepted an order involving four activities with an assurance of delivery at 5-00 p.m.

Activity –1- takes five hours to complete.

Activity –2- takes two hours to complete.

Activity –3- takes four hours to complete.

Activity –4- takes five hours to complete.

If all these activities are to be completed at 4 p.m. (one hour before the delivery time) we would have to start activities one and four at 11-00 a.m., activity two at 2-00 p.m. and activity three at 12-00 noon. This programming would enable us to save labour time by engaging the labourers at the time scheduled to start the activity.

The organisation undertaking work requiring sequential activities involving time of different length, the same technique will have to be used in modified form to deliver at target time, with quality ensured at lowest cost.

(5) Tally Chart and Histogram

An organisation selling cars has fixed the target of delivering ninety cars every month. But it is likely that the same number of cars may not be delivered/purchased every week and also every day of the week. From Tally chart and Histogram drawn on the basis of data from tally chart, it can be found which were the days and weeks of heavy delivery and of lean delivery. On the basis of this information measures can be taken to streamline and even out the swings in delivery performance. This is illustrated in Figure 2.11.

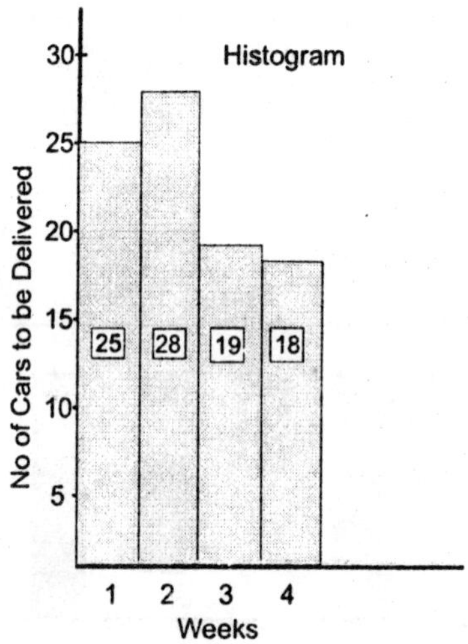

Figure 2.11
Tally Chart and Histogram Exhibiting Delivery of Cars

Tally Chart

Days Weeks	1	2	3	4	*Total*
Monday	||||	||||	|||	|||	15
Tuesday	||||	𝍸	|||	|||	15
Wednesday	||||	||||	||||	||||	16
Thursday	||||	𝍸	𝍸	𝍸	19
Friday	||||	𝍸	|||	||	14
Saturday	||||	𝍸	|	|	11
Total	25	28	19	18	90

(6) BS 5750 and ISO 9000: The British Standard Institute has instituted nationally and internationally recognised standards for purity and quality of different products. This was developed in 1984. It was adopted at international level in 1987 as ISO – 9000 and is known for third party certification. These certifications are guarantee of quality of product and service. India has instituted certification for process as well as quality of product under the auspices of Indian Standard Institute and processes and product that qualify these standard tests are awarded ISI mark. In respect of agricultural and food product India has instituted AGMARK indicating the standardization of process and purity of product.

(7) Performance Indicators: There are a number of indicators whereby we can assess whether the quality is delivered or not

They are –

(a) $\text{Total factor} = \dfrac{\text{Value of total output}}{\text{Value of labour} + \text{material} + \text{energy} + \text{capital}}$

(b) $\text{Partial factor} = \dfrac{\text{Value of total output}}{\text{Value of labour employed}}$

(c) $\text{Individual factor} = \dfrac{\text{Value of actual production}}{\text{Value of expected production}}$

(d) $\text{Rejection factor} = \dfrac{\text{Value of actual rejection}}{\text{Value of expected rejection}}$

Achievement of quality can also be measured by time standard achieved with the help of time studies, work sampling as well as by undertaking activity analysis.

The measurement of quality achieved is reflected in each of these elements – specification, conformance, and reliability, cost (value) and delivery. In addition to these tools the methods of measuring progress are discussed at the end of section on Tools of TQM.

Let me conclude the discussion done in the last three sections. Quality must be the watchword of the entire world community. It is not only in business firms but in all our activities we must endeavour to achieve, maintain and improve quality of our life. The goal of our very existence, of our activity is satisfaction, self-satisfaction, and satisfaction of the community. Thus, Total Quality Management is the concept based on number of ideas. It means thinking about quality in terms of all functions of the enterprise. TQM is a start to finish process that integrates inter-related functions at all levels. It is a systems approach that considers every interaction between the various elements of organisation and also of the organised community.

In TQM the main thrust is on implementation of the plan. The plan is to get other people to change their approaches, attitudes and behaviour. The emphasis is on changing one's own behaviour and thereby making others to follow to change their outlook, their behaviour. TQM is the vehicle for eliciting greater commitment of all through shared decision making to solve the problems that ultimately result into better quality and better life. TQM can further be taken to use strategically the involvement of employees, of people to introduce forms of self-management.

The concept of Total Quality Management is broader in context, wider in application and better in results. In 21st century if the firms have to survive, prosper and make mankind enjoy fruits of their toil, they have to implement total quality at individual level, at corporate level, at community level, at national level and finally at the universal level.

Total quality can be achieved, as we will discuss in succeeding chapters by implementing various concepts, tools and programs like benchmarking, supply chain management, six sigma management and relationship marketing. These concepts, tools and programs will have to be strengthened by managing knowledge, intellectual capital and focusing on core competence and corporate governance. These programs will develop a new organisational culture that will make 21st century a memorable century in the history.

References

(1) Timings Roger and Tooley Mike. *Basic Manufacturing*, Newnes, 1999.

(2) Gawin David A. *Managing Quality*, New York, The Free Press, 1988, pp. 40-46.

(3) Mohamed Zaire – *Bench Marking for Best Practices*, Butter – Worth – Heinemann, 1996.

(4) Sang M. Lee and Marc J. Schniederjans. *Operations Management*, First Indian Edition, All India Publishers and Distributors Regd, p. 574.

(5) Ross Joel E. *Total Quality Management*, Kegan Page Ltd. 1993.

(6) Reynolds Larry. *Beyond Total Quality Management*, Scheldon Press, 1999.

(7) *What is Quality Control?* The Japanese Way. Engle Word Cliffs, N.J. Prentice Hall 1985 and Guide to Quality Control, Tokyo, Asian Productivity Organisation, 1983.

(8) Kilman Ralph H., Saxton Mary J. and Sepra Roy. *Issues in Understanding and Sharing Culture*, California Management Review, Winter 1986, p. 89.

(9) Crosby Philip B. *Eternally Successful Organisation*, New York, McGraw-Hill, 1988.

(10) Kermally Sultan. *Management Ideas in Brief*, Butterworth Heinemann, 1997.

(11) Ross Joel E. *Total Quality Management*, Kogan Page Ltd., 1993.

GENERAL REFERENCES

(1) Drimmond Helga. *The Quality Movement*, Nicolas Publishing 1992.

(2) Gattis Gorden F. *Total Quality Management*, Cassell, 1996.

(3) Jaffries David, Evans Bill, Raymonds Peter, *Training for Total Quality Management*, Kogan Page Ltd. 1996.

(4) Macdonald John, *Understanding Total Quality Management*, Hoddar Stoughton, 1993.

(5) Marshall Sashkin and Kiser Kenneth J., *Putting Total Quality Management to Work* – Benett Kechler Publishers, 1993.

(6) Scherkenbach W.W. *The Deming Route to Quality and Productivity*, Mercury Business Books, 1982.

(7) Sultan Kermally. *Management Ideas in Brief*, Butterworth, Heinemann, 1997.

(8) Williams Richard L. *Essentials of Total Quality Management*, American Management Association, 1994.

APPENDIX 2. A
PHILOSOPHY OF TQM

Quality is an inbuilt concept of product or service. Quality is the characteristic of the product or the service that meets customer needs. Quality is that which satisfies internal and external customer. Quality management is an organisation-wide activity and not a technical task. To maintain quality is the responsibility of management. Management must create the systems and processes that generate quality. Top management must take quality improvement seriously. Everyone, through education and training must acquire skills and capabilities to produce quality products. A quality product combines a good design with effective production methods. Total quality can be achieved by good product design, manufacture, test and sales followed by market surveys and redesigning the product if required.

Organisation must adopt customer driven approach based on mutual co-operation between labour and management. They together must maintain competitive environment. They must develop quality habit. To achieve this and maintain it all must undergo effective training and refresher courses. So that we can achieve conformance to customer requirements. Total Quality Management is not the objective, it is the tool to achieve conformance to the customer requirement; customer delight.

APPENDIX 2. B
STRATEGY FOR TOTAL QUALITY

The company devotes itself fully and wholeheartedly to achieve the highest quality of the product, maintains it and to make concerted efforts to improve the quality continuously. The company values people who create value for customers and shareholders by deploying, producing, selling and supporting state-of-the art products for our customers. The company constantly tries to find out the requirements and desires of customers by means of surveys, seminars, and research papers and tries to exceed their expectations. The company desires to expand its customer base by reaching the customers in rural area. The economy of the country has turned around the corner and is achieving higher rate of growth. Our core values are to provide best of the product to our valued customers at competitive lower prices. The company desires that all stakeholders – suppliers, employees, owners, distributors, should lend full support in making our mission successful.

APPENDIX 2. C
POLICY FOR TQM

The company having decided to improve the quality of the product restructures the organisation by de-layering it and making customer focused.

The products will be redesigned as per the needs of the customers and on the basis of benchmarking would be produced best of the class from beginning to delivery. All the employees will be given full information of the project.

Various teams would be organised to improve processes, functions and activities and members of the team would be given full freedom to invent, innovate and reengineer products and processes.

All the employees will be fully trained in all aspects of TQM. They will be trained in state of art technology, computer and information technology. They will be given freedom to make suggestions and would be adequately rewarded for suggestions improving quality of the products and reducing product cycle time.

❑ ❑ ❑

3 Supply Chain Management

Companies have come to focus their attention on stakeholders' satisfaction from as back as 1970s. Stakeholders constitute suppliers, suppliers' suppliers, shareholders, employees, distributors and customers. All these stakeholders expect companies to deliver exceptional result every time and all the time. This puts enormous pressure on corporate management. Management has to sell-off non-core business so that it can increase its earnings to satisfy the demands of stakeholders. This continuously changes manufacturing and managing topography. Under such circumstances it is absolutely vital to regain all the corporate activities from the point of acquiring resources, processing them into products or services and delivering them on time to the end user to his delight. Thus, the suppliers, vendors, manufacturing, distributors, wholesalers, retailers and customers all constitute an integral part of the organisation which we name as the 'extended enterprise'. The flow of goods from one end of supplier to the other end of the customer is a chain which needs to be so managed that our corporate objective of satisfying all the stakeholders is achieved.

This presentation needs to be completed by adding a number of dimensions. The first dimension is that, from nineties the process of globalisation has changed the very reference of geographical limits within which the companies were operating. All companies have become global. As a result the space in which companies compete has become enormous as well as complex. Companies have to remain competitive permanently and all time. In doing so they have to take into consideration second dimension, that alongside, globalisation, a number of trading blocks have emerged. Each block, while supporting globalisation, has certain unique characteristics of rules and regulations, trade practices etc. Global companies, that have stakeholders spread over the entire world, have to acquire competitiveness within each block, *vis-à-vis* in the world. The third dimension that these global companies have to encounter is the local character of stakeholders. In each region, in each country, the suppliers, the vendors have their own values, characteristics, behavioural patterns, employees have their own 'work cultures', financial institutions have their peculiarities of providing capital and expectations of return on capital invested. A global company while functioning on world scale has to consider and honour these local characteristics. That means such a company has to act on global scale as well on local level, we call this cultures as 'GLOCAL' culture. They have to think global but act local.

In doing this 'tight rope walk', companies have to flow raw materials, semi-finished products and components received from suppliers and vendors from one end to the other in least possible time and at least possible cost. Supply chain has to keep moving each of its links with all responsibilities and accountabilities. Initially the concept of supply chain was referred to the flow of raw materials from its sources to the company and then inside the company to areas where it was needed. This concept did not include the function of order generation, taking it and fulfilling, that is demand chain. But as these two concepts are interrelated they have been integrated as supply chain. Thus, supply chain refers to flow of materials, information and services from raw materials and component suppliers through factories and warehouses to the end customers. A supply chain does include the organisation, processes that create and deliver these products, information and services to the end customer. It involves many activities such as purchasing, materials handling, production planning and control, production, logistics, warehousing, inventory control and distribution and delivery.[1] Supply chain encompasses all activities associated with the flow and transformation of goods from the raw materials stage, through the end user, as well the associated information flows. In other words, supply chain includes sourcing and procurement of raw material and components, production scheduling, order processing, inventory control, warehousing, customer service, management information systems and disposition of packaging and materials. That means supply chain comprises of internal functions, upstream suppliers and downstream customers. Internal functions consist of various processes that transform inputs provided by suppliers into a finished product. In case of large firms the network of suppliers is extensive and complex. Upstream suppliers are providers of components, raw materials and various assemblies that go into making a final product. Downstream arm of the supply chain constitutes all distribution channels, processes, warehousing, transportation of goods to retailers and there from to the end customer. Of late, downstream arm of the supply chain has come to acquire reverse process of 'disassembling' used product, transport it back to production process location and put usable, serviceable parts and components into new products. Such extended enterprise also comprises of 'repair network' to provide services facilities included in the warranty contract and repair, replace worn out parts of the product. So supply chain includes 'forward logistics' as well 'reverse logistics' to attain the customer critical criteria.

Managing such a complex and spread over supply chain is a difficult task. Therefore, we need to have a very precise idea of the concept of supply chain management. Fred A. Kuglin defines supply chain management as 'the manufacturer and his suppliers, vendors and customers — that is, all links in the extended enterprise working together to provide a common product and service to the market place at a price that the customer is willing to pay for.' Kuglin considers the customers as the key role in the management of supply chain extended enterprise and therefore, insists that the product must be as desired by the customer at a price agreeable to him so that he can be bound for throughout the life cycle of the product and service. Thus, he includes 'total relationship marketing' strategy as a part of supply chain management. Supply chain management is the act of integrating all these activities through improved supply chain relationships to achieve competitive advantage.

Every company, each organisation, small and big alike, local, domestic or international is a part of some supply chain. This is true of every area may it be manufacturing, processing, servicing, financing, banking or education. This is true of every sector may be government, public, private or co-operative. All are pipe lines that constitute an inseparable part of a complex, all inclusive supply chain. Constituents as well as management of supply chains in each of these activities may differ in content and detail, but their overall logic, logistic and operation is governed by the same principles, objectives, goals and strategies. I will discuss the general outline of such a supply chain and its management. The discussion is divided mainly in four sections. In the first section, I will discuss the need for development of an extensive, efficient and effective supply chain, its objectives, modus operandi and management of such a chain. Second section will be devoted to preparing people by providing them required training through different modes and leveraging them to effectively participate and work in intra-functional, inter functional teams so as to make movement of goods, ideas, and information fast and quick. Movement of information in a supply chain is as much important as movement of products, may it be physical goods or financial services. This enables the supply chain organisation to achieve its objectives, and goals. Thus, creation and collection of data, transformation of data into information, presenting it into formats that can provide foundation for decision making by different people and various teams is the basis on which manufacturing activity is founded. Data from the point of ordering through delivery of the product and follow up are vital in the organisation. In the third section of this chapter I have discussed all these aspects of information management, enterprise resource planning and e-commerce. In the final and fourth section I have drawn conclusion based on discussion in preceding three sections and have discussed the future of supply chain management.

Every company is a link in one or the other supply chain. Within the company manufacturing products, output of one department is the input of the next process department. That way, all process departments are successive links in the supply chain. Along with this internal supply chain, the manufacturing company has external links in the supply chain. This is equally true of companies like banks, insurance companies, financial institutions, consultancy firms providing services. In the present economic scenario all companies trying to acquire competitive advantage have to focus their attention on satisfying, delighting customers by achieving 'customer critical criteria'. In such a situation the company must achieve 'six sigma' criteria of its final products so as to maintain 'total quality'. The company has to respond intelligently to the demands of the customers and other stakeholders and find solutions to their problems quickly and successfully. If the final product is to attain 'six sigma' criteria quality of component produced by each supplier, dealer and each of the department must be higher than the 'six sigma' level. To meet this target, the organisation has to move through a challenging movement of 'readying' the organisation to conceive, adopt, engineer and implement.'supply chain' philosophy.

PREPARING THE ORGANISATION

To begin with the company should evaluate its present supply chain, performance of each of the link in the process and identify losses in terms of delay in movement, inventory accumulation, non-value added activities, increased cycle time, delayed deliveries, irregular billing, non-conformance of, non-compliance of consumer specifications and follow-up activities. In case of multinational supply chain lower performance may be caused by different customs practices resulting into delays in movement of goods, cultural differences, environmental regulations etc. All these factors may lead to loss of competitive advantage.

Performance of existing links in the supply chain must be assessed with the help of objective criteria as related to (1) products and services offered, (2) sales, (3) market share, (4) cost, (5) quality, (7) cycle time, (8) assets utilised, (9) responsiveness, and (10) customer service. It is very difficult to gather information for internal supply chain activities because departments in the organisation though willing to receive information are not ready to part information they have. Together with this the company has to collect information about performance of the suppliers. This endeavour encounters difficult obstacles because practices with different upstream suppliers and downstream distributors are not the same as that of the principal company. Thus, performances of the different constituents of the chain are to be transformed on same parameters so that they would become understandable and comparable. It is necessary to impress upon the minds of all constituents of the supply chain that it is to the benefit of all that the information must be shared and must be communicated fully and in its real form. This problem of collecting information from internal and external sources can be overcome by installing enterprise resource planning (ERP) software. It integrates all departments and functions across a company into a single computer system that can serve the entire enterprise's needs. Adoption of decision support and business intelligence capabilities to ERP system helps in streamlining the practices of all upstream and downstream arms of the supply chain.

Once the performance of existing links in the supply chain is evaluated, the company can identify which links in the supply chain are strong and which are weak. The company should benchmark the best practices within certain of its suppliers, dealers and departments or within the industry or outside the industry so that the organisation can strengthen strong links further and leverage weak links. It is not necessary that the best practices need to be identified in the same industry. Even practices in non-relevant activities can teach us innovative procedures to improve performance. It is suggested that internal processes should be reduced to the minimum, number of suppliers should be kept as few as possible and down stream movement of goods should have B2B or B2C strategy. This will enable the company to achieve six sigma level of the final product. In other words, upstream supply chain, internal supply chain and down stream supply chain should have minimum links, that is, as short as possible.

PREPARING SUPPLY CHAIN MAP

Once the benchmark partner is identified, the company should prepare a map of her own current practices. Benchmarking teams comprising of employees possessing interdepartmental and inter-functional skills and having knowledge of their mission and task should be formulated. These teams should identify what to benchmark and collect information by finding relevant data from company publications, stock exchange handouts, industry reports and if required from the responsible persons in the benchmarked company. It is quite likely that the information so collected may not be in consonance with the practices in our company. Therefore, the benchmarking teams would have to analyse the information and transform the same into usable and comparable format. Thus, the benchmarking teams would be able to identify the gaps. Benchmarking enables us to focus efforts on those areas that need most improvement. These teams can suggest measures to improve the performance of the weak links. This helps in reengineering the supply chain.

All the concerned employees in the company and the constituent links in the supply chain should and must be associated with this exercise from the beginning because it is their performance which is conditioning the performance of the producer company. Now the company is set to proceed further to reengineer its supply chain.

In the first place the company has to conceive, charter and develop internal supply chain. This task is much complex and demanding in a multi divisional, international organisation with many businesses. In such an organisation, a division considers other divisions as external entity in the form either as a supplier or as a customer. A team consisting of members from a division performing cross functional jobs, is organised to process a map in the form of a flow chart of movement of goods in the division. Members of such a team are trained to have thorough knowledge as to what is a supply chain, what are its objectives, what strategies the company proposes to adopt to achieve these objectives and the role of the division in the supply chain. They must know the language that is to be used in the extended enterprise of the supply chain. The character of the process map of the division depends upon its sequential position in the organisation, whether it is at the entry point, or in the middle or at the end point of the production process in the organisation. Considering that the department is at the middle of the production process, an hypothetical flow map would look like presented in Figure 3.1.

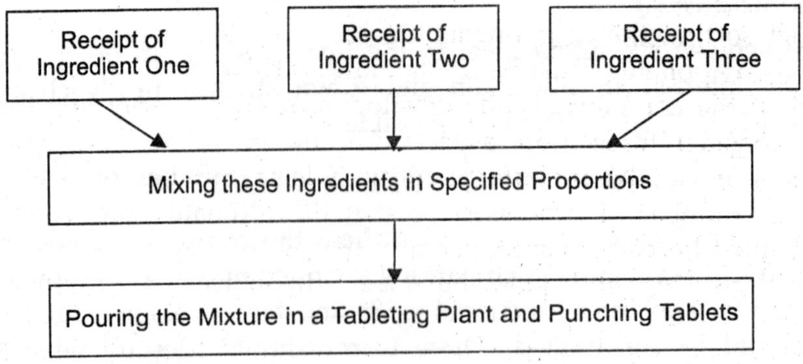

Figure 3.1
Flow Chart of the Department at the Middle of Production Process in the Division

Having prepared process maps of each of the department in a division, the task of preparing interdepartmental process maps is undertaken. A number of interdepartmental task teams are organised. The members of the teams must have inter functional, interdepartmental knowledge; they must know their role in the total supply chain and how their role interfaces with other members of the supply chain. Team members should possess knowledge of common mapping conventions that are being used and common language and practices that are being employed. This exercise would prepare a supply chain map for the division. Process maps of various departments in a division would look something like one in Figure 3.2.

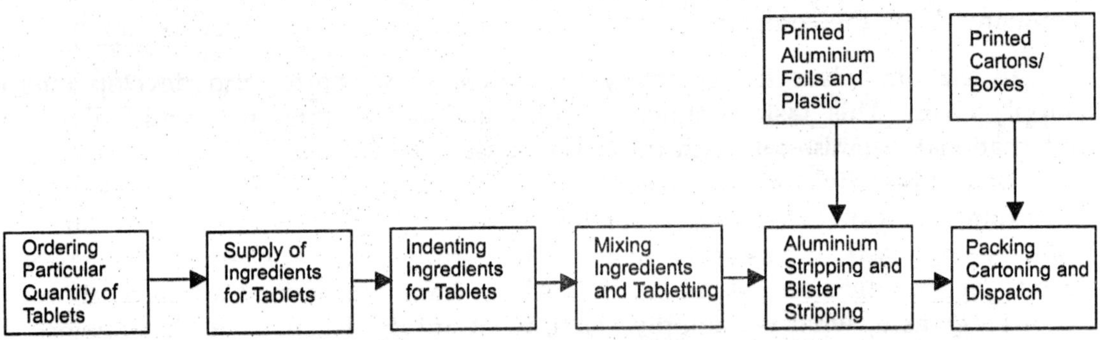

Figure 3.2
Flow Chart of Various Departments in a Division

Once the process-maps of each of the divisions in the organisation are prepared, we set upon to organise interdivisional inter-functional teams consisting of members from procurement (purchase), order planning, manufacturing, packaging, warehousing, shipment, marketing, sales, finance and human resources departments. An extensive and intensive training is given to these members and common workshops, brain-storming exercises are organised so as to have personal interface for each to express his point of view and learn points of view of other members of the team. They set upon to prepare an extensive supply chain map of all the divisions in the organisation. In doing so they would have to consider redesigning of the product so that the components are easy to manufacture, and convenient to transport. The components must be so standardised that they can be used in various like products of the company. While developing such a supply line the committees will have to consider three more aspects. The design of the product should be so engineered that it can be manufactured with least number of dealers and there should be least number of processes. So that the ultimate product would be fault free. Product must be easy to manufacture; that is the key to quality. Designer has to put many things in mind; parts must be light in weight, low in cost and easy to manufacture. Second aspect the committees have to consider is that a properly designed and implemented benchmarking program is necessary to cover the entire supply system. This program should examine the company's role in the supply chain, looking upstream the suppliers and down stream the distribution channels. The third consideration that the committees will have to bear in mind is that production of such output should not emit effluents that endanger the environment. We need to have a 'Green Supply Chain'. Another important matter the team would have to consider is to develop a flow map of information. Internal supply chain comprising of various divisions in the organisation would look something like that exhibited in Figure 3.3.

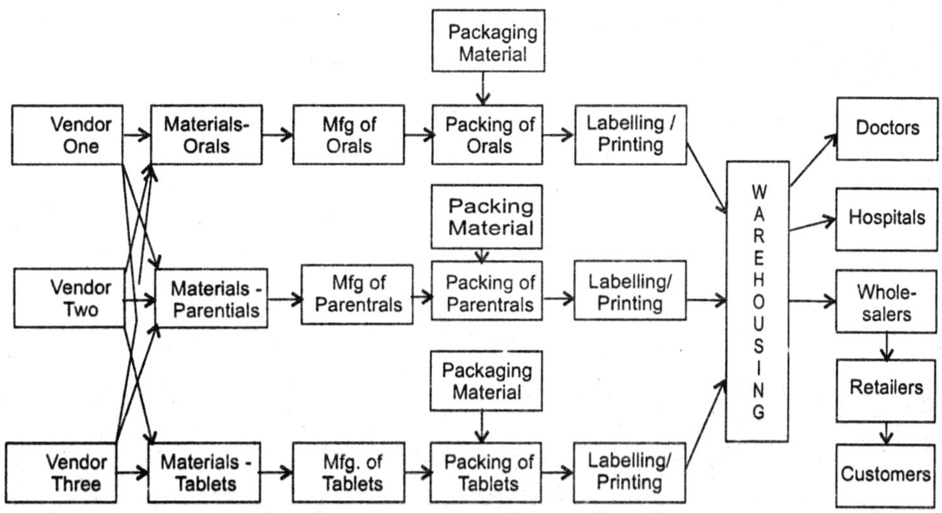

Figure 3.3
Supply Chain Map of the Organisation

After having prepared a flow chart and supply chain map of existing order we set up to design a new supply chain. In designing a new supply chain, it must be taken into consideration that because of changing dynamics of global environment traditional stakeholders in the supply chain are going to be joined by new stakeholders. Telecommunication providers, information technology partners, logistics vendors and financial institutions will join hands in making the supply chain more flexible, responsive, efficient and effective. These new stakeholders in the supply chain will enable us to identify and focus on our core competencies. New supply chain is to be so structured that it would be capable of absorbing new ideas quickly, would be able to adopt to new circumstance, mobilise appropriate resources, would be able to create well developed knowledge base and be able to resolve problems efficiently. New supply chain is intelligent supply chain. There has been a shift in the power from manufacturer to the retailer, to the customer; therefore it is necessary for the organisation, to be successful, to align its competencies with core competencies of partner companies. So that the life cycle of the product can be reduced and the product or the service can be reached to the consumer quickly, at the low cost and with high quality. One important point must be taken note of, customers have been demanding new and better products to suit their particular requirements at lowest possible cost. R and D departments have been developing new models, better products constantly. As a result the shelf life of the product is reduced considerably and existing products, models are becoming outdated very early. This development is fast communicated from customers to producers and from laboratories to producers very quickly by the information network that is woven in the new fabric of supply chain. Thus, competence of new stakeholders in the supply chain, need to be aligned with competencies of all partners in the supply chain (i.e. extended enterprise). The ability of the new supply chain is to be leveraged so that it can conceive new ideas, new designs, new products and offer such new products as quickly as possible to the consumer before he defects. This will change the total management style, economic parameters and break even production levels.

Such a supply chain structure developed by the intra-organisation inter-functional teams should have to provide for recruitment, training and turning of new generation 'technocrats' possessing the knowledge, capabilities to take decisions at split of a second and exhibit courage to implement these decisions in least possible time. Such people will not be employees of the organisation but associates and leaders of the team.

IDENTIFICATION AND SELECTION OF PARTNERS

Having prepared flow chart of supply chain within the organisation we embark upon to prepare process map of key suppliers and customers. It is necessary to have a face to face talk with representatives of the suppliers and customers. This provides us an opportunity to improve our internal supply chain flow chart and align the supply chain maps with those of the vendors and customers. While undertaking this exercise, we try to identify key supply chain members that are critical to organisation's supply chain management efforts. External members, especially suppliers must be chosen on the basis of predetermined objective criteria. It is necessary to know how competitive are suppliers in the world market and how will be integrated into our company's own core business process, product design, product planning and order fulfillment. Once the potential partners are identified it should be ascertained whether they have interest in becoming alliance partners. The organisation and chain partners must perceive that significant benefits would be derived from forming alliance. Supplier is to be chosen very carefully because the organisation purchases not only supplier's products but their capabilities as well.

There are two different approaches of using objective criteria for choosing and selecting suppliers. One is based on Fuzzy Logic principles and the other is the ability and behavioral attributes of the supplier. Let us discuss both one after the other.

FIRST APPROACH

Fuzzy logic principle[2] adopts mainly three tests for selection of a supplier- (1) Supplier monitoring system, (2) Delivery time measurement, and (3) Weight average for supplier defect rate assessment

(1) Supplier Monitoring System

This system is exhibited in Figure 3.4

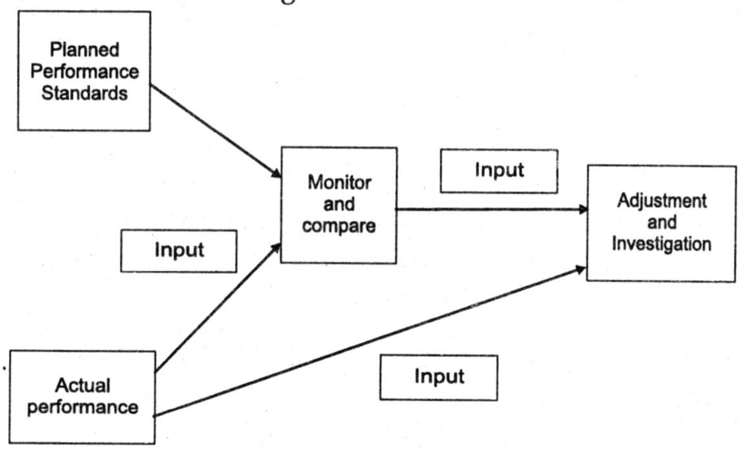

Figure 3.4
Supplier Monitoring System

If investigation gives an input that actual performance of the supplier is adjustable with planed performance standards then the supplier is acceptable.

(2) Delivery Time Measurement

Table 3.1 describes the variation in the delivery time in column one and whether this variation is fine, acceptable or not, is shown in the column two of the table.

Table 3.1
Delivery Time Measurement

Delivery Time	*Standard*
More than 4 days early (< 4)	Not acceptable
Four days early (4)	Acceptable
Three days early (3)	Acceptable
Two days early (2)	Acceptable
One day early (1)	Fine
Promised delivery day	Fine
One day late (-1)	Fine
Two days late (-2)	Acceptable
More than two days late (> -2)	Not acceptable

This can be expressed in the form of Figure 3.5

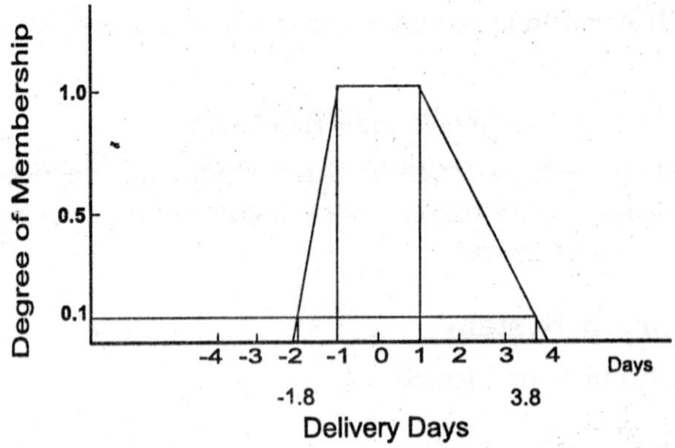

Figure 3.5
Fuzzy Set of Delivery Days

If we need to have one degree membership then only those suppliers who have an established record of delivering components one day early or one day late than the promised delivery date can be chosen. However, if we relax our norms and satisfied with 0.1 degree of Membership though standards of acceptance allow us to choose suppliers delivering two day late from the promised day of delivery or four days earlier to that day the figure indicates that only those supplier who supply 1.8 days late or 3.8 days earlier than the promised day of delivery are acceptable.

(3) Weight Average for Supplier Defect

we make a supplier time assessment over the period for last four years. We calculate weighted average of supplier time. This will enable us to generate a fair performance assessment. If the supplier has supplied components for one year only, then he has only one record. He is given the highest weightage of 100%. But if the supplier has been supplying components for four years then the record for latest year is given weightage of 40%, second year 30%, third year 20%, and the fourth year is given a weightage of 10%. Equally so we calculate weighted average for supplier defect rate. We take the percentage of components received with defects and multiply it by the weightage as enumerated above. Both these are explained in Tables 3.2 and 3.3 respectively.

Table 3.2
Weighted Average for Supplier Delivery Time Assessment

Records Completed	*Weighted Methods*	
1	Delivery time of Record of	1 X 100%
2	Delivery time of Record	1 X 75%
	+ Delivery time of Record	2 X 25%
3	Delivery time of Record	1 X 50%

	+Delivery time of Record	2 X 30%
	+Delivery time of Record	3 X 20%
4	Delivery time of Record	1 X 40%
	+Delivery time of Record	2 X 30%
	+Delivery time of Record	3 X 20%
	+Delivery time of Record	4 X 10%

Table 3.3
Weighted Average for Supplier Defect Rate Assessment

Records Completed	*Weighted Methods*	
1	Defect Percentage of Record	1 X 100%
2	Defect percentage of Record	1 X 75%
	+Defect percentage of Record	2 X 25%
3	Defect percentage of Record	1 X 50%
	+Defect percentage of Record	2 X 30%
	+Defect percentage of Record	3 X 20%
4	Defect percentage of Record	1 X 40%
	+Defect percentage of Record	2 X 30%
	+Defect percentage of Record	3 X 20%
	+Defect percentage of Record	4 X 10%

The data presented in Table 3.3 can also be exhibited in a different form as we did in case of table 3.1 and corresponding figure can show acceptable level. This is done in Table 3.4 and corresponding figure 3.6.

Table 3.4
Quality Measurement

Quality Value (Defect Percentage)	*Standard*
≤ 1	Fine
2	Acceptable
3	Acceptable
4	Acceptable
5	Acceptable
> 5	Not Acceptable

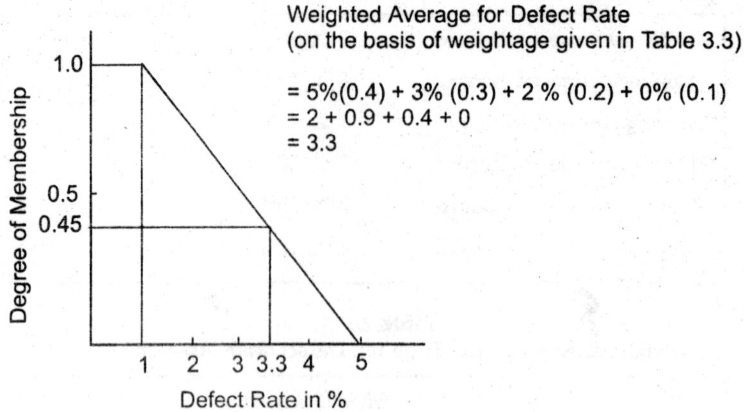

Figure 3.6
Fuzzy Set of Defect Rate

Considering the defect rate in percentage and delivery time in relation to promised delivery time, we can fabricate an hypothetical table 3.5 giving both these aspects of a supplier.

Table 3.5
Defect Rate and Delivery time

No.	*Defect Rate(%)*	*Delivery time (days)*
1	5	-2
2	3	-2
3	2	-1
4	0	-2

On the basis of weightage given in Tables 3.2 and 3.3 we can calculate weighted averages for defect rate and Delivery time

Weighted average for defect rate	*Weighted average of delivery time*
5% × 0.4 = 2.0	(-2) × 0.4 = -0.8
+3% × 0.3 = 0.9	+(-2) × 0.3 = -0.6
+2% × 0.2 = 0.4	+(-) × 0.2 = -0.2
↑+0% × 0.1 = $\frac{0.0}{3.3}$	↑+(-2) × 0.1 = $\frac{-0.2}{1.8}$

These figures in respect of data exhibited in tables 3.2, 3.3 and calculated the below are exhibited in figures 3.7 and 3.8.

Figure 3.7 exhibits data given in Table 3.2 in graphic form.

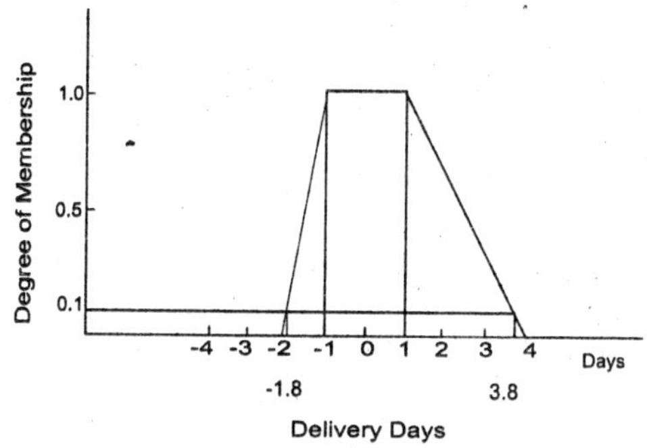

Weighted average of delivery time
(On the basis of weightage given in table 3.2)
= (-2) (0.4)+(-2) (0.3)+(-1)(0.2)+(-2)(0.1)
= (-.8)+(-.6)+(-.2)+(-.2)
= (-1.8)

Figure 3.7
Weighted Average of Delivery Time
(Adoption of Fuzzy Logic)

Thus, the supplier who can provide components 4 days earlier to 2 days late, the promised delivery day may be selected as partner in the supply chain.

Figure 3.8 exhibits in graphical form the data given in Table 3.3.

Weighted Average for Defect Rate
(on the basis of weightage given in Table 3.3)

= 5%(0.4) + 3%(0.3) + 2%(0.2) + 0%(0.1)
= 2 + 0.9 + 0.4 + 0
= 3.3

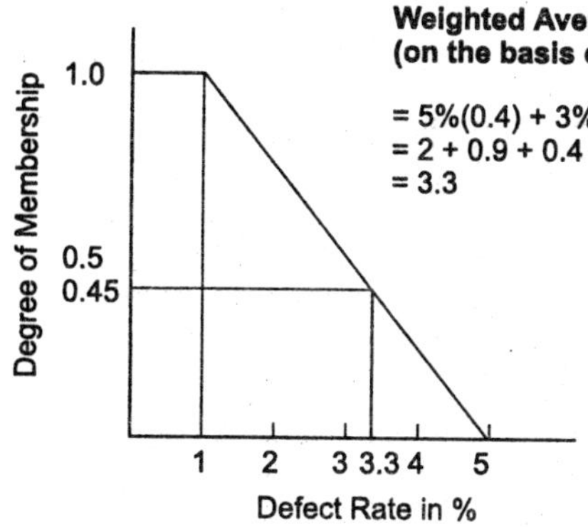

Figure 3.8
Weighted Average for Defect Rate
(Adoption of Fuzzy Logic)

On the basis of discussion done in preceding pages we can say that the fuzzy logic gives us guidelines regarding selection of a supplier for our reengineered supply chain. The data given in Tables 3.1, 3.4 and 3.5 is assembled in Table 3.6

Table 3.6
Performance of the Supplier According to Four Latest Records

No.	*Defect rate (%)*	*Quality Standard*	*Delivery time (days)*	*Delivery Standard*
1	5	Acceptable	-2	Acceptable
2	3	Acceptable	-2	Acceptable
3	2	Acceptable	-1	Fine
4	0	Fine	-2	Acceptable

Guidelines described above give a wide choice of fuzzy set. It specifies a fuzzy distribution as choice. In some cases where single discrete answer is required we will have to de-fuzzify, the process of reducing the fuzzy set (as in Table 3.6) to a single point. If ours is a six sigma organisation we would have to give more weightage to quality where defect rate is zero and compromise on delivery standard time. Thus, our choice would be number FOUR supplier.

SECOND APPROACH

The second approach to choosing and selecting suppliers on the basis of ability and behavioral attributes consists of ten tests to be applied to the supplier. They are —

(1) Suppliers should not be direct competitors among themselves and also with the organisation.

(2) They must be enjoying competitive advantage in the production segment.

(3) As constituents of the extended organisation the suppliers should be pursuing, if not identical, at least similar goals, so that the direction of their activity becomes compatible with overall supply chain management initiative.

(4) Suppliers must exhibit financial capability and stability.

(5) They must be practicing total quality management philosophy and programs.

(6) The suppliers have to have process and technology capability.

(7) The suppliers must be complying with environmental regulation.

(8) Suppliers must be convinced that the present exercise of developing supply chain is beneficial to all and they must enthusiastically involve themselves in development and functioning of the supply chain.

(9) They must be ready to sign and observe confidentiality agreement; and

(10) Suppliers so chosen must be ready and willing to participate all information by way of delivering and receiving it. They must utilise the information fully to the advantage of entire supply chain. Suppliers should not dwelve with this information to any other party.

The inter-functional teams preparing supply chain process maps should discuss in detail with the representatives of the supplier the objective of developing supply chain, the strategies and policies to be adopted. The members of the team should personally visit the plants of the supplier so as to assess the tool-room facilities, knowledge as well as capabilities of the employees of the supplier to meet the strict code of quality that the supply chain expects to ensure. As a matter of fact the supplier should be regarded as partner in the organisation.

Having selected the supply chain vendors the company should organise person to person meetings between key personnel of supply chain members. Workshop sessions should also be convened. This will enable the company as well as supplier to discuss current business practices and the new practices that are required to be followed. The supplier must be doing their jobs 'good' according to them but they must be able to perform the job 'the best' from the point of view of all members. Delays, wrong ordering problems can be identified and corrected immediately. Face to face discussions can unearth the problems that the supply chain is likely to face in future and solution can be thought of. Such meetings will prepare all to respond positively to critical situations. Members of such groups can visualize possibilities of joint projects between 'sub groups' of the supply chain members. Such joint projects may encompass a few but critical activities that would improve performance of the entire supply chain. Inter-organizational cross-functional teams may meet as often as required by the situation, even weekly, to improve performance, cut short processes and resolve problems then and there before they assume monster form. These teams can discuss the measures to be adopted for reducing product cycle time and chart out the measures to do the same.

The discussions between members of inter-organisational cross-functional teams and contracts drawn must develop trust between the members of the supply chain. Trust is really a multidimensional phenomenon. Trust can be developed by acting as discussed by both or all the parties in the supply chain. Supply chain relationship based on trust can be developed by creating a process that implements decisions with fairness and equity. It can also be done by improving level of competence within the organisation, especially for individuals who will be acting as key liaison with partners in the supply chain. All members of the supply chain must involve themselves fully in all activities so as to add value to the customer.

While contracting with the supply chain members, the inter organizational teams must envision possibilities of disputes and conflicts between parties. The contracts must be so designed that there should be least room for such instances. Even with these precautions would there be any dispute or conflict between the supply chain members, provision must be made in the contract itself to resolve the disputes. Solutions provided by commercial law to resolve such disputes being lengthy, time consuming and costly must be avoided. The provisions in the contract should make room for an hierarchy of alternative means to resolve such disputes beginning from face-to-face negotiations between parties involved though arbitration, mediation, mini-trial or renting a judge from court. It must be mentioned that solutions to such disputes depend upon the sincerity and willingness of affected parties to end the dispute even by compromising and sacrificing a little by both the sides.

Desires and expectations of customers must be given highest consideration while developing a blue print for effective and efficient supply chain. Fred A. Kuglin in his book 'Customer Centred Supply Chain' argues that the very purpose of developing an efficient supply chain is to meet customer critical criteria and delight the end user. The supply chain must be so tightly woven that there will be hardly any room for waste of resources, money and time. He states, 'the design of the order-to-cash supply chain should focus entirely on the final product and the consumer'. Reengineered supply chain must prepare for relationship marketing. It must innovate methods, processes for value refinement to satisfy the needs of the supply chain customer. It must find ways to creation of value that would satisfy unmet dreams of the customers. It is very important here that value creation efforts usually establish new linkages between supply chain partners. Value addition activities innovated in one link of the supply chain must be carried forward through the chain to the end user. This can be done by leveraging core competencies which enable the chain to migrate values from one link to another.

Reviewing the existing operations of supply chain is the first act of the supply chain management. Deciding objectives and strategies for new supply chain, preparing a blue print of process flow and putting it to work is the second act of the management. Tasks of management become more complex and challenging as the supply chain begins to function. I am preparing to discuss these management functions.

MATERIALS AND TIME MANAGEMENT

Management of the supply chain organisation has to carefully and continuously watch flow of materials through the links of the chain. Most suppliers are simultaneously members of various supply chains. These suppliers offer a number of products and services to various organisations. To make them play their role efficiently in our chain is very critical to survival of our organisation. Therefore, management has to ensure that right materials arrive at right locations at right time. Improvement in the supply base must be initiated and driven. To make the components move fast in the pipe line, product design should be simplified so as to make it easier to manufacture and assemble. This calls for a new approach to ordering and inventory management. Cost of operating supply chain is major part of the operating costs of the organisations, in some cases even rising to 75% of the total operating costs. Therefore, every opportunity to improve the flow of materials across the supply chain must be grabbed and made full use of. On one hand products are becoming less standardised because customers are demanding options that are tailored to their requirements. The organisation, to be successful, has to develop ability to 'mass-customise' their products.[3] When we talk of simplifying product design, actually products are becoming complex to provide greater variety of options to a greater variety of shrinking market 'niches'. Mobile phone has come to acquire so many functions that in addition to 24 functions it performs it can take photographs and it can act as a remote control to issue directives to a domestic robot. Product life cycles are shrinking from years to a matter of 2 to 3 months. Tom Peter describes 'many global markets are comparable to the fashion industry in which products go in and out of style with every season.[4]

Manufacturing companies, service organisations have to develop very efficient and effective logistics. Logistics refer to the movement of materials within a production facility, the shipment of incoming materials from suppliers and the shipment of outgoing products to customers. Materials include all the physical items used in the production process such as fuel, equipment, tools, office supplies and so on. In many a manufacturing units the architecture of the plant building is so laid out that the supplier provides the components, not to the stores, but at the location in the plant where they are used. To speed up the matter further all the supplies are 'invoice-less purchasing' and 'stockless purchasing' so that the producing company maintains no inventory at all. The materials received just-in-time are directly taken on the assembly line. Cement manufacturing companies prepare such a layout of the plant that the bags of cement are directly transshipped on conveyor belts from packing point to the railway wagon wherefrom it is transported directly to the retailer or if possible to the consumer. Many a companies producing electronic consumer goods and catering for foreign markets have shifted production facilities on the ship itself. The suppliers reach the required materials to the port and the ship and the goods are assembled while the ship sails to the destination port. In brief, innovation in logistics has no bounds. The objectives are to reduce inventory to as little as possible, make the flow of materials as fast as possible and reduce operating costs.

R. H. Ballou argues that extended organisations, to be successful, have to put emphasis on logistics control since it ensures that the goals around which logistics plans are developed are also achievable. Besides deploying successful logistics controls, it is also essential to build and maintain good business relationships with the partners for adoption of technologies and algorithms, i.e., deploying a methodology that must be able to provide enough flexibility to measure quantitative values. Even then there are likely to be some areas in real life situation where making a decision about selection of a particular supplier may be difficult. Such indecisive area of decision making is called as gray area. Fuzzy logic can help us to resolve the problem. The method of selecting a supplier explained with the help of data given in Table 3.6 can be used here.

Organisations have to be alert so that any and every mistake can be avoided, that is because even a small mistake in supply chain is likely to cost life of the organisation. Supply chain expects 'perfect orders' so that they can respond quickly, precisely and provide quality products every time. This is a time based competition. Organisations have to move men, material and money as quickly as possible. savings in the time result into savings in cost and increase in profit level. Robert Handfield and Ronald Pannesi argue that 'time based competition enables the firms to grow fast and earn higher profits, increase in profit share through early introduction of new products, control overheads and inventory costs'[5] Strategy to satisfy 'impatient customers' translate time saved into profits gained. Time management enables the organisation to reduce the amount of inventory flowing through chain. Outsourcing 'data processing' to India from the U.S.A is an example of reducing inventory, saving time and reducing cost of production. The 'due to stock' method described in the illustrations given in preceding and this paragraphs reduce rework, improve product quality and less overheads through every link in the supply chain. Robert Handfield and Ernest. L. Nicolas (Jr.), state that, 'such a supply chain system has internal benefits such as simplified organisations, shorter planning loops, increased responsiveness, better communication, coordination and cooperation between functions'. This brings all parties in the supply chain 'on the same wave length'.[6]

Organisations have to compete on the basis of time, keeping quality of their product high, price low and performance better. It is one of the objectives to participate in supply chain to reach products earliest to the end consumer. Organisation must integrate its supply chain so close that least possible time is taken to respond to the customer demand. Time sensitivity presents a number of challenges and opportunities to the organisation. Organisations must improve their capabilities to compete on the basis of time. Time is the area where a number of opportunities are present for improvement. The point can be illustrated with the help of an live example. Bajaj Auto Ltd. exports 28 per cent of three wheelers produced by it in India. Most of these utility vehicles are exported to South Eastern Asian countries. The organisation has decided to set up fully-owned subsidiaries or joint ventures with local players to assemble three wheelers in Indonesia, Philippines, Thailand, Vietnam. This will enable the organisation to customise production to cater to the local needs and reduce cost of production. Such a decision strengthens the supply chain.

The most important method to compete on the basis of time is to reduce 'cycle time'. Real work consumes not more than twenty per cent of the cycle time. Rest of the time is taken by a wide range of activities that hardly add value to the product or the service. Supply chain management faces a challenge and opportunity in identifying and reducing or eliminating such unproductive uses of time and assets. Reduction of cycle time improves effectiveness of the organisation. Many an areas consuming time unnecessarily can be identified and can be either eliminated completely or reduced considerably. Performance in reducing cycle time can be improved if all information available with the supply chain members. Information sharing-that making information available to all partners in the supply chain is the main leverage to improve cycle time performance. This can be done by developing "Inter-Organisational Information System" (IOIS).

Supply chain management must ensure that no time is wasted in waiting between process steps, especially when the productive activity is multi-step process. Activities that are redundant in the productive process must be identified and howsoever deep-rooted in the routine must be ruthlessly eliminated. They add little or no value to the current environment. Process that can be activated simultaneously should be run right first time, this avoids repeat processes under the guise of improving quality. If the process is run right first time it maintains the quality and shortens the cycle time. Batching of production should be so streamlined that time elapsed in transferring production facilities from one batch to another is eliminated or at least reduced to the minimum. A cost benefit analysis should be done to find out which rules, procedures add to the cost and not to the benefits. Such rules, regulations and procedures should be repealed. Poorly designed procedures should be discarded. Forms seeking the same information again and again should be either streamlined or should be done away with. Just in time practice should be strictly adhered to, to hasten the movement of materials, avoid early arrivals causing storage, warehousing and material handling problems. All members in the supply chain should reengineer their production facilities, material handling facilities and information platforms by adopting the state of art technology. Suppliers, dealers and manufacturing company, all constituents of the supply chain should periodically or as and when available adopt newer technology so as to keep an edge on the competitors. All members of the supply chain should simultaneously train their employees in implementing and using new technology and latest environmental expectations. They should introduce new concepts in management so as to make all proficient in their jobs and thereby become quality organisation. Supply chain management should ensure that the communication system is fully integrated so that there is no gap in the information system of suppliers and dealers on one hand and manufacturing system on the other hand. Such information system should provide all necessary and required information to all those who need to use it, up date it regularly. Management should base their decisions on this up-dated information. Employees in the entire supply chain must be trained to put in the necessary information into the network and draw therefrom required information so as to make the material move fast. Employees in various links of the supply chain as well in the organisation must communicate with each other as often as possible so that there would be perfect co-ordination in the activities of all the partners in the chain. Associates (employees) in the entire chain must be charged with enthusiasm and devotion so that they co-operate fully to make their mission achieved. To put in a nutshell, link to link supply chain should be alerted regarding materials planning and scheduling, purchase order cycle, inbound transportation, manufacturing process, customer order processing, warehousing operations, outbound transportation, return material and reverse logistics. The steps of material receipt, inspection and review have been omitted purposely because in a supply chain, adoption of total quality criteria, and six sigma methodology leaves no space for these steps.

It is quite clear that opportunities and means to reduce cycle time in each supply chain and in many a links in a supply chain are bound to be different. Even there can be different right ways to reduce supply chain process cycle time. However, the various aspects to which supply chain management should pay attention to, as described above, remain to be almost the same. H. James Harrington[7] has suggested that every supply chain should organise a Cycle Time Reduction Team consisting of persons having analytical capabilities and coming from each functional area and each organisation involved in the given process. Members of the team should be given thorough grounding in various processes in the supply chain. Members of the team should study fully and carefully the process map, flow chart and on the basis of thorough examination of the map and chart, identify opportunities for improvement in performance and reduction in cycle time. The team should prepare a plan of measures to reduce cycle time and the method of implementation of the measures. The team should articulate the time expected to be reduced by means of implementation of these measures and time span they would expect to achieve this reduction in the cycle time. These measures can be classified into five major areas, namely (a) organisation design and management

(b) human resources, (c) product management, (d) operations, and (e) inter-organisational issues. These measures along with expected results and time limit set for should be made known to all members of the extended organisation. Reduction in inventory held by the extended organisation and reduction in cycle time is a continuous exercise. There is always a scope for further improvement and that must be done to maintain competitive advantage.

Managing Organisational Relationship

Developing organizational relationship with all stakeholders and especially with suppliers and customers is another area where supply chain management has to function positively. This helps developing trust among various links of the supply chain. Developing trusting relationship among and with partners in the supply chain is an outcome of the deliberate and concerted efforts. It can be created by performance and demonstration of reliability in organisations. The organisation can evaluate trust by assessing feeling of suppliers 'loyalty, good feeling about integrity and openness'. Partners in the supply chain are trustworthy if they are reliable, competent, loyal, vulnerable and exhibiting goodwill. Relationship in all links of the supply chain can be long lasting if all act is as committed and in a predictable manner.

Organisation has to give complete understanding of the objectives, strategies and policies to all the constituents of the supply chain and it has to act as per promises given and decisions taken. This behaviour must be continued with suppliers' suppliers also. Such consistent behaviour on the part of the organisation alone can develop trust and trust is the foundation of relationship. Relationship thicknes further into an alliance with supply chain partners. All the constituents in the supply chain need to have competencies in the same core. Matching competencies as we can call it, is an asset on which to build relationship. Such relationship need to be reviewed if the organisation has to make a change in the strategies because exogenous factors like actions of global companies, industry consolidation, technological changes or new route of distribution or retailing have emerged. Closer supply chain relationship provides the best opportunity for achieving strategic goals.

Continuation of relationship may come across a number of storms which need to be taken care of. It is quite likely that over the period of time one or a few members of the supply chain may begin to wield greater power. Such power imbalance may jeopardise cordiality of relationship. It is usually observed that buyer organisation enjoys greater power that enables it to squeeze terms and advantages from client or dealer supplier. Such imbalanced power hits at the root of supply chain relationship. Therefore, the agreement, with suppliers, itself must provide safeguards against such power imbalance. One more point needs to be considered. It is quite likely that one or few partners in the chain may behave in a way that is injurious to alliance or block the scarce resources to benefit self at the cost of other members of the chain. The relationship agreement has to provide for such traits of unscrupulous members. In other words, all members must be accountable to all members for every act of theirs.

An effective and well knit communication line is to be established with suppliers and customers and used on a regular basis. Even saying 'hello' occasionally strengthens bonds of relationship, wards off misunderstanding and fosters trust. This smoothens the way of sharing information. As the degree of trust between organisation and suppliers as well as with customers increases and is firmly established, a smoother flow of materials and information within the supply chain takes place.

As a part of the corporate governance the organisation must disclose to the shareholders information about suppliers, major buyers and their stake in the supply chain. This practice of transparency brings discipline in the working of the organisation. People develop confidence; trust in the organisation which becomes helpful in raising capital at reasonably low cost. People remain assured about the ethics, values that the supply chain and organisation cherishes.

Major suppliers, buyers, representatives of investors and financial institutions should meet face to face periodically. This enables all links in the supply chain to perceive changes in relationship and operational practices. Such communication provides a conduit for feed back to all the partners in the supply chain. All the members in the supply chain compare actual effectiveness with perceived effectiveness, adherence to predetermined operational standards with promised standards. It is quite likely that, with all such open door policy, a few problems, grievances are likely to crop up. The well knit, trust based, face-to-face relationship enables all members to look to such problems objectively and resolve by realigning objectives and priorities.

Schmitz J.M, Frankel R and Frayer D.J. have gone much ahead in the process of developing and strengthening relationship by establishing horizontal and vertical alliance between suppliers, organisation and consumers. Supply chain members should be willing to devote time and effort necessary to create a strong supply chain relationship. Efficient Consumer Response Alliance Model can do so by developing a special type of relationship which the authors call as 'strategic alliance'. This enables supply chain members to exchange and share confidential information, to undertake joint projects by investing assets and pursue all-round improvements. The authors define — 'strategic alliance is a process wherein participants willingly modify practices to reduce duplication and waste while facilitating improvement in performance. The schematic figure from the book 'ECR Alliance— The Best Practice Model'[8] is reproduced in Figure 3.9.

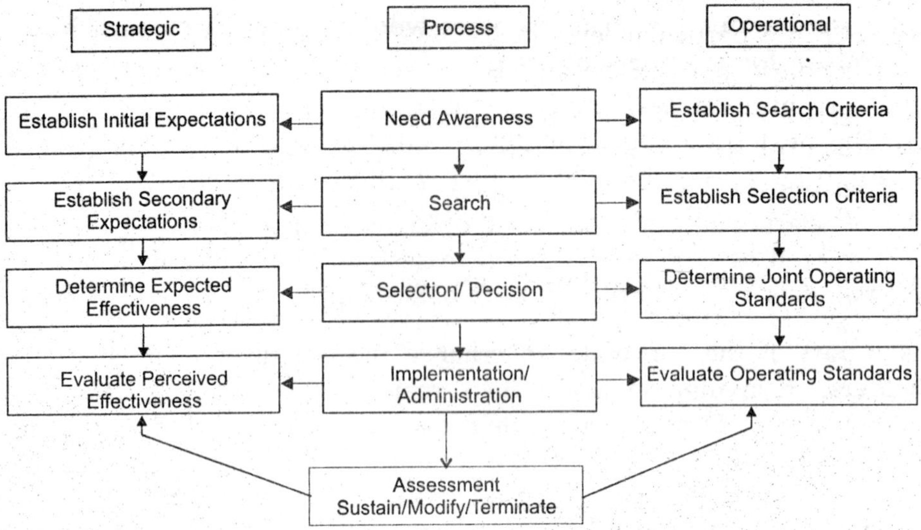

Figure 3.9
Efficient Consumer Response Alliance Model

Vertical components of the figure show that strategic component examines how strategic expectations and evaluations of alliance effectiveness develop as an alliance progresses through development stages. The process component outlines stages of alliance's development that show the required steps for information, implementation and maintenance of alliance. Thirdly, the operational component explains the development of search and selection criteria and operating standards for managing alliance. When horizontal stages are discussed it is necessary to consider in which vertical stage this horizontal stage occurs. As indicated by downward pointing arrows in each vertical component, the management has to take into account strategic, process and operational issues that come in each horizontal stage.

After having identified partners for linkage, the organisation assesses suppliers' strategies and competencies as we see in the first box on left hand side of Figure 3.9 where initial expectations are determined. This is an initial but strategic move. The organisation then perceives whether the partner chosen is aware of the role he has to play in the supply chain, responsibilities he has to shoulder. The organisation ascertains whether mindset of the partner is prepared to welcome changes in internal activities as well approach to the external members of the supply chain. At operational level, in initial stage, the organisation develops criteria on which the chain partner is to be evaluated. Partner's performance in various areas is evaluated. If the supplier partner passes these three criteria at conceptual level, alliance modalities are taken to the next, second level.

In the second level of alliance, as we can see in the Figure 3.9, boxes from left to right tell us how the organisation moves to pursue the alliance. The organisation indicates secondary expectations from the chain partner. It is evaluated whether the supplier possesses flexibility and capability of introducing successfully changes that would be required to make alliance successful. Reduction in inventory, performance improvement to a particular level in specified time, degree of achievement expected are the secondary goals. Expectations are set forth. Setting such secondary goals helps the organisation to identify strategic and operational characteristics of the partner. The next box, middle in the second level, tells us that the organisation would search processes that the partner is practicing and would try to find out whether they are in line with the processes that the organisation tries to develop in the supply chain. It is assessed whether the partner feels that such an alliance is beneficial to both the parties. These are the criteria on the basis of which operationally the partner is found suitable to be a member of the supply chain. Such alignment is helpful in deriving benefits expected by both the parties.

At the third horizontal level in the Figure 3.9, the box at the left hand reads that the organisation expresses strategically the effectiveness expected from the alliance. Considering the above criteria the organisation selects the supply link partner. He has the effectiveness to make the potential alliance a success. The chain partner is thus selected and an agreement is contracted to develop mutual understanding as to how the alliance will be strategically managed to achieve its goals. There may arise a situation when the partners may experience managerial imbalance as required support is not provided by participating links. Partners may also experience power imbalance especially when buying organisation wields greater power or a supplier providing catalyst component may try to dictate his terms. In such a situation cohesive arrangements based on management styles and corporate cultures must be nurtured to develop suitable match between the parties. Even arrangement to allocate benefits among chain partners can make the alliance function frictionless at the process stage. At this horizontal stage at operational level partners have to develop mutual agreement on specific joint operating standards. Supplier would have to upgrade performance to 'zero defect' level so that the final product will reach 'six sigma' level to achieve 'consumer critical criteria'. Supplier would have to agree to avoid duplication of efforts and establish accountability procedures when doing day-to-day business. Organisation and suppliers would have to work out the quantum and quality of human, physical and financial resources so as to make alliance function operationally.

Once the contract agreement is reached between the suppliers and the organisation regarding the terms, involvement, commitment and resources to be invested the alliance comes into force. At the fourth level thus on strategic plane the partners would have to begin evaluating how far every link in the chain is 'true to his words'. Members of the extended enterprise have to have determination to manage relationship smoothly. No doubt, problems are likely to arise, no, they do arise, either because of situation, environment or lapses on the part of partners to remain true to their words. If all the members have confidence at the bottom of their mind that the alliance is beneficial to all, then they would definitely find out way to resolve problems and make the supply chain function smoothly. Partners must abandon traditional strategies and operational practices, incompatible system of doing business. They must invest human, physical and financial resources promised while agreeing to the contract. A mechanism must be developed to compare achieved effectiveness with perceived and expected effectiveness and a feedback from that mechanism should be continually used to align both so as to make the alliance successful. Implementation and administration of supply chain on these lines makes the process smooth and workable.

When this program works for a predetermined period, the performance of the supply chain and of each of the partner in the supply chain is evaluated on strategic and operational dimensions. Achievement of strategic goals and operational standards is compared with expected and perceived effectiveness. This comparison tells us whether there is a need to change strategic goals and operational standards because the competitive conditions, business environment, government policies have changed. The comparison also tells us whether continuance of alliance is going to add to the benefits derived so far. If the comparison gives us neutral results, we should have to modify our strategic goals and operational standards to make the supply chain relationship beneficial to all. It needs to be noted that effectiveness of new modified goals and standards should be evaluated, compared and modified till they give positive results. Negative results of the comparison tolls a warning bell. Even then there is a possibility of revising goals and standards if the partners are keen on making the relationship become successful. Comparison may give a red signal probably because technology on which the alliance was working has become outdated or the product has outlived its life cycle. In such a situation it is wise to terminate the alliance.

REENGINEERING SUPPLY CHAIN LOGISTICS

'Logistics is a process of planning, implementing and controlling the efficient, effective flow and storage of goods, services and related information from the point of origin to the point of consumption for the purpose of conforming to customer requirements'. This is how Robert Handfield and Emest Nicolas Jr. define logistics. It is very necessary to make a supply chain enjoy competitive advantage and become efficient, effective and successful. It must be seen that goods, ideas and information move as fast as possible. Logistics is capable of overcoming time and space obstacles in movement of physical goods, managerial decisions and information bits. Logistics strategy helps management in movement of products through supply chain intimately and cost effective manner: Rumler - Brache have suggested six steps in their Process Improvement Approach for reengineering supply chain management and logistics. These six steps are-

(1) The organisation should identify critical business issues and critical processes that need to be studied.

(2) A Process Improvement Team should be organised and members of the team should be imparted training as to the objectives of development of new methods of logistics.

(3) The Process Improvement Team should map the current logistics process that we have decided to study.

(4) The team should analyse all the links and details of logistics process, identify process wastes and search for the factors that cause these wastes.

(5) The team should develop, reengineer the new logistics process, work out its details and prepare a thorough map of movement of materials, information, management decisions and ideas along with each other. This flow of information and ideas specially must be two way to provide feedback to the decision makers. Information and information technology are the main stay of supply chain management and logistics management.

(6) The Process Improvement Team should recommend to the organisation how the new logistics system is to be implemented, what results it is expected to reap and measurement of these results.

Having mapped the movement of components, spares and assemblies from supplier's supplier to supplier and therefrom to the main organisation; then from successive processes in manufacturing sections to final product and therefrom through distributor, retailer to the end consumer, the logistics design has to make plan for movement of components, spares and assemblies from one link of supply chain to another on "just in time' basis. Even movement of various components from one stage of process to succeeding stage of process without loss of time is to be planned by logistics. This is more important in case of food and perishable goods. The whole supply chain has to develop an integrated logistics strategy. Each individual partner in the supply chain should manage its logistics activities independently but within the framework of logistics strategy of extended enterprise. Any organisation that wants to grow fast must develop effective and integrated supply chain and logistics. Such organisation must select strategic and structural approaches that would guide logistic operations. The company must make efforts to integrate excellence of logistical operations and development of solid supply chain relationship. Company must align supply chain competency, manufacturing excellence and high level of logistics to make the organisation enjoy competitive advantage.

Logistics has to arrange bar coding, so that with the help of computer readable codes on items it improves flow of products and information. Dispatch of goods to centers of warehousing and distribution till it reaches the final consumer on dot time is vital in logistics. Information technology is important tool to improve the quality of logistics and implementing measures to reduce logistics costs. High level information availability is very critical in an integrated logistic environment. Information technology improves speed and reliability of movement of goods, helps reduction in inventory and product cycle time. It enables the organisation to reach the customer at appointed time and maintain delivery schedule. However, information technology is an enabler and its utility, usefulness, reliability depends upon how well integrated, defect proof logistics map is drawn and systems reengineered. Use of internet improves company's efforts in globalising and streamlining procurement operations.

It is advocated that logistics activities be outsourced. This provides the organisation 'best in class' expertise which complies with ever-changing global environment. This reduces risk and uncertainly. It makes the logistic process flexible; reduces investment requirements, improves customer service, provides spring board to respond quickly to competitors. Role of third party logistics providers is always greater in organisation implementing integrated supply chain management. Outsourced logistics provides a number of opportunities to improve performance of the organisation. It improves organisation's competitive advantage. Use of sophisticated logistics enhances scope for capturing global markets.

Logistics adds one more dimension in the functioning of organisations playing at global level. Development of trading blocks, removal of trade barriers because of integration of nations or because of WTO conventions or policies of regulation require a fundamental change in supply chain strategy. This would necessitate creation of a new logistical model. Multiplicity of national markets, time differences, geographical distances, diverse supply and demand conditions, wage rate and work culture differences, suppliers attitude, their margin requirements and performance standards, consumers religious, ethical and regional preferences add vexity to the complexity of situation in which multinational supply chain functions. Multinational corporations have to take into consideration seemingly small cultural differences that add to the complexity of task of managing logistics within the region. Logistics would have to take into account the behavioural traits of foreign supply chain partners. In such an environment we need a well integrated, co-ordinated and well founded logistics model. Naturally, integrated information system required to support and smoothen the functioning of logistical program must also be sophisticated to that level. The logistics model would have to consider customs practices, tariff classifications and rates, subsidies, product adaptation requirements while reengineering the entire process. It would have to rationalise supply chains by changing locations and transportation modes, make efforts to reduce buffers of inventory and time between successive steps in the supply chain.

The discussion on logistics to support and make supply chain more effective brings us to a conclusion that supply chain and logistics must integrate with each other so closely that they become one and inseparable parts. Supply chain supporting the logistics and the latter supporting the former.

HUMAN RESOURCES FOR THE SUPPLY CHAIN

Knowledge and skill that people require to man a supply chain organisation are to be multi-disciplinary, multi-dimensional and versatile. Such people have to perform duties of queer nature and of complex dynamics. Let me first discuss what duties have they to perform, what responsibilities have they to shoulder. People employed in such organisation have to carry out various processes used in transforming the inputs provided by the supplier network. Process owners in six sigma projects are required to perform as a part of their duties of developing and managing supply chain the function of their processes and comprehending the linkage of six sigma process to other processes. Co-ordinating and scheduling of internal flows is very challenging and exacting work specially in large organisations. They have to work with extensive dealer network to ensure that the right mix of spare parts, service parts are available so that dealer can meet the needs of the customers. They have also to undertake another internal function of production scheduling translating orders into actual production task. They have to integrate information requirements and inventory flows across multiple tiers of customers and suppliers. Thus, they have to work with material requirement planning (MRP) systems and schedule work centers. All these functions are to be performed so quickly and accurately that customer critical criteria are met on schedule and he is delighted. These people must exercise capabilities of reducing cycle time. They must implement redesigned cross functional process to utilise cross-selling opportunities and capture the channels to reach the customer. Managers in a modern supply chain have to make all partners in the supply chain to co-ordinate their activities so that strategies, policies and practices of all links in the chain become unidirectional. They have to cultivate inter organisational relationship based on thoughts, ideas, promises, acts and trust.

Information and information technology are very critical to the working of a supply link. It is more so if the organisation is multi-product, multi-national and multi-directional. Thus, the managers must know what data crops up in operational exercise of the extended enterprise, how can it be transformed into meaningful information. They have to develop format for making this information available to various disciplines so that decision makers can draw meaningful conclusions and base their decisions on these conclusions. So this information can function as decision support system. They need to know what characteristics the logistics system must possess to make the goods move quickly to the desired destination.

Choosing, selecting and developing people to form such multi-multi-dimensional, inter-organisational and cross functional teams is a big training task. I suggest a long running comprehensive, extensive training program to prepare people to man such challenging, satisfying and rewarding jobs. It is well known that there are no set rules or decisions. Therefore, in these training programs I do not pretend to provide them a tool box giving set rules of decisions. My emphasis is on developing aptitudes, attitudes, traits and capabilities.

We organise group discussion sessions, role playing exercises, psycho-social tests to identify youth who possess that spark to face the challenge, those who have passion to fight, those who thrive on crisis. Then upon we grind them rigorously on building physical capacity, concentration capability, observation trait, analytical power, liking for interpersonal communication, patience to listen and delay in response. These mutually inclusive as well as in some part mutually exclusive behavioural pathos can be inculcated with the help of various training programs tailored by training institutions. It is important to note here that the nature and content of such programs would depend upon the nature, activity, spread and size of the supply chain. These volunteers will have to be trained in financial jargons, cost cutting alternative pathways, new methods of marketing products and ideas; developing inter-personal relationships with different people of different organisations motivated by various objectives. They need to be given intensive training in information technology. They should be taught to use as much information as is available from intranet and internet. Their reluctance to use the information that is available must be broken. Equally so they are to be given thorough understanding of mathematical and statistical tools. Such tools are very useful in assessing and evaluating whether we have been achieving required standard and value addition to the product or service that we provide. Training in mathematical and statistical tools is to be given because a supply chain has to achieve six sigma standards to be a total quality organisation; and these tools are necessary for green belt and black belt personnel. That is why the effort.

After completion of this initial training they are put into the functional seat and are continuously put under strain to align situations. They are to be inducted in refresher courses as often as possible; they are required to participate in symposia, seminars, workshops, present papers based on their unique experiences and participate in discussions. Deputation to renowned, reputed supply chain organisations for exposure and gaining experience is a necessary step in training our people.

As a part of making supply chain more efficient and effective, organisation install enterprise resource planning software. Such customized software are provided by SAP, Oracle. They provide ERP as well as CRM software with defined system of working. Such system specifies the roles the user has to play. Modules with various functions and capabilities are provided to each user employee. Many a employees are not computer literate and do not know how to operate the module. Thus, along with training in supply chain functioning, employees are to be trained in using the system, in maintaining the system, in detecting the error and in removing the error. Each employee is to be taught how the events flow. We can see from the chart that there is a central data base. Each and every entry made by the user employee is recorded and stored in this data base. Figure 3.10 exhibits this chart. Therefrom each employee can resource the data he is authorised to resource.

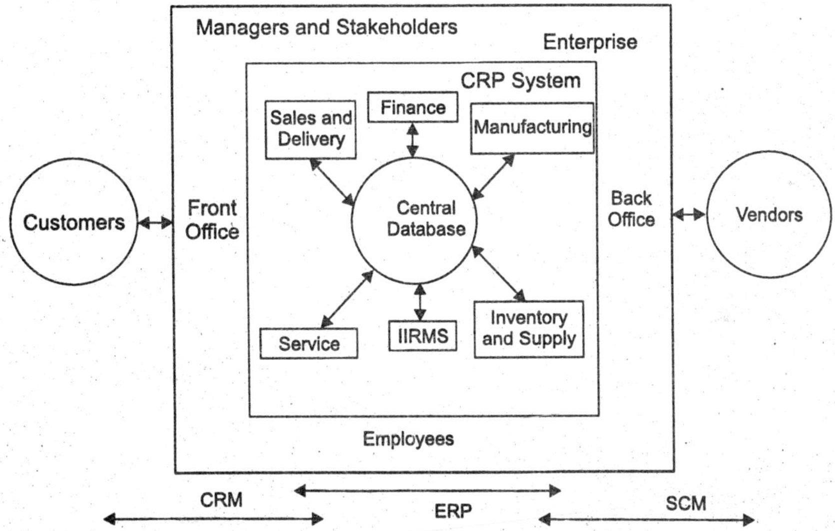

Figure 3.10
An Enterprise Resource Planning System

Employees are to be taught how the mouse is to be clicked, how are the keys on the board to be operated to make the data appear on the screen and how the work is to be processed. Thus, each employee is provided with a module for the function he is to perform and is to be trained how much authority can he exercise and what limits his authority has. He cannot operate the module beyond the authorised limits. And if he has to, he should get the system approval from the policy and/or strategy framers. Each employee is to be trained as to how the charts are to be read and interpreted; how necessary information is to be clicked on the screen. They must know how to generate reports from the system.

Employees in sales and delivery department are to be trained to operate base rate, carrier select and match pay systems so as to compute freight costs, compare transportation mode rates, analyse service and cost effectiveness of carriers so as to select most effective and economical transportation system. Employees in front office, finance and manufacturing need to be trained in operating and using supply chain planning software program to ascertain demand, replenish inventory accordingly and manufacture goods to achieve accurate planning and scheduling these activities. It is suggested that employees having the responsibility of planning, problem solving and decision making should be trained in operating geographic information system. With the help of geographic information system (GIS) they can prepare spatially oriented or geo-coded digitalized maps for capturing, checking, integrating, manipulating and displaying data for planning and decision making as well for solving problem. This improves productivity of the entire supply chain.

Information technology employees are to be imparted training of maintaining the system, and get various parameters set by the authorities. They need to be trained in cleaning up the database of information worthy of deletion and servers to be restarted. IT employees need to be trained so they can know, what are the formats of charts to be prepared, how are the rows and columns to be filled in and to which screens these charts are to be displayed. IT people have to specify which part of the data can just be seen on which screens and which data can be operated by which employees. They have to develop skill to prepare graphs, exhibits, diagrams that will be useful for module users and decision makers.

These ERP and CRM systems are usually got programmed, installed and commissioned from expert organisations. Consulting and planning of such system accounts for about 23 per cent of total cost and training of employees in ERP and CRM systems costs around eleven per cent of the total cost.

Training in a supply chain is not one time program, it is a continuous process. It must be practiced diligently, and scrupulously by human resource department. Success of a supply chain, its competitive advantage depends upon the richness of the human resources in respect of initiative, imagination, intuition and experience of the world. Supply chain must be a learning organisation, it must be knowledge organisation, it must be an intelligent organisation.

SUPPLY CHAIN PROBLEMS AND SOLUTIONS

Addition to value, in supply chain, though essential for achieving and maintaining competitiveness is limited by many problems along the chain. Capacity of the supply chain organisation in finding solutions to these problems determines its competitiveness and chances of success. Lack of supply chain strategy, failure to recognise the breadth of organisational implications, misconception that good supply chain management can be attained solely with the help of ERP system are the major problems. However, uncertainties arising out of demand forecasting that is influenced by various factors, uncertainty in delivery time are the typical problems faced by supply chain organisation. Demand forecasting is influenced by factors like changes in competitive environment, price fluctuations, weather conditions and technological developments. Uncertainties in delivery time are caused by machine failures, load shedding of electric power, unfavourable road conditions, traffic jams, customs clearances, production time delays, varying quality of raw materials. Customers not getting the products of the quality they want, at the time they need and place where they need are the problems resulting into poor customer service. This is also a problem that many supply chain organisations suffer from. All the problems listed here cause higher inventory costs, loss of revenue and extra cost for special shipment or extra cost for expediting shipments.

Different solutions are suggested and experimented to resolve these problems. Vertical integration of as many activities as possible was the usual solution that was implemented. Factors that cause uncertainties must be clearly identified. Effects of these uncertainties on the activities of the organisation, on the activities of the suppliers and on the customers' satisfaction need to be visualised. Ways and means to eliminate or reduce these uncertainties must be clearly identified; must be thought of and weighted in order of effectiveness and prioritized. Building own chain shops is experimented to resolve the problem of retail trade uncertainties. Some sugar factories undertook sugar cane cultivation to ensure regular and assured supply of sugar cane. Many a sugar factories installed high pressure boilers and generated electricity for self use and thereby overcame the problem of uncertainty of electricity supply. However, management of such non-core activities itself becomes a new problem.

Holding adequate inventories was another experiment carried out by supply chain organisations to ensure smooth and speedy supply of raw materials, spares and components. However, difficulty faced in this solution is determining levels of inventory correctly. A production organisation uses hundreds and thousands of components and spares and to determine accurate level of inventory for each item itself becomes a problem. The technique of just in time supply of spares and components is a better a solution to this problem. Penalty for inaccurate inventory stocks are heavy. Therefore, supply chain organisations have begun to rely on decision support system to manage levels of stock. Bar-coding system provided great help in this respect. This enables the organisation to make decisions and coordinate various activities and links of supply chain. So that components, spares and finished products move smoothly through chain to maintain delivery schedule. Bar-codes are being replaced by Radio Frequency Identification Device (RFID). Suppliers affix a band-aid sized tag onto merchandise and retailers install readers that collect the data once the tags come into range. This technology is used to track merchandise from the manufacturer to the store. It helps to control inventory. The information system automatically debits the items sold from stock register and orders the supplier when stock register at the central data base gives signal for order. Therefore, the RFID resolves the problems of co-ordination of activities of suppliers, manufacturers and customers. Supply chain organisations need to co-ordinate the methods of creating, building, sharing and transmitting the information that forms the basis of decision making. I will discuss in the next section as to how information and information technology is used as an effective tool of improving efficiency and effectiveness of supply chain and forms the decision support system.

Turban and Aronson[9] have suggested a number of solutions to the problems that supply chain faces. We see today that these solutions are used in most of the corporations with enthusiasm and effectiveness. They suggest —

(1) During the times of demand peaks as many functions as possible should be outsourced. However, our feeling is that, outsourcing should be done as a strategic policy rather than a measure of unloading activities, processes and functions

(2) Buying products rather than making them by the company is another solution. The company can market it with the name and fame achieved by it and confidence of the customers developed over a period of time.

(3) Configure the optimal shipping plans. In sea food industry the processes of cleaning fish, slicing, processing and canning are done on the ship that purchases sea food from fishermen. As a result canned sea food is ready for delivery at any and every time.

(4) Crete strategic partnership with suppliers. There are a number of stories where companies have withdrawn from supplier-contracts because the credentials of suppliers were not scrutinised rigorously, intensely and closely.

(5) With the help of computerized information system and selection of small number of well qualified tier one suppliers, manufacturers are able to reduce inventory to almost zero by making them deliver their products just-on-time. However, they have observed the discipline of making payments immediately on turning the final product out of factory. Companies have insisted on selecting suppliers' suppliers, that is tier two suppliers, as rigorously as they do in selecting tier one suppliers. This has improved supplier buyer relationship. Many companies have involved suppliers in strategic decisions. Such close relationship with suppliers improves accuracy in demand forecasting.

(6) Electronic commerce (e-commerce) system should be introduced for booking orders and enabling the customers to be in a position to monitor progress of their orders. Use of extranets can reduce lead time in selling the products and buying components. Most of these solutions are part and parcel of Enterprise Resource Planning.

With these many solutions suggested there should be no problem in a supply chain. However, with reality of life being beyond imagination new problems are bound to rise and new solutions found to resolve them.

INFORMATION AND INFORMATION TECHNOLOGY IN SUPPLY CHAIN MANAGEMENT

Introduction of computer based information technology has changed the very face and composition of supply chain management. Information technology is the process of innovation through which knowledge is converted into wealth. It began with inventory management system and billing having an objective to reduce cost, expedite processing and decrease errors. Such applications were developed in the functional areas independently of each other. However, as activities in supply chain are inter dependent and interlinked material requirement planning model was developed and MRP software package was introduced. Inventory and purchasing operations being related to financial and labour resources, fully-integrated Enterprise Resource Planning and Supply Chain Management packages were developed and introduced. With information systems, encompassing suppliers, suppliers' suppliers, producers, service providers and customers, we have added one more partner, to the supply chain, namely information system. Inform tion systems, need to be well managed to manage the supply chain efficiently and effectively. With coming of internet electronic data interchange, electronic funds transfer, automated voice mail, CD-ROM catalogs, we are able to online communicate with suppliers, manufacturers, distributors, retailers and customer in least time regardless of locations. These technologies are supply chain 'enablers' and have reduced lead time and non-value added activities. We can achieve global visibility into transportation, global inventory management, global sourcing, inter-company information access and data interchange. Information technology has enabled us to effect just-in-time deliveries between every link of the supply chain and also to the end user customer.

Extended enterprise creates huge data, from the point of purchases of raw materials, through various stages of processes to the point of delivery to the end user. Materials required, their cost, taxes, materials utilised, materials wasted, blockages to the flow of materials, spares, components, time wasted because of blockages and cost increases to the organisation, inventory accumulated and status, quality of final product are some of the items of data created in the activities of supply chain. Order receiving, its processing, ordering to the suppliers, production scheduling, delivery of goods to the customer, payment receipt from the customer, follow up are other items of data that spring up during the process. Human resources consumed, in this process, labour hours wasted, investment required, capital and assets utilised, capital and assets lying idle, funds flow requirements are alongside data created during the functioning of the supply chain. Data in such raw form is just a heap of figures which do not convey head and tail of the story. It is the function of the information technology to collect all this data, wherever and whenever created, and transform it into usable meaningful format. This data is very heterogeneous, complex and varied. To put it into orderly cohesive form is the function that information technology has to perform. People working in different departments and in various capacities do need information, but not all this, and they need the information that is required by them and as they want to look at it. Metallurgist would look to the information as to how much iron, aluminum and chromium is used to make the casting, metallurgy-analyst would look for porosity, physical properties, while cost accountant would look to the cost of material, labour hours put into this casting, input-value-output value; as against this financial analyst would try to find out how much investment has gone into this casting and for what time is it blocked-trying to find funds out flows and inflows. Thus, the data created just in casting S J Iron component need to be cast in various formats from various angles so that the information can form a basis for decision to be taken. Requirements for information are so varied that we have to look to information system as a function with cross-functional data because much information needed to make decision in a given function comes from sources outside that function and sometimes from outside the organisation. And all this is to be done with the sole objective of providing goods to the customer on time, satisfying his critical criteria.

Having discussed the importance and utility of information in a supply chain extended enterprise, let me come to discuss what information system needs to be created, how is it to be integrated and how can it be made use of.

Information is very critical to the very existence of a supply chain. Twenty first century supply chain having all its activities integrated with each other requires integrated functional software systems using the same language and communicating with each other. This has brought tangible benefits like reduction in inventory, reduction in number of personnel, financial close cycle improvement and intangible benefits like information visibility, customer responsiveness. All this improves supply chain management. Considering its critical importance firms that have extended supply chain crossing functional, geographical and political boundaries create an 'Inter Organisational Information System[10] (IOIS). IOIS is an integrated data-processing and data communication system used by all links in a supply chain. Computer based electronic link is established which records order booking, passing it on to production scheduling for preparing a plan to process the product, requirement of components and spares from clients with prescription of quality, quantity and time schedule of delivery, funds requirements, labour requirements, etc. Over the period of time it does check the order status, reviews inventory levels, tracks shipment schedule and receipt of price on time. IOIS tracks transaction transfers. Within the IOIS, supply chains opt for Electronic Funds Transfer (EFT) system so that the funds flow is automatically and optimally operated. IOIS provides computerised support for an increased number of non-routine applications. The decision support system enables supply chain to take computer supported non-routine and partially structured decisions in terms of the design of products that smoothen the flow of inventory through various links in the supply chain. It also enables decision-makers to reach at the solutions in operation of the supply chain and enables them to identify opportunities for improvements across the supply chain. I will discuss separately the information system technologies used for effective supply chain decision support system.

In developing and designing (programming) Inter-organisational Information System we can make provision for the inclusion of various partners participating in the supply chain and also organisations that are outside the supply chain. Equally so, organisations working at higher level and lower level can also be allowed to participate in such an information system. Donald Stephaive Berrett and Benn Konsynski have professed five ways as to how individual firms can participate in inter-organisational information system. They discuss, the first way of participation is Remote Inter-organisational Node-Member firms located at remote places but participating in the system can have access to information and/or can provide information to extended enterprise. The second way is, Application Process Node-The partner in the supply chain needs and therefore shares information having single application. It may need information regarding the system how order is processed and therefore shares network for that application only. Third is Multi-participant Exchange Node – An organisation, either a member of the supply chain or otherwise, participates in the information network to interlink itself with its suppliers or suppliers' suppliers having business relationship to collect and share various types of information. The fourth way the firm can participate is Network Control Node-Partners in the supply chain use the network to develop as well as share information that can be put to diverse applications along with a number of lower level applicants. The fifth is, Integrating Network Node-partner in the supply chain has high level computer infrastructure with internet network. Utilising this network, it undertakes to process data, transform it into meaningful information that can be used by many participants for various applications. Robert B. Handfield and Ernest L. Nicolas Jr. suggest sixth level of participation. Participating Network Node — A participant shares the information network with diverse applications with any number of participants with whom he has established business relations.

The Inter-Organisational Information System needs to determine what type of information they need to process, so that it can be utilised by member links. They would have to determine the objectives they wish to satisfy. Technique used to identify information required in the supply chain is multidimensional. In the first instance the participating members would have to decide a common language in terms of planning, format and priority across several and vastly different constituents. This common language will enable them to describe, analyse, measure and improve the information. Secondly, they would have to decide which information do they, their managers and decision-makers require. Many a times, the information actually required by them is much different from the information asked by them. This becomes much difficult if the extended organisation is multinational and multi-product. To find out which and what type of information is required, the organisation should prepare a 'portfolio of information requirement determination' rather than depending upon one method like group interview of managers or individual interview of managers. This can be done by using technique of 'Business Systems Planning of Structured Interviews'. Business planning decisions should be listed and information required for such decisions should be listed and information required for such decisions can be identified. 'Critical Success Factors' of each link partner in the supply chain should be identified for that purpose. This can be prepared in a tabular form. The information system must be capable of supporting an integrated supply chain which needs a formal structure of information to ensure balanced and widespread exchange of information. Thirdly, the standard of information that is to be collected, analysed and disseminated must be articulated. The table so prepared would give us in last column all points of information required to take all types of decisions and to solve all problems that crop up in operating a supply chain. The information jotted in last column is then categorized on the basis of 'entity-attribute-analysis'. Customers, suppliers, products are the entities. Attributes are their characteristics. Customers need particular type of product with reference peculiarities. To illustrate, college going young students prefer a smart, good looking, stylish, high pickup motor bike. Thus, we can prepare a format of information that we would require and have to collect taking entities in rows and attributes in columns in the matrix. This gives us an overall profile of information needed to develop the prototype for the Inter-Organisational Information System for the entire supply chain. We assign a code number to the field from where the information is generated and assign unique identifiers for the function to which the information of particular category is to be supplied. Computer operational program based on such prototype can satisfy all the needs of all the users in the supply chain.

N. Venkatraman[11] argues that such supply chain Inter-Organisational Information System is well suited to the enhancement of supply chain management. It helps the management to arrange resources on just-in-time basis; it can ensure quick and efficient consumer response and continuous replenishment. All members and partners of the supply chain rely on such information made available through latest technology. Even then it depends upon the users of such information how to extract maximum values from such information. There are many software titles that address specific aspects of supply chain management. It is a challenge before the extended organisation and software providers as to how to develop an all inclusive information system for the particular supply chain with greatest benefit to all. With the help of electronic commerce, documents pertaining to order booking, order processing, dispatch noting, billing, receiving payment can be transcribed between suppliers, manufactures and customers. It ensures that the entire process is handled electronically. Electronic Data Interchange can be used to link supply chain members together to improve efficiency, accuracy in respect of order processing, production, inventory, transportation and accounting.

Discussion in the foregoing paragraphs explains clearly the need and importance of developing integrated information system and merging it with the supply chain pipeline. The explanation clearly warns us as to how difficult it is to program such a customised all-usable information system and how challenging it is to extract maximum value from such a system. Three more aspects of information system in a supply chain need to be discussed. The first is Decision Support System; the second is Enterprise Resource Planning and the third is E-commerce. They are discussed in the following paragraphs:

(1) Decision Support System

It is a part of the entire information system developed for supply chain management, but with a little different application. Decision Support System (DSS) provides computerised support for increased number of non-routine applications. The basic objective of DSS is to provide computerized support to complex non-routine and partially structured decisions. With the help of DSS, opportunities for improvement across the supply chain can be identified and measures as well decisions can be taken and implemented to improve design of the supply chain and operation of the extended enterprise.

Frontline decision making is the process by which companies automate decision process and push them into the organisation and out to partners. It includes empowering employees by letting them devise strategies, evaluate metrics, analyse impacts and make operational changes. Frontline decision making serves line managers, sales executives by incorporating decision making into their daily work. The line managers, sales executives need to know what questions to ask, where the information resides and the components of any metric, so that they can take advantage of ordinary frontline 'ecision making support system. Software packages provide in a single browser based self-service solutions to standard problems and support system to line managers and sales executives in taking routine decisions.

Executive Support Systems provide answers to complex real time situations. Online Analytical Processing (OLAP) system provides multi-dimensional spread sheets, databases along with organisational decision support systems. Such systems are easy to learn, easy to use and easy to navigate and they have enough intelligence to automatically determine the tasks to be performed. Such systems perform these tasks directly or guide executive users to perform such tasks. These systems may suit to some extent highly individualised work styles of executives. However, they have certain limitations of not being able to change the basic way in which the executive user interacts with the systems. These executive support systems provide facilities of visualisation of various data including multi-media documents.

Enterprise support systems have multi-tasking capabilities and therefore these programs can be run simultaneously in separate windows and can be accessed from cell phones and wireless devices. As a result the top executives and directors of supply chain extended enterprises can take decisions regarding introducing a new product or service into other countries and distributional channels in other countries. Such systems can provide a business intelligence capability to supplement ERP. The 'Strategic Enterprise Management System' developed by SAP have inbuilt enterprise information systems. Such integration has leveraged the capabilities of existing ERP and reduced their costs.

Thus the decision support systems at frontline, executive and enterprise levels are implemented with the help of ten technologies suggested by B. H. Flickinger and T. E. Baker. Most commonly, a prototype of decision support system (which is also known as iterative design or evolutionary development) with a set of menus, displays prepared reports, and demonstrates to the users. So that they can see what they were going to get from the prototype. They can also visualise whether the proposed DSS would be giving exactly what they had needed for longtime. Such prototyping DSS reduces development time and feed back time from users.

Ten technologies suggested by B. H. Flickinger and T. E. Baker[12] are :

(1) DSS must be capable of seeming as data concentrator. For that it should develop Structured Query Language interface for direct links to common database. With the help of this database, supply chain management can take a number of decisions regarding demand forecast, product information as to changing requirements of the customers, inventory scheduling, process operations etc.

(2) On the basis of this database various schedules are produced to determine forecast, product requirements etc. These schedules are tested for validity and if found valid policy proposals are recommended for saving costs.

(3) These schedules convey us signals to determine what should be produced, when and how much and in which strategic business units. So that we can balance the capacities of different strategic business units; we can

sequence the production, decide the lot size, and prepare just-in-time schedule and adjust material flow accordingly.

(4) The software prepared/programmed tool should have the capability to formulate any linear, non-linear or mixed-integer model. Decisions that need to be taken under the conditions of risk and uncertainly, especially in large organisations, can be taken with the help of special algorithms.

(5) In case of supply chains involving significant sequences, in industries like chemical reactors, plastic extruders, paper machines, continuous blenders, packaging lines, printing processes where operations are many a times blocked, even algorithmic approaches do not work. In such cases a combination of linear programming and expert system rules will alone be useful as decision support system.

(6) Most of the organisations catering for world market are multi-plant having multistage processes. The software described in fourth point, above, can be used to allocate production across plants in such a way that while plant capacity is optimally used the product mix is to the requirement of the market. Of course software needs to be upgraded to provide data on availability of raw material, cost of alternative raw material, plant capacities, and capabilities of all supply chain entities. The Bill-of-Material structure of the software providing different combinations of raw materials and processes enables the organisation to route the raw materials with different combinations for making a product at each distinct stage of production.

(7) With the help of a powerful graphical user interface we can create online custom windows, presentation graphics for developing new applications in as little a time of few days.

(8) Large metrics prescribing various applications of database should also be user definable for knowing bills of materials, product flows, inventory status etc.

(9) The software developed to support decision taking process must also be capable of providing information to the customers to know immediately whether the products they want are available at the moment or at least to know whether the capacity to turn their product is immediately available. In competitive environment the companies will have to make customers partners in their production process so that their queries can be heard and responded instantaneously.

(10) The information network has to provide data to the company regarding the demand status at least in near future so that the extended enterprise can gear up its activities to meet predicted demand.

All these technologies Flickinger and Baker prescribe, can be integrated into one multi-faceted information network to be used for various purposes including decision making process.

(2) Enterprise Resource Planning

ERP is a single software program that serves the needs of all departments and vendors and customers in a supply chain. The name ERP is somewhat misleading because the software does not concentrate either on planning or on resources. Each entity in the supply chain has its own computer system optimised for particular function that department or dealer performs. ERP combines them all together into a single, integrated software program that runs off a single database so that various departments can share information more easily and communicate with each other. There are hundreds of data tables, which store data generated as a result of diverse transactions; but they are not confined to any department or functional boundaries, rather it is integrated to be used by multiple users for multiple purposes and at multiple places. It is important that much value can be extracted from this software if it is correctly installed and used. Formerly it required sophisticated information technology infrastructure. However, with declining cost of P.C., advent of client server technology and Scalable Relational Database Management, installation of ERP system has come within the reach of small organisations. ERP replaces standalone computer systems into one single unified software program with software modules that can be used by different departments. ERP is a back-office software. ERP integrates order fulfillment process, that includes recording customer order, providing a software road map automating different steps through fulfilling the order. Front office selling process is automated by CRM software. When one department finishes its part with the order, ERP automatically routes it to the next department. The order process moves very quickly, so customers get their orders fulfilled fast and without error. If one wants to know the status of the order one has to simply login the ERP system and track it down. Introduction of ERP needs total change in the attitude of all people in the organisation and change in the way companies do their business. Value addition done by ERP depends basically upon changing the ways people do their jobs. Companies have to change long established ways of doing business and shake up important people's responsibilities and roles. ERP helps enhancement of performance of supply chain by integrating financial and customer order information, by standardising and speeding up manufacturing process, by reducing inventory and by standardising HR information. The organisation can reduce production and delivery lead time by improving co-ordination and by making commitment more realistic. Installation of ERP software costs about $ one million to $ 30 million, however if implemented fully and whole heartedly the system begins to pay back in around two years and annual savings are about $ one million. About 44 per cent of the ERP costs is on hardware and software purchases. It must be remembered that, once installed, ERP system dictates the process design and people must be ready to change overnight. It is also suggested that ERP system may be installed initially as a pilot project covering a few important processes or departments in the organisation and on the basis of experience gained it can be installed fully. It is observed that the benefits of installing full ERP system are greater than installing computer system in each of the department in the organisation.

It has synergic effect where the whole is larger than the sum of its part. It is so because ERP instead of treating each transaction separately as stand-alone activity, considers them to be the part of the interlinked processes that make up the business. It is also necessary to build two new channels of access to ERP systems. Customers demand information regarding status of their order and billing of their work. Thus, we need to build an access to customers which is commonly known as B2C or SRM. Suppliers, vendors and partners need information regarding components they have to supply, schedule of delivery, quantity, rate contract etc. We need to build an access to ERP for them that is commonly called as B2B or SCM. These two accesses to ERP are to be independent because both stakeholders need different type of information and information provided to one need not be provided to the other party. A schematic presentation of this ERP system and its access is given in Figure 3.11. It is to be read in connection with Figure 3.10.

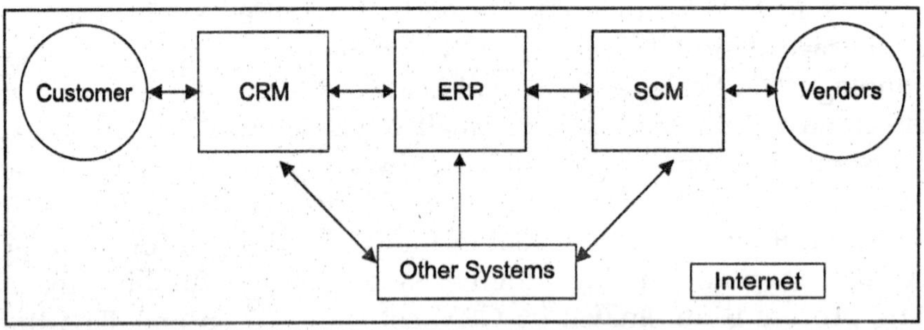

Figure 3.11
An Enterprise Application Integration (EAI)

ERP helps organisation to satisfy internal need to stay competitive, to deliver shareholders value and dominate the market. ERP enables organisation to share information, convert it into knowledge, empower people and improve decision making environment. It helps to bridge the gap between having the information and coming to the user level. This makes the organisation an 'Intelligent Corporation'. It improves Corporation's IQ, not because the company has employed people with better IQ, but because it enables organisation to create a real time knowledge environment in which various functions and individuals can react efficiently in order to solve any challenge their corporation might be facing. Intelligent corporation has ability to absorb new ideas quickly, ability to adopt to new circumstances, ability to solve problems efficiently, ability to mobilise appropriate resources and ability to efficiently accumulate experience

Dell Computer Corporation, with a view to find ways to build more value into relationship with suppliers, launched in 1999 a web site www.valuechain.dell.com – a secure extranet acting as a portal allowing Dell suppliers to collaborate in managing supply chain so that inventories can be reduced, materials management can be improved and relationship with suppliers can be enhanced. The site provides the suppliers with an 'eye' that can follow their material as it winds its way through Dell Corporation. Dell Computer Corporation purchases almost ninety per cent of its direct material supplies on line worth $ 26 billion every year. This web site has reduced the number of suppliers from 1000 three years ago to 100 in the year 2003. This has provided strength to Dell Computer Corporation in maintaining links with suppliers and customers.

(3) E-Commerce or Consumer Resource Management

ERP provides information to the various departments of the organisation and not the consumers. However, consumers demand information on order status, billing of their work etc. If this information is to be provided, and needs to be provided to maintain transparency and competitive advantage, we have to build up a new channel in ERP system which is called Consumer Resource Management (CRM). It is a front door access to limited information by the consumers. It is rather difficult to integrate this channel with ERP system available with the web. We need to have a software vendor experienced in developing e-commerce ware. It is advised that internal staff be associated with software vendor so as to make the channel fool proof as well user friendly. It is necessary that ERP should not be directly linked to the web; rather a flexibility should be built up between ERP and e-commerce web so that e-commerce applications can be kept running on the web while ERP is shutdown for upgradation. Middleware and Enterprise Application Integration (EAI) software are an alternative software to solve the problem of keeping web running when ERP is shutdown. These applications act as software translators that take information from ERP and convert it into a format that e-commerce can understand. Middleware is an application that solves many of the biggest integration woes that plague IT these days.

Buyers find on the screen of their PC connected to internet a typical display of products. Keyboard search function lets the customer find the specific item. When the consumer finds the specific product he wants, he clicks on it and then proceeds to the 'check out' a form into which the information of the buyer such as his name, address, credit card number are entered and he signs the order. The company finds the order booked and dispatches the goods ordered within a specific time period.

There exists an array of electronic commerce agents which help buyers in various aspects of their transactions. For example Salesmountain.com helps people looking for certain items when they are put on sale. Even there are electronic agents which negotiate for buyers. Tête-à-Tête agent negotiates a number of different parameters like price, warranty, delivery time, service contracts, return policy, loan options and all these negotiations on Tête-à-Tête are argumentative. Electronic agents enable customers to correct mistakes made in filling an electronic order form. Fraud is a big problem in electronic commerce as buyers cannot see products or the seller. Agent based fraud detection system like eFalcon (www.ehnc.com) driven by neural computing helps to prevent frauds.

Every supply chain tries to add and maximise value delivered to the customer. So every supply chain is a value chain. The generic value chain model developed by Michael E. Porter consists of five types of primary activities involving creation and delivery of products and four types of support activities supporting primary activities. Figure 3.12 exhibits the model.

Output of the first is the input of the second and each time an input changes into output value is added. Maximising value addition is the objective of supply chain management. Supply chain benchmarking is done by either focusing on entire change or by focusing attention on one aspect like core delivery process. Such benchmarking enables the supply chain organisation to achieve its objective in a better way. There are various ways to add this value and this can be done by taking right decisions at right time and by implementing them fully. It is also necessary to evaluate their input.

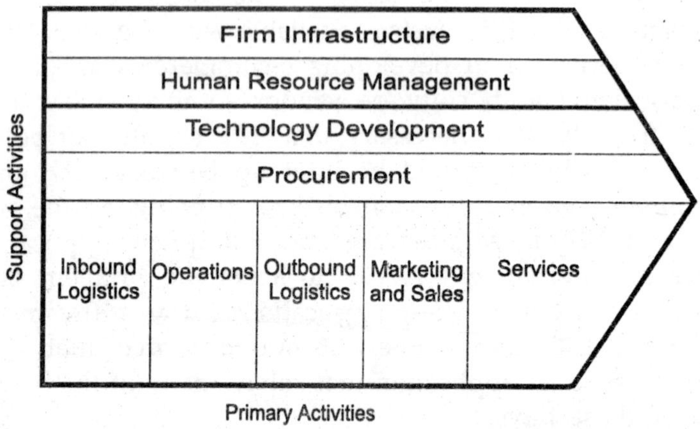

Figure 3.12
The Generic Value Chain Model

In inbound logistics it must be decided where, when and how much to buy at what price. One has to choose the right mode of transport for shipping inbound and outbound materials. In each link of the chain, decisions must be made on movement of information, material and money so that maximum value is added at minimum cost. Supply chain management software are available for supporting decisions to be taken both in primary and supporting activities. They are optimisation of manufacturing process, scheduling, inventory management and procurement. However, one must take care to see that benefits derived from installation of such support system and information technologies must be much higher than the cost incurred on installation. And such benefits must be passed on to the consumers and other stakeholders. These decision support systems must have adequate flexibility to accommodate changes in activity, environment and processes.

E. Fraim Turban and Jay E. Aronsons say that the goals of modern supply chains are to reduce uncertainly and risks in the supply chain thereby positively affecting inventory levels, cycle time, processes and customer service. All these contribute to increased profitability and competitiveness. Benefits of supply chain management are, increased efficiency and effectiveness that are critical for survival.

References

(1) Turban E. Fraim and Aronsons Jay E. *Decision Support System and Intelligent Systems.* Pears Education (Singapore) Ltd., 2002 p. 323.

(2) Lak H.G.W. Pang Wankai and Wong Christina W.Y., *Methodology for Monitoring Supply Chain Performance: A Fuzzy Logic Approach, Logistics Information Management*, 2002, Volume 15, No.4, pp. 271-80.

(3) Pinet B. J. *Mass Communication: The New Frontiers in Business Competitions, Boston*, Harvard Business School Press, 1993.

(4) Tom Peter. *Liberation Management*, Alfred K. Knopt, New York, 1992.

(5) Handfield Robert and Pannesi Ronald. *An Empirical Study of Delivery Speed and Reliability*, International Journal of Operations and Production Management, No.12(1992), pp. 60-74.

(6) Han field Robert and Nicolas Ernest L. Jr. *Introduction to Supply Chain Management*, Prentice Hall, 1999.

(7) Harrington H.J. *Business Process Improvement: The Breakthrough Strategy for Total Quality, Productivity and Competitiveness*, New York, McGraw-Hill, 1991.

(8) Schmitz J.M, Frankel R. and Frayer D.J., *Efficient Consumer Response Alliance*, The Best Practice Model – Joint Industry Project on Efficient Consumer Response, 1995.

(9) Turban E. Frain and Aronsons Jay E. *op.cit.* p. 329.

(10) Barrat and Konsynski, *Inter-organisational Information Sharing System*, MIS Quarterly, 1982, pp. 74-92.

(11) N. Venkatraman. Beyond Outsourcing – Managing IT Resources as a Value Center Sloan Management Review, Spring 1997, pp. 51-64.

(12) Flickinger Bernd H. and Baker Thomas E., *Supply Chain Management in the 1990s*, APICS, The Performance Advantage, February 1995, pp. 24-28.

❑ ❑ ❑

4 Six Sigma Management

In the last two decades of 20th century a number of changes with far flung effect on business world, took place. On one hand establishment of World Trade Organisation obliged many a countries to open up their boundaries and welcome industries, trade and service companies and on the other hand obliged them to introduce new agricultural practices. This added complex dimensions to the intensity to competition. Organisations, particularly in developing countries had to shed off old structure, old strategy, old way of thinking, existing attitude. Organisations in developing countries were obliged to embrace new style of management, better methods of corporate governance, concentrate on strengthening core competence, shift corporate strategy from management of investment and physical assets to management of knowledge, improve intellectual capital so that the company can command competitive advantage. Spread of information technology necessitated this still more, because no organisation, no country can survive on competitive advantage of factor endowment. Techniques of production have changed regularly and frequently. A number of new products, new models are constantly introduced in the market. Japanese producers are introducing new models with differentiated features so frequently that they have begun to carve new niches in the world market for their products. In the year 2003 alone, Japanese Automobile Companies introduced 40 new models of cars.

While these changes were taking place in organisational environment, market ethos was also changing completely. Incomes of customers were rising; advertising was becoming aggressive; there was quest for new life style. Information of new products was spreading fast. These factors changed customer attitude. Customers started demanding more value from the product, the services that they bought in the market. Naturally the reigns of control over economic activity came from the hands of organisations to the minds of customers. Customer satisfaction, customer delight became the goal to be achieved by organisations. Companies began to re-organise themselves by mergers and acquisitions on one hand so as to strengthen core competence further, and on the other hand they began to introduce new and newer concepts of managing production activity so as to put more value into the product, improve its quality continuously and reduce cost of production further and further. Companies have made all out efforts to make their products as defect free as possible and make them as efficient as the technology would permit.

So, pressure from both the sides, from within the organisation and from without the organisation have obliged companies to focus their attention on customers. They are obliged to produce goods with almost accuracy so the customer need is fully satisfied. Companies put all their efforts, concentrate all their energies, utilise all their strengths in developing, in improving total quality of the product. Six sigma management is an effort in this crusade on quality. It is a thought to reach to the highest perfection, zero defect, of the product or the service. Twenty first century needs a new organisation capable of facing and accepting new challenges. Such a new organisation will have to reengineer its activities and manage its functions so as to face global competition and local demands. This effort is called– GLOCALISATION. An organisation implementing all methods of improving quality will alone be successful. They can do this by producing zero defect or near zero defect products. In technical terms such effort is known as six sigma deployment. Total Quality, Six Sigma, Bench Marking, Total Relationship Marketing, Core Competence, Knowledge Management, Intellectual Capital Management, Corporate Governance are the various aspects which companies will have to integrate in their strategies, policies, plans and projects to deliver to customer's delight. All these efforts are to be simultaneously exercised so as to achieve the target goal of customer delight. These efforts are mutually inclusive.

WHAT IS SIX SIGMA ?

Six sigma is a highly disciplined process that helps organisations to focus on developing and delivering near perfect product or service. Six sigma is a statistical concept that measures a process in terms of defects. It is a set of business concepts and methodologies developed to satisfy customer's demand for high quality of the product or service which is called as 'Customer's critical criteria'. Sigma is eighteenth Greek letter. Capital sigma (Σ) is used to denote summation of numbers. Small sigma (σ) is a note used in statistics to measure standard deviation of the population. The standard deviation σ is the square root of that variance. It is from the small sigma (σ) the six sigma draws its meaning as a measure of performance. Each sigma represents a standard deviation. In its business use, it indicates defects in the outputs of a process and helps us to understand how far the process deviates from perfection. A sigma represents 691462.5 defects per million products. That means 40.854 per cent products are perfect or rather about 60 units per hundred are defective. Really a poor performance. It is quite acceptable that we cannot produce all output without any defect – zero defect. However, our endeavor is to reach as near to the perfection. If each sigma represents a standard deviation; six sigma would mean six standard deviations from the mean on both the sides. Standard deviation from the mean is measured on either directions. If we raise efficiency of our production process to three sigma level then we will have 66807.2 defects per million products. In percentage terms this mean 6.681 defects per hundred products. In other words we will deliver about 94 per cent non-defective or defect free products. Even though this performance is better than the earlier one sigma performance, it is still far from the level of perfection that we cherish to achieve. If we state that acceptable performance of a process is said to be three sigma, then amount of variation covered by three standard deviations is all that is acceptable for that measurement. This level tells us that 6.681 defects per hundred products will be acceptable. The sigma level tells us what the chances are that there will be performance outside the acceptable range. If the organisation is working at four sigma level then it will turn out 11875 defective parts per million. That means the organisation has achieved 98.81 per cent level of defect free production level. We would have to go still further towards perfection. If the organisation achieves six sigma level then it will turn out 9003 defective units of the product per million. In percentage this would come to 00.01 defective units per hundred. In other words the organisation achieves 99.09 per cent perfect or zero defect products or 3.14 defective units per million. This is exhibited with the help of normal distribution diagram in Figure 4.1.

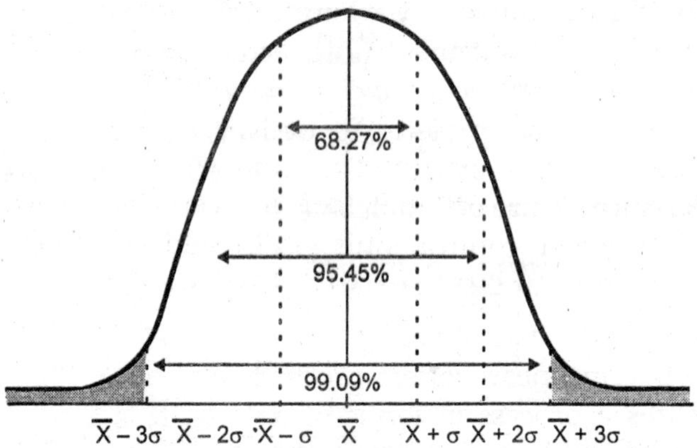

Figure 4.1
Distribution in Terms of Standard Deviation

Six sigma level (i.e. $\bar{X} - 3\sigma$ to $X + 3\sigma$) determines the tolerance levels from Lower Tolerance Level to Upper Tolerance Level, the level that is acceptable and the shaded area beyond that exhibits level of defects not acceptable. This corresponds to the process capability ratio. A process is capable if it has a process distribution whose extreme values fall within the upper and lower specification (tolerance) limits for a product or a service. As a general rule, most values of a process distribution fall within plus or minus three standard deviation (_ + 3 σ) of the mean. If a process is capable, the difference between upper and lower specifications called the tolerance width must not be greater than six standard deviations. The process capability ratio can be calculated with the help of following formula.

$$\text{The process capability ratio } C_p = \frac{\text{Upper specification} - \text{Lower specification}}{6\sigma}$$

If Cp is 1.0 the actual process outputs are within the range of tolerance range. The Cp index is a common measure for describing the potential of a process to meet the specifications.

The bell shape diagram drawn in Figure 4.1 can be compared with Taguchi loss function developed by Gerichi Taguchi. Taguchi loss function is drown in Figure 4.2.

Figure 4.2
Taguchi Loss Function

Customer tolerance is the 6σ limit that is acceptable to achieve quality. This is limited by customer lower control limit (LCL) and customer upper control limit (UCL). Customer quality standard in figure 4.2 corresponds to $\bar{X}$ point exhibited in figure 4.1. Production with a quality beyond LCL and UCL is not acceptable as shown at the top of the diagram. Taguchi argues that when process output performance reaches the specification limit. (Upper or Lower Specification Limit) the customer's economic interest in the item is neutral, that is, the losses will exactly offset any gain from having the item.

There appears to be an element of fuzzy logic in the sense that any process capability between $\bar{X} - 3\sigma$ and $\bar{X} + 3\sigma$ (as shown on horizontal axis in figure 4.1) is acceptable.

Many efforts on total quality management and other popular initiatives failed to deliver the promised improvements because there was no focus or business reason driving many of the efforts. I cannot resist the temptation of narrating an anecdote. A company asked its supplier to provide components of the machines with not more then three defective components per million pieces. The supplier company delivered the order with a letter that said, 'As per your advice we are dispatching herewith million pieces packed in cartons. Three defective pieces are packed separately because we have a process guaranteeing' Zero defect production. The cost of processing defective components being higher, they are priced separately.' This assurance of accuracy and quality is what we aim at.

Six sigma has three different meanings depending upon context in which they are referred to. However, when we talk of 'six sigma' as a tool of management all the three meanings are integrated. These three meanings are—

(1) Six sigma is a management philosophy, in the sense that defects in product or service are expensive because they may cause defection of customer. Customer will be satisfied and will remain loyal if we provide him highest value at lowest cost. Thus customer satisfaction is our strategy and six sigma is a means to achieve that goal and this is our philosophy.

(2) Six sigma is a statistical measurement that determines that there would not be more than 3.1 defects per million products.

(3) Six sigma is a process used to define, measure, analyse, improve and control (DMAIC) production.

(4) Greg Brue states one more meaning. Six sigma is a symbol of quality.

Customer expects the product, that he purchases, should perform perfectly, critically and sustainably. This is customers critical criteria. Customer would purchase from that organisation which assures, promises products that would satisfy his critical criteria and keeps its assurance and promise. Customer's critical criteria is not limited to the product, but spread over to delivery, billing, collection and contact after installation or delivery assessing the satisfaction enjoyed by the user. If all this happens that company satisfies, meets customers criteria. Six sigma tries to meet this criteria driving defects to the lowest level. Organisations which are short of this target should take up six sigma project so that they can maintain their share in the market and enhance it by the 'Word of mouth' of the satisfied customer.

Organisation receives a number of signals of its failures, the company affairs department of the government points out that the organisation has defaulted on the front of maintaining quality of the product, in reporting the inter-organisation transfer of funds. The quality control authority withdraws its quality certification because of inappropriate proportion of ingredients, defaults in design etc. The finance rating organisation lowers the rating because of default in repayment of loans, deposits, or because of inappropriate debt – equity ratio. Reduction in market share, rejection of products by customers, defection ratio, failing repeat orders are good signals to tell us that we need to make efforts to improve situation of the organisation. Comparison of our organisation with that of world class organisation (benchmarking) does tell us whether we need to do something to improve our performance. These facts are a place to undertake six sigma project.

Six sigma initiatives focus on improving quality of the product to zero defect level so as to achieve customer critical criteria. Along with that the organisation desires to improve profitability. Six sigma project is a method to resolve long term problems that encompass the organisation at all levels. Our objective in introducing this project is to reengineer the entire system of the organisation.

At almost every point of time there exist opportunities to improve performance of the organisation. Six sigma is a program, philosophy to take advantage of these opportunities and produce zero defect products. WIPRO started six sigma initiative in 2000 with an object to introduce defect prevention practices at project level. Six sigma is a management program driven by customer's critical criteria and organisational strategic focus. Successful implementation of six sigma project can surely add at least two per cent to the revenue, make organisation competitive and improve bottom line. In carrying out six sigma project we can be successful only if we can develop zero defect attitude.[1]

Total quality management has changed the way thousands of companies conduct their operations. Corporations adopting TQM have undergone a major paradigm shift, a transformation of 'unlearning previously believed themes about business to create better products and services.' Quality does not require higher costs but more reliable and efficient processes that deliver defect free output. That is why, TQM is an excellent foundation from which to build toward the next level of quality management, represented by six sigma approach. Companies that have implemented TQM have secured larger market, have achieved outstanding financial results and have developed a disciplined, pragmatic plan for improved financial performance and growth.

PREPARING ORGANISATION FOR SIX SIGMA

Once it has become clear to the organisation that it is losing competitive advantage, the management has to make efforts to find out, to identify causes of lowering market share, defection of customers, increased cycle time, late deliveries, reluctance of financial institutions in releasing finance etc. The organisation should appoint a committee consisting of people having cross-departmental, cross-functional skills capable of analysing the situation objectively. If it is found that the percentage of defective products is larger than tolerable level or the products are returned for not meeting the customer criteria or the products do not provide expected services then it is time to think seriously of considering steps and measures to improve the quality of the product. This we may call to be a situation for 'SIX SIGMA INITIATIVE.'

The organisation should constitute executive quality council consisting of six to nine chief officers as members who ordinarily determine strategy of the organisation. The council determines the process or processes that are mainly responsible for deterioration in the quality of the product. Having identified the processes that hamper the quality of the product, the council prioritizes those processes in order of importance, or in order of impact on the quality of the product. The council selects process/processes from among those claiming high priority to be taken under six sigma project. Feedback should be taken from employees, customers, suppliers, competitors, bench marking technology to identify and select six sigma project(s).

There may be very many projects that need to be initiated under six sigma program. Out of them the management must select a good, viable and promising project. Selection of a good six sigma project has long term impact on the success of the organisation. It is quite likely that initially the whole project may not be identified, but problems encountered, signals bipped by various key indicators detected on time may suggest bits of the places where the shoe is exactly pinching. Setting this jig-saw-puzzle in order would give us full fledged account of the project. Naturally, for this the organisation must have build up an ongoing long term relationship with customers and suppliers and must have sharp ears to hear their cry. The organisation must also have a proactive attitude to respond to these challenges, opportunities immediately. Informed discussions among employees may also be tapped in search of bits of problems. The organisation can draw on the results of good market intelligence. What I am suggesting is that there are plenty signals indicating opportunities for improvement in administration, management, process and products. Most important thing is that the executive quality council must lend its attention to such signals and select therefrom a good, feasible and effective project for implementing six sigma philosophy. Selection of right project aligning with the key objectives and strategic plans of the organisation is a sure road to the success of the initiative.

As a part of the preparation for adoption of six sigma initiative in the organisation, the management has to decide its strategy.

(1) If the organisation aims to achieve cost leadership, six sigma is to be designed to improve internal processes, so as to reduce complexity in design, reduce cycle time, appoint suppliers that are competitive in the world market and provide services at low cost so that productivity and yields will improve.

(2) If the organisation wants to be price leader, six sigma project is to be aimed at reducing cost by controlling overheads, idle time, inventory, wastes, labor cost and capital cost.

(3) If the objective is to gain customer loyalty, then six sigma project has to achieve highest quality in product design, product quality; it has to have just-on- time delivery schedule. It must develop a practice of following up the customer so that the product exceeds the customer expectation.

(4) If the organisation wants to be a development leader then six sigma initiative would have to be focused on de-layering organisation with inter departmental and inter functional barriers pulled down, so that a very sound knowledge base can be built up and extensive intellectual capital can be created. This will provide strong support to the leader beyond organisation.

That means with various strategic objectives the organisation pursuing six sigma initiative can be aligned to the strategic objective that it wants to achieve in particular. Those various aspects of the philosophy of leadership help to strengthen it's values, beliefs and principles which form the basis of the vision. Our leader must be a JANUSIAN LEADER who can see into the past and see the future. He best presents the spirit of movement. The capacity to look ahead and to look back is critical to learning and leadership. The vision is an image of the purpose of the organisation. A well articulated vision provides a sharp focus of the purpose of the organisation.

Six sigma project is to be implemented by the people in the organisation. All persons in the organisation from CEO to every employee down the ladder must be prepared as a measure to gear the company to accept, adopt and make six sigma project successful. It is necessary to transform the people and the process. Six sigma considers all people in the organisation an asset rather than a liability. Shifting the perspective of considering people an asset is the basis of six sigma. If six sigma projects that are aligned to the strategic objectives of the organisation are selected and management has firm belief in the efficiency and effectiveness of the six sigma project, the management developes interest in the project and supports it wholeheartedly in all its aspects. Executives and managers must be trained in identifying opportunities of introducing six sigma projects. This can be done by detecting deficiencies, defects in the present process. They must have knowledge of customer's critical criteria. They must be trained to assess project on the strength of their feasibility and impact. Employees usually have base level skills. They need to be given additional training so that they can participate in each and every activity of six sigma project. Every activity or job needs some level of technical skill that must be mastered by employees in order to reach acceptable defect free level of the process. More importantly, they must be motivated to utilize all their skills they were trained in. The organisation must provide all opportunities to use the skills acquired in training; so that they can be held accountable for giving adequate returns of training. We must change the way that employees look to the processes so that they can detect, understand the vital few factors that cause waste, error and rework. Once they know vital few factors to look at, they can make improvements that deliver dramatic results.

It is very necessary that people's objectives, goals, values, plans at work and their spiritual, familial, social, physical, financial and mental goals in personal life must be made coherent. Then only people can put whole attention, whole heart in the endeavor to satisfy customer. It must be made to be his commitment. If both these aspects, namely values and commitment are coherent then people can perform their best in implementing the organisational strategy. Usually employees are engaged for a job at the age of 19 to 20 years. Process of socialisation of these adolescents begins at the age of 21 and at this age their belief and value systems begin to take shape. These become strongly held paradigms for much of their lives. The organisation designing to introduce and implement six sigma project must make conscious efforts to inculcate sound beliefs and values in personal life that are coherent to organisational six sigma strategy. Organisation has to mould their attitude and direct their behaviour so that lasting motivation is created. In almost all organisations this aspect of life is not known and not taken care of. As a part of preparation of organisation for six sigma project this must be done deliberately, consciously and consistently so that people and teams that are required to define, measure, analyse, improve and control the project are groomed.

Six sigma is perceived as a statistics and measurement program. Statistics is used as a tool for interpreting, analysing and clarifying data. We have to develop six sigma company. To achieve that level of quality we require not just statistics but changes in the culture of the organisation, changes in the attitude, approaches of the people. We require deep commitment of the top management and that sense of deep commitment must permeate the entire organisation. We need to develop key people for actively implementing the six sigma project.

We have discussed in this section that six sigma project cannot be and should not be taken up instantaneously. A full scale ground work, home work needs to be done if the project is to be initiated, implemented and completed successfully. It is to be evaluated by the organisation whether we are losing ground in the market and then with a view to improve the situation the organisation has to think of six sigma initiative.

Strategy of the organisation should be restated by organising Executive Quality Council. The council identifies the process, factors that hamper the quality and selects those which need to be corrected on priority basis. Out of these processes to be improved one or a few are selected for six sigma project. Such projects must be viable and feasible. Then the council decides the goals of the six sigma project and outlines the strategy to satisfy these goals. This is done in such a way that there can be perfect alignment between organisational strategy and project goal. People in the organisation need to be trained in six sigma methodology, project skills and attitude to give best to the organisation. Thus, the organisation is readied to take up six sigma project on strategic, technical and H.R. aspects of the organisation.

IMPLEMENTING SIX SIGMA PROJECT

Six Sigma signifies that the final product or service that reaches the consumer must meet his critical criteria of being defect free or nearly defect free. Many a writers indicate that each part or component going into assembly line must satisfy six sigma criteria, meaning, there should not be more than 3.14 defective parts per million. My consideration is that the final product and not each part or component must satisfy this test. My reasoning is that, if there are 10 components in the final product and in respect of each component six sigma test is applied then in final product, proportion of defective products would be 31.4 per million. Our very objective may be defeated. That means each component making the final product must be fully defect free. We know this is difficult goal to achieve; however, various technologies, state of art and management skills have made this possible and feasible.

Six sigma products are interrelated and integrated with total quality, bench marking and supply chain management. As we will see, champions have to benchmark the processes that help achieve customer critical criteria and have to develop and manage supply chain to provide zero defect components.

To begin with a process flow diagram is drawn in which we decide the minimum defect level we want to achieve, the cycle time we want to reduce and thereby the quality of the product we can determine. On the basis of the process flow diagram and actual working we can determine where the defects lie in the process. We will have to take into consideration the defects cited by customers as well as by employees. This enables us to calculate cost of poor quality by measuring scrap, rework and lost capacity cost. To this we would have to add field failures, warranty cost, complaints, returned material and lost business. Internal and external cost of poor quality, outlined above, can be saved if we endeavor to eliminate these costs. The management begins to identify which of these process losses cost more and can be removed. This we will call as prioritising opportunities for the project. Here we come to implement six sigma project.

Six sigma Signifies specific methodology steps for managing a project that is selected for achieving defect free or zero defect production. It must be remembered that much needs to be done in spirit in and beyond the five steps of implementing six sigma methodology. Such six sigma project must be implemented fully with total focus on achieving targeted goals. Then only the project can make a significant real contribution. At its core, six sigma revolves around six key concepts. They are —

(1) Critical to quality – We must provide all attributes in the product that are most important to customers.

(2) Defect – Failing to deliver what customer wants.

(3) Process capability – We have to develop a process that can deliver what customer wants.

(4) Variation – The customer sees and feels that the commodity delivered to him and service provided to him is different than perceived by him.

(5) Stable operations – We have to ensure consistent, predictable processes to improve what customer sees and feels.

(6) Design of the product in six sigma – We have to design the product to meet customer needs and process capability. For that we have to develop 'quality function deployment' method – In this method cross sectional teams translate customer requirements into appropriate design requirements at each stage of the product development process. However, technical product specifications are very difficult. Customer requirements are often vague and many a times they conflict with each other. Moreover, technical product specifications are expressed in a 'different language ' than are the needs of the customer. 'The voice of the customer' is often lost. With all this we have to develop a product that fully meets the needs of the customer 'Quality Function Deployment' (QFD) is an excellent way for the organisation to capture the voice of the customer. Quality Function Deployment determines both, what will satisfy the customer and secondly, translating those customer desires into target design. QFD is used early in the production process to determine what will satisfy the customer and also where to deploy quality efforts.

The management of the organisation must make financial, physical and well trained, qualified and skilled human resources available for the project as and when required. It is very interesting to see that at General Electric, a pioneer company in introducing six sigma philosophy, all employees are trained in strategy, statistical tools and techniques of six sigma quality. The management must provide leadership support and exhibit full involvement and commitment in the project. Six sigma project is usually run through five steps as described below – DMATIC. Some organisations also follow five step different model known as DMADB for designing a process using six sigma project. Various kinds of trained people required for the project are also discussed in technical terms. Equipping them with knowledge, skills, training and experience is discussed in a separate sequence.

FIVE STEPS OF IMPLEMENTING SIX SIGMA

Almost all Organisations implementing six sigma project follow a five step pattern. It is discussed below —

(1) Define

Leaders define the core processes that are to be covered in the project. Leaders outline the scope of the project, expectations in respect of quality improvement, reduced cycle time, reduced costs and resources that are to be committed to the project. They identify performance gaps in various activities and identify areas that need improvement. They also set the time in which the project is expected to be completed and results to be delivered. The core process selected by leaders for inclusion in the project are taken as task given to the Green Belts. Green Belts work as project team members. Thus they analyse customer's critical criteria and on the basis of that decide or validate the improvements that need to be brought into the process so as to achieve zero defect components of the final product. Green Belts prepare a detailed document as to how the processes are to be reengineered. If these processes are out sourced to suppliers, Green Belts will have to see that suppliers adopt the improvements that need to be brought to make their components defect free. In most of the cases enterprise resource plan is implemented whereby each user with specific Id can introduce computerised process so as to attain required quality, eliminate inefficiency and remove waste. Not that each process improvement will require additional investment, but if required the process has to justify investment by measuring gains from improvement in quality. Wipro have developed their own six sigma software which marries six sigma methodology and software development process. This is specialization of six sigma for software. They have a Quality Management System for software. They have a Quality Management System proprietarily developed named as Veloci-P.

(2) Measure

Black Belts act as project managers. They undertake SWOT analysis so as to find out where we are. Six sigma approach to management involves cultural change. Essential to this cultural change are key players known as Champions and Black Belts. They act as agents to facilitate that change. Black Belts use benchmarking technique to identify the difference between targeted goal and present position. They take into consideration customer critical criteria with a view to understand his requirements, cost of meeting such requirements, understand his personal preferences, would he consider our product if his requirements are met, differences in expectations of different customers etc. Black Belts then undertake an exercise to assess existing defects per unit and the target to be reached of defects per million units, activity costing and calculate process capability index. On the basis of this they prepare a control chart exhibiting upper and lower statistical control limits and the average that can be achieved. This helps to improve quality on one hand and reduce cycle time on the other. Reduction in cycle time improves delivery schedule which is critical for staying in the market where competition is very intense.

Black Belts calculate contribution of the project and potential value it can generate by viewing the achievements from various perspectives. Black Belts perceive the satisfaction the customers is likely to derive from this improvement, the satisfaction that the shareholders are likely to derive from this development. They identify the processes in which the project has to excel to succeed. They also try to find out the project teams ability to change and improve and undertake measures to sustain this ability. Kaplan and Norton call this exercise as – (1) Customer perspective, (2) Financial perspective, (3) Internal business process, and (4) Learning and growth perspective. This exercise enables the organisation to measure the progress of the project and identify critical factors that have contributed to the success and how can we do better in these critical factor areas.

So, the project manager Black Belt is in a position to assess that the project is proceeding at right pace and in right direction. He can also measure the benefits the project has derived in its journey. The Black Belt project manager and Green Belt team members can decide which actions are correct and should be followed and which actions were wrong and should be avoided. They document all this and on that basis prepare reports for higher authorities.

(3) Analyse

The project team under the guidance of champions undertake analysis of the data regarding performance of the project. On the basis of this analysis the team decides the opportunities that can be exploited for improving performance of the project. The project team tries to identify input variables that affect critical – to — quality attributes. Thus, the team is able to establish a relationship between critical – to – quality defect measurement and the inputs that affect it. The team can formulate an hypothesis and statistically test it to determine which factors are critical to the outcome. Thus, the Black Belt team managers compare these options so as to identify promising options. This enables the Black Belt manager to make decisions as to what should be accomplished and in how much time. Thus, analysis of performance data is very important from the point of view of making right decision.

Statisticians and experts have suggested various tools and tests to analyse the performance of the project and to formulate different options of actions to improve performance of the project. The tools that are used to test the hypothesis are —

(1) Failure Mode and Effects Analysis (FMEA): Project may be falling short of performance because of the defects in the design of the product or shortcomings in the manufacturing process. Data analysis reveals the counts on which the project is failing and its effects on the progress of the project. On the basis of this analysis a number of measures can be thought to remedy the situation. The project manager can select the measure that can make maximum contribution to hasten the progress. Thus, FMEA tells us the factors that are causes of failure and the actions that can be taken to correct the situation.

(2) Pareto Analysis: It was revealed by Vilfredo Pareto that eighty per cent of the problems arise because of twenty per cent of causes. Pareto analysis helps us to find out which are those twenty per cent causal factors that hamper the progress of the project. For example, if in a unit producing nuts-and-bolts (fasteners) the efforts to improve quality of fasteners were hampered by various causes, the six sigma team would try to identify the factors that mainly hindered the progress. On the basis of data analysis the team could draw a Pareto chart (Figure 4.3) and pinpoint the factors that were most responsible for failure of the project.

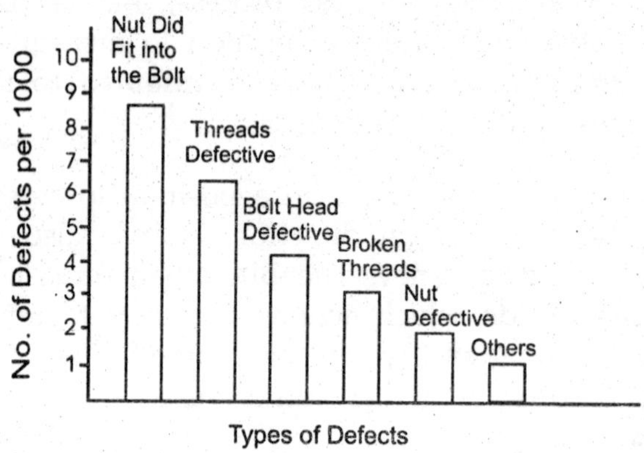

Figure 4.3
Pareto Chart Showing Proposition of Causes Leading to Failure

This chart reveals that CNC lathe process is defective causing most of the problems. Therefore solution is to repair CNC lathe and set it right.

(3) Analysis of Variance: It is a statistical technique that classifies variations shown in the data into meaningful parts. As a result the analyst is able to identify specific sources of variation. Variation in the cycle time, delivery time may be caused by a weak link in the supply chain; quality might have impaired by Peter's principle stating that 'every employee tends to rise to his level of incompetence' or delivery time may be missed because of defects in customer resource management.

(4) Histograms: This graph displays the factors or processes in which the six sigma project has achieved good success and in which it is yet to achieve the target goal. A typical histogram is shown in Figure 4.4.

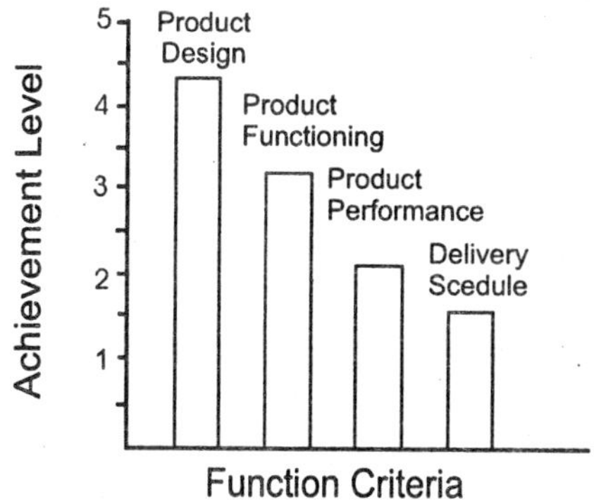

Figure 4.4
Histogram Exhibiting Levels of Success

Histogram in figure 4.4 tells that in achieving six sigma level of various activities the organisation has to move much in maintaining delivery schedule though the product design is to the satisfaction of the consumer and product provides services as per the expectations of the consumer. However, it falls short in providing expected performance. This also indicates that product design facilitates better movement in supply chain.

(5) Cycle Time Chart: The time taken by the manufacturing process from the point of inflow of input to the point of outflow of output is exhibited in this chart and compared with the cycle time achieved. This concept is applied in financial institutions and banks also. The time taken for granting home loan from the point the prospective loanee submits his papers to delivery of cheque of the amount of loan is cycle time. If it takes time more than that targeted by the organisation there is a need for six sigma initiative. This cycle chart is exhibited in Figure 4.5.

On the basis of cycle time chart we can draw another graph that tells us which function has fallen short of requirement.

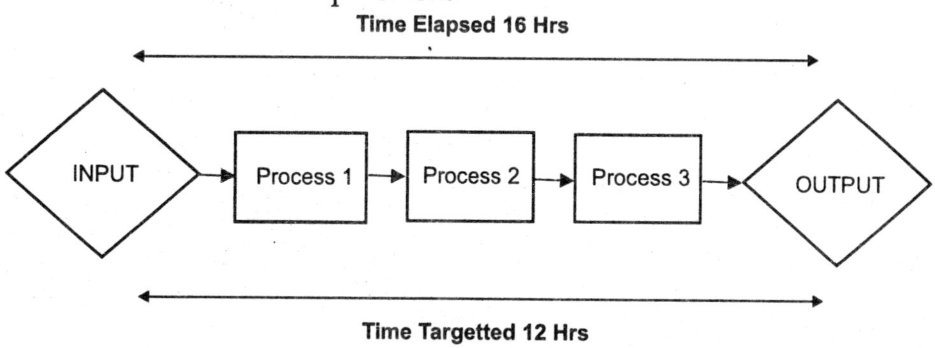

Figure 4.5
Cycle Time Target and Achievement

(6) Reliability Engineering Chart: Chart 4.5 tells us that there are three processes that go into making the product and each process, if requiring equal time, should not take more than four hours each, so that we can achieve the cycle time target of twelve hours. However, process one takes six hours and process two takes four hours while process three takes six hours increasing the cycle time to sixteen hours. Thus, we would have to find out causes of detainment of process one and three and remove them.

Reliability engineering is a relatively new discipline concerned with the design, manufacture and assurance of products having high reliability. Common methods of reliability engineering are —

Standardisation – High reliability can be ensured by using components with proven track records of reliability over years after actual use. Use of standardised components achieves higher reliability and reduces costs since standardised components are used in many different products. This gives economies of scale.

Redundancy – We provide back –up components that can be used when failure of that component causes failure of the entire system. Redundant components are designed in a stand – by configuration or a parallel configuration. Redundancy is crucial to systems in which failure can be extremely costly.

Physics of Failure – Many a times systems fail because of deterioration caused by chemical reactions over time. We can eliminate potential failures by studying physical properties of materials and their response to environment.

De-rating Practice – De-rating is the assignment of a product to operate at stress levels below its normal rating. Designers use this data to achieve reliability by using parts at lower working conditions and low ambient temperatures. De-rating is a method of determining more scientifically the factor of safety so that the reliability is increased and failure rate is reduced.

Reliability Testing – The reliability of a product is determined principally by the design and the reliability of the components of a product. Reliability of a product being a complex issue needs to be tested by simulating environmental conditions to determine a product's performance, operating time and mode of failure.

Burn-in – Burn-in is component stress testing involving exposing integrated circuits to elevated temperatures in order to force latent defects to occur. Burn- in tests ensure long, trouble free operating lives. Some function tests are performed during the Burn-in cycle to save testing time.

Failure Mode and Effect Analysis – It is a detailed study of product design, manufacturing operations or distribution network to determine which features are critical to various modes of failure.

Fault Tree Analysis – Fault Tree Analysis (FTA) is a logical procedure for listing potential hazards or undesired states. It tries to prepare a list of causes of failure. FTA diagram shows the logical relationship between failure and its causes.

These eight methods used as tools and tests help the project team to analyses the rate of progress of the project, possibility of reaching the target and time required for it. Six sigma project venturing to delight customers can find evidence of its success or otherwise in clients paying bills on time, in deducting billing adjustments to negligible level, in improved accounts receivable outstanding days to almost negligible level, in increasing referrals by customers to potential buyers substantially and in increasing client retention rate significantly.

(4) Improve

If the analysis of the project's progress done with the help of various statistical tools, as described above, drives us to conclude that the six sigma project has not met the customer critical criteria then the Black Belt project manager identifies the lacunae left in performance. These shortcomings in the performance are listed as per priority of strategy, and their effect on performance. Black Belt manager finds solutions to resolve these problems, selects the most suitable and effective method. In other words the Black Belt manager confirms key variables and quantifies the effect of those variables critical to – quality outcome. This enables him to identify the maximum acceptable range of each variable to ensure that the measurement system can actually measure the variation. Each variable can be modified to keep it within the acceptable range. Black Belt project manager is assisted by Green Belt team in this entire exercise. It may be found necessary to make experiments to identify the maximum acceptable range of variable and to take trials as to find out the best solution. It should be the effort of everybody to select solution that provides benefits at multiple levels simultaneously. If improvement can be registered in various areas the synergetic effect will be much appreciated. Improvements must register that the organisation can deliver quality goods fast and at cheap price. Improvements achieved can be measured with the help of various tools. These tools are discussed below –

(1) Gantt Chart: The performance achieved in a given period is compared with the targeted achievement. This enables the six sigma team to find out where did it excel and where did it fall short. On the basis of further investigation it can be found out as to what factors, which measures helped the project to win and which to lose. Gantt chart is drawn in Figure 4.6.

The figure explains that the un-shaded part is the target the organisation cherished to achieve and shaded part exhibits actual achievement. The chart indicates that the organisation has excelled in achieving customer satisfaction, it has just reached the target of controlling financial cost but the organisations performance in maintaining relationship with suppliers falls short and needs attention.

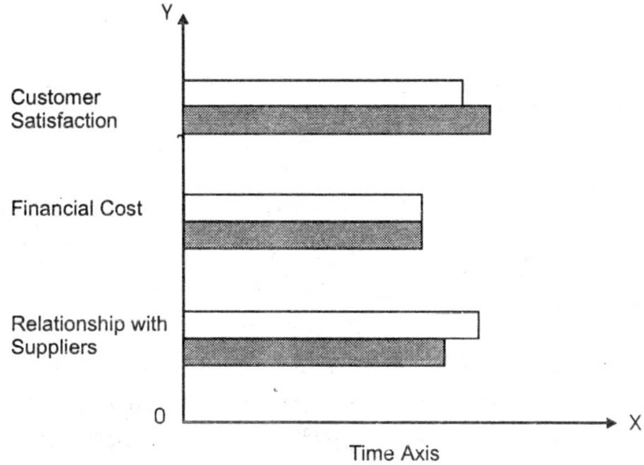

Figure 4.6
Areas of Success and Failure (Gantt Chart)

(2) Design of Experiment: The six sigma team undertakes an exercise to find out key variables in achieving targeted performance. Better and sustained relationship with suppliers, total relationship marketing, moral and ethical support of management, sustained training and updating are the key variables that are found to be important in achieving performance. This is a way of determining and measuring the importance of two or more factors on the outcome of the process, by experimenting with many factors and variables simultaneously. This method is also known as multivariable testing. These factors interact upon each other in such a way that they strengthen contribution of each of them.

Greg Brue has listed fourteen steps of design of experiment. They are – (1) Define the problem. (2) Establish the objective. (3) Select the response variable. (4) Verify the measurement system for factors and responses. (5) Select the independent variables. (6) Plan logistics. (7) Manage logistics. (8) Create set-up procedures. (9) Collect data. (10) Analyze data. (11) Draw statistical conclusions. (12) Replicate results (validation). (13) Draw practical solutions and (14) Implement solutions.

It is important that Black Belt project managers have to be patient in gathering results and in ensuring that sufficient time is allocated to conduct and complete Design of Experiment. Black Belt has to plan to work properly. If done in this way Design of Experiment saves time and resources.

Set Limits on Parameters – The project team identifies and selects few and most important parameters on which attention is to be focused to make the project success. Market share, E.P.S., repeat business and new customers, product returns, warranty claims, defect level, environmental performance are the parameters that are usually considered. Usually the champion in the project set time as well as numerical success considerations that must be achieved.

(5) Control

It is necessary to maintain the gust, speed, enthusiasm and efforts in the implementation and execution of the project so that the project can yield desired results. The project team under the leadership of Champions, Black Belts and Green Belt project teams must reach higher and higher standards. Control phase enables us to maintain a higher level of quality and productivity. The project manager can do this by mapping processes, and then measuring and analysing each factor that needs to be improved and controlled. These control mechanisms can be both macro and micro in scope. This way we can achieve continuous improvement through constant striving – the process which Japanese call as KAIZEN APPROACH. Control on project progress is exercised by means of performance tracking mechanisms and measurements to achieve incrementally better standards and not to let the gains once achieved lost over the period of time. Every year the financial gains earned in the project should be evaluated to ensure that improvements are not transitory. Such controls can be exercised with the help of (a) control charts, (b) Audits, and (c) process capacity index.

Control charts like the Gantt chart (figure 4.6) can be gainfully used to gauge achievements over the period of time in relation to targets fixed. Audits are undertaken to compare profitability of the project with established profitability objectives, review the environment outside the corporate level. Audits are carried out to calculate cost of poor quality (COPQ), to identify contributors to profitability and to compare performance achieved with performance base line. Process capacity index can be calculated with the help of formula $\frac{(\text{USL–Mean})}{3\sigma}$

Let us suppose that the upper specification limit (USL) for a six sigma project is the maximum tolerance limit below which the defect level must be achieved. Mean level is the mean of various tolerance levels achieved in production and 3 σ is 99.3 per cent accuracy. Thus if we have achieved zero defect level that is hundred per cent accuracy and that is specified to be USL and mean level achieved is 80 per cent accuracy, arithmetic would work out to be

$$\frac{100-80}{99.73} = \frac{20}{99.73} = 0.2$$

The result calculated indicates, we can still utilise twenty per cent extra efforts to achieve six sigma level of our product. Taguchi Loss Function (figure 2.1) indicates that the tolerance level of designing product is limited by upper specification limit and lower specification limit. Variations lesser than these tolerance limits alone would enable us to achieve quality of highest level. We can do this by determining the functions that the consumer expects the product to perform; then we build up a prototype conforming these functions. Taguchi specifies this as system design. We identify controllable as well as uncontrollable factors that affect the performance of the product and then by fixing combination of controllable factors we try to improve the quality of the product to six sigma level. Taguchi names this as parameter design. Then by using better raw material, better machines and by developing new process we can achieve the target six sigma quality level of the product. Taguchi states this as tolerance design.

PERSONNEL AND TEAMS OF SIX SIGMA PROJECT

I have discussed in earlier chapters that the organisational activity, competitive environment and nature of business have become so complex that days of individual heroism are history and teams consisting of interdepartmental, international, multi expertise personnel are the rule of the day. This enables the organisation to achieve competitive performance for the organisation. Team structure, composition, cultural integration and work performance that I have discussed in earlier chapters applies to six sigma teams in most aspects. Therefore, one need not get scared as to how many types of teams are to be organised for attaining total quality, making supply chain function smoothly, benchmarking, total relationship marketing, knowledge acquisition, storage and dissemination or to improve core competence.

Careful selection of persons, intensive and focused training to man various jobs is required to develop the product to the six sigma level. These persons are to be organised into a well knit, closely co-ordinated teams so that six sigma target of meeting customer critical criteria can be achieved in scheduled time frame. The team leaders such as Master Black Belts or Black Belts heading these teams must be proficient in transferring skills to the members of the team. They must be capable of transferring personal effectiveness to team effectiveness. These team leaders have constant contact with team members and thus have good opportunity to sharpen the skills of the team members. The organisation of six sigma project team is generally as depicted in Figure 4.7.

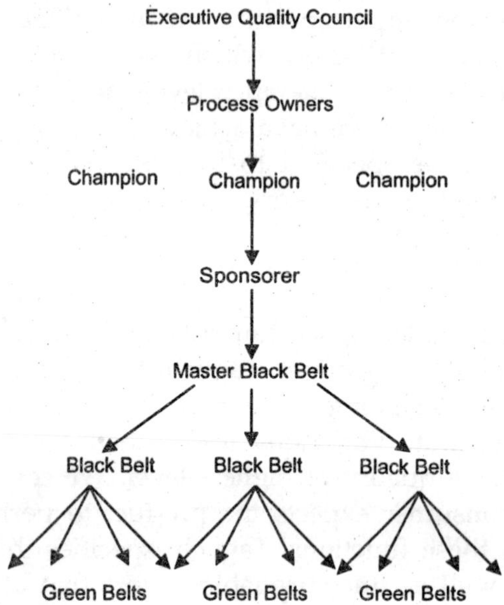

Figure 4.7
Organisation of a Six Sigma Project Team

I will discuss in detail in the following paragraphs personnel and teams, their constitution, responsibilities, functions and training to be imparted to them so as to equip them to discharge their duties successfully, efficiently and effectively.

(1) Executive Quality Council

Executive Quality Council is the topmost team in the organisation undertaking six sigma initiative. The council consists of six to nine chief officers who determine strategy of the organisation. The executive quality council has to overlook the six sigma project end to end. Members of the council possess cross functional expertise on the basis of which they manage critical functions in the initiative. They have to sense, define and regularly update their understanding of customer's critical criteria so that the project initiative can be navigated accordingly. They have to develop crystal clear and complete descriptions of the factors that achieve customer's delight. They are the leaders who have to be at the vanguard of the project, therefore, they must exhibit determination, confidence, patience and integrity. They need to scrutinise periodical progress reports prepared by Black Belts and presented through champions. The council should assess the performance of the project in terms of real time and initiate corrective actions that address the problems. The council should improve existing tools and innovate new methods and processes that would better the organisation's performance levels, competitiveness and profitability.

Functions of the Executive Quality council are –

(1) Initiate six sigma project, develop clear and comprehensive map of ' value delivering activities' within the organisation and direct these activities to manufacture 'zero defect' components of the product.

(2) Prioritize the six sigma projects according to their feasibility and impact, develop inventory and strategy improvement priorities.

(3) Monitor periodically the progress of six sigma initiative so as to ensure that the targeted results are achieved in assigned time.

(4) Use existing tools and if required develop new tools to measure the performance of the project. If necessary corrective actions should be taken to maintain the movement along track and expedite the achievements.

(5) Take measures to sustain the achievements of the project over long period of time.

(2) Process Owners

Once the Executive Quality Council has initiated the six sigma project, process owners are given charge of the project from inception to completion. They have to procure resources, assemble personnel, search expertise, generate and acquire knowledge from within the organisation or outside the organisation. They have to identify supply chain partners, make alliances with them and if necessary make them partners in the endeavor of the organisation. Such suppliers must possess enthusiasm, expertise, technology and time management techniques that keep the links of the supply chain to the minimum and attend zero defect level of the components they are entrusted to produce. It is the ultimate responsibility of the process owners to ensure and achieve hundred per cent success in the project. They are accountable for each of their action to the organisation.

Their functions are –

(1) Prepare a detailed, comprehensive map of processes to be carried out from the beginning to the end to deliver defect free product/service to the customer.

(2) Bench mark the processes that are critical and important in producing zero defect products. Bench marked processes need not be from the same region or from the same industry but they must be effective and feasible to reach ultimate goal.

(3) Assign to the Black Belt project manager particular process or processes for carrying out necessary changes and improvements so as make the components hundred per cent perfect.

(4) Comprehend and co-ordinate processes that are carried out by Black Belt project managers so that their efforts become complementary to each other.

(5) Initiate Black Belt project managers to constantly improve their processes so that better results can be registered year after year.

(6) Make use of existing tools and develop new tools for monitoring performance of the project.

(3) Champions

A champion is a person who has successfully completed two or three six sigma projects and has accumulated experience. Champions are in a way a link, a laison between the executive quality council and the project. Their expertise is related to initiating, guiding, counseling, training Black Belts. They have to train Black Belts in financial as well as accounting methods so as to evaluate progress and performance of the project on the basis of cost benefit analysis.

Their functions are –

(1) To ask for and maintain adequate financial budget to cover various expenses like installation of computers, provision of software, training, development of office space, travels etc.

(2) To assist management in identifying potential Black Belts and seek next two potential replacements for each Black Belt.

(3) To review progress of project management activities of Black Belt project managers and to assess the skills and expertise of Black Belt project managers in six sigma project methodologies.

(4) To sponsor presentation of completed six sigma projects. These reports are got to be prepared from Black Belt project managers.

(5) To present an independent evaluation of completed six sigma projects and decide that the gains claimed in the project reports are real and as per expectations. They have added to the bottom line of the company. If the project is found to be not worth continuing champions can halt that project and report council accordingly.

(4) Sponsors

The Sponsors decide whether the six sigma project can improve the situation by trying to reach near zero defect level of the product by studying annual reports of the company and other factors like customer defection rate. They evaluate various proposals for attaining this level of quality and select viable as well as feasible proposals; prepare a draft of six sigma project on the basis of these selected proposals. Sponsors present these project plans to the executive quality council and get approvals and funds for these projects. Sponsors assign these projects to a team of Black Belts to be assisted by Green Belt teams. This is done on the basis of information and reports gathered about the project and capabilities of Black Belt. A master Black Belt is advised to lead such projects. Sponsors are the authorities to sanction and make adequate expenses out of the funds allotted by Executive Quality council for the project.

(5) Master Black Belts

Persons who have completed successfully one or two six sigma projects are promoted as Master Black Belts. They shoulder dual responsibilities. On the one hand they serve as project managers for very large six sigma projects from end to end. On the other hand they take responsibility of educating, training and career planning of the Black Belts. They have expertise in peoples' soft skills and that empowers them to prepare next generation Black Belts.

Their functions are —

(1) To advance the organisation's capacity within the boundaries of six sigma philosophy, methodologies and techniques.

(2) To serve as project managers for large six sigma projects from the stage of inception to completion. Divide this large project into small projects, allot them to Black Belt project managers, guide them in carrying out and in completing their projects. Master Black Belts should co-ordinate their project activities so that they become complementary to one another and advance the large project of which they are a part.

(3) To facilitate continuing education of the Black Belt and Green Belt personnel. They have to chalk out the course curriculum, classroom lectures, practical as well as exposure sessions to educational module. They have to arrange for on job training for these personnel.

(4) To participate in the career planning of the Black Belts they coach.

(5) To host and facilitate Black Belt sharing sessions.

(6) To coach Black Belts on their projects.

(6) Black Belts

These persons act as six sigma project managers or as managers of sub-projects that are discussed in the foregoing paragraph. They are fast track, ambitious, energetic, well educated and well trained people. Wipro has over 150 Black Belt personnel well trained and well groomed and Wipro has rolled out about 1000 six sigma projects and has about 500 ongoing projects. General Electric, Satyam Computers, Cummins are the organisations that run six sigma projects all round the year and have adequate Black Belt personnel to man these projects. In the first instance, they are well grounded in the technology the firm uses, may be in the field of production, service, banking, insurance, business or trading. They are high performance people who have demonstrated capacity of standing above all. In addition they must have proficiency in computer operations, proficiency in advanced and appropriate statistical techniques as well in computer based statistical methods. They are persons who have completed training in six sigma methodologies and tools. They work at senior manager level in the organisation. They are 'best and bright' in the organisation possessing speciality knowledge like design of experiments, failure mode and effective analysis, reliability engineering and must have flavor for inventive problem solving and project management initiatives. In most of the organisations persons seeking management positions must first become Black Belt qualified.

There has been much debate about the number of Black Belts an organisation should have. Some relate their number to the six sigma project numbers as well as the project value. The number of six sigma projects is fixed by the Executive Quality Council and usually adequate number of Black Belt project managers are educated, trained and promoted. Considering the need for new projects on annual successive basis an ongoing program is instituted. Some experts argue that in organisations having large number of unskilled workers, number of Black Belt managers should be between half a per cent and one per cent of the employee base; however, in organisations having majority of workers skilled and having fast implementation plans, this proportion may rise to four per cent of the employee base. Some people are even in favor of hiring qualified Black Belts or appointing consultants as Black Belts for particular six sigma projects. However, this view is not endorsed and favored because requirements of an organisation are unique, culture distinguished and ethics and values personalised. Black Belts are best sourced by training best of the volunteers from within the organisation.

Most of the organisations do not have formal rules and procedures for selecting persons to be elevated to the level of Black Belts. Some organisations keep a track record of brilliant, intelligent, enthusiastic and knowledgeable persons and from among them people are picked and deputed for training. In some organisations prospective candidates are chosen from main activity of the organisation. While in some organisations such persons are chosen from support activities like corporate services, network and analysis services, quality department, finance and H.R. They are identified as change agents.

I have discussed characteristics, qualities, capabilities, expertise of persons who are or can be Black Belts. I have also talked about recruitment and promotion policies of Black Belt managers at such a length because they are the kingpin in the whole process and procedure of the six sigma project.

Their functions are –

(1) To conceive project design to achieve six sigma level of the product or service in the light of customers' critical criteria.

(2) Plan and map the project and submit the project report to executive quality council through sponsors, champions and process owners.

(3) To act as a manager of six sigma project or sub-project as assigned by the Master Black Belt.

(4) Get to the detail of each act in the project with the help of green belt project teams and search and research every measure, methodology, technology to achieve not more than 3.14 defects per million products.

(5) To prepare and submit progress report of the performance of the project to the Master Black Belt if it is a sub-project or to the process owner for consideration and presentation to the executive council.

(7) Green Belts

Managers who offer to participate in six sigma projects are trained as Green Belts. In some organisations all managers are trained as Green Belts whether they participate in such a project or not. Green Belts are usually found in two roles – first, as the assignment ranks, where they learn six sigma philosophy, techniques and tools. Second they are in the role of team members, where they acquire competence to participate in six sigma projects. Some organisations require all managers to be Green Belts qualified; While some organisations do not promote a person to manager's post unless he or she is Green Belt qualified.

Most of the persons who are qualified Green Belts perform full time managerial role and work on six sigma project as a separate assignment. They are usually selected to work on particular project before the project starts. Once they are assigned to a project they are given intensive education and training. They are taught six sigma philosophy, methods of selecting a project, use of fundamental tools of mapping and improving six sigma process, major steps of Define, Measure, Analyse, Improve and Control. Green Belt team members are invariably selected from within the organisation. This is done firstly to open up avenues and opportunities of furtherance to hardworking, enthusiastic and capable persons. Secondly, they are conversant with the nature of the product or service offered by the organisation. They are closely acquainted, on one hand, with suppliers and on the other with the customers, and as such they know strengths and weaknesses of suppliers and customer's critical criteria. They are chosen from within the organisation because they are a part of that corporate ethics, culture, strategy and policy. Many a times they have lent their hand in formulating these corporate ethos. They have become valuable because they have worked for longer period in the organisation; they become more familiar with the business of the company, they learn more and thus they become more valuable. These employees deal directly with customers day after day and therefore have powerful impact on the loyalty of the customers.

Their functions are —

(1) To assist Black Belts in carrying out the project.

(2) To identify the defects in the products and/or services, study them and innovate methods, technology, machinery to remove those defects.

(3) To get such work done from the shop floor employees by enthusing them to produce "defect free components and defect free assemblies". Guide the employees in attaining that perfection of skill and expertise.

(4) To evaluate work of suppliers, provide them necessary technological inputs and bring them to the level of zero defect supplier.

Thus, Green Belt team members are the persons who actually implement the work practices that make the products foolproof and are the persons charged, sparked with a mission 'Let Us Do The Things Better".

TRAINING

Six sigma objective is not a philosophy practiced in isolation. It is very much a part of total quality management approach to productive activity. An organisation initiating six sigma project is a link in the supply chain — internal as well as external. The process owners in the six sigma initiative benchmark best of the practices. Organisation initiating six sigma project has to search, assimilate, create and disseminate best of the knowledge so that best of the brains, thoughts and ideas can make our efforts come true. Therefore, the training program organised for six sigma project personnel must encompass all these aspects of the functioning of the organisation. At the same time there is an unique phenomenon where tiffin carriers of Mumbai carrying tiffin carriers from places of residence of employees to their work places and returning back in the evening have achieved success greater than six sigma without any formal education or training, The story is –

SIX SIGMA – MUMBAI DABBAWALAS
Logistics at its Best

Around 5000 tiffin-wallas deliver 1,75,000 lunches everyday and take the empty tiffin boxes back. They make one mistake in two months. That means there is one error on every 16 million transactions. The percentage of correctness is 99.999999.

Lakhs of employees commute from suburbs of Mumbai to their workplaces in South Mumbai. They leave their homes so early that they can neither have their lunch before they start or cannot carry their lunch boxes with them. Out of this necessity the institution of tiffinwallas came into existence. People coming from rural places to Mumbai to earn their livelihood undertake the job of picking up tiffin-boxes from residences of these commuters and reach them at their workplaces before lunch hour.

The meals are picked up from commuter's homes in suburbs around Central Mumbai long after the commuters have left for works. Each tiffin carrier has painted on its top, a number of symbols which identify where the carrier was picked up, the originating and destination railway stations and the address to which it is to be delivered. After the tiffin carriers are picked up from homes of the commuters, they are taken to the nearest railway station where they are sorted according to destination station.

Between 10.15 a.m. and 10. 45 a.m. they are loaded in crates on to the baggage cars of trains. At the destination station they are unloaded by other tiffin-wallahs and re-sorted, this time according to street address, and floor. The 100 kilogram crates of carriers, carried on tiffin-wallas heads, hand-wagons and cycles are delivered at the work place at 12-30 p.m. After the lunch time is over they are picked up at 1.30. p.m. and returned where they were brought from. Since one tiffin-walla does not pickup more than 15-20 tiffins, he can easily recognise the destination to which they are to be delivered. The tiffin-walla can also recognise the place of origin and can return the tiffin-box exactly at the place wherefrom it was picked up in the morning.

The charges for this extraordinary services are just Rs. 150/- ($ 3.33) per month. Tiffin-wallas do not own the crates. They pay a charge of Rs. 60/- as rent of the crate, Rs. 120/- per month to the railways for transport, the average tiffin-walla earns about Rs. 3250 per month., Rs. 10 are contributed to the tiffin-men's association. The association collects in this way around Rs. 50,000 per month. The association deducts minimum administrative charges; and the rest of Rs. 50,000 a month goes to charitable trust that feeds the poor.

This system has uniqueness. It extends the design and uses tiffin-wallahs, the end user and their cognitive and memory structure as well.

These tiffins carry only

X A symbol (not name) of the originating station

X A symbol for the destination station.

X A symbol for the building where the tiffin-box is to be delivered.

Most of the people who run this are illiterate.

Even then they have achieved the level of

ONE ERROR ON EVERY 16 MILLION TRANSACTIONS.

Most of the organisations have proprietary programs for training employees Black Belt skills. Quality Assurance Institute of India conducts examination for Black Belt certification. Motorola University certifies methodology and persons who can certify Black Belts. Some organisations run Black Belt training program spread over to three sessions called as three waves. Each wave consists of a week's program where-after a gap of two days is given before beginning the second wave. Most of the training is class room training.

The course contents are -

(A) Enterprise Development –

(1) Value of six sigma, Business systems and processes, process inputs, outputs and feedback.

(2) Leadership – Enterprise leadership, Six sigma roles and Responsibilities.

(3) Organisational goals and objectives – Linking projects to organisational goals, Risk analysis, Closed loop assessment and knowledge management.

(4) History of organisational improvement – Foundation of six sigma.

(B) Business Process Management –

(1) Process versus functional view – Process elements, Owners and stake holders, project management benefits, project measures.

(2) Voice of customer – Identify customer, Collect customer data, Analyse customer data, Determine data, Determine critical customer requirements.

(3) Business results – Process performance metrics, Benchmarking, Financial benefits.

(C) Project Management –

(1) Project charter and plan – Charter/plan elements, Planning tools (Gantt chart, PERT Chart, Planning Tree), Project documentation, Charter negotiation.

(2) Team leadership – Initiating teams, Selecting team members, Team stages.

(3) Team dynamics and performance – Team building techniques, Team performance evaluation, Team Tools.

(4) Change agents – Managing change, Organisational road blocks, Negotiation and conflict resolution techniques, Motivation techniques, Communication.

(5) Management and planning tools.

(D) Six Sigma Improvement – I

(1) Project scope

(2) Metrics

(3) Problem statement

(E) Six Sigma Improvement – II

(1) Process analysis and documentation – Tools, Process inputs and outputs.

(2) Probability and statistics – Drawing valid statistical conclusions, Central limit theorem and sampling distribution mean, Basic probability concepts.

(3) Collecting and summarising data – Types of data, Measurement of scales, Methods of collecting data, Techniques for assuming data accuracy and integrity, Descriptive statistics, Graphical methods.

(4) Properties and Applications of probability distribution – Distributions commonly used by Black Belts, Other distributions.

(5) Measurement systems – Measurement methods, Measurement system analysis, Metrology.

(6) Analysing process capability – Designing and conducting process capability studies, Calculating performance versus speculation,

Process capability indices, Short-term versus long-term capability, Non-normal data transformations, Process capability for attributes data.

(F) Six Sigma Improvement - III

(1) Exploratory data analysis – Multi – vari studies, Measuring and modelling relationships between variables.

(2) Hypothesis testing – Fundamental concepts of hypothesis testing, Point and internal estimation, Tests for menus, Variances and proportions.

(3) Paired – comparison tests – Goodness-of-fit tests, Analysis of variance, Contingency tables, Non-parametric tests.

(G) Six Sigma Improvement - IV

(1) Design of experiment – Technology, planning and organising experiments, Design priorities, Design and analysis of two-level factional experiments, Taguchi robustness concepts, Mixture experiments.

(2) Response surface methodology – Steepest ascent/descent experiments, High order experiments.

(3) Evolutionary operations.

(H) Six Sigma Improvement – V

(1) Statistical process control – Objective and benefits, Selection of variables, Rational sub-grouping, Selection and application of control charts, Analysis of control charts, PRE control.

(2) Advanced statistical process control.

(3) Lean tools for control.

(4) Measurement system re-analysis.

(I) Lean Enterprise -

(1) Lean concepts – Theory of constraints, Lean thinking, Continuous flow manufacturing, Non-value added activities, Cycle time reduction.

(2) Lean tools.

(3) Total productive maintenance.

(J) Design for Six Sigma –

(1) Quality function deployment

(2) Robust design and process – Functional requirements, Noise strategies, Tolerance design, Tolerance and process capability.

(3) Failure mode and effects analysis.

(4) Design for X.

(5) Special design tools.

This is the curriculum developed by the examination development committee.

Adam's six sigma plus (+) program has five blocks in which the curriculum for Black Belts is divided. These five blocks are –

Block 1

(1) Introduction to Six sigma Black Belt manager training.
(2) Strategy and Six sigma Black Belt project managers.
(3) Service for Six sigma Black Belt project managers.
(4) Six sigma Black Belt project manager defect measurement.
(5) Understanding behaviour for six sigma Black Belt project manager.
(6) Six sigma Black Belt and the use of data.
(7) DISC profile for six sigma Black Belt.
(8) Use of statistical tests by six sigma Black Belt.
(9) Six sigma Black Belt team empowerment.
(10) Leadership for six sigma Black Belt.
(11) Six sigma Black Belt project work.

Block 2

(1) Six sigma Black Belt project manager and customer service.
(2) Create a service plan for six sigma Black Belt project manager.
(3) Six sigma Black Belt basic finance.
(4) Six sigma Black Belt financial controls.
(5) Measurement systems for six sigma Black Belt project managers.
(6) Six sigma Black Belt use of repeatability and re-producibility.
(7) Economic evaluation for six sigma Black Belt project manager.
(8) Cycle time improvement introduction for six sigma Black Belt manager.

Block 3

(1) Project management introduction for six sigma Black Belt.
(2) Six sigma Black Belt project define.
(3) Six sigma Black Belt project plan.
(4) Six sigma Black Belt project budget.
(5) Six sigma Black Belt project people.
(6) Six sigma Black Belt project execution.
(7) Six sigma Black Belt project reporting.
(8) Six sigma Black Belt project closing.
(9) Reading control charts for six sigma Black Belt.

(10) X Bar and R control charts for six sigma Black belt.

(11) X m R and R control charts for six sigma.

(12) C and U control charts for six sigma Black Belt.

(13) P and n p control charts for six sigma.

Block 4

(1) Graphical view of design of experiment.

(2) Six sigma Black Belt interpretation model.

(3) Fractional factorials used by six sigma Black Belt.

(4) Importance of replication and randomness.

(5) Six sigma Black Belt planning of design for experiment.

(6) Use of root cause analysis by six sigma Black Belt.

(7) FMEA as a six sigma Black Belt project manager tool.

(8) Fault free analysis used by six sigma Black Belt.

Block 5

(1) Writing procedures for six sigma Black Belts.

(2) Six sigma Black Belt and audits.

(3) ISO 9000 and six sigma.

(4) Six sigma Black Belt project manager use of reliability engineering.

(5) Presentation skills for six sigma Black Belt project managers.

(6) Theory of inventive problem solving.

(7) Closing six sigma Black Belt.

The vigor and intensity of the program indicates the importance Black Belt personnel have in six sigma project.

Thus, six sigma projects are programs and methods for all-round development of the organisation. It is a philosophy to achieve competitive advantage. Probably, this is an important measure to delight the customer.

In conclusion I state that the success of any organisation in this competitive age depends upon management leadership. Management leadership is the single most important ingredient in the six sigma project. Personal direct involvement and personal time are the two major leadership initiatives. Management's and champion's roles, responsibilities and duties are critical to six sigma deployment. If the company decides to accept and implement six sigma initiative to improve its competitive advantage, it has to shake up its organisational setup, delayer hierarchy and focus all its attention on satisfying customer's critical criteria.

References

(1) Zaire Mohamed. *Benchmarking for the Best Practice*, Butterworth Heinemann, 1996.

❑ ❑ ❑

5 Benchmarking

Every organisation trying to acquire competitive advantage has to achieve total quality in its activities, may they be production, service, business, banking or insurance; and every firm doing so has to benchmark best of the practices and absorb them fully and totally. This is because benchmarking is critical to total quality management. Total quality management entails benchmarking in twenty-two areas classified into three tiers. First tier critical factors cover management behaviour. Second tier benchmarking entails production and problem solving activities, and third tier factors relate to attitudinal and improvement activities.

In good old days organisations used to borrow employees, artisans of proven outstanding qualities from other organisation for a specific period of time. This method of deputing best of the people called as SHUKKO was the most effective application of the principle of benchmarking. Such legend employees spread new practices that helped the organisation move forward. It helped transfer of technology, acquisition of specific knowledge and developing, leveraging the performance of managers creating abilities to take bigger tasks. I have discussed in earlier chapters on supply chain, Six Sigma project that benchmark best of the practices and adopt them to add more value to products and/or services to delight customers.

Sarah Cook defines, "benchmarking is the process of identifying, understanding and adopting outstanding practices from within the same organisation or from other business to help improve performance." Sultan Kermally defines, 'benchmarking is a method of improving business performance by learning from other companies how to do things better in order to be the best in the class'. 'Benchmarking is a continuous systematic process of evaluating companies recognised as industry leaders to determine business and work processes that represent best practices and establish rational performance goals'. 'Benchmarking is a continuous process of analysing the best practice in the world for the process of goals and objectives leading to world class levels of achievement'.

Events that have taken place in the last two decades of the last century in the fields of technology, management, product innovation and development, trade, social ethos, political and military strategies have compelled the organisations, to be alert and attentive. They have to sharpen their tools to gain competitive advantage in every possible way. Benchmarking is one of the best practices to achieve the goals of sustainable levels of growth and profitability. Thus, organisations have come to benchmark in the areas of manufacturing, operations, finance, marketing and customer services so as to improve organisational performance and effectiveness. New and rising industries like bio-pharmaceutical have carried out exercises on benchmarking practices in almost all areas like staffing, generic competition, industry leadership, company objectives, quality manufacturing, quality assurance, quality control etc. Even governments of newly created states in India have got benchmarking done from reputed institutions to create best class corporate governance in government administration.

Any type of improvement the organisation desires to achieve needs a systematic, planned and thorough approach. It is so with benchmarking project. Benchmarking is an ongoing process and therefore benchmarking studies need to be monitored regularly. We need not wait till one program of benchmarking exercise is completed. That is because benchmarking is a method of identifying new ideas, new ways of performing processes and adopting innovations that come any time and every time. Benchmarking program must be well conceived, well designed and meticulously implemented. It must take total system approach so that it can look to the suppliers and distributors in view of the company's goal. This enables the company to integrate entire production and distribution systems into company's core business. Such benchmarking leverages company's capabilities to develop product design that will smoothen the movement through chain of suppliers. It will help avoiding unnecessary processes, steps and stages in production, and make the product as small in size. As a result product will become universal in application and as customer delighting. That will make practices of our company benchmarking practices for others.

Mohamed Zaire argues that benchmarking is adopted with six views in mind. They are (1) to help transfer of technology, acquire specific knowledge lacking in the organisation, develop the performance of employees and create abilities to take bigger tasks, (2) benchmarking is a good strategic planning method and as such avoids strench objectives and sets credible and easy to reach targets, (3) benchmarking exposes organisation to state of–art practices and by instigating a continuous learning process, can help in the cultivation of a culture based on change and continuous improvement, (4) benchmarking is a good vehicle for peoples education, involvement and empowerment. It helps in optimising creative potential of the employees in the area of innovativeness. Sarah Cook adds, (5) benchmarking helps the organisation to add value to its customers and distinguish itself from competitors, (6) it helps the organisation to focus on the external environment and improve process efficiency.

Organisation small or big, public or private, production or service can undertake benchmarking program. However, it must have inner urge to match with the best, it must have burning leadership. Such an organisation must have ethos and drive for continuously seeking better ways of managing process. The organisation must recognise that benchmarking is a proven tool of initiating a continuous improvement process. For many companies benchmarking has become key component of their

TQM program.[1] It should be understood that there can be various and different 'best practices' of doing things. Bestness of a practice is related to the dimensions of social, religious and political culture, state of art and strategy of the organisation. Thus, the organisation implementing benchmarked best of the practice has to realise that such practice cannot just be imported and copied. Such best of the practice needs to be moulded to the requirements of the organisation at the present state of its development. Best of the practices are to be chosen from different organisations in different fields and are to be co-ordinated into single cohesive well-knit practice that makes the organisation best in the field.

Benchmarking concept was introduced, it is practiced and will be practiced in future because it is a thirst quenching exercise in the organisational atmosphere. It provides satisfaction, good feeling, and happiness of achieved desired objective. Benchmarking if done properly, implemented painfully and executed rigorously does bring a number of benefits. Rather it is the benefits of benchmarking that justifies benchmarking.[2] Quality should be one. Godling has matrixed the benefits of benchmarking. They are enumerated in Table 5.1.

Table 5.1
Benefits of Benchmarking to the Organisation

	Benefits	*How is the benefit derived*	*When is the benefit accrued*
(1)	Improved performance and profitability.	Improving efficiency and effectiveness of processes, reduced costs associated wastes and reworking errors.	Initially when processes are analysed; continuing throughout the 'life' of benchmarking in the firm.
(2)	Clarity of leadership.	Discussion on what improvements would bring biggest benefit.	Prior to starting the benefit.
(3)	Clarity of management enhanced communication.	Focus on key processes helps manage where it matters.	In the first three months.
(4)	Saving and better utilisation of resources.	Analysing processes and finding out exactly what is going on.	In the first three months.
(5)	Increased efficiency of operations.	Remove error, rework and duplication of process.	In the first three months.
(6)	Greater value creation or reduction in non-value adding activities.	Questioning which activities in the process add value and eliminating those which do not.	In the first three months.
(7)	Challenge current thinking.	Learning from others' mistakes saves time and speeds up the learning curve. Also increases speed of learning about new things in the organisation.	When networks are accessed or potential partners contacted-benefit-on going.
(8)	External focus and tapping into innovations in other sectors or countries.	During data search and collection as well networking of information.	Begins within first three months but becomes evident within 12 months.

(9)	Reduces fire-fighting and improves quality of working life.	As processes become more efficient and effective.	Gradually from month one onwards.
(10)	Beneficial impact on customers and suppliers.	By taking their perspective and views into account as you tighten up process.	Gradually from month one onwards.
(11)	Opens doors to other organisations.	The technique provides a purpose and common language.	As external benchmarking progresses.

Sarah Cook states the benefits of benchmarking in rather general terms. She states, when an organisation adopts benchmarking program it sets realistic performance goals. Benchmark program demands all-round change in the organisation. As benchmark program is to be completed in fixed time frame, it helps accelerate and manage change. All processes in the organisation are improved. All persons in the organisation that adopts benchmarking exercise begin to think in an unconventional manner that takes them 'outside the box'. People in the organisation come to know what world class standards are. This understanding of world class performance kindles their urge to reach that level.

Joel E. Ross looks to the benefits of benchmarking still from a different perspective. Benchmarking initiates cultural change among the employees in the organisation. It is very difficult to convince our people that there are people out there who do things better than we do. In the process of benchmarking these very employees, who collect, data and see for themselves how better others do the things, set new performance targets which are realistic in their own belief. They begin to believe in the capacity, capability and also in credibility of these targets. Benchmarking inculcates initiative culture.

Benchmarking helps organisation to improve its alround performance. Comparison of benchmarked performance level and our performance level identifies gaps in performance. This enables us to select processes that are to be improved. These gaps provide us the set of objectives to be achieved and action plan to be framed to promote improved performance for individual and group participants.

Benchmarking initiates HR development activities. Employees having seen for themselves the gaps between what they are doing and what best-in-class are doing understand the need and importance of training and development. This enables the management to understand the need for personnel to be involved in techniques of problem solving and process improvement. Moreover, the synergy between organisation activities is improved through cross-functional co-operation.

TYPES OF BENCHMARKING

Objectives of benchmarking can be different for different organisations. Sometimes the whole organisational process is benchmarked and sometimes particular product, particular process, quality system, supplier partnership, supply chain management or customer service and customer satisfaction are the areas that are chosen for benchmarking. Many a times a combination of these various types of benchmarking is taken as a project. Some important types of benchmarking are discussed below.

(1) Strategic Benchmarking

It aims at strategic changes like change in management style, marketing policy and prioritised resource allocation. It tries to develop measures for a business unit, which quantify its key strengths and weaknesses. It enables you to find out how well you are prepared to compete in a market segment and helps you to find out best-in-class competitor. This is usually done by constructing Key Success Factor Matrix with the help of field study. We try to take a number of characteristic features of the product and note customer rating of various companies. This is shown in Table 5.2.

Table 5.2
Key Success Factors of a Product

Characteristic feature	*Weight*	*Customer Purchasing Rating*			
		Our Company	*Competitor One*	*Competitor Two*	*Competitor Three*
Price Performance Durability Availability Reliability Consistency					
Total					

The company producing goods that passes highest rating score is taken for benchmark. Data on its production method, processes, technology, training given to human resources are collected and analysed and then implemented. In the same way data on management style is gathered. Openness of management can be assessed with the help of suggestions made by employees, suggestions accepted and implemented. An index of openness of management can be computed with the help of this data. The company with highest value of index can be selected for benchmark. Strategic benchmark enables us to adopt a new policy, different strategy to improve our performance.

(2) Operational Benchmarking

Particular activity in the functional operations is selected and focused for collecting data. If a company is pricing its product of good quality at lower level then we try to find out where does it save on the cost of production and data about cost incurred on that activity is collected, analysed and that practice is benchmarked. Some companies capture larger share of the market by differentiating their product from others. We collect data on the factors that are highlighted in differentiating the product. Producers of motorcycles differentiate their bikes by highlighting style, sleek design, pick up, control, fuel efficiency, road grip, suspension etc. We collect data as to what characteristic features out of these attract buyers and collect data on that. So we try to find out the factors that affect/influence customer purchasing decision and benchmark those factors and implement them.

This type of benchmarking is also known as process benchmarking. Some companies compare processes of its own divisions in the same country or in other countries. Processes of leading service providers can also be benchmarked. This is usually done in a company having longer supply chain. For example, we find out the core delivery process of a company that is best-in-class chain store. Collect data on that aspect of the process that makes the whole company stand out as an example. Collection of data in this way is very difficult and a rigorous task because small small things count in making a big difference. Catching attention on such small small things is rather difficult.

(3) Product Benchmarking

Many a companies try to find out what makes products of some producers move fast than our products. Sometimes this exercise is of the type of introspection, where the company tries to discover characteristic features of it's own old products that made them move fast. Thus, we can take lessons partly from ourselves and partly from best of the Class Company of today. This company need not be from our industry. Discovering the trick, technology, recipe of making better product is important and collecting data on that aspect of the product is key to product benchmarking.

(4) Benchmarking Quality Systems

People in general and buyers in particular have confidence in the product, service of an individual company. Such a company enjoys competitive advantage. A company develops such a system of procedures and practices, values that makes it stand as a quality system. Usually auditing is an important activity in quality systems. The company has set standards of doing each and everything and auditing ensures that these standards are complied with at all stages, at all places and at all times. We study this system of procedures, practices and values. This system is commonly known as quality program. It is difficult to collect data on such soft matters because their success depends less on words in the procedure book but on the devotion, commitment to follow them in good manner.

(5) Benchmarking Innovative Management

Some companies add to their reputation and status by providing extra dimension of quality that differentiates the product or service through newness and originality. Any and every activity of the company that impacts, enhances customer satisfaction, customer delight is innovative management. The degree of newness is time related, it has to be replenished and has to be recreated on continuous basis. New product launches and timeliness of such launches increases the sales by about 28 per cent and boosts the profits by about 20 per cent. We have to study in such benchmark study the way various organisations exploit opportunity and deliver what the customer wants in the fastest, most effective and economically viable manner. Patterson argues that many companies manage innovation through Innovation Life Cycle time that is the interval between the moment the window of opportunity opens 'the moment the first customer is satisfied.'[3]

We have to study how various companies master the movement in various stages of new product development that is to be smooth through effective integration. We must understand how other companies have created specific tools, techniques and build up involvement of teams. Core innovation activity must be well resourced and supported by management. It is rather challenging to collect such data and put it in project form so that strategic benefit can be ensured.

(6) Benchmarking Supplier Partnership

Success of a supply chain depends upon how best supplier has been chosen and how good relations are developed with them. Thus, a company would have to decide criteria for choosing suppliers. R. Halhead argues that from 1990, companies have adopted strategy of vendor-managed inventory to improve productivity, ensure customer satisfaction and meet global demands.'[4] Effective supply chain partnership can be developed by selecting a group of suppliers based on industrial reputation and transaction records, price charged and quality of the product. This is done by setting up a supplier assessment program. Then we choose those suppliers whose supply chain management strategy is closely aligned with the company's strategy.

There are two models developed for benchmarking supplier partnership. The first model is Supply Chain Management Group (SCMG). We identify relationship strengths and weaknesses on both sides in the context of best practices with the help of 'relationship positioning tool'. It enables the company and supplier to develop joint agenda for improvement activities. Quality, delivery, cost and innovation are the factors examined in respect of the supplier because they determine the present and future performance.

The second model is Lamming model. We search for fewer larger and more talented suppliers who can play more complex and more critical role in the whole manufacturing process. We try to identify supplier who has more than ten production lines and who has presence in various markets. Even suppliers with global presence are scanned.

These types of benchmarking can be used separately or jointly. We can use one type of benchmarking to achieve one goal and another type to achieve another goal. Use of particular type benchmarking depends upon whether we are seeking best of the class practices outside the organisation or within the organisation. These are the benchmarking practices related to strategies, operational processes, products, quality, management practices and people.

PREPARING FOR BENCHMARKING

Total quality management has to be total and for that the organisation has to carry out a planned time bound program of satisfying customer critical criteria, of delighting the customer. The organisation has to streamline its activities so as to produce zero defect foolproof products at lowest cost of production and deliver it to the customer at the place where he wants and at the time when he wants. This can be done by adopting and adapting the processes of best of the world producers in our organisation. Though apparently it appears to be a technical job it has organisational, managerial, attitudinal and psychological dimensions. If our product is to be technically, technologically the best in the market the organisation on one hand has to install best of the machines incorporating state of the art technology and train its work force in nano-technology that will enable us to configurate various technologies. So that goods of molecular size and precision can be produced at very low cost. It will enable us to develop self-replicating manufacturing systems.

It must be remembered that all aspects of business operations can be benchmarked. In achieving organisational transformation all aspects of business should be benchmarked but priority should be given to those areas which have maximum impact on the performance of the organisation and which provide utmost opportunity to gain competitive advantage. It is argued by some authors that, factors like product development, marketing, on time delivery; customer care – the factors that maximise customer value as well as shareholders value – should be given priority. Benchmarking is an integral part of total quality management program. Therefore, a team approach is adopted under TQM banner to identify the areas that are to be improved and generate well implement measures, remedies to achieve that improvement. Thus, as a preparation it must be made clear as to what objectives the organisation perceive of benchmarking program. Some organisations adopt benchmarking program as a means of continuous improvement because such an exercise offers external perspective, which is also called as 'helicopter vision'. This is done in quest of better quality of service and customer delight. Such an approach takes us much beyond the benefits of benchmarking. However, it must be remembered that benchmarking is not the only, but one of the tools and techniques that can improve business processes. Sarah Cook expresses, 'benchmarking is an useful vehicle of learning.' This discussion gives us an understanding of strengths and limitations of benchmarking and those must be borne in mind while launching benchmarking program in our organisation.

While preparing organisation for benchmarking project, the management has to do a number of things. The management has to select a senior, well experienced, expert person as a 'sponsor' or 'champion' to carry out the project from 'end to end' and see that benchmarking program yields expected results in a given time frame. Benchmarking team usually consists of executive champion, leader, and project coordinator, facilitator and team players. The skills required by them and level of benchmarking experience as well the time they are required to allocate to project work is exhibited in Table 5.3.

Table 5.3
Members of the Benchmarking Team, Their Skill and Experience

	Team Role	*Time To Be Allotted To The Project*	*Key Skills Required*	*Level Of Benchmarking Experience*
(1)	Executive champion	10 per cent of usual work time	Leadership, communication	Executive overview fit with strategy
(2)	Project leader	Half of usual work time	Leadership, team building, communication, presentation	Overview and awareness of practicalities
(3)	Project co-ordinator	Full time on benchmark project	Project management and presentation	Theory and practice of methods of benchmark project
(4)	Facilitator	Half of usual work time	Facilitation and communication	Theory and practice of methods of benchmark project
(5)	Team player	25 per cent of usual work time	Process analysis, documentation, data scanning, information search	Overview of methods of project and required skill mix
(6)	Customer/supplier	10 per cent of usual time	External perspective of the process, objectivity and communication	Executive overview, process analysis

The management has to set objectives of the benchmarking programs in clear terms, set the time frame in which the targets must be met. The project team needs to be given parameters in which it has to operate. The organisation has to select appropriate persons as members of the team. They are to be taught to work as a team, not as a bunch of individuals. They must have full knowledge of the benchmarking process and must exhibit enthusiasm, devotion and dedication for the task. It is necessary that they should be imparted adequate education and training before they begin their assignment. Training program should concentrate on benchmarking process, data gathering and data analysis skills, research techniques and more importantly the pathos of the team working must be imbibed in them. The entire benchmarking team should be lent all moral, physical, financial and authority support by the management. The catalyst requirements of benchmarking project are people and time. Thus, all members as well as the management must be committed to devote as much time as required to run the project and make it through.

Usually the objectives of benchmarking project are to incorporate best practices in our business processes. It may be alright to initially pilot the project to cover a few strategic processes, but over the period of time it must encompass all aspects of the business. Best practice cannot sustain in isolation of the whole business. Secondly, synergy effect of best practices in all areas and activities of the organisation is greater than the sum total of individual effects. The organisation should try to exceed the best qualitative results achieved by the world class leaders. With this exercise the organisation has to attain level of maturity in the process of production, finance, human resources, distribution and management so it becomes a model to be benchmarked.

Thus, the organisation in preparing for initiating benchmarking exercise has to set up proper infrastructure, develop corporate culture of quality, information systems, process controls and human resource programs. Such organisation can set to undertake the benchmarking exercise. Benchmarking is a process of improvement and customer delight and satisfaction of all the stakeholders.

STARTING BENCHMARKING PROGRAM

Having prepared the organisation to initiate the program the management has to set the stage for action. It must be understood that there is no standard approach, approved and recognised blueprint for benchmarking program. Even the stages, steps in the program may slightly vary. Usually planning, analysis and integration are considered to be three broad stages of the program. Papers presented by IBM, ICL, Rank Xerox and Milikan at Benchmarking conference convened under the auspices of The Economists Conference outlined ten steps of benchmarking program. They were categorised under three heads – namely – planning, analysis and integration stage discussed by the conference. The three steps discussed below are covered in planning; fourth step of our program is covered in analysis stage, while fifth and sixth steps in our analysis are covered in integration stage of conference. Steps seven, eight and nine recommended by the conference are like Deming Cycle-Plan-Do-Act-Review. Joel Ross has listed five stages in benchmarking program. They are (1) Determine the functions and processes to be benchmarked. (2) Select key performance variables. (3) Identify best in class. (4) Measure your own performance, and (5) Action to close the gap. We discuss below in a broad outline steps in benchmarking program from beginning to end.

(1) Identify the Subject to be Benchmarked

Determine the functions and/or processes to be benchmarked. Organisations may experience shortfall in different areas or in the strategy and policy. Therefore, the management has to first decide which specific attribute of the product is failing in attracting customers, or which function and/or process in the organisation is not up to the standard. Shortfalls in customer service may also be a subject to be benchmarked. Even blurred, shaky corporate vision may need to be benchmarked. Attributes of products in fast moving consumer goods and vehicles especially motorbikes are very important. Catchy name of the product (Hudibaba), product design (sleek, stylish), product qualities (pickup, fuel efficiency, control), packaging, colour, smell are very important attributes of products like motorbikes, toilet soaps, shampoos, tooth pastes, potato chips, namkeen which may need to be benchmarked. In Indian market price and ready availability of FMCG are very sensitive aspects. Style, sleekbody, manly appearance, pickup, control, fuel efficiency are supposed to be important attributes of motor cycles that are benchmarked. Customer service in respect of banking services has become catalyst. In banking industry a number of value added services are being provided free of cost to the customers to lift up the sinking bottom line of banking enterprises. Banks have realised that not making the customer to come to banking premises to meet his needs can be a value addition action to the customer and saving of employee time for the bank. Providing electronic payment/clearing payment facilities to the users of electricity, telephone, municipal services was benchmarked as value adding facility. If we examine each link in the value chain we can identify various activities that need to be improved. This can be done by benchmarking program of core activities that are critical to customer satisfaction. Feedback from the customers themselves can tell us which activities if improved may enhance their satisfaction. Employees can provide clues in identifying factors that are critical to organisation's success or the factors that have maximum influence on the organisation's performance. Suppliers and people who work with you can provide external perspective as to which activities need to be improved and which are the companies that excel in these activities.

On the basis of this introspection the organisation can draw a map expressing links between and within processes, decide which links are weak and are falling short of performance. Identification of exact weak link is most important for the success of the program. Inappropriate method of selection of employees or outdated training curriculum, a weak link in the support process like this may cause shortfalls in the performance. This shortfall in performance may be experienced in primary process like inbound logistics, production operations like machining, milling, boring, assembling the product and outbound logistics. Thus, shortfalls in the performance of primary process are caused by weak support process links. What we want to emphasise is that the cause of inferior performance in one area or in one activity may not always be in the same area or activity. Finding this root cause is the kingpin in the success of the program. To make this exercise fruitful, project team members have to study the activities that make process and relationship of the process with other parts of the business. This can be conveniently done by drawing fish bone diagram, process flow diagram, and information flow diagram or supply chain diagram. A process flow diagram can be shown in Figure 5.1.

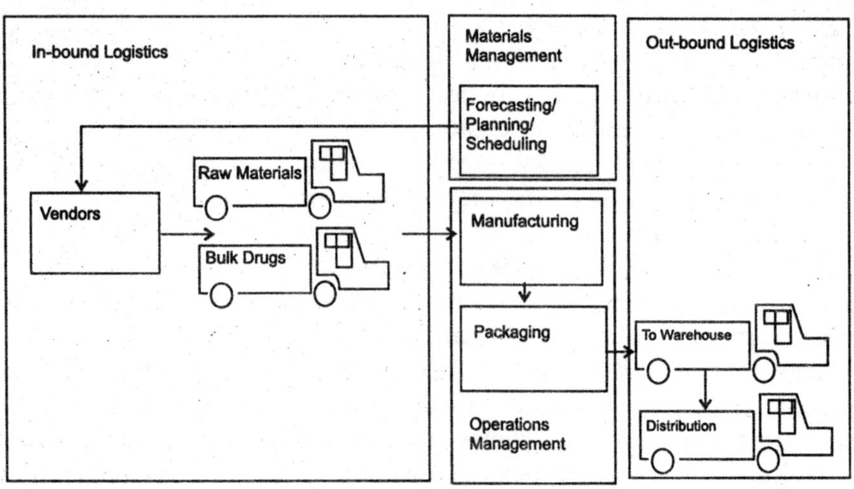

Figure 5.1
Process Flow in a Pharmaceutical Organisation

In the process shown in figure 5.1 there are about seven links in the chain. Shortfall in performance or weakness in a link in the chain can deteriorate performance of the whole process. Therefore, each link must be examined and it must be ascertained that the potential of the link is fully utilised.

(2) Identify who to Benchmark

The organisation must have a clear idea what it wants to benefit from benchmarking program. It has already identified the gaps in performance and has earmarked the functions, the processes that are to be benchmarked. Now, we venture upon in search of benchmark partner. M. Syrett has notified eight key success criteria to be benchmarked. They are (1) manufacturing cycle time, (2) on time supply and delivery, (3) shipment, (4) concept of market, (5) supplier delivery, (6) return on assets, (7) return on technical investment, and (8) revenue per employee. The benchmark team can prioritise the areas and decide which benchmarking project is to be taken first.[5] The study would have to begin accordingly. Benchmarking may be singular or combination of more than one of the types of benchmarking discussed.

Benchmarking partners need to be chosen very discretely and carefully. Benchmarking may be done within the organisation itself. That process or link in the process adds maximum value to the name of the organisation can be studied and its catalysts be made known to other links in the process to be adopted. This is the first route to choosing benchmarking partner. In the second instance, we may look to 'best in the class' strategic business unit in our industry itself. This can be known from the information that market provides. Third route to identifying benchmarking partner is to pinpoint well-reputed well-known unit in our geographical area. The top officials, managers, employees, suppliers can help us in this task. Fourth method is to identify a partner from other competitive business. Sugar factories producing sugar from cane can think of studying data of factories producing sugar from beat. Fifthly, the organisation may consider to choose a benchmarking partner known to be 'world best' or 'best in class' irrespective of industry, sector or location. States in India have benchmarked watershed projects in Maharashtra for their water conservation program. There are a few organisations that provide benchmarking services to companies. Tefen Ltd. has completed benchmark study in 2003 for Bio-pharmaceutical industry.

Usually a brainstorming session of members of the project team is conducted in which prospective benchmarking partners are selected. In many a cases suppliers and customers are also co-opted in such brainstorming session. From among the benchmarking partners enlisted a few are short-listed. Complete background information in respect of the shortlisted partners, regarding their corporate culture, corporate climate, ethics is collected and verified so as to find whether these aspects of benchmarked company match with our company. It is ascertained whether such company would readily co-operate in benchmarking program.

(3) Data Collection

We decide the areas on which the information is to be collected; not only that we have to pinpoint the function or process on which we have to collect data from each of the area. Success of the project depends to a large extend on collection of right type of data. The project team should prepare a document of checklist of data collection clarifying the objective of data collection, the nature of the data the team needs and the additional information that would be helpful. The team should enlist in detail the parameters on which quantifiable data on performance of the benchmarked company would have to be collected. The team should also write down the data it should have to collect on qualitative aspects of the company. This data may relate to company culture, management style, employee attitude, working practices, communication and information system, decision making process etc. The team would have to decide the depth of the information that it would need. Product wise, process wise data needs to be collected. The team has to decide the number of years for which the data is to be collected. The information is to be collected on day to day and on month to month basis. The project team should review the resources in terms of time, people and money that are at its disposal for conducting and completing the projects.

These are various routes and sources of collecting data and cross verifying them. Major methods of collecting data and information are –

(1) Published or secondary data: Much of the information of benchmarked organisation is readily available from corporate publications, directories, industry journals, trade associations, industry network, media reports, seminar papers and conference presentations, professional institutions, consultants. Project team members, individually and collectively, must make all-out efforts to participate in the collection of such data. These efforts would make them familiar with the company to be benchmarked and would acquaint them with the benchmarking process.

(2) Priced data: There are a number of firms, organisations institutions that collect, analyse and draw conclusions from company data, industry segment and also industry data. Centre for monitoring Indian Economy, EPW Research Bureau, Economic Times Research Bureau do perform such research and that information is available at a price. Some institutions undertake the work of collecting data for their clients.

(3) Data collected from potential partner: If analysis of data and information collected from earlier two sources brings us to a conclusion that the potential partner is a good company for benchmark, members of the project team, who know officials of the benchmark company, make an initial contact with these officials indicating their purpose, objectives etc. It is suggested that officers of both the companies, who write articles in industry journals, who present papers in seminars or participate in industry conference, are likely to know each other and can be better contact points. Members of the project team proposed to make initial contact must discuss and decide in what manner should they introduce and present themselves. They should decide the points and details of benchmarking project that should be disclosed to the representative of Benchmark Company in introductory meeting. On successful negotiation and affirmative response of the benchmark company, an exhaustive questionnaire should be prepared. It should be classified into different sections beginning from general information and including the areas, processes, functions that are agreed upon to be benchmarked. If we have chosen different companies to benchmark different areas, processes or functions, we would have to prepare different questionnaires pertaining to each company and quite likely in different languages. Nature of the questionnaire would vary according to the type of benchmarking being done. Tefen Limited and Consortium seem to have followed the same procedure in benchmarking exercise for biopharmaceutical industry.

The answers provided to the questions in the questionnaire should be scrutinized scrupulously, studied closely and analysed objectively. On the basis of this analysis interviews should be arranged with appropriate and responsible persons from benchmark companies. The interviewees must be knowledgeable to clarify our queries and authorised to provide information and discuss points that we need to get clarified. Tefen Ltd. and Consortium had surveyed approximately 30 industry executives for their benchmark study for biopharmaceutical industry.

The final step in the data collection stage is to visit the benchmarked organisations. Sites of visits will be so selected that they have in practice, areas and functions covered in the benchmark study. If we have to study innovation management, the project team would have to visit research laboratories of benchmarked organisation, to find out the way the extra dimensions of quality are incorporated in the product. On the other hand if we are to benchmark quality systems we would have to visit quality control department of the organisation. While for benchmarking various aspects of manufacturing the project team would have to go round the workshops and mills of the company. The project team has to decide and plan carefully and meticulously, the functions and processes it has to study and fix the sequence. Better the homework done in this respect better would be the information collected. Before commencement of the visit a confidentiality agreement has to be signed and protocol of such site visits is to be observed. Members of the project team should go round the workshop with responsible people involved in the process studied. Extensive notes should be taken while going round the site and all points should be discussed honestly and openly. Team members should look, listen, observe and question so as to return with all information needed because there would hardly be a chance of second visit. Visiting persons should validate the data they have already collected. At the end of the site visit a return visit invitation should be extended to the persons from benchmark organisation with which the team members have discussed. And on return make thorough notes of their visit when the points are fresh in the minds of the team members. The discipline of writing down the observations is the first step toward making it happen. Tefen Ltd. had collected about 1600 data points in their study.

(4) Analysis of the data and identifying the gaps: After having collected the relevant data an exercise is undertaken by the project team of interpreting the information. This is done in two stages. In the first stage the data is reviewed, the gap between best of the practice and our practice is gauged.

Review of the data is done again in two parts. Quantifiable data is one part, soft data is another part. Numerical information and factual data can be studied with the help of metrics, and various charts – flow charts, fish bone charts, scattered charts, bar charts, histograms, pie charts and radar charts or cobweb charts – that used in total quality management program. An illustrative matrix of numerical data is given in Table 5.4.

Table 5.4
Financial Data of Partner Organisation

Revenue per Employee	*Advertising Cost per Employee*	*Cost per Rupee of Sales*	*Advertising Cost per Rupee of Sales*	*Value added per Employee*
Rs. 45000	Rs. 29000	Re. 0.35	Re. 0.20	Rs. 18000

Soft data collected in descriptive and numerical form will have to be converted into quantifiable form. Suppose, the project team wants to find out how much open is the openness of the benchmark organisation. The team can collect numerical data on various aspects that exhibit openness of management. For example it can collect data on (a) number of suggestions received from employees, (b) number of suggestions accepted per employee, (c) number of awards given to employees for cost saving and quality improving suggestions.

Let us suppose that an organisation employs one thousand workers, sixty suggestions were submitted in a year, out of which twenty were accepted and fifteen were implemented. Thus, the formula

$$\frac{\text{Number of suggestions submitted}}{\text{Number of total employees}} \times \frac{\text{Number of suggestions implemented}}{\text{Number of suggestions accepted}}$$

Would give us an aspect of openness of the organisation. Our illustration gives us-

$$\frac{60}{1000} \times \frac{15}{20} = \frac{18}{400} = 0.045$$

Thus, our illustration gives us the value (0.045) of the index of the openness of management in one of its aspects. In the same way employee motivation index can also tell us a number of facts. Proportion of absenteeism among employees, employee turnover, number of strikes in a year can tell the story of employee satisfaction. Customer satisfaction is exhibited by customer retention, number of repeat orders, number and types of complaints from the customer. These facts can be converted into hard data. Mohamed Zairi has developed a concept of force field analysis to convert soft data on organisational environment. The facts can be understood and noted on the basis of observations done at the time of site visits and interview talks. Proportion of well trained machine operators, application of just-in–time principle, open style management, ISO 9000 certification, age of the plant, receptiveness of managers to change, inventory-to-turnover ratio, can be converted into hard data to assess the organisational environment.

Still there appears a necessity of a tool to compare best practices with the help of measured criteria. We must be able to compare and explain differences in performance of organisations as well of different sectors of the industry. The concept of Five Forces Analysis developed by Michael Porter is an useful framework of that kind for determining competitive position of an organisation. The bargaining power of the suppliers and customers, competitive environment and size and structure of industry in which the organisation operates determine the competitive advantage of the organisation. Thus, (a) Bargaining power of the customers, (b) Bargaining power of suppliers, (c) Rivalry amongst competitors, (d) Threat of substitutes, and (e) Barriers to entry are the five forces that determine competitive position of the organisation. Higher the value count of these five forces better are the practices of the organisation.

Thus, the data of the benchmarked organisation collected with the help of published and secondary sources, priced publications and contacts with potential partner are analaysed with the help of metrics and charts. Indices of openness of management, of employee motivation, of customer satisfaction, results of force field analysis and of five forces analysis help us to determine the gaps in our performance and that of the bench mark organisation. In the second part of our discussion we will analyse as to how the gaps in our performance and performance of benchmarked organisation can be identified and measured. This will enable us discuss target levels of performance and criteria of performance. Comparison between target performance and actual performance would give us an idea of the gap. If the actual performance is higher than targeted performance, the organisation is enjoying 'positive gap'; while in areas where actual performance is lower than the targeted performance the organisation is suffering from 'negative gap'. The project team has to quantify the size of the gap and identify the factors that have led to 'positive gap' as well to 'negative gap'. A matrix in table 5.5. exhibits the gap in the performance.

The project team would assess the gap in a form similar to that exhibited in Table 5.5. Then the project team would discuss the situation and take appropriate decisions. In the first place the team would decide whether the organisation should be satisfied by matching the benchmarked practices or should it try to go beyond and better than the performance of the benchmarked practices. If the performance gap is too wide, the team would have to first assess whether the organisation has capability to achieve that level of performance. If the desired level of performance is beyond the reach of present capability of the organisation, the project team would have to set a time frame program to achieve the benchmarked level of performance gradually. So we are near the stage of implementing planned measures to achieve objective of benchmarking project.

Table 5.5
Actual versus Target Performance Matrix

Performance criteria	*Actual performance*	*Target performance*	*Best practice method*	*Current method*	*Nature of gap*
Price	Rs. 35	Rs. 30	Price quoted at the time of call. Details of service provided.	Price given to the customer after the job is completed.	Negative
Delivery schedule	3 hours	2 hours	Engineers on completion of earlier job, call for next job on mobile phone.	Service engineers report to the base after completion of each job and get the next job.	Negative
Customer service score	90 per cent	100 per cent	Call time agreed with customer on booking. After completion of the job customer called back to confirm quality of service and satisfaction.	No call time agreed with customer. No follow-up done after completion of the job.	Negative

(5) Plan for implementing the measures and actions for improving the performance of the organisation: The first thing that would have to be undertaken is to decide the areas and functions that are catalyst to improvement. Improvement in these areas or functions would improve performance in secondary areas or functions. Fundamental functions and primary areas that need to be prioritised for improvement of performance can be short-listed in the second round of in-depth discussion. The functions or areas to be chosen for benchmarking project should have to be evaluated on the cost benefit analysis matrix. Direct as well as indirect costs and quantitative and qualitative benefits would have to be viewed.

Second step in preparation of the plan is to consider the measures to restructure the organisation to make it capable of attaining goals. Delayering the organisation, increasing the number of technically qualified directors in the board, reducing product cycle time by breaking down the walls between quality and manufacturing, setting up electronic quality systems in the manufacturing arena itself, recruitment of employees from other and non-related industries are a few suggestions to reengineer the organisation of the company.

As a part of the plan, one important consideration can be evaluated. Considering the potential, capability, tool room facilities, managerial and employee skills, information networking infrastructure, upstream suppliers may also be selected to ensure quality of performance in production of components that are catalyst to the product. It must be remembered that such outsourcing is to be done on strategic consideration and not just for offloading our work and responsibility. Performance scenario within the organisation can also be improved by installing automated computer numerically controlled machines and spreading information network in the entire organisation together with well trained and skilled employees taken on roll. It is needless to say machines guarantee inbuilt quality. Even facilities provided on regular basis for updating skills can make a difference.

Sarah Cook has suggested that we prepare a blue print of the plan with new and efficient process design chart without consideration of improving existing system. This would formulate a process following the ideal flow and keeping the process as simple as possible. Unnecessary steps in our process flow and stages of production can be weeded out. Sarah Cook calls this plan as 'Green field design'. Short of this suggestion of creating a new set up of organisation it is also suggested that critical functions and areas that have maximum impact on performance of the company can be redesigned.

On the basis of the discussion in preceding four paragraphs the project team prepares a project report. The report would state the targets to be achieved and explain the criteria on which these targets are earmarked. If necessary the team may redraft the vision statement. The project team should enlist various resources – moral support, managerial leadership financial and human resources, information backup, research and development infrastructure — all resources should be stated preferably in quantifiable terms and time frame. The committee should specify the commitments required, responsibilities earmarked and accountability determined. With implementation of this plan the results expected by the team must also be presented in terms of increased market share, higher customer satisfaction, increased productivity, improved quality, less rework, less complaints and increase in profitability. The project team should pointedly recommend organisation of a high power committee to monitor periodically the progress of the benchmark project. If the time span over which the project is spread is longer annual breakup of inputs required, organisational changes expected, training facilities to be established and information network infrastructure is to be laid down should be given. Along with that, improvements in the performance for every year should be stated. An outline time-table need to be given to senior managers so as to decide what should happen and when. The performance achieved in every quarter of the year should be made known to all in the organisation.

(6) Review: High Power committee recommended to be organized by the project team, to periodically monitor the progress of benchmark program should examine the ongoing project on regular basis without waiting for completion of the same. The committee should compare at each stage the results achieved with the targets fixed for that stage.

The committee should review the result of benchmarking projects in terms of organizational performance. The performance achieved in given stage has to be matched with the objectives set by project committee for that stage. It should highlight the changes that have taken place and the factors that have been helpful in bringing these changes about. If necessary a SWOT analysis may be undertaken to assess (1) the strengths that have emerged as a result of process and how can strengths be further built up, (2) weak links discovered in the review study that have either hindered or slowed down the process of achieving performance, (3) the opportunities that have come forth, further development of which can strengthen the process, should have to be noted, and (4) the factors that may emerge and threaten the achievement would have to be foreseen and measures suggested to ward them off. The review committee should note significant improvements brought about in the process of the organisation because of measures suggested by the project committee. The review committee should study the willingness with which the organisation welcomes the change and supported the benchmarking program.

In the second part the committee should review the lessons learnt, experiences gained during the period under consideration and also state how far these lessons were implemented in furtherance of the project. The committee should express improvements achieved in the abilities of employees, leveraging of the capability of employees to face and complete the tasks. The committee should underline the new practices that have proved to be sure-shot in achieving targets. The capabilities of project team members improved should also be described. The committee should try to find out how far has this program motivated the organisation and its people to change for the better. Confidence gained by all members participating in the program should be discussed.

TRAINING

Project team need to understand the activities that make the process and relationship of the process with other parts of business. Therefore, the team members need to be trained in the entire activity of benchmarking. The training program includes educational module that has a curriculum on the theory of benchmarking, factors that necessitate benchmarking, methodology of identifying benchmark partners, benchmarking areas and functions identification, creating benchmarking program and report writing. They need to be given understanding responsibilities of participating team in running the benchmark program through. They are to be taught leadership qualities, team building methods, role they have to play and communication skills.

Team members are to be taught the skills of constructing graphs, diagrams, tables and interpreting them. This can help them in measuring achievements in performance. They should be taught specifically (1) understand importance of benchmarking, (2) document objectives achieved and manage the lessons learned to identify additional opportunities, (3) establish key performance metrics and prepare appropriate project documents, (4) plan the benchmark project using tools such as Gantt chart, Pert chart, planning trees etc. (5) apply team facilitation techniques such as coaching, mentioring and facilitation techniques to guide the team, (6) apply team tools such as nominal group techniques, force-field analysis, multi-voting and conversion/diversion, (7) use management and planning tools like (a) affinity diagrams, (b) interrelationship diagraphs, (c) tree diagrams, (d) process decision program charts, and (e) activity network diagrams, such a detailed education and training program will prepare the benchmark project team well to shoulder every task and complete it successfully.

Benchmarking is not an organisational objective. It is a program undertaken to achieve the objectives of total quality and six sigma. Thus, it is to be looked at as a tool, as a very effective tool to satisfy customer critical criteria and achieve competitive edge, competitive advantage. It must be remembered that benchmarking is not a one time program, it is to be adopted as an all time going process to do the thing better and better every time and each time. This is because total quality and six sigma are all time going program.

References

(1) Ross Joel E. *Total Quality Management*, Kogan Page Ltd., 1993.

(2) Brian and Godling. 'Dynamics of Best Practices' *Benchmarking for Quality Management and Technology*, 4(2) pp. 96-103.

(3) Patterson M. *Accelerating Innovation, Technology Strategies*, Nov. 1993, pp. 23-25.

(4) Halhead R.,'Breaking down the Barriers of Free Information Exchange', *Logistics Information Management*, 1995, Vol. 18, No. 1, pp. 34-37.

(5) Syrett M. *The Best of Everything – Human Resources*, Winter 1993-94, Issue 12, p. 83.

General References

(1) Sultan Kermally. *Management Ideas in Brief*, Butterworth – Heinemann, 1997.

(2) Mohamed Zairi. *Benchmarking for Best Practices*, Butterworth – Heinemann, 1996.

(3) Cook Sarah. *Practical Benchmarking*, Kogan Pages Ltd., 1995.

❑ ❑ ❑

6 Relationship Marketing

It has become imperative for all corporations to develop long term, sustained relationship with customers and buyers, so as to strengthen competitive edge in satisfying and delighting the customer.

Globalisation, intellectual property rights, trade related property rights and free movement of capital have added new dimensions to creating, developing and sustaining continued relationship with customers. Theories and practices of marketing management developed in pre-globalisation era, therefore, need a second look. On the basis of experience of three years full of change, we would have to develop a new strategy for marketing, if we have to provide a sound basis for marketing management in 21st century. In the last century we had different concepts for marketing customer products, industrial products and for marketing services. Over the period of time, it is visualized and realized that companies producing and marketing consumer as well as industrial goods have to market services to develop competitive edge. Companies providing and marketing services have to innovate and market new service products. Thus, we need a strategy based on new theory that can encompass marketing of anything and everything in this new environment. We had a marketing management function different from corporate management. However, marketing having become first function of business, we have to discuss and develop marketing management strategy that will be an integral part of corporate management.

Secondly, globalization, institutionalization of WTO with its emphasis on freeing trade of goods, services and finance, have added one more dimension to this situation. Disintegration of erstwhile Soviet Union on one hand and integration of European countries on the other, have created an environment in which companies establish their production, service and marketing facilities in a number of countries. Communities in these countries, though have adopted products and services of international character, have maintained their own distinguishing features in respect of products, their tastes, ingredients, components etc. As a result, the multinational companies have to produce and provide products and services that can suit the requirements of global market as well of local markets. War heads, aeroplanes, automobiles, two wheelers, electronic equipment used for medical diagnosis, entertainment, communication and health and skin care products, eatables, all such products are no exception to this. Therefore, companies functioning either at national or at international level have to develop such marketing paradigm that suits at global as well as at local levels. This calls for new perspective for developing and sustaining relationship with customers and buyers.

One more change we must take note of, it is the new modes of communication that have developed in the last twenty-five years. As a result a new perspective in communication has developed to interact between the seller and the buyer that begins before selling, remains in the selling and in consuming process and remain so in post-consumption period also. Communication between seller and buyer has become two way and has become effective through different platforms like advertising, sales promotion, public relations, personal selling and direct marketing. Community has developed new, better, cheaper and faster media of communications with the help of which the company can reach masses as well target groups simultaneously. The message as well as the choice of media chosen to communicate this message has acquired immense importance. Selling messages are so visualized and audited that they muster attention and positive response of the buyers and consumers. New communication media, and language have changed the very philosophy of production process, inventory management, movement of goods, selection and training of personnel, financial management and structure of organisation. Thus, we have to conceive and deliver an entirely new strategy of marketing in fast changing business world. These global communication forces have affected and have continued to affect everyone's business and personal life.

Finally, technologies involved in producing and delivering goods and in providing services have come to change so fast that they have revolutionised organisational perspective in every activity and walk of life. Genetic engineering has evolved genetically modified crops that have changed the agricultural practices, need for chemical fertilizers, pesticides and insecticides. Genetic engineering has opened doors wide for development of new branches, challenges and opportunities in bio-medical sciences. Digital revolution has made many products and services smarter than before. Intelligent robots have invaded and captured many a productive activities. Invention of transistors, xerography, new petroleum solvents called DF 2000 and Dryel used for ecofriendly dry-cleaning of clothes, virtual reality technology that lets users interact with computer generated world through sight, sound and touch, enables buyers to move around inside the future home and experience yet un-built house. Introduction of Ecuspun squared fiber having moister management properties has changed the marketing environment. Technological developments have brought new tools in the hands of sales persons and as a result their role in marketing has drastically changed. Company websites, e-mails have brought customers in direct contact of the company. Therefore, the old paradigm of the sales persons of providing products or services that come closest to meeting the needs of the customer is replaced by new model called as "relationship marketing" wherein the sales persons sell long term partnership. Here the seller company and the buyer collaborate on identifying latter's needs and developing and updating products that delight the customer, Sales person has truly gone "electronic" because of technological developments. This enables companies to develop strong brand and position them on world shelves. It must also be remembered that the role of pricing has changed. Pricing must be a part of total marketing strategy. Most of the time price is anchored not on cost but on customer's value.

There are a number of technological developments that have automated services that have improved productivity and reduced cost of rendering services. Theodore Levitt has developed a new concept which he named as "production line approach to services".[1] Hotels use self-service machines to facilitate guest check-in and check out and billing bed and breakfast (B and B) charges automatically. Airlines have installed ATM-like machines facilitating self service ticket purchasing and boarding passes.

Developments, in the spheres of industrial product and service marketing, eco-geographic environment, communication and technologies discussed in preceding paragraphs have forced companies to adopt new approach to marketing products as well as services.

APPROACHES TO MARKETING

There are four major approaches to marketing. They are – (1) Marketing Mix, (2) Service Marketing, (3) The Net work or Industrial and Business Marketing, and (4) Quality Management Market. They are discussed below.

(1) Marketing Mix[2]

Marketers try to sell maximum to the buyers. They influence the buyers to do so by employing various means. E. J. McCarthy has classified these means into four groups namely products, price, place and promotion — commonly known as 4 Ps. Marketers use various combinations of these means to reach the buyers and achieve the objective. Combination of these means is known as "Marketing Mix". Marketing mix is the set of means that marketers use to achieve their objective by influencing the buyers. The definition of marketing suggested by American Management Association is based on marketing mix thinking. AMA defines[3] "marketing is the process of planning and executing the conception, pricing, promotion and distribution of ideas, goods and services to create exchanges that satisfy individual and organisational objectives". Various components of each of the P are detailed in Table 6.1.

Firms use various combinations of these thirty-two components to hook the buyer. This combination may vary from product to product, region to region, economic status of the buyers, intensity of demand, market environment etc. Firms innovate new means to influence the buyer. Firms try to impact the market by manipulating factors that are under control – price, product, promotion and place and by exercising influence on uncontrollable factors – consumer tastes, economic condition in the market, laws of the nation, taxation etc. Power to influence these factors beyond the control of the firm depends upon size of the firm, nature of the product/service provided, political alliance, creativity and status of the board of directors.

Table 6.1
Components of 4 Ps

Product	*Price*	*Place*	*Promotion*
Product quality	Notified Price	Channels of delivery	Advertising
Product variety	Discounts	Geographical coverage	Schemes of discount
Shape	Allowances	Location	Free samples
Design	Schemes	Mode of transport	Pre-purchase tests
Features	Credit-period	Delivery Schedule	Demonstration
Size	Installments	Assortments	Gifts/Bonus/Rebates
Colour/smell	Credit terms	Public Relations	
Brand name			Counselling
Services			Direct Marketing
Warranties			
Replacement			

Firms change some of the factors under its control in short period; for example they change the price, advertising expenditure, promotion policy, but it cannot change the design of the product or cannot develop new product, cannot change brand name, cannot alter delivery channels in short period. There appears to be a tendency in selling firms to make as few changes as possible, in a short period though situation demands so. This is because change in one factor – say price of the product – imbalances the entire composition of marketing-mix. Creating such balance again may be hazardous, time consuming and detrimental to the image of the company.

Philip Kotler argues that marketers try to stimulate sales by modifying marketing – mix elements. He expects that along with changes in the price of the product or service, the decision-maker should try innovative channels of distribution to boost up the sales. Companies producing FMCGs, insurance companies, banks have tried this by developing sales/service facilities on petrol pumps. Marketers may also make experiments with advertising wherein we find the same theme being imposed on the consumers in banners, electronic media, print media, and brochures handed over at corners. With change in the age of the product we find this mix being changed. Methods of sales promotion may also be taken help of. Providing gift hampers of different products to the winners and/or participants of various competitions screened on various channels is a new method of sales promotion that is experimented to make the marketing-mix more realistic. Many a companies introduce personal selling by opening up special product divisions as in pharmaceutical industry – respiratory track medicines division, gynaecology product division etc. Banks also open separate branches like home loan branch and women branch. This enables sales persons to focus on doctors specialized in that field and patients suffering from specific ailment. Bank employees can specialize in completing home loan procedure quickly. Even services can be tried as an instrument of marketing products. Many a companies have reduced delivery time. Installation of products like domestic water purifiers, domestic water heating systems is done free of additional cost. Most of the vendors selling cars in collaboration with banks have instituted zero interest car loans schemes to boost up the sales of cars. Major question that Philip Kotler has tried to raise is how to decide which of these measures be adopted, to what extent, in which proportion and at what time should they be implemented. Marketing Decision Support System framework developed by Efraim Turban and J. E. Aronson[4] on the basis of Kotler's prescription indicates that marketing decision system support package can give us directive about media mix, site location, product design, advertising budget, web evaluation with the help of intelligent agents. Enterprise computing i.e. enterprise system promoter helps in analysing the effects of promotion and advertisement on sales especially in packaged goods industry.

Customer needs and customer satisfaction are at the centre of focus of the marketing concept. Marketing-mix concept suggests that the seller company by introducing and executing a judicious mix of thirty two factors should persuade the customer to buy a product. Seller Company can do this by selecting right measurers in the right combination and with right intensity. This is discussed by R.F. Lauterborn[5] that sellers 4Ps correspond to customer's 4Cs. Ajay Menon[6] and Anil Menon state that there is emergence of corporate environmentalism as marketing strategy. Customer finds solution to his need (first C) in the product supplied by the seller (first P); cost of the product to the consumer (second C) is the price charged by the seller (second P); consumer buys the commodity at a place convenient to him (third C) is the place at which the seller provides the product (third P) and consumer receives the information from communication channel of the seller (fourth C) it is promotion chosen by the seller (fourth P).

Marketer, in spite of the fact that he does not know what is in the mind of the buyer, tries to extract a response, a buying decision as he needs by providing stimulus-pressure on him through combination of thirty two components of 4 Ps. Marketer, many a times does not receive the response that he desires from the buyer; then he tries another combination to elicit the desired response and goes on doing so till he makes the buyer behave to seller's advantage. Marketer does not know which combination will receive which response from the buyer and he cannot take for granted that the response he received from the buyer to a particular mix last time will be repeated this time. Thus, it is a game of hide and seek every time. That marketer who receives response greater than expected from a particular marketing-mix is the successful marketer. Thus, the marketer tries to strike optimal mix, satisfying mix that receives superior response from the market and adds to his profits. There are very many different factors operating in the market every time those make the situation so uncertain and so complex, that no rule can be set about an acceptable marketing-mix. It is the analytical rationality, experience and vision of the marketer that initiates him to strike right marketing-mix.

Marketing management tries to strike a balance between Profit Impact of Marketing Strategy on sales volume, acceptability and market share. However, such profit impact marketing strategy can at the best give guidelines of co-variation between marketing strategies and responses of the buyers.

All this discussion makes it amply clear that marketing-mix theory is related to consumer goods that are produced on large scale. However, as it discusses distribution channels, a part of it can be helpful in theorizing marketing strategies for industrial goods and services because there marketing uses almost the same distribution channels that are used for mass consumption of standardized consumer goods. The later versions of marketing-mix theory discuss means of pressurising buyers by means other than 4 Ps, areas like complaints handling, invoice, design and production are not included in the discussion. As a result marketing-mix theory has remained to be only a theory of marketing management and has not become integral part of the total corporate management. The theory is totally dissociated from the individual consumer. It does not cover the process of mass–customization where goods are produced on a mass scale, but are individually designed. For example, body-scanning technology is used by apparel manufacturing companies to tailor clothes at particular measurement that will fit many buyers. Present knowledge based society clamors for customized mass marketing; a terminology which is probably paradoxical in meaning.

However, there are a few factors in marketing-mix approach that can be integrated with the total relationship approach to marketing that is relevant to the corporate management in twenty-first century. As a part and parcel of promoting sales, the marketing-mix approach suggests person-to-person, face-to-face encounter between the sales person and the buyer with a view to persuade, induce the buyer to purchase the product. Such close relationship is the foundation of sustained loyalty of buyers. It develops confidence in the marketer's ability to deliver quality reliably. This is the first factor. The second factor is that the competition between seller and buyer in regard to product, price and place is the outward expression of relationship. It is experienced that intense the competition of this nature, closer is the relationship. Thirdly, the channels of distribution, geographical coverage, locations, mode of transport and delivery schedule developed by the marketer are to meet the requirements of the buyer that strengthen the bond between the seller and the buyer. The fourth factor in marketing-mix approach that contributes to development of para-social relationship is the brand equity and brand image that is impressed upon the mind of the buyer. The new approach to marketing that we are to discuss in the third section of this chapter will draw much from these four factors on which relationship between seller and buyer stands.

(2) Marketing Services[7]

Marketing-mix approach is basically confined to marketing physical consumer products. However, in later half of the twentieth century service sector has grown so much and so fast that marketing services has become as important or rather more important than marketing physical products. About 49 per cent of India's gross domestic product is generated in service sector, and 33 per cent of the labour force is engaged in this sector. Though it is stated that services are intangible; this has only a face validity because in many a cases the factors like bus, aircraft, railway (transport service), ATM (financial service) through which these services are provided are tangible. Services are less standardized than physical goods. Services of management consultants, lawyers, architects, though highly customised contain standardized modules. However, they are variable depending upon who provided them and when they are rendered. Services are produced and consumed simultaneously wherein consumer plays a role of co-producer. Services cannot be stored. These salient features of services bring customer and marketer in close contact leading to relationship in marketing. That is why great attention is paid on quality of services while rendering or marketing services and quality of service as perceived by customer depending upon the value and satisfaction derived by him. B. H. Booms and M. J. Bitner[8] suggest additional 3 Ps to the 4 Ps that are required to be attended in marketing-mix. They are people, physical evidence and process. Most of the services are provided by people. Therefore the satisfaction derived by consumer from a service depends upon the way, the method, the mode in which it is rendered to the consumer. That is why, front line people, rendering service actually to the consumer must be well selected, trained and motivated to differentiate the services rendered by them in comparison to those rendered by others. Frontline people must be competent, responsive, possessing caring attitude and exhibit initiative to solve the problems of the customers. Marketers must produce evidence of their services being excellent, outstanding and courteous. Cleanliness, good up keep, diligent housekeeping, presentation, interior, equipment, furniture, attractive physical environment, superior delivery process are the means of the superior physical evidence. Process of rending service must be pleasing, acceptable and satisfying to the customer. Customer must feel that he is treated as an individual who is welcome on the premises. Customer must be able to feel the high touch as a result of functional quality and high-tech as a result of technical quality of the service. Service provider must exhibit such a skill in rendering the services that it should become an interactive marketing. The consumer must be able to clearly evaluate the quality, the standard of service before receiving and while consuming the service.

Development of service marketing models has focused on quality of service, that is customer perceived quality, customer satisfaction and value for customer. After receiving service, customer compares perceived quality of service with expected quality of service. Customer expectations are the true standards for judging quality. To reach that level, service marketers strive to present realistic picture of their service to the customer. They ascribe highest priority to provide best service right the first time; they see that the right message is communicated in the right manner about the quality of service to the customer. They make every effort to exceed the expectation of the customer. Problems faced by customers are perceived as opportunities by service providers. Service marketers make continuous efforts to evaluate and improve their performance in providing services. A. Parsuraman, V. A. Zaithavi and L. L. Berry[9] pioneered research in service quality in marketing and measurement instrument SERVQUAL was developed for assessing it. Originally SERVQUAL consisted ten dimensions which were reduced to five by pooling some of the dimensions together. That has been exhibited in Table 6.2.

Table 6.2
Dimensions of Service Quality

	Ten Dimensions (Original Model)		*Five Dimensions (Later Model)*
(1)	Tangibility	(1)	Tangibility
(2)	Reliability	(2)	Reliability
(3)	Responsiveness	(3)	Responsiveness
(4)	Competence	(4)	Assurance
(5)	Courtesy	(5)	Empathy
(6)	Credibility		
(7)	Security		
(8)	Access		
(9)	Communication		
(10)	Understanding the Customer		

Three of the original ten dimensions *viz.* Tangibility, Reliability and Responsiveness remained intact. Assurance and Empathy were the two new dimensions introduced by pooling Competence, Courtesy, Credibility, and Security under Assurance and Empathy covering Access and communication. S. J. Delvin and H. K. Dong[10] have identified five determinants of service quality. They are –

(1) Reliability: It depends upon service provider's ability to perform the service according to promises. Buyer tries to calculate product life-cycle cost which comprises of purchase price and discounted cost of maintenance and repair less the discounted salvage value. It is the responsibility of the marketer to fulfill buyer's reasonable expectations of trouble free service. Manufacturers enhance reliability of their products by offering facilitating services such as installation, staff training, maintenance, repairing and financing. By undertaking follow-up activities, product marketers add value augmenting services.

(2) Responsiveness: Readiness and willingness to help customers and to provide prompt services determines responsiveness of service providers. Service marketers can make customers experience responsiveness of the service providers by increasing their awareness, knowledge, liking and preference for the particular service. Service marketers develop thereby effective message to gain attention, hold interest and arouse desire and coerce the customers to take action to buy service from them and them only. So by initiating responsiveness of service consumers, service providers increase their responsiveness to satisfy the consumers. It is the effort of the service marketers to convert responsive marketing that attempts to satisfy existing needs to anticipative marketing which tries to satisfy needs of services that he may feel in near future.

(3) Assurance: The Service providers try to create confidence in the minds of the service consumers and thereby trust the providers and services provided by them. Service marketers exhibit knowledge about the existing and future needs of the consumers and exhibit courteously that they possess this knowledge. This helps the service marketers to interact with the consumers and develop long-lasting relationship. Top management of service marketers maintains close watch on the financial performance and on the service performance. They audit their service performance by conducting customer surveys, appealing customers to put in their suggestions and complaints in respect of accuracy, responsiveness and timeliness of services provided by them.

(4) Empathy: Service Marketers make every effort to pay individual attention to the customers. They make extensive and intensive provision for caring-caring employees as well caring customers; because cared employees can care customers. Caring employees does not depend upon the salary paid to them but on a number of factors. These factors are- providing better service conditions, sympathy and help in their distress, listening to their suggestions. These suggestions should be implemented as and when required with acknowledgement of the suggestion maker. Top officials of many service providers make personal calls on customers to show courtesy for their patronage. Such companies carry periodically customer importance and company performance surveys and thereby find out which attributes of the services are rated highest by the customers and which elements in the service bundle fall short of expectations. Satisfaction of customers depends upon empathy where services are people based and personal need. Job done right the first time is the attribute of service that creates feeling of caring in the minds of service consumers. Availability of service when needed, not providing extra service (perform only necessary services), cleanup after service are the most important attributes of service which creates feeling in the minds of the consumer that they are cared for.

(5) Tangibility: Consumers are given a feeling that all the physical facilities, equipment that would make them comfortable are present and available. Communication channels are well in order and pleasantly greeting the customer. Availability of toll free phone number for registering complaints improves customer satisfaction even if he has no complaints to make. Quality of service and quality of goods must go hand in hand. Satisfaction of the customer depends much upon tangibility where services are equipment based and also services that are business need.

The five determinants of service quality, which we have discussed in preceding paragraphs, categorically underpin that interaction between service provider and customer is at the central focus of service market. That means relationship; close and persistent relationship is at the very heart of service marketing. Marketing and production of services must work hand in hand because on the marriage of marketing and production depends the quality of service and that is the core of the service marketing approach. This brings marketing functions and technical functions closer that determine and guarantee total quality. Internal marketing is service marketing and this integration has made service marketing applicable to general marketing.

In recent past because of development of electronic media, service marketing has added one more dimension to relationship marketing. This dimension is data processing and transmission have earned primary importance in service companies. This aspect of relationship marketing has become universally applicable because all companies whether providing tangible goods accompanied by minor services, hybrid marketing providing goods and services in equal proportions or major service with accompanying minor goods or pure services, use electronic media for speeding, improving and perfecting their services. Services whether provided by part-time or full-time marketers, on commercial or service basis, bring close interaction between service providers and consumers. Services, whether provided internally in an organisation by one department to another, by one function to another or externally between organisations or between organisations and individuals have resulted into close interaction between two parties. That is why, service marketing approach has provided many concepts, various dimensions to total relationship marketing which has become the slogan, the watchword of corporate management in the twenty first century.

There is an illustration how services of providing products to the consumers are being revolutionised. It is announced by Domino's Pizza test-base in Milton Keynes in England that they have been harnessing new technology and systems to invent new methods of delivering Pizzas on time and with minimum of fuss and heat loss. They have already in use patented Heat Wave Bags for keeping Pizzas hot during transit. Internet and interactive T.V ordering account for thirteen per cent of Pizzas delivered in UK and Ireland. Now they are innovating technology to introduce remote controlled airships, amphibious cars capable of traveling along rivers rather than busy roads to get pizzas to customers. They are also researching on introducing air bikes to deliver hot pizzas to the customers right on time.

(3) Marketing Industrial Products

This is also known as network approach to marketing. Industrial goods are materials and parts or components that are sold by one manufacturer to another manufacturer. Materials are either farm products or natural products. Manufactured materials are component materials and component parts. Installations like buildings, offices and equipment like generators, main frame computers, lift trucks are capital goods. Operating supplies like computer peripherals, ink cartridges, stationery and maintenance and repair items like toilet cleaners, naphthalene balls, hammers, spanners, are also included in industrial products. Marketing of such industrial products depends upon width, length and depth of product mix produced by a company. Width, length, and depth, of the product mix is increased by line stretching-either by down market stretch, up market stretch or two way stretch. With a view to bring and fix industrial or consumer products in the eyes and minds of the buyers, products are branded and labeled. Brand extension. Multi-branding, co-branding are the major strategies used to create relationship between product seller and buyer. B2B marketing broadens the application of the term industrial marketing by including consumer goods sold to intermediaries.

Liberalisation and globalization policies adopted in last decade of last century have brought many foreign companies in Indian market; likewise many an Indian companies, especially through merger and acquisition have entered foreign markets. Indian agriculture, horticulture, aquaculture are no exceptions to this. Indian software industry has made its footprints firmly rooted in many foreign countries. These global companies have to plan operate and coordinate their activities on a worldwide basis. Many an Indian small industrial units have carved for themselves a global niche. Most of the Indian MNCs have adopted and proved worthy of international standards. They have suitably amended product features, brand names, labeling, packaging, prices, and sales promotions, advertising themes, advertising media and advertising execution. Many an Indian MNCs have established manufacturing facilities, have developed marketing policies, financial flows and logistical systems. They implement simultaneously global as well as glocal production and marketing strategies.

P. Ford, H. Hakansson and J. Johansson[11] argue that the marketing thought has developed from Industrial as well as International Marketing and Purchasing group to network approach. Marketing company is a node in an ever widening pattern of interactions. In such interaction marketers participate directly, in some they participate indirectly and some interactions occur without participation of any company. Such interactions, whether between single buyer and single seller or between many buyers and single seller or between many buyers and many sellers or between single buyer and many sellers, is so complex that it is difficult to describe fully and analyze fruitfully. In essence, the network approach perceives industrial as well as international marketing as an interaction in a network of relationships. This network consists of the company/companies and its stakeholders such as customers, suppliers, distributors, retailers, advertising agency with which mutually profitable business relationships are built up. In the network approach of industrial marketing a distinction is made between three types of connections mainly-activity, resources, and actors which form a B2B relationship between buyers and sellers. Interaction is a process in which sellers and buyers enter into active contract with each other. Activity links include technical, administrative and marketing effort. Resource ties include exchanging and sharing tangible resources like machines and intangible resources like knowledge and skill etc. Actor bonds are created by people who interact and exert influence on each other and form opinions about each other. Thus network interaction and core variables like activities, resources, and actors form the complex relationship in industrial and international marketing.

Such relationships constitute the partner base and the organisational total network made up of companies and their stakeholders. It is quite possible that many a times these relationships may be visible and active but on many occasions they being passive may be so much embedded in the network that they exercise their influence on the three connections explained above, namely, activity, resources and actors. It is found that important general properties of commercial relationships are many a times complementary and inclusive while some times they are competitive and exclusive of one another. These properties are exhibited in Table 6.3.

Table 6.3
Properties of Commercial Relationships

Complementary	*Inclusive*	*Competitive and Mutually Exclusive*
Collaboration	Trust	Closeness and Remoteness
Commitment	Risk	Formality and Informality
Dependency	Power	Openness and Routinisation
Importance	Longivity	
	Frequency	
	Regularity	
	Intensity	

The nature and character of relationship between seller and buyer companies is influenced and determined by product types, degree of standardisation, technical complexity of product and frequency of transactions between companies. This network of relationship consists of nodal company, its suppliers, supplier's suppliers, intermediaries, distributors, customers, customer's customers and other collaborative parties like power suppliers, transporters etc. Relationship between two companies is subsystem of this larger relationship network. Relationship between global companies marketing on international level is formal, legal and intensive while relationship between companies trading at national level is informal, casual and intimate. They are more accommodative.

Network approach to industrial as well as international marketing emphasizes that the relationships between nodal company and stakeholders should be permanent and stable. All the players in the market should collaborate with each other extensively so as to improve efficiency of market economy. They should actively participate in developing economy so that their competitive power, knowledge, technology, logistics and procurement strategies should improve and benefit all parties. Network approach has helped us to rethink about consumer goods marketing and service marketing and integrates all the three (consumer goods marketing, service marketing, and industrial marketing) into total relationship marketing. In this way network approach has made unique contribution to marketing thought. The network approach to marketing uses interaction in network of relationships as the vantagepoint. Network approach to marketing clarifies that customer and seller are many headed and the relationship between them being of mega-character is influential. The approach also makes it clear that introduction of modern technology that improves quality and utility of the product does have positive effect on marketing.

(4) Quality Management Marketing

The term quality was used in a very broad sense in the discussion of marketing. However, since the introduction of the concept of the management of quality, zero defect production in 1950 by W. Edwards Deming, the concept of quality has taken articulate and definite meaning not only in production but also in marketing. Quality means consumer perceived quality. That means marketing has to provide such service to the buyer, to the consumer that he is satisfied and delighted. Marketing has become value-adding function.

F. W. Taylor introduced the concept of quality in the areas of management. G. S. Radford introduced quality considerations in product design stage. Philip Crosby developed the concept of 'Zero Defect'. In late 1970s approach to quality changed from reactive to proactive — from quality assurance to strategic approach to quality. That means systematic approach to quality management was basically related to quality of product with very little consideration of quality of marketing. However, the quality perspective that was initially limited to shop floor spread over to entire corporation. There are criteria that are fixed to make quality happen. Quality cannot be achieved unless all activities, unless all functions in the company are directed towards quality. Involvement of management is not enough to achieve all-round quality, all employees must develop set of mind directed to quality and this can be done only if a close relationship is developed in all functionalities of the company. Daniel Beckham[12] stated that "we have to think of ourselves as customer satisfiers — customer advocates focus on the whole process. Marketing managers have to deliver marketing quality alongside production quality."

Increased global competition and the appearance of high quality products in the market led buyers to consider their purchasing decisions more carefully. Buyers began to expect high quality and reliability in goods and services at a fair price. Consumers now compare, evaluate and choose products critically for total value comprising of quality, price and serviceability. Quality excellence has become the watchword among producers and consumers. This has necessitated a close relationship between technical functions and marketing functions. As a result interhierarchical and interfunctional collaboration has become more intense and fruitful. The relationship quality is at the very centre in service marketing because interaction between production of service and its delivery process affects the quality of service. Customer relationship is the outcome of employee relationship. Better the quality of employee relationship, employee satisfaction, better is the quality of customer relationship. Professional as well as social relationships are inseparable aspects of quality relationships. Producers must know the factors upon which their credibility depends and this must be experienced in their approach and activity. They must also show concern for customer perceived quality of their product and service. This human touch to the activity of the producer marketer differentiates products and services. Relationship quality depends upon personal relationships and social network woven out of this personal relationship.

Thus, let us conclude that, marketing-mix approach, service marketing approach, the network marketing approach and quality management marketing approach though focusing on consumer goods, services, industrial goods and quality goods have one common thread running through them. Relationship between the nodal company, its suppliers, supplier's suppliers, employees, stakeholders, distributors, and transporters, marketing outlets, administrative machinery and buyer or customer is of vital importance in developing marketing. Marketing is not a separate but, an integral part of the supply chain that adds to the value of goods and services till they are consumed by the ultimate customer.

Before we embark upon discussing relationship marketing that a corporate body must practice in twenty-first century, two concepts that are developed in last twenty years must be explained. Companies have come to realize the importance of non-financial assets and have come to understand their role in the development and reputation of the organisation. Accounting of customer base and customer retention has come to exert great influence on decision making in a corporate body. A balanced score card developed by Kaplan and Norton[13] where financial measures are balanced against customer, process and innovation measures, helps organisation from being financial driven to being mission driven. Accounting of intellectual capital, knowledge capital is supporting sound relationship marketing applications. Relationship marketing considers that each and everyone who has impact on the success of the company should be included in the network of relationship. Existing customer base and customer relationship are investment in marketing. That is why we have to pay more attention to customer capital, relationship capital, human capital, knowledge capital and social capital. Capital is 'something of value' a resource that adds to the efficiency, performance and bottom line of the organisation. Individual capital consisting of employees, their qualities, behaviour, motivation and network of relationships is cultivated over a long period and that culminates into the trust and confidence established among customers. Power and prestige of employee capital, individual capital are important in many headed customer, supplier relationship. There is capital built into an employee who can quickly gain and win customers' confidence. This quality of QUICKLY gaining confidence is particularly essential to sell goods, services or ideas in competition with other organisations. Migratory knowledge, that remains with the individual and embedded knowledge which is inseparable from environment, from organisation, both are essential for developing relationship. Such relationships are tied to culture, systems, contacts, and image and network developed over a period of time.

Customers are classified as lost customers, part customers, young customers and complete customers. Customers migrate between these groups. It is the role of the individual capital and structural capital to transform customers from lost or part customer category to complete customer category. This can be done by improving customer relationship and extending them to longer period and by focusing on profitable customers. Customer retention is financially always cheaper than attracting new customer. It is not certain that newly attracted customer will become buyer and then client or defect soon. Customer retention can be strengthened by either erecting high switching barriers or by delivering high customer satisfaction. Of these two methods delivering high customer satisfaction is better approach to customer retention. Creating customer loyalty is known as relationship marketing and of all the five levels of marketing, partnership marketing is the best method. Satisfied customer index can be gauged by calculating five functions-

(a) $\dfrac{\text{Money value of Annual Sales}}{\text{Number of customers}}$ = money value of sales per customer.

(b) Customer Lost every year.

(c) $\dfrac{\text{Number of total customers}}{\text{Number of customers transacting in the year}}$ = average duration of customers relationship

(d) $\dfrac{\text{Number of orders received from customers}}{\text{Number of customers}}$ = rate of repeat customers.

(e) $\dfrac{\text{Money value of orders received from customers}}{\text{Number of customers}}$ = average customer purchases

(f) $\dfrac{\text{Number of customers contacting company}}{\text{Number of customers}}$ = average contact by customers

(g) $\dfrac{\text{Days spent by employees on visiting customers}}{\text{Number of customers}}$ = average days spent per customer

Gronros Christain[14] makes distinction between three types of costs that hit both the customer and the company. In addition to the price paid by the customer for the service, there are costs to correct mistakes caused by customer which are called as direct costs; costs caused by provider that are indirect costs and mental and social discomfort caused by correction procedure is psychological cost. If the relationship between service provider and customer is perfect, these costs disappear. In other words, if quality of service is high, relationship cost is low and customer satisfaction is better. That is why creating, maintaining and strengthening relationship is very essential in marketing. Richard Norman and Rafael Ramirez[15] state that shared value-creating process depends upon relationship and interaction with customer. Suppliers and customers are co-producers, co-managers and co-developers of a product or a service. Marketing is a function that distributes value to the customer. More so, value is created through concerted efforts of various functions inside the organisation, suppliers outside the organisation and customers themselves. This is so because value is created while manufacturing a product and also while consuming a product.

Thus, non-financial capital, specifically intellectual capital, knowledge capital and every empowered employee is a vital functionary in creating, maintaining and strengthening relationship with the customer. Therefore, corporate bodies in the twenty first century must focus their attention on those facts of financial as well as non-financial capital in strengthening relationship marketing. They can introduce frequency marketing programs and club cards.

One more concept that we have to discuss, before formulating a new approach to marketing, is RETURN ON RELATIONSHIP. Return on relationship is the long-term net financial outcome caused by the establishment and maintenance of organisation's network of relationship. Customer relationship life cycle is a link between good internal quality and high profitability. This is exhibited in figure-6.1.

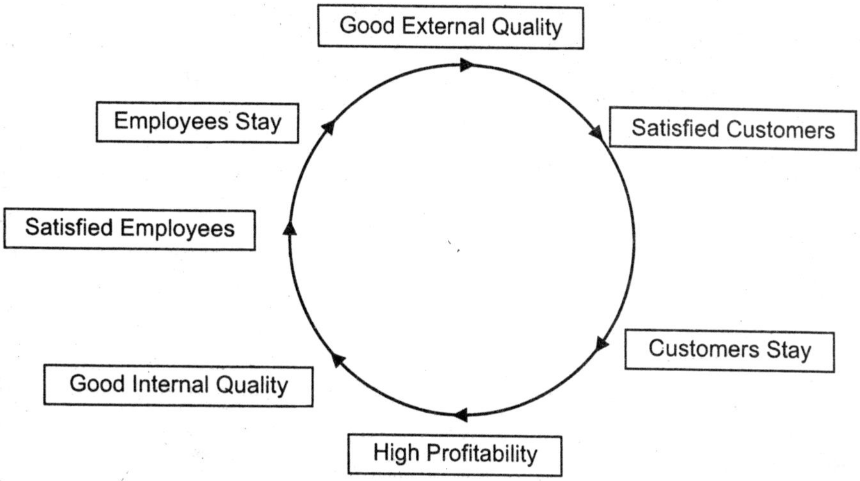

Figure 6.1
Customer Relationship Life Cycle

However it is argued that, return or relationship is not well correlated to satisfied or very satisfied buyers who are loyal buyers. Loyal buyers may be good advertisers by their word of mouth, but they are not necessarily most profitable customers. Storebacka, Kaj, Strandvik, Jore and Gronros Christian have given a relationship profitability model in which they have shown how stages and properties of the relationships between suppliers and customers have linked together. Customer expects certain quality, utility from the product or service that he needs. He has to make some sacrifice, incur some cost for getting, acquiring this utility. This utility net of the cost or sacrifice is the value perceived by the customer from that product or service which is termed as customer's satisfaction, his delight. V.J Kasturinrangan, Rowland T.Moriarty and Gordens Swartz[16] state that relationship buyers are second most profitable group. Programmed buyers are highly profitable segment. His commitment to buy from the same marketer (i.e. loyalty) and his bond with the marketer is dependent upon customer satisfaction. Strength of the relationship is determined by customer satisfaction. Stronger the relationship between supplier and customer, both perceive fewer alternatives; supplier is not ready to search new customers and customer is not interested in trying alternative products and/or services. Gronros Christian calls this as single sourcing strategy pursued by the customer gives the supplier a hundred per cent share and maximum revenue. Economists term this situation as monopsony. The revenue received from buyers with longer bonds is relationship revenue and the cost incurred to create, maintain and strengthen customer relationship is relationship cost. Relationship revenue minus relationship cost is A RETURN ON RELATIONSHIP. Return on relationship depends upon three factors (a) the duration of relationship — how long does the customer buy from the same supplier, (b) the retention rate — percentage of customers who continuously buy from the same supplier, and (c) the defection rate — percentage of customers who stop buying from the same supplier. Arguments are advanced that sellers should invest and try to meet new buyers rather than retaining existing buyers and there is some truth in this argument. Though the cost of netting new buyers is higher than the cost of retaining existing buyers, revenue from new buyers is much higher and therefore profits too. Thus, the central question in relationship marketing is how much should a supplier spend on retaining existing buyers and extending period of relationship and how much should he spend on netting new buyers.

Discussion on total quality management leads us to believe that fifteen per cent of buyers terminate relationship because they are not satisfied with the product, and sixty eight per cent buyers quit because of the indifferent attitude of the supplier towards buyers. Thus, by characterizing customer needs, by prioritizing customer needs and by linking these needs to the needs of the design of the product or service the first fifteen per cent buyers can be retained. Genichi Taguchi has recommended (a) system design — that prepares prototype design that meets performance and tolerance specifications of the buyer, (b) parameter design — develop such parameters of the design that optimize the performance, and (c) tolerance design — to minimize the cost by achieving sub-optimal but allowable tolerance variance. These three links in the quality chain to design quality into the product are recommended by Genichi Taguchi.[17] The sixty eight per cent of the defector buyers can be retained by designing a fool-proof mechanism to hear and respond to the voice of the customer. How is the voice of the customer heard? Who hears the customer and how is the voice of the customer evaluated and how quickly and satisfactorily his voice is remedied can do much. Frederick F. Reichheld and W. E. Sasser (Jr.)[18] observe that customer loyalty cannot be earned in isolation. It is closely dependent upon loyalty of employees and of investors. Companies that initiate relationship with customers, employees and investors are amply rewarded.

Enterprise computer or enterprise system can help decision-maker to analyse the effects of quickly redressing customer grievances and hearing customer voice. This system provides decision support system to decide how much return on relationship can be improved by particular actions. These actions may be improving process capabilities, giving and observing commitment to customer, improving technical and behavioural standards, developing one-to-one or face-to-face contact between customer and deliverer of the service. This does improve customer retention rate and also return on relationship.

Return on relationship can be improved by identifying customers who provide very little business to the company and do lot of hedging on prices, terms etc. It is necessary to weed out such unprofitable customers. To identify and classify migrating buyers and loyal buyers, purchase probability scale can be gainfully used. We must be able to identify customers who over time yield revenue streams that exceeds by an acceptable amount the company's cost stream of attracting, selling and servicing that customer. The 80:20 rule states that 20 per cent buyers provide 80 revenue to the company. We have to find out those 20 per cent buyers. Even profit links between different products, services must be calculated, so as to identify profitable buyers. Return on relationship can be improved by making investment in individual and intellectual capital. Empowering the employees, caring the employees helps them keep satisfied, loyal, devoted and committed. Satisfied employees alone can keep customers satisfied. Roles of different players in the marketing network can be outlined and on the basis of that the interaction between suppliers and customers can be planned. This helps to maintain relations streamlined and extract more returns from the same. Having taken review of four measures to improve return on relationship, we have now to take stock of their impact on return.

Approaches to marketing those we have discussed are definitely an evolution from transactional focus on marketing to relationship focus on marketing. The journey from earlier approaches to new approach is well summarized by Sultan Kermally and is exhibited in Table 6.4.

Table 6.4
Transaction Marketing and Relationship Marketing

	Transaction Focus		*Relationship Focus*
(1)	Orientation to single sales	(1)	Orientation to customer retention
(2)	Discontinuous customer contact	(2)	Continuous customer contact
(3)	Focus on product features	(3)	Focus on customer value
(4)	Short term sales	(4)	Long time sales
(5)	Little emphasis on customer service	(5)	High customer service emphasis
(6)	Limited commitment to meeting customer expectations	(6)	High commitment to meeting customer expectations
(7)	Quality is the concern of production	(7)	Quality is the concern of all staff

In pre-second World War period most of the companies were selling simple goods and the principle of personal selling and negotiation was to initiate and complete particular sale. That means the seller as well as the buyer viewed each exchange as a transaction to be terminated as soon as the exchange is completed. This was transactions focus of marketing. However, as competition began to become intense and companies began to offer complex goods and marketing accompanied by services, they needed to build a long-term relationship with customer. They began to demonstrate superior capabilities to serve the customers. Nil Rackham[19] argues that sales persons should make preliminary enquiries with susceptive buyer, having found him to be a prospective buyer, sales persons should investigate his needs and demonstrate to him company's superior capabilities to meet his present as well as future needs, thereby obtain a long-term commitment from both sides. This transformation from immediate sale to developing a long-term customer relationship is an evolution in approach to marketing.

TOTAL RELATIONSHIP MARKETING

Though it is difficult to state who discovered the term 'relationship marketing' and when, we find it being used first in late 1970s by Barbara Bund Jackson[20] in her project on industrial marketing and in 1983 by Leonard Berry[21] in his writings on service marketing. A number of authors, researchers have defined relationship marketing in their own way indicating that relationship marketing is a challenge to established marketing management theory and practice. Evert Gummesson[22] in his concept of 'Total Relationship Marketing' has added two more dimensions namely networks and interaction to the original dimension of relationship. He defines 'Relationship Marketing is marketing seen as relationships, networks and interaction.'

Philip Kotler's[23] concept of total marketing has much different connotation than that of Gummensson's concept of total relationship marketing. Kotler lists ten critical players in a company's environment differentiating between firm's immediate environment and its macro environment. Immediate environment of a firm has four players, namely, suppliers, distributors, end users and employees while its macro environment has six players, namely, financial firms, government, media, allies, competitors and general public.

Relationship is person-to-person, face-to-face, close contact between marketer and buyer. It is argued that the contact may be established, retained and developed through various media. Contact is the major feature of relationship. Frequency of contact determines continuity and intensity of relationship. Thus, relationship in marketing is continuous contact between marketer and customer. Relationship can be strengthened by establishing contact continuously either in person or through some media. Marketer's behaviour of keeping the promises he has given establishes and improves credibility of relationship. Collaboration and competition both are necessary to strengthen relationship. There must be complete openness in thoughts, expression and dealings if relationship is to be strengthened and put to the benefit of all the parties. Business relationship can be strengthened by; evaluating the terms of contract, planning and engineering the product and/or service, delivery and installation of equipment at right time and at right place, providing service, follow up after completion of contract and final evaluation of the deal by both the parties.

Network is the agglomeration of various actors in the marketing process. Network is extended enterprise with components from suppliers, their suppliers, to customer and customer's customers. Network also includes all stakeholders of the company, shareholders, board members, managerial staff, employees, bankers, insurers, consultants and various administrative and government departments. Scope of network depends upon size of enterprise, nature of activity and geographical area covered by the company.

Interaction is the play between various components of the network, especially between seller and buyer. Interaction may take place by personal contact or through various media depending upon the nature of the business. Interaction between seller and buyer may relate to price, quality, and quantity of goods and/or services, conditions of contract, execution and completion of contract as also penalty for non-fulfillment of terms of contract.

The interaction between customer and provider is referred to as service encounter or in popular management jargon as 'the moment of truth'. Interaction can be between providers' contact personnel whom we know as front line person and the customer. Customer and customer may also interact with each other. The contact between physical environment, provider's product and customer and providers service system is also an interaction. These four types of interactions are perceived in Gummesson's concept of interaction.

Evert Gummesson in his theory of Total Relationship Marketing has shifted the very focus on marketing from 'delivering a customer service' to developing a long term 'RELATIONSHIP'. Not the service alone but the relationship should be the basis, the objective of marketing. Creation of relationship bonds with customer and other players in the market includes customer service. Customer service is a process that encompasses all activities before, during and after the sales transactions. This approach is much broader than the traditional approach discussed in marketing-mix, service marketing, network marketing and quality management marketing. The concept of 'total relationship marketing' brings together customer service, quality of service and network in marketing. What we need is a company-wide alignment of purpose towards meeting the customer requirement.[24]

According to Gummesson, relationship, network and interaction are the necessary conditions of total relationship marketing. He has developed thirty aspects of relationship in marketing that can be classified into four categories. A classic market relationship is the first class of such relationship. That includes relationship between supplier, customer, competitor, and distribution channels. Second category is named as special market relationships and includes fourteen aspects of relationships concerning various types of buyer seller interactions. A mega relationship is the third category of relationship that exists above market relationships and provides a platform or markets relationships and concerns the economy and society in general. Among these mega relationships are included efforts like lobbying, public opinion, political power; mega alliances such as North Atlantic Free Trade Association setting new stage for marketing in North America and social relationships such as friendship dealing between friends and friends of friends, ethnic bonds. Fourth category of relationships proclaimed by Gummesson is Nano Relationships that are found below market relationships. That is relationship inside an organisation like relationship between different departments, different divisions and different functionaries. But this category also includes relationship with external entities like advertising agencies, market research institutes, financial institutions etc.

On the basis of thirty aspects of relationships developed by Gummesson, total relationship marketing is defined as based on relationships, network and interaction. It recognises that marketing is embedded in total management of the network of the selling organisation, the markets and society. It is directed to long term win-win relationships with individual customers and value is jointly created between parties involved. It transcends the boundaries between specialist functions and disciplines. It is made tangible through the thirty market, mega and nano relationship.

It is observed that Gummesson's concept of total relationship marketing represents various players in the market and different characteristic features of the relationships between these parties and players. Inclusion of both these aspects (players and characteristic features) has made his concept broader in scope and has reduced inconsistency in approach. But equally so, it has become all embracing. He emphasizes that there should be long term collaboration between market players and that should benefit all the Constituents. This collaboration benefits all because all the players in the market are active. Gummesson recognises relationships and service values to be more prominent and persistent than bureaucratic and legal values. It is true that these three generic relationship characteristics are inherent in the relationship.

Total Relationship Marketing Theory is extension and comprehension of the four theories and two genesis that we have discussed in the second section of this chapter. The theory covers all types of products and services and customers and bears on all marketing situations. It takes into account uniqueness of each marketing situation. The theory develops a coherent framework encompassing traditional marketing and sales management. It is an extension of the concept of total quality management to marketing because the theory states that long term relationship and collaboration can be built up by providing customer perceived quality goods and services. It is crystallisation of six sigma philosophy because providing each unit of the product or each service, the quality required by customer amounts to zero defect; the objective of six sigma process. Total relationship marketing theory encompasses the genesis of supply chain management. The theory expresses that maximum value must be delivered to the customer which means that from suppliers' supplier to the end consumer each link of process must add value to the product or service passing through it. The relationship is extended to merge suppliers, producers and consumers into an organisation. All the parties become active so as to create value for mutual contribution. Therefore, competition and collaborations become essential functions of the market economy. Thus, we develop new perspective into relationship, networks and interactions which Gummesson calls 'relationship eyeglasses' a new angle to understand relationship.

Human activities have thrived on two fulcrums, namely collaboration and competition, that result into long term and harmonious relationship between all players in the market in a particular sense and in the society in general sense. Higher degree of collaboration and limited degree of competition enables the parties to develop, sustain and maintain intense relationship. Physical, mental and emotional closeness between various parties in the market strengthens the bonds of relationship. Therefore, it is advised that suppliers, company, people, customers, competitors, consultants, administration and government people should keep on meeting each other preferably personally or at least through some contact media. Frequent visits, regular spoken contact and intensity of communication strengthens relationship. Even, they may associate with each other privately. Closeness strengthens the feeling of security. Closer collaboration between various parties in the market, in the society leads to trust in each other. Thus, much collaboration coupled with limited competition; physical and emotional closeness, meeting and speaking to each other and trust are the characteristic features that develop long-term relationship and it is the pillar of total relationship marketing. Marketers build images of products and/or services by developing brand equities and value monopoly. This develops para-social relationships involving objects, symbols and other less tangible phenomena with branded products. Commodities like Surf, Lux, LML Freedom (bike), Splendor (bike) are product images or symbols that are marketed through corporate body language transforming products into symbols which is usually seductively low key. It is subtle marketing. If this strategy of marketing is looked through 'relationship eye-glasses', we find that corporate bodies try to develop long term permanent relationship with society. They also undertake permanent social projects like ITC Academy for Music, Firestone Football Academy. Relationship marketing has the aim of building long term, mutually beneficial and satisfying relationships with all parties.[25] Marketers achieve this by compromising and delivering high quality services and products at fair prices to the customers.

Relationship marketing culminates into developing marketing network. A marketing network consists of the nodal marketing company and aligned supporters ranging from customers to university research team. This network is the asset of the nodal company. The limited competition to which we made a reference in foregoing paragraph is between these marketing networks. Naturally that company, which has built up an extensive, close and lasting network wins the market. James Anderson, Hakan Hakansson and Jan Johanson state, "build an effective network of relationships with key stakeholders and profits will follow". To be successful in marketing, the firm has to build competitive advantage beyond its own operations, to its suppliers, suppliers' suppliers, distributors, wholesalers and retailers. The best way to have total quality, zero defect and six sigma process spread over to these stakeholders is to develop alliances, partnerships, joint ventures, with them. This is called as 'value – delivery network' or 'value supply chain'.[26] K. Shridhara Bhat argues that 'Nodal company should build up virtual companies relying on a variety of supplier relationships to provide services on demand. Virtual companies have fluid, moving organisational boundaries enabling them to create an unique enterprise that makes them capable of meeting changing market demands. It improves efficiency of performance and attains exceptionally good performance. These virtual companies are also known as 'hollow companies' or 'network companies'. There are a good number of software packages that make nodal company to manage network relationships effectively and efficiently. With the help of Alertview (Intel Corporation) nodal company can monitor network resources. Webcasting enables the company to make the information about the network appear on user's screen in a ticker – taper format.

In a network of stakeholders there is a firm commitment of all the players because they depend upon each other. As a result the risk arising out of uncertainly in the market is distributed and/or avoided. No doubt a long time is taken to build up and develop such closely-knit network in which power of position of all parties is balanced and is symmetrical.

Interaction between different players of the market is important because it emphasizes observance of routine procedures that are necessary for achieving efficiency and cost effectiveness. Interaction beginning on the springboard of formality develops into informality. Such informality strengthens formal nature of interaction. As a result of this, all the players in the network relationship begin to share data, information and knowledge freely. This openness is the very success of interaction. In case of physical products consumers can judge, search qualities, experience qualities and credence qualities by referring to the information manual provided with the product. Washing machines, refrigerators, air conditioners, hairdryers, even clothing, jewellery, and furniture fall in this category. In case of such goods personal interaction plays a very limited role. However, in case of many a services like dental root canal, medical diagnosis the patient consumer finds difficult to evaluate technical qualities of such services. Therefore, functional quality becomes more important for consumers to derive satisfaction. The functional quality is exhibited by employee's skill in serving the client who is called interactive marketing.[27]

Gummesson has added one more dimension in his thirty-relationship list. People having become conscious of the hazards of chemical fertilizers, harmful pesticides and fungicides in respect of agricultural products and characteristics of products that are detrimental to health, firms have taken up green marketing as a sub-set of total relationship marketing. Most of the firms now proclaim that their products are environment friendly and in no way harmful for human consumption. Such firms make this factor inherent in their business mission and express genuine desire to be a good citizen.

All this discussion brings us to the end of the journey of tracing development of marketing theories. Formerly marketing management theories were independent of corporate management theories. However, total relationship marketing theory has made marketing management an integral part of corporate management. As a result the management of 21st century intelligent corporation has become cohesive, comprehensive and efficient. It can achieve better its objective of attaining consumer satisfaction, consumer delight by making every aspect of corporate activity quality oriented.

With all this discussion on marketing management one thing remains to be discussed as to how in the environment of uncertainty the exchange between seller and buyer would take place. The customer wishes to have the demand satisfied without he wooing the seller or seller pressurizing him. Equally so, the seller wishes to sell his product without running after the buyer or buyer pressurizing him to sell his product at buyer's terms. This fussy situation calls for an innovative solution based on the principles of fuzzy logic. We can do this by constructing a series of three 9 x 9 grids. The first grid represents the customer, the second the seller and the third grid brings us to a unified solution by defuzzification of the situation. This is done by superimposing customer grid on seller grid and noting the square where the buyer as well the seller will have a stable equilibrium.

In all the three grids we begin from left low corner to vertical and horizontal axes exhibiting higher level of satisfaction. These grids are sequentially numbered as 6.2, 6.3 and 6.4; the earlier (6.2) representing customer grid, the second (6.3) the seller grid and the third (6.4) former superimposed on the latter.

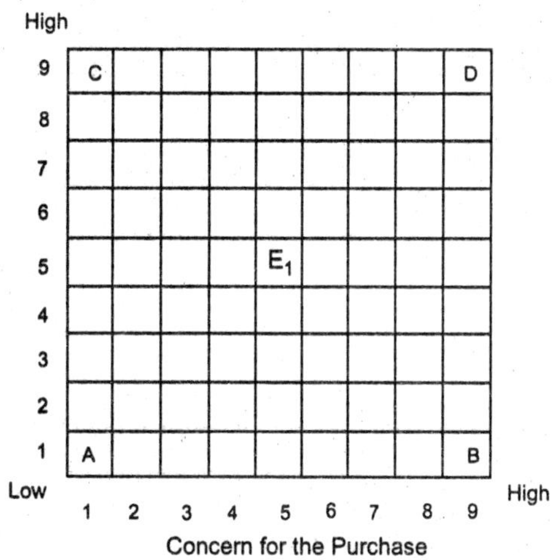

Figure 6.2
The Customer Grid

Situation A: The left-hand lowest point (square 1–1) shows the least satisfaction that the customer derives. The customer in such a situation tries to avoid the sales person, as far as possible, because the sales person pressurizes him and bothers him. This situation is named as 'care less' situation in which the customer cares least about the sales person.

Situation B: The right hand lowest corner (square 9–1) exhibits the position of a defensive buyer. The buyer would not allow the sales person to take disadvantage of this position. In such a situation the buyer would want to dominate the sales person and would try to extract maximum value for price of every rupee spent by him. Of course the sales person being at disadvantage would not like to transact at this point.

Situation C: The left hand highest point (square 1–9) is a comfortable position in which the sales person recommends a product or products to the buyer genuinely and the buyer, also believing in his recommendation, may buy the product. The buyer may be so impressed by the recommendation of the sales person that he may buy more than he needs and repent afterwards for not buying many a things suitable to him. This is 'pushover situation.'

Situation D: The buyer knows (square 9–9) what he needs and is in search of a product that will satisfy him the best, but he would pay for such a product a price that he can afford and not the price that the salesman quotes. He is known to be a 'solution buyer.'

Situation E_1: The buyer would be guided by the experience of others who have tested this product for a long time. This is a prestigious product and the buyer feels that his prestige is enhanced if he buys this product. So square 5–5 exhibits 'reputation buyer.'

Thus, in such a fuzzy situation as to what position on the customer grid should the buyer choose to indicate his purchase is indicated by point E_1.

Figure 6.3 exhibits the sales grid that would analyze fuzzy situation from sales person's point of view.

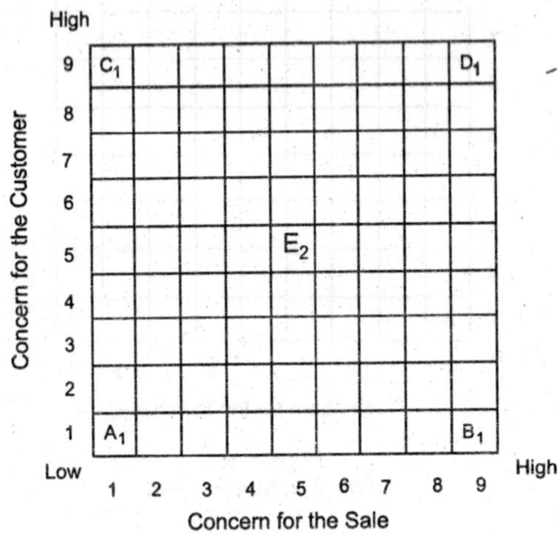

Figure 6.3
The Sales Grid

Situation A_1: The sales person at point A_1 (square 1-1) cares very little about the buyer. He exhibits the product to the buyer. The product gets sold as and when the buyer takes it. This situation is 'take it or leave it'.

Situation B_1: The sales person at this position (square 9-1) takes charge of the customer, pursues him hard and makes him buy it. This situation is 'push the product'.

Situation C_1: At this position (square 1-9) known as 'personality oriented, 'the sales person plays the role of being customer's friend. The sales person listens to the buyer, understands him and responds to his feelings. The sales person tries to know how much is he liked by the customer. This relationship leads to a personal bond and makes the buyer purchase the goods.

Situation D_1: This situation (square 9-9) is 'problem solving situation'. The sales person appeals the customer to tell him what his needs are and which needs sales person's goods can satisfy. The sales person in conversation with the buyer and consultation make a sound decision. This benefits the buyer and the buyer is satisfied as he gets the product on his terms.

Situation E_2: at square 5-5 with sales technique oriented strategy the sales person tries routine method and makes the buyer purchase the goods. Thus, the customer is able to choose and buy a product mix that satisfies him most.

Thus, in such a situation the sales person and customer travel through 9 x 9 grids and finally arrive at a solution exhibited by E_1 in Figure 6.2 and E_2 in Figure 6.3. This position is win-win position for both because the objective of the sales person to delight the customer is satisfied and buyer's objective of getting maximum value is also met. This is exhibited by super imposing Figure 6.2 on Figure 6.3 and is shown in Figure 6.4.

Figure 6.4 configurates the total relationship marketing theory and fuzzy logic so as to present a firm situation at which seller and buyer would strike at a long-term relationship with benefit to all in the market.

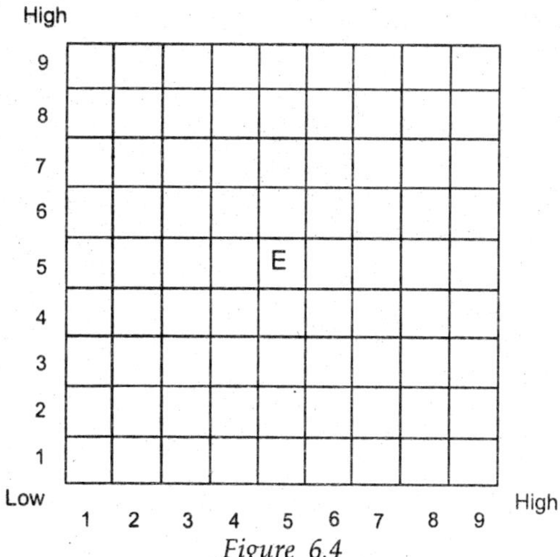

Figure 6.4
Total Relationship Marketing and Fuzzy Logic

In Figure 6.4 we find, Figure 6.2 superimposed on Figure 6.3. The conclusion of the results that, we had drawn at the end of discussion of Figures 6.2 and 6.3 is that the market will enjoy long-term sustained relationship at point (E) as shown in Figure 6.4.

References

(1) Levitt Theodore. *Production Line Approach to Services*, Harvard Business Review, Sept.-Oct.-1972, pp. 41-52 and *Industrialisation of Services*, Harvard Business Review, Sept.-Oct.-1976, pp. 63-74.

(2) Borden Neil H. *The Concept of Marketing Mix*, the Journal of Advertising Research, June 4, 1994, pp. 2-7.

(3) American Management Association, *Marketing News*, 1985.

(4) Turban Efrain and Aronson J.E. Decision Support System and Intelligent systems, Pearson Education Asia, Sixth Edn. p.112.

(5) Lauteborn R.F. *New Marketing Liteny – 4 Ps Passe-c-words Take Over'*, Advertising Age, October 1, 1990, p. 26.

(6) Menon Ajay and Menon Anil. *Entrepreneurial Marketing Strategy*, Journal of Marketing, Vol. 61, January 1997, pp. 51-67.

(7) Henkoff Ronald. 'Service Is Everybody's Business' Fortune, 27 June 1994, pp. 48-60.

(8) Boom B.H. and Bitner M.J. 'Marketing Strategies and Organisational Structure for Service Firms, in 'Marketing of Services', Edited by Donelly and George W.R.(American Marketing Association) Chicago, 1981, pp. 47-51.

(9) Parsuram A, Zaithani V.A. and Berry L.L. – 'A Conceptual Model of Service Quality and Its Implications on Future Research' *Journal of Marketing*, Fall 1985, pp. 41-50

(10) Delvin S.J. and Dong H.K. – 'Service Quality From the Customer's Perspective' Marketing Research, *A Magazine of Management and Application*, Winter, 1994, pp. 4-13.

(11) Ford P., Hakansson H. and Johanson J. 'How Do Companies React?' *Industrial Marketing and Purchasing*, Vol. 2, No. 1, 1986, pp. 26-27.

(12) Beckham J. Daniel. 'Expect the Unexpected in Health Care Marketing Future', *The Academy Bulletin*, July 1992, p. 3.

(13) Kaplan R.S. and Norton D.P. *The Balanced Score Card Measures that Drive Performance*, Harvard Business Review, Jan.-Feb. 1992.

(14) Gronros Christian. 'Facing the Challenge of Service Competition: The Economies of Service' in 'Quality Management in Service' edited by Kunst Paul and Lemmik Jos; Assen/Maastricht, Van Gorum 1992, pp. 129-140.

(15) Norman Richard and Ramirez Rafael. 'From Value Chain to Value Constellation' Harvard Business Review, July-August, 1993, pp. 65-77.

(16) Kasturinrangan V., Moriary Rowland T. and Swartz Gordon S. 'Segmenting Customers in Mature Industrial Market', Journal of Marketing, October 1992., pp. 72-82.

(17) Basterfield Dale H. 'Total Quality Management', Pearson Education, Asia, 2nd Edition, p. 69.

(18) Reichheld F.F. and Sasser W.E. (Jr.). *Zero Defections: Quality Comes to Service*, Harvard Business Review, Sept.-Oct., 1990, p. 105.

(19) Rackham Neiland. *Vincentis John De-Rethinking the Sales Force*, McGraw-Hill, New York, 1996.

(20) Jackson Barbara Bund. *Winning and Keeping Industrial — The Dynamics of Customer Relations*, Lexington M.A., Heath D.C., 1985.

(21) Berry Leonard. 'Big Ideas in Sevice Marketing,' *Journal of Consumer Marketing*, Spring, 1986, pp. 47-51.

(22) Gummesson Evert. *Making Relationship Marketing Operational, Service Industry management*, Vol. 5, No. 5, 1994, p. 5.

(23) Kotler Philip. 'Total Marketing', *Business Week*, Advance Executive Brief, 1992, p. 4.

(24) Bank John. *The Essence of Total Quality Management*, Prentice Hall, 1992, pp. 185-186.

(25) Christopher Martin, Adrinpayne and Ballanlyne David. *Relationship Marketing: Bringing Quality, Customer Service and Marketing Together*, Oxford, U.K. Butterworth-Heinemann, 1991.

(26) Magnet Myron. *The New Golden Rule of Business*, Fortune, November, 28, 1994, pp. 60-64.

(27) Zeithaml Valarie A.- 'How Consumer Evaluation Processes Differ Between Goods and Services', in Donnelly and George (Ed.) *Marketing Services*, pp. 190.

❑ ❑ ❑

7 Knowledge Management (Third Evoloution in Management)

Now we are at the threshold of the third evolution of organisational management. The Industrial Revolution of 1769-76 gave birth to large sized organisations based on the principle of limited liability. It resulted into capital based production activity and organisation matching that. Criteria measuring the productivity, efficiency and development of organisation were based on return on capital. How does the organisation use capital and how much does it earn per rupee of capital invested was measured on the indictors developed in 1860 named as balance sheet, profit and loss account, and income expenditure statement. Ownership of capital and unlimited authority to use it was the characteristic feature of these organisations. This system culminated into perfection by the time of American Civil War of 1861 - 65 and Franco-Prussian War of 1866. First evolution in the structure and organisation of such corporate bodies came around in the decade of 1895 to 1905. Ownership rights and management right were bifurcated and management was recognised and established as an independent function. George Siemens in Germany introduced this reform by handing over the reign of his organisation to a professional. J. P. Morgan, Andrew Carnegie, John D. Rockfeller popularized these developments by reorganising their enterprises. Pierre S. DuPont began second evolution in about 20 years by introducing centralised organisation based on the principle of command and control. After those in a few years time Alfred P. Slones reorganised General Motors on these principles. This organisational system began to use Central Service Staff, personnel management, budget and controlling measures and separation between policy and operations as its characteristic features. This model was perfected by organising General Electric in 1950 and accepted all over the world including Japan.

Peter Drucker by introducing in 1963 the concept of knowledge worker spearheaded the third evolution in the organisation of enterprise. The world is changing fast from 1960 and the business world is changing still faster. The changes are going to be still faster in twenty- first century. Naturally, enterprises have to face unprecedented challenges. Expectations of customers are changing over last thirty years because of information blast and entry of global brands in international market. Enterprises have to accept and face the challenge squarely of satisfying and surpassing these expectations of customers. Revolution in expectations of customers is spearheaded by pervasive computing and Internet. Prospective customers are adopting new life style based on information received on Internet. Present customers show no respect and loyalty about brands, they expect maximum value for the price paid. They expect availability of new products and new service every day. As a result such change in the mindset of customers, markets have become customer oriented, competitive and location and time unbound.

As a result of such changes in the mindset of customers the mindset and behaviour of enterprises have also undergone a change. Market oriented every enterprise has to focus its every activity on customer value addition. Method of reengineering enterprise organisation formerly used to reduce the size of the body is now used to facilitate communication with the customer. Increasing pressure of information technology has embraced all functions within and outside the organisation. Technique of production is continuously refined and it is being made known to all because of fast flow of information.

Along the changes in the mindset and behaviour of organisations discussed in forgoing paragraphs, changes in approach and behaviour of employees that need to be discussed here have also taken place. Employees now instead of concentrating their attention on work are focusing on customers and their changing expectations. Employees pay greater attention now on how to develop commodities and services having maximum value. They are endeavouring to raise their productivity to the highest level. They are exhibiting maximum capability to reduce the learning time required to change their functions and roles to match the changes in the organisation. Effectiveness has become more pervasive than efficiency. Efficiency is the product of division of output by input while effectiveness is the product of division of actual production by expected production.

One more dimension of reorganisation of unit needs to be discussed. Business enterprises have developed a practice of outsourcing components and spare parts of their products. In the process, outsourcing is given greater scope calling for development of new systems of relationship between the principal and outsourcers and suppliers. They are being considered as principal partners of the organisation. They must develop and possess capability to supply components that match with changing requirements of the market. Enterprises in this new environment have to face three major challenges - (1) To develop new system to attract and provide services to new Internet and e-commerce customers. (2) To develop capacity to absorb expertise in information technology and to transform it into practice so as to make enterprise market oriented. (3) To reengineer the mindset of knowledge workers in such enterprises and to develop a system to institutionalise their individual and professional training. Organisations need to identify sources of knowledge present in the units to face these three challenges squarely. It is necessary to share this knowledge with others, to disseminate the same in the organisation and to search necessary knowledge from the stock of it so as to transform the capability of employees of satisfying expectations of customers. Thereby the organisation can add to the process of search for knowledge. To examine such sources of knowledge, to nurture such knowledge, transform it to those who need it and store in computers are the system that can be called as knowledge management.

Capability to handle a job, system or relations between individuals, relations between organisation and customers as well as between individuals, groups and institutions more effectively is called as knowledge. Many a times the terms, information, knowledge and wisdom are used as interchangeable. Conclusions drawn by processing data and making it available to those who are authorised to use it at tip of finger is Management Information System. If the experience of handling this or like situation in the organisation, ideas, thoughts and practical wisdom are added to information then the knowledge of handling every transaction is generated. The terms, information and knowledge are mostly used as synonyms and people are confused about them. Information and knowledge are different things and they project different concepts. Information totally related to activities and enriched with individual explanations and expertise is knowledge. Wisdom is born as a result of deep insight to understand inner knowledge and inner self. Even if it is possible to manage such wisdom it is not always so because wisdom is slippery and subtle. Formerly, people used to talk about managing information, now people discuss about managing knowledge. However, it is wise to leave wisdom as it is rather than to mechanically handle it.

There is a difference between information and knowledge. Information is objective and knowledge is subjective. Knowledge is always related to reference. Knowledge cannot be utilized or explained unless its reference is taken into consideration. Transformation of data, information and knowledge is exhibited in Figure 7.1.

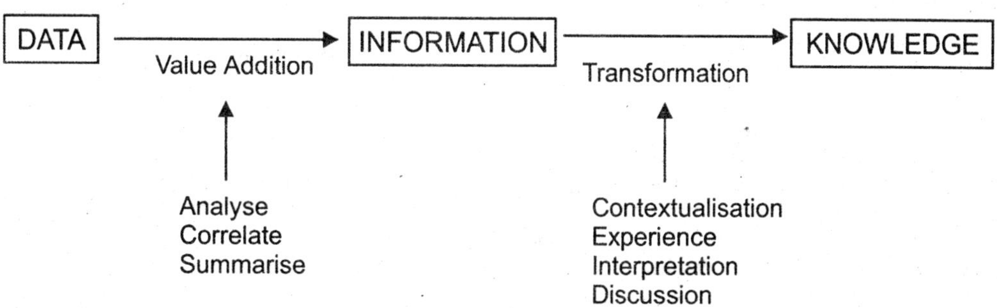

Figure 7.1
Transformation of Data, Information and Knowledge

The data in its raw form tells nothing. It is to be analysed as to what type of interrelation exists between different items of data. Then these interrelated facts are to be correlated. Conclusions of such interrelated facts are to be then summarized. This is a process of adding value to the data to transform it into meaningful information. The information so arrived at is then put along with reference to which it relates. Experiences as related to these references are added. The results thereof are interpreted and discussed so as to arrive at fruitful conclusions. That is crystallized as knowledge. So information transformed into conclusions is knowledge.

Knowledge is an asset from the point of view of an enterprise. It is knowledge asset. Knowledge about market along with competing constituents, products, process and technologies is knowledge asset. All these four constituents of knowledge asset have important place in knowledge asset. They play important role in the success of the organisation. Management of knowledge asset is necessary to retrieve maximum returns from all the constituents of knowledge asset. Management of knowledge asset is as important in knowledge management as is in the management of factors in the process working on it. Generation of knowledge, preservation of knowledge and use of that knowledge are the processes that are related to knowledge asset.

Generation of knowledge includes acquisition of knowledge, synthesis of components of knowledge and creation of knowledge. Preservation of knowledge includes, decision as to which type of knowledge is necessary for construction of the organisation, to acquire that knowledge, to choose that knowledge which is needed by the organisation without getting lost into its chaos, to broaden the base of structured and unstructured knowledge and prepare knowledge map. While using knowledge it is required to disseminate the knowledge in the organisation that remains implicit and isolated with the people who run the organisation. That means, in disseminating and in sharing the knowledge use of knowledge is maximized. It is very necessary from the point of maximizing the use of knowledge to spread the knowledge of required type and at required destination. It is important to develop mechanism required for that. Technology plays important role in such transformation of knowledge. The process of transformation of knowledge is exhibited in Figure 7.2.

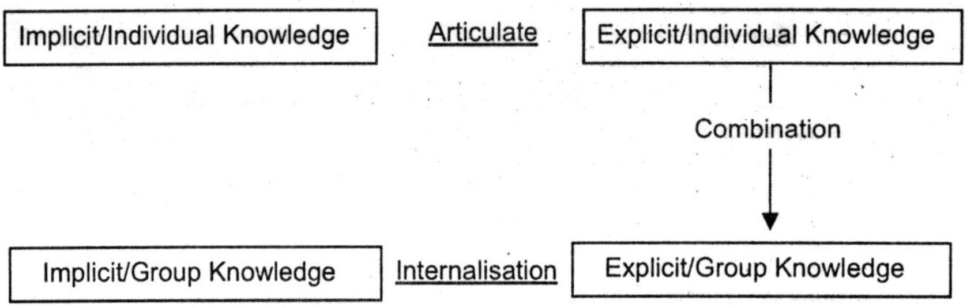

Figure 7.2
Process of Knowledge Transformation

Knowledge gap is the difference between the knowledge required to combat the competitive situation in the market and the knowledge that the organisation has. It is necessary to fill up the gap by human resources development. It is necessary to take the fact of filling up knowledge gap as a process of knowledge management. Imperatives of knowledge gap and solutions of these imperatives are given in Table 7.1.

Table 7.1
Knowledge Gap and Solutions

	Imperatives of Knowledge Gap		*Solutions for Filling up Kowledge Gap*
(1)	To develop customer oriented business system.	(1)	To align business system of the organisation with e-mail.
(2)	To search out measures to achieve first class performance.	(2)	To acquire all knowledge related to the business of the organisation.
(3)	To select right person for right job.	(3)	To integrate knowledge by knowing who possesses what knowledge.
(4)	To understand promotional role of information technology.	(4)	To perfect information technology by using all possible means of knowledge management.

People working in the organisation possess huge knowledge. Knowledge workers know much about the economy, social behaviour, expectations of customers, the industry of the organisation in which they work is a part of; they also know many things about their organisation in which they work. Employees using this knowledge and co-operating with those who use each other's knowledge are 'knowledge workers'. Peter Drucker has defined knowledge worker as 'an employee whose major contribution depends upon his employing his knowledge rather that his muscle power and co-ordination is a 'knowledge worker'; frequently contrasted with production workers who employ muscle power and co-ordination to operate machines.[1]

After introduction of computers in 50s, many were doubtful about the future of middle management cadre. However, barring the time of recession, the number of middle managers increased. However, the middle-management cadre of today is fundamentally different from that of earlier middle-management cadre. Knowledge function has become the principal job. Middle managers of today are knowledge professionals. Middle managers of earlier days were leaders; middle managers of today are suppliers of knowledge. Traditionally middle managers of today are responsible to colleagues and superiors. Middle managers of earlier days were not required to perform routine jobs, they even did not take decisions; they used to implement decisions. They were required to run the system which they had not created and which they were not expected to change. Present day middle managers being knowledge professionals their decisions and functions affect directly and importantly on the capability of the organisation and direction of function. They are neither line managers nor are they staff. They perform operating work. Even though they are not in the category of top management on the grounds of status and salary, however effect of their activities on the performance of the organisation is as much as that of the work of top management.

The middle management knowledge system of 1970s and 80s is now transformed into knowledge organisation. Organisations using middle management cadre effectively have recorded a growth rate much higher than that of other organisations. While this is happening, it is observed that there is a need to reorganise individual approach and organisation of corporate bodies. In knowledge organisation all jobs from bottom to top need to be focused on the objectives of the organisation. Business unit needs to be organised according to assignment. Organisation must match the status of the individual and flow of information to destination. And this need to be done to suit decision-making process. Because, in a knowledge organisation downward authority system does not work, we need a multi-dimensional authority system. Everybody in the knowledge organisation must have the opportunity to contribute maximum to achieve organisational goal. There must be a limit to the authority of everybody in the knowledge organisatioı It must be clear as to which decision is to be taken at which level. As a result the structural organisation of knowledge organisation is much complex and not line organisation. The organisation of knowledge organisation must be capable of facing much greater risks. It is emphasized to strengthen the organisation by taking new decisions rather than running the organisation as usual. Employees of such knowledge organisation are at the centre. Such knowledge workers do much productive work. They must be put in those areas or on jobs in which they have potential to offer required results. It is insignificant as to in which way they work. The key to productivity of knowledge workers is in assignment control. It is important for that to understand what are their strengths. It is necessary to assign them on such jobs where they, by using their strengths can perform the best. That means they need to be assigned where opportunity exists and where appropriate opportunity exists. Then only we can reap good and quality results. Knowledge jobs cannot be got performed from machines or mechanically. Capital investments create greater scope for knowledge function.

In all developed countries knowledge workers have become center point of work force. By the end of 80s number of knowledge workers has outstepped the number of blue-collar workers. Because we are substituting workers by capital and knowledge, we are shifting from labour intensive industries to knowledge intensive industries. Manufacturing industries are also becoming knowledge intensive. Organisations are reducing in size. Plant size went on becoming larger in the twentieth century; Probably economies of size must be beneficial to them. Modern management system is also developed to suit such large sized organisations. However, this picture is changing in the last 15-20 years. Small and medium sized organisations are growing fast. The size of large enterprise is also shrinking. New concepts, new models of managing such knowledge intensive small sized organisations are emerging. Knowledge management is one such model.

Evolution of the model of knowledge management can be discussed as below. Douglas McGregor in his book 'The Human Side of Enterprise (1996) discussed two theories; 'Theory X' and 'Theory Y' of managing workers. And he explained that 'The Theory Y' was practical. The theory professed that there is only one way of managing all workers. However, Abraham H. Maslow in his book 'Eupsychain

Management' argued that 'Theory Y' was wrong and stated that different people need to be managed in different ways. Both these theories were based on the hypothesis that people working in the organisation are employees. However, Peter Drucker in his book, 'Management Challenges of 21st Century '(1999) argued that people participating in the knowledge organisation are not employees but associates. All people working from bottom to the top management are associates and not subordinates, as knowledge workers know their jobs better than their superiors. Superiors will not be able to perform their jobs properly unless they are provided all information of their jobs in respective areas performed by knowledge workers. That means supervisors in determining their directions depend upon knowledge so much as the knowledge workers depend upon superiors for direction. Knowledge workers are more mobile than their predecessors because their 'means of production' - knowledge is possessed by them. Therefore, not only different groups of knowledge workers are to be managed differently but knowledge workers of the same group are to be managed differently at different times. Because, they are partners in the process of production and all partners are equal. Therefore, the foundation of new theory of management is not going to be 'managing the work of people' but 'managing the performance of people'. Formerly, managers used to discuss extensively productivity of manual workers, raising that productivity and used to focus on that. Now they are focusing on what is productivity of knowledge workers, on which factors does it depend and how to raise it. Our present goal is how to make the knowledge and strength of knowledge workers more and more productive.

It was believed forty years back that the technology outside the organisation in which we are working would not affect the technology in our organisation. However, it needs to be accepted today, that, the technology beyond our area of work does make a great impact on the industry and organisation in which we work. The transistor invented by Bell Telephone Company is no doubt much important in telephone industry but it has revolutionised many industries. However, it is equally important that the inventions that revolutionised telephone industry like digital switching, fiberglass cable took place outside the research laboratories of telephone industry. Therefore, the assumptions that there is a technology of self in the management of the organisation and there is some definite customer using our products need to be placed aside. That means, technology and end use will not be the basis of management in the new theory of management. Decision about division of disposable income by the customer and customer values are going to be the basis of new theory of management.

Over 35 years ago, Peter Drucker observed that a company's first task is 'to create customer'. But today's customers face a vast array of product and brand choices, prices and suppliers. Customers of today are value maximizers, within the bounds of search costs and limited knowledge, mobility and income. They form an expectation of value and act on that. They want to maximize customer delivered value, which is the difference between total customer value and total customer cost.

Michael Porter proposed that 'Value Chain' is a tool for identifying way to create more customer value. Every organisation is a collection of activities that are performed to design, produce, market, and deliver and support its product. The value chain identifies nine strategically relevant activities that create value and cost in a specific business. These nine value-creating activities consist of five primary activities and four support activities that are exhibited in Figure 7.3.

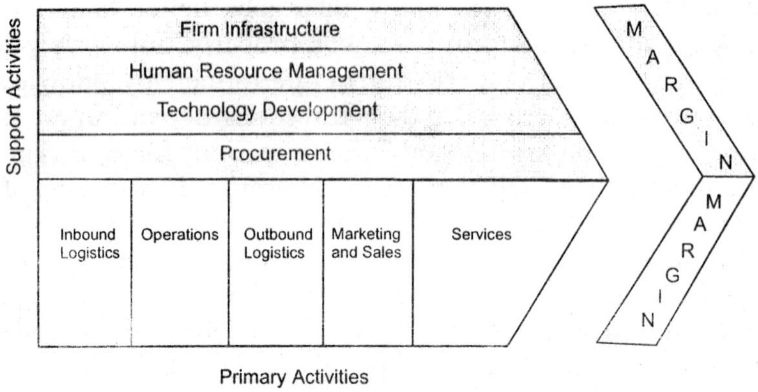

Figure 7.3
The Generic Value Chain

(*Source* –Porter Michael — Competitive Advantage: Creating and Sustaining Superior Performance, Free Press 1985. Kotler Philip — Marketing Management, the Millennium Edition — Prentice Hall of India Pvt. Ltd. 2001, p. 34).

The organisation would reach its goal only if it follows this path. Fulfilling the task given to a knowledge worker is based on autonomy granted to him, his innovative power, continuous teaching, continuous learning, his output and its quality and his intention to devote fully to the task of organisation even by keeping aside all alternative opportunities.

Objective of knowledge management is to make the organisation customer oriented by speeding up the decision process, to raise productive competency of the organisation to the highest level and maintain it at that level. Knowledge management is not an end; it is a means to improve competitive competency of the organisation. Knowledge management means: to identify information assets of the organisation, manage these assets and integrated and systematic method of sharing this information. This includes integration of individual workers implicit skill, experience, information, documentation and procedure. Fundamentally, knowledge management is to make available information to him who uses it knowledgeably and adds to its stock the collective information and experience of the organisation. This continuous cycle includes learning organisation, initiates co-operation and empowers employees to do their tasks still better. Annier Brooking in her book titled 'Corporate Memory'[2] argues that beginning of an organisation, its history therefrom, method of working in the organisation, principles and values of organisaton are its memory. All employees must know this and make them known all this is an inseparable part of knowledge management.

There are various techniques of transforming implicit knowledge into explicit knowledge. They are-

(1) To interview experts with the help of prestructured questionnaire — Experts possess knowledge in respect of experience they have gained. Even information can be sought from them on exceptional occurrences of business situations.

(2) Explanation of decision-making process — Experts and chief executive officers explain the process as to how did they arrive at particular decision. This gives us knowledge about decision-making process.

(3) Observation — we can observe a live situation in which the expert or the decision-maker has arrived at a particular decision. This gives us knowledge about decision-making process.

(4) Computer based methods of using knowledge — Decision process, decision matrix, rules of making decisions and methods of mapping the factors that affect decision-making process are some of the means that enable us to form basis of acquiring knowledge.

METHODS OF KNOWLEDGE MANAGEMENT

Five thinkers have described different methods of managing knowledge. They are –

(1) Eight-step method described by Jay Liabowitz.
   (a) Transform data into knowledge.
   (b) To verify the knowledge by acquainting with it.
   (c) To preserve knowledge by acquiring it.
   (d) To arrange bits of knowledge and arrange them in sequential form.
   (e) To utilize knowledge fully by economizing it.
   (f) To collect as much knowledge as possible.
   (g) To create knowledge.
   (h) To disseminate knowledge or make it available at a price.

M. Macwartz, K. Wig and Von Ur Spek have described four-step method of managing knowledge. They are put in Table 7.2.

Table 7.2
Four Step Methods of Managing Knowledge

	M. Macwartz		*K. Wig*		*Von Ur Spek*
(1)	To acquire knowledge	(1)	To create and acquire knowledge	(1)	To develop new knowledge
(2)	To create knowledge	(2)	To edit knowledge and transmit it	(2)	To acquire existing and new knowledge
(3)	To transmit knowledge and use it	(3)	To spread knowledge	(3)	To spread knowledge
(4)	To store knowledge	(4)	To utilise knowledge and earn value for it	(4)	To collect and preserve knowledge that is available

Hall Sapple and Joshi have suggested six steps of knowledge management.

They are—

(1) To acquire knowledge

(2) To choose knowledge as per our need

(3) To cultivate knowledge in the organisation

(4) To utilize knowledge fully

(5) To create knowledge, and

(6) To transmit knowledge outside the organisation

Above discussion clarifies that knowledge management comprises mainly of four factors, they are — (1) to acquire knowledge, (2) to create knowledge, (3) to assimilate knowledge, and (4) to spread knowledge. Strategy of knowledge management includes web-based mapping of knowledge of experts who are due for retirement and to develop a system of stocking knowledge continuously. Method of mapping knowledge, of experts is known as 'expert system'. There are various 'expert systems'. All they comprise mainly four factors. These factors are — (1) Conversation between expert and the person acquiring knowledge, (2) To resolve problems is the second factor. This enables us to test how far our hypotheses and objectives are realistic, (3) Real happenings in specific sector and *ad-hoc* decisions taken therein helps us to acquire and store knowledge. This is third factor, and (4) In this 'expert systems' we provide an opportunity to the knowledge seeking person to ask questions to explain as to how did he reach to this decision.

The second method of knowledge management is mechanistic centred on technology. It contains little information; it is articulated and easy to manage. It relates to functions like accounting, comptrolling etc. the second aspect is organic with a focus on people. Most business functions represent this world. The flow of information is interactive. Every one is encouraged to contribute to the dialogue. Tools include : (a) small group discussions — people representing different functions and part of the organisation are connected through network. This develops common understanding. (b) Organised dialogue groups — Groups of five persons discuss specific topic, which is the choice of the organisation and their work. The group reports their key conclusions to a group of next five through Intranet. Thus, common understanding is generated through multi-layered and multi-phased dialogue. This may result into over flow of information causing chaos. It is necessary to learn to manage chaos and benefit from the overload of information in order to generate new knowledge. It is necessary to expedite the process of innovation to new products and they are transferred to mechanistic world.

'Experts systems and mechanistic centred system are two inseparable aspects of knowledge management. The first two factors in experts system enable us to acquire knowledge and keep it safe. Knowledge store system can be developed from the third and fourth factors of experts system. That means most of the aspects of knowledge management can be achieved by experts system and mechanistic centred system of knowledge management. It is imperative that information technology is extensively used in knowledge management. A number of functions of knowledge management can be performed with the help of information technology.

Following six functions of knowledge management can be performed with the help of information technology. It reaps a number of benefits.

(1) To test, evaluate important knowledge and keep it safe.

(2) To utilize best knowledge to perform our functions efficiently.

(3) To learn as to how can we do our work in best way and to develop new methods of doing this.

(4) To prepare a new layout of work place and work process.

(5) To provide maximum information to people related to the organisation and to general public.

(6) To develop new products and new services.

These functions of knowledge management can be performed with the help of following information technology based means:

(1) E-mail,

(2) Video Conferencing,

(3) Knowledge mapping,

(4) Seminars,

(5) To collect information of new products and new production process,

(6) To educate and train knowledge-workers,

(7) To study new cases and best methods of knowledge management,

(8) To collect knowledge from world wide websites,

(9) To study knowledge based methods of producing goods and providing services,

(10) To study and understand methods of supporting performance and decision-making process,

(11) To take support of information about management, and

(12) To acquire knowledge from available information to improve work system,

Management of knowledge done in this way provides following benefits:

(1) Innovations are done in larger number.

(2) Method and process of doing work are improved.

(3) Customers' satisfaction is enhanced.

(4) Capacity of knowledge workers to work is enhanced and the system of organisational learning is improved.

(5) Capability to prepare report of work done is improved and customer queries are more efficiently answered.

(6) The time required by knowledge workers to learn work process is reduced.

People centred aspect of knowledge management contains almost all functions of a business organisation. In this aspect flow of information is interactive and everybody is induced to participate in such interaction. Group discussion and efforts on the part of everybody to understand all the things is the first method of interaction. People performing different functions and working at different levels are interconnected with the help of network. Second method of developing interaction is to arrange a discussion of a group of four or five persons on topics that are related with people but selected by the organisation. This group transmits to the next group. Such multi-staged and multi-phased discussion creates general coherence of understanding. Sometimes such flow of information creates problem. However, it is important to learn how this problem is to be resolved and to create new knowledge from this situation. It is necessary to accelerate the process of developing new products, through such innovations.

KNOWLEDGE MANAGEMENT FRAMEWORK

The framework of knowledge management consists of six types of core services.

(1) Knowledge Administration: To prepare a structure after identifying groups of knowledge workers of the organisation, people facilitating acquisition of knowledge and managers.

(2) Analysis of Knowledge Needs: To find as to which knowledge does the organisation need to achieve its goals. To assist in systematically understanding the needs of knowledge workers. It facilitates storing of knowledge.

(3) To identify the nature of knowledge that the organisational system possesses. This knowledge may be in the form of books, papers, booklets, project reports, e-mail, internet or in the form of multimedia. This facilitates knowledge mapping.

The collective knowledge base, until recently was relatively limited in breadth and depth. Information entropy was not a consideration. However, today not only the knowledge has become vast but the mutating influence of electronic media has made it imperative to adopt knowledge mapping. The intention of knowledge mapping is to increase the sustainability of collective knowledge base.

The model of knowledge mapping developed by Professor Robert Wright attempts to reconcile aspects of knowledge mapping. The knowledge mapping process consists of four contiguous spaces: the dialogue space, the construct space, the operational space and the synthetic space. The definitions and the connections between these spaces can be explained as below:

(a) Dialogue space: The dialogue space represents the medium or media within which people communicate with one another. In the absence of technology, this would reduce to oral conversation, but in the present, it includes a vast array of available means. The significance of dialogue space to any knowledge mapping system is its role in sharing awareness of significant opportunities, issues and problems. Once these have been identified and the intent of their resolution is clear, the information, which enables resolution, can be assembled.

(b) Construct space: Construct space represents the rationale supporting the intent of a resolution of a problem or issue. It deals with the assembly of information used to establish measures of the problem or issue. These measures foster common understanding. In order to resolve complex problems and issues, a large number of constructs are required. Problems like environment, rights of aboriginals require construct involving various disciplines.

(c) Operational space: Operational space takes the constructs and manipulates them in attempting to resolve the problem or issue. Operational constructs include approaches such as computer simulation models or analog process such as policy development or legislation. The significance of the operational space is in its role as a translator of intent and rationale into a particular resolution of the problem or issue. It identifies explicit linkages between constructs, which are in turn linked to dialogue.

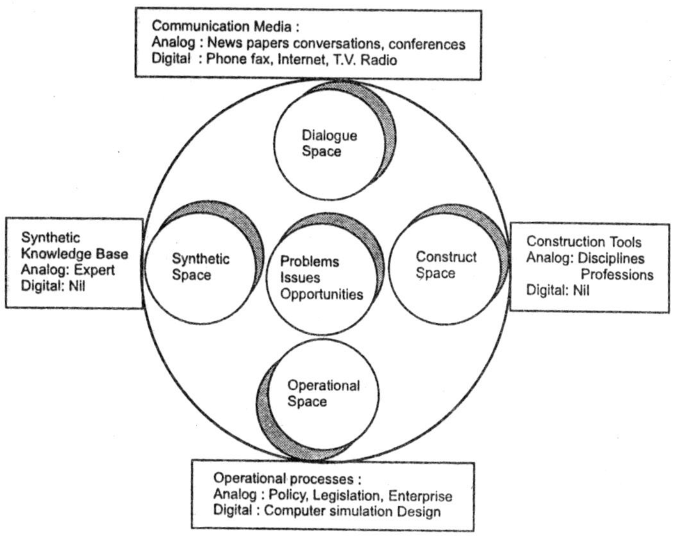

Figure 7.4
Spaces of Knowledge Mapping

(d) Synthetic space: Synthetic space synthesizes the adequacy of a resolution to a problem or issue, in terms of intent, supporting rationale and operational approach. The better the fit of a resolution with reality, the more likely the resolution strategy is to be employed again under similar circumstances. Appropriate resolution strategies form strong conventions within a culture. Access to this synthetic space however, is typically restricted to dialogue with experts. As implicit and as difficult as it may be presently to access this synthetic space, it has the potential to become explicit and accessible to all knowledge mapping spaces.

A knowledge mapping cycle will nearly always involve these four contiguous spaces and most problems and issues will require a large number of interactions. There can be three different types of processes of knowledge mapping – intra-disciplinary, multi-disciplinary and trans-disciplinary. The knowledge maps so drawn should ideally contain a record of all such interactions to enable independent validation and androgogy.

Besides Rebert Wright, Jay Labowitz has also developed a model for knowledge mapping. To exhibit knowledge in the form of a diagram is a technique of mapping various concepts. Knowledge diagram is a web of concepts. In such diagrams concepts are depicted with the help of dots or crosses and the relationship between them or exhibited with the help of one way or two-way arrows. Complex constructs are mapped to create, to develop new ideas, new concepts. Knowledge maps are drawn with various intentions. Such maps are drawn to explain concepts developed by integrating old and new knowledge. Such maps are also drawn to find out how far are the concepts understood and are there any misunderstandings about them. From such knowledge maps a new vocabulary helpful to knowledge-management develops. Knowledge maps are helpful in understanding the nature of new problems and to create a free dialogue based on constructive knowledge that can solve these problems. This makes implicit knowledge available to all the people. Concepts can be very clearly explained with the help of knowledge maps. Knowledge maps are useful in showing concepts and their interrelation. On the basis of that we can identify the shortfalls in knowledge in our organisation. Knowledge map is a two-dimensional figure. Dots and arrows showing relationships between them explain the concepts and their interrelations. A schematic graph showing various divisions in an organisation and their interrelationships is drawn in Figure 7.5.

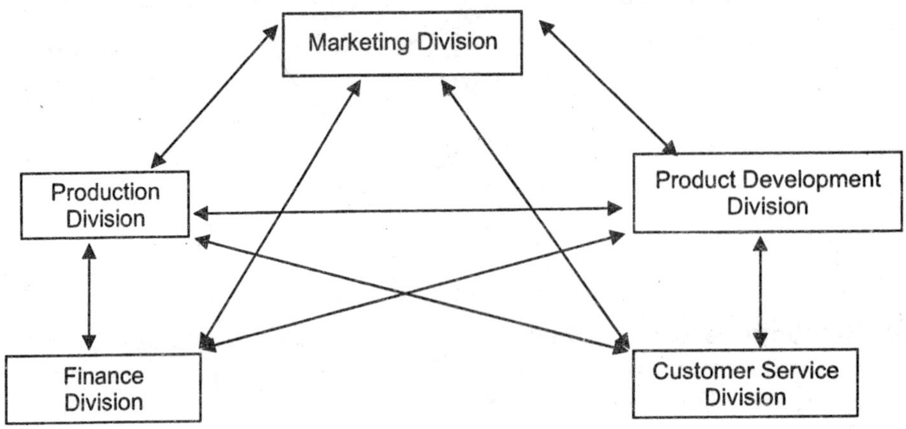

Figure 7.5
Map Exhibiting Different Divisions and Their Interrelationship in an Organisation.

Figure 7.6 depicts important network showing the knowledge nodes and interrelationship between them.

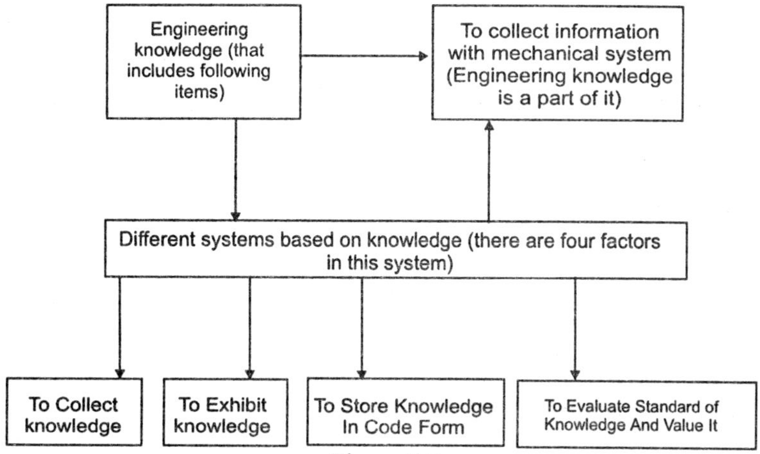

Figure 7.6
Knowledge Nodes and Interrelationship between Them.

This map helps us in utilising practically the methods of collecting knowledge.

(4) Knowledge Dissemination: Knowledge gets disseminated among groups. It enables them to perform any work by collaborating among themselves. It enables them to invent and develop process for doing such work. Knowledge dissemination can be achieved by creating facilities for virtual teams at shared workplaces. Effective groups of knowledge workers can be organised if strengths of knowledge workers are known to the management. Such groups can perform complex jobs very well.

(5) Knowledge Refinement: Information about new products, new process of producing these products is continuously flowing. In view of this it is necessary to refine the knowledge that the organisation has. This can be done by using different control methods for refining knowledge stock with the organisation.

(6) Knowledge Enhancement: A vast volume of knowledge is becoming available because of the explosion in information technology that has taken place in the last decade of last century. It is necessary to acquire this knowledge and use it to the maximum extent to improve competency of the organisation. Knowledge enhancement is possible in following ten ways:

(1) Knowledge is generated out of experience gathered from job performed.

(2) New technology and modern knowledge can be acquired by hiring people from outside.

(3) Knowledge can be gathered from various programs and project reports.

(4) Knowledge can be acquired by knowledge workers by giving them particular type of education and training. Their knowledge can be updated by providing them facilities of on line learning by enrolling on web-based courses.

(5) The knowledge of knowledge workers can be enhanced by analysing the happenings in our organisation and in the industry.

(6) New knowledge can be acquired by interacting with outside world.

(7) Knowledge can be generated by discussions in the workshops and brain storming sessions.

(8) Knowledge is acquired by talking and discussing with various types of people.

(9) Knowledge can be developed by educating and training knowledge workers continuously.

(10) Horizons of knowledge can be broadened by self-intuition.

Knowledge management is imperative to utilise to the maximum extent the knowledge of workers so as to enhance capability of the organisation in competitive situation. Tools discussed in the foregoing paragraph must possess following characteristics so as to implement them successfully.

(1) They must possess sensitivity to context.

(2) The organisation must be sensitive to those who use these tools.

(3) Tools of knowledge management must be flexible.

(4) These tools must possess capability to adjust to heuristic functions.

(5) Different factors implementing knowledge management must possess capability to understand suggestive interactions.

Every knowledge organisation must be learning organisation. Organisation learning is the process that enables an organisation to adopt to change and move forward by acquiring new knowledge, skills and behaviour and thereby transform itself. In successful learning organisations, individual learning is done continuously; knowledge is shared by the company. Such company developes a culture that supports learning. Employees are encouraged to think critically and to take risks with new ideas and all individuals are valued for their contributions to the organisations.[3] In a learning organisation people find benefited by working together, they share stories and lessons learnt. That means they teach each other the practice. J. S. Brown and P. Duguid name such groups of knowledge workers 'Communities of Practice'. An organisation practicing knowledge management must encourage formation of 'communities of practice'. Communities of practice are formed to grow competency to ensure that its members can take full advantage of the community's collective knowledge. 'Communities of purpose' are formed to address a market opportunity by applying knowledge of various competencies to come up with best solutions.

Consideration of emotional intelligence is an inseparable part of knowledge management. Proportion of success depends upon how do we perform our job knowing oneself and others and get the job done. It is important to have a conscious, as to which things must be observed, which things must be appreciated while performing a task. Emotions, capability, status of the people must be appreciated under whom we perform our job, with whom and from whom we get the jobs done. If this appreciation comes and if it is co-ordinated with knowledge, then the quality of success is good. Managing feelings is emotional management. To express emotions carefully, to behave in a sober and balanced manner, to express thoughts effectively in appropriate words, to develop unified attitude in performing job and in getting job performed are the factors that are important in knowledge management. The secret of success lies in studying capabilities and induct in them qualities and virtues. To create confidence about one's work, to develop skill and capability of performing job and to create confidence about work are the factors that help in creating emotional competence. That is the key to knowledge management.

Improving capabilities of individuals is a necessary step in knowledge management. Organisational capabilities are improved by individuals sharing their knowledge. An infrastructure is created to increase connections, decentralize and create as many information repositories as possible on Internet. This helps corporation to grow into big organisation but act like a small company. Knowledge management or organisational learning efforts of individuals must be connected with firm's most pressing strategic initiatives. Organisation must change its thinking about knowledge and learning. Latest talent, creative solutions and capabilities to compete and change must be made driving philosophy. Capabilities can be built by moving money, people and ideas throughout the firm. Walls between business units, functions, geographic locations and ceilings between hierarchical layers must be broken. Walls between the firms, customers and suppliers must be broken.

Company, that does not have critical knowledge functions does not have the right profile of staff it requires to achieve its corporate goals. Choosing the right person for the right job requires knowledge about both the individual and the job at hand. It is the right mix between the problem and individual or client and individual that enables the company to perform best. A psychometric profile of an individual must be prepared before assigning him a job. It is necessary to have an idea as to how to use talents of employees who work best for the organisation. Employees who possess serendipity are an invaluable asset and to know that employee who has such gift is equally valuable. Employees who do the nuances of doing business with other culture have knowledge that is difficult to transfer from one person to another. Knowledge of how to put together teams can be a critical knowledge function where teamwork is essential for the operation of the organisation. In some organisations where teamwork is mission critical, the strength of the team can literally mean the difference between life and death.

KNOWLEDGE MANAGEMENT PROGRAM

Nine point program of knowledge management to improve competency can be discussed as below—

(1) **Analytical skills:** Workers must be trained to analyse problems by analysing data exhaustively, generate alternatives for action and evaluate these alternatives, develop optimal and creative solutions that maximize performance.

(2) **Communication:** Employees of the organisation are taught to receive information clear and accurately. They need to know the importance of

transforming information promptly and accurately by using appropriate methods of communication.

(3) **Customer focus:** The workers are trained to anticipate customer needs, develop contact with customers. They are also taught to actively seek feedback from customers and act on feedback received from the customers. They are expected to proactively design systems to fulfil customer requirements.

(4) **Decision-making:** workers are required to identify and analyse issues, generate solutions for timely decisions. They identify information required to take decisions and use this varied information. They take decisions with the overall strategic view in mind. After having identified areas of risks in such decision-making, they take calculated risks.

(5) **Interpersonal skills:** Interaction between persons and/or groups of persons is of great importance in managing knowledge. As a part of knowledge management individuals are trained to appreciate others view points, deal with social situations with objectivity and empathy; proactively take moves to resolve conflicts, develop relationships.

(6) **Innovation:** Knowledge workers are trained to think outside the obvious frames of thought and thus innovate new modes of action; they are expected to be open to accepting new ideas; be inquisitive and look for new ideas enthusiastically and thereby contribute in area of work other than his own.

(7) **Planning and organisation:** Once new ideas about action are generated it is necessary to prioritise the different courses of action; evaluate these priorities and sequences of action; empower subordinates to achieve desired results by using resources optimally and process effectively.

(8) **Strategic thinking:** It is necessary to find out and differentiate between short-term and long-term perspectives of the actions that are accorded highest priority. The actions are conceptualized and transformed into results so as to improve the competitive advantage of the organisation.

(9) **Team work:** This task is to be so organised as to be performed in synergy with a group of people. The roles and responsibilities of team members are clarified and they are supported so as to achieve higher level of performance. It is necessary to encourage collaborative teamwork among members.

When two firms merge it is necessary to find out what people know, who knows what and to leverage what they each know to converge two corporate cultures. Merger company and merged company have to share knowledge about clients, skills, experience expertise, methods and policies. It is necessary to provide up-to-date information on post merger integration activities. Ganesh Natarajan and Sandhya Shekhar recommended, in their work titled 'Knowledge Management: Enabling Business Growth' that knowledge creator's contribution and knowledge users rate are important in knowledge management. This can be done by documenting their names as thought leaders, sending 'thank you' notes, awarding 'knowledge bucks' prizes for contributing good ideas and announcing spot bonuses for exemplary knowledge sharing efforts.

Many a problems arise in introducing and practicing knowledge management. However, solutions to these problems are not available out of box. Different solutions are to be searched for the same problems in knowledge management. To create culturally and technologically congenial atmosphere for sharing knowledge is the major contribution in resolving these problems and in making knowledge management a success.

It is necessary to align main function and program of the organisation with knowledge management. With a view to do that we must plan a program of knowledge management on permanent basis and become successful by continuous functioning. Knowledge management and knowledge sharing depend to a large extend on the ethos of the organisation. The four-point program of knowledge management is K-need, K-acquisition framework, K-net design and K-net implementation. Success and impact of knowledge management on the competitiveness of the organisation can be measured on indices comprising of – customer satisfaction, cost reduction, change in employee attitude, better time to market, sales effectiveness, new product sales, employee turnover, number of knowledge management initiatives, increase in sharing management responsibility, improved productivity at the individual and organisational level.

About eighty percent of the organisations in the developed countries have introduced knowledge management practices and are reaping advantages of that. With globalisation and integration of national economies into global economy, it is imperative that organisations in developing countries adopt these modern practices of management to gain and retain competitive advantage.

References

(1) Drucker Peter F. *An Introductory View of Management*, Harper and Row Publishers Inc., 1997, p. 580.

(2) Brooking Annier. *Corporate Memory*, International Thomson Press, 1999.

(3) Senge Peter. *The Fifth Discipline: The Art and Practice of the Learning Organisation*, Double Day Currency, New York, 1990.

❑ ❑ ❑

8 Intellectual Capital

It has been realized in last twenty-five years that companies are paying more attention to soft capital and nurturing it, caring it, so that they can grow faster than those concentrating on development of physical and financial capital. Karl Eric Sweshi puts this argument in his book knowledge Company, He further argues that human capacity to collect, assimilate and use knowledge is unlimited. Many a companies create huge wealth by utilizing this knowledge fully, efficiently and effectively. Intellectual capital increases by sharing it with others. Discussion on intellectual capital began in all seriousness with Tom Starwarts article titled Brain Power published in Fortune magazine in 1991. Management of organisations began to realize that there is huge treasure of implicit knowledge in our companies that must be transmitted in explicit knowledge and used to create wealth. However, people were puzzled as to how to do it. Capacity of intellectual capital to create wealth is much greater than the capacity of traditional factors namely land, labour and capital.

Economics has come to discuss from ages the fundamental factors of production-land, labour and capital. However, discussion on intellectual capital is hardly a quarter century old. Intellect of employees in an organisation is company's asset; however, it is necessary to identify where it resides, what is its nature. Unfortunately it is difficult to describe. That is why there is no universally acceptable definition of intellectual capital. People seem to be defining intellectual capital as per their interests and approaches. Academics interested in knowledge and education describe intellectual capital as human capital and concentrate on its constituent factors. People connected with knowledge management consider computer based information system as intellectual capital. Development of "ideas and concepts" is creation of intellectual capital and the essence of management of intellectual capital is in creating more effectively "new ideas and concepts". People related with capital market consider intellectual capital as business asset and think it imperative to provide information to shareholders of intellectual capital in terms of rupees and sterling pounds and dollars. Shareholders try to analyze from annual reports of companies how is intellectual capital utilized by the company. Managers of business houses considering intellectual capital as business asset and pay more attention on maximizing its value creation capability.

MEANING OF INTELLECTUAL CAPITAL

Knowledge that can be transformed into profit is intellectual capital. Business organisations earning profit by utilizing intellectual capital are knowledge organisations. Power of Intellect leveraged and given formal form for creation of wealth is intellectual capital. Meaningful experience, technology used in business organisation, relations established with customers and trade related skill are intellectual capital. As a result of the intellectual capital business organisation acquires competitive advantage in the market. Some thinkers include logos, trade marks, leadership in technology, training programs run for employees and the speed with which response is given to customer demand, in intellectual capital. Intellectual capital is imbibed into people in business organisation, structure of the organisation and customers of the organisation. Intellectual capital can be implicit as well as explicit. Some people believe that intellectual capital is created by interaction between people in the organisation, organisational structure and customers of the organisation.

Intellectual capital must be comparatively competitive. Business organisations can leverage competitiveness of their knowledge workers by doing following four things (1) by inducing the workers to suggest new ideas, (2) by making them agree to share knowledge that they have with colleagues, (3) by making employees eager to learn new things, novel ideas and modern technique, and (4) by making them give importance to create loyal and active customers. Intellectual assets are the knowledge stored in codified form. To get explicit knowledge of a person recorded in some media is the knowledge stored in codified form. If this knowledge is secured legally it becomes intellectual property. This form of intellectual capital is exhibited in Table 8.1.

Table 8.1
Intellectual Capital and Its Components

	Human Capital	*Intellectual Assets*	*Intellectual Property*
(A)	Experience	Programs of education and training	Patents
(B)	Knowledge of producing goods or providing service	Search and Research	Copyright
(C)	Skill	Work	Trademark
(D)	Innovativeness. Production process, Documentation, Graphs, and Maps.	Stock of information	Business secrets.

Discussion in foregoing paragraphs makes it clear that human capital, organisational capital and customer capital are the three factors that make intellectual capital. Let me discuss the three constituents of intellectual capital in greater detail in the next section.

UNDERSTANDING INTELLECTUAL CAPITAL

Every entity, individual or corporate takes stock of its status, rate of growth, direction of development, rate of return on investment. Present reporting format of this state is based on a model of financial statements developed over a period of century from 1868. Balance sheets, profit and loss account, income expenditure statement, trading account, the components of this model are stock statements and historical records. They fall short in predicting how the entity would fair in future. Accounting process on the basis of which these statements stand is well set in their ways. But they have trouble in doing the traditional auditing of financial assets. The existing methods and concepts of accounting, budgeting and planning are biased against anything that is not tangible asset. Tangible things get disproportionate attention and intangible things get sloughed away. These methods equip users with tools to value, measure and manage only tangible assets and woefully few tools to maintain and increase competitive advantage and generate wealth. If management focus and company valuations continue to be based on traditional accounting numbers, then the result will be serious distortions in the effective operation and value of companies.

Intellectual capital does not replace the financial system of a company, but rather complements it to be able to visualize and thus manage the system based on the total value of the company. The increasingly technical complexity of modern business and relatively more time required for personnel to gain experience in many vital areas promise to continue the trend towards making human capital the most critical resource an organisation possesses. While financial performance is easily measured, it is just tip of ice berg. The organisations true validity and promise or conversely its weakness and sources of potential disaster lie below the water line. When the whole agenda is dominated by the financial results of the firm, it is difficult to understand how you can invest in human capital and know that when you are investing in such intangible things that you are actually getting a tangible outcome. Whereas financial accounting provides a rear view perspective. The new system of accounting intellectual capital promises to help the firm more thoroughly examine its competitive capabilities and future prospects. We need to measure intellectual capital and concentrate more on the developmental factors that keep the intangible value.

Formerly managers' functions were to plan, organise, execute and measure (POEM). In Knowledge Company his jobs are more essentially human tasks, namely, sensing, judging, creating and building relationship. An organisation that is not managing knowledge is not paying attention to business. Till now intellectual assets have gone unmanaged, that negligence has cost much – the money wasted and the opportunities squandered. Intellectual capital is knowledge that exists in an organisation that can be used to create differential advantage. Knowledge is tacit rather than explicit. On this assumption that knowledge is tacit, the organisation adopt values, principles and ways of doing things which in turn determines how it makes decisions and shapes the collective behaviour of its members. This process makes tacit knowledge so as to produce higher value assets.

For companies to succeed in the next century, they will have to find a way of managing present by looking to the future rather than the past. Doing things inside old context will not be enough. A corporation has to shift from being a place of production to place of being thinking. This improves, doing something better, faster, cheaper and more the planned efficiency gains, productivity gains. A rupee invested in human capital returns eight times more than a rupee spent on machinery because human capital leads to innovation. The knowledge company does not care much about owning physical assets because intellectual assets replace physical one. In fact fewer the assets better. So long as a company has intellectual capital, the company gets the revenue without the burden and expenses of managing and paying for assets.

Intellectual capital is the intellectual material that has been formalized, captured and leveraged to produce a higher value asset. Intellectual capital is the possession of the knowledge, applied experience, and organisational technology, customer relationships and professional skills that provide the company a competitive edge in the market. Many authors extend the concept of intellectual capital to include brand names, trademarks, technology leadership, and ongoing employee training and even speed of response to client service calls. Intellectual capital is located in people, structures and company's customers. Once intellectual capital is identified, it becomes possible to ask questions that allow you to identify and measure tacit as well as explicit capital. We have to seek ways to tangiblise-hidden value. Intangible capital is raw material from which financial results are made. Intellectual capital is created from interplay among human, structural and customer capital.

HUMAN CAPITAL

Human capital is the capabilities of the individuals required to provide solutions to the customers. It is the source of innovation and renewal. There must be knowledge flow. Success hangs on employees informed and full-hearted willingness to offer ideas and learn new tasks. That is on human capitals wringing gains out of physical capital. Employees must understand that their ideas can make a difference. They are immensely valuable assets. Protecting the equity in a career is a lot more important than protecting the equity in a house. The management value of investing in human capital is about three times greater than the value of investing in machinery. It is important to hire a mind than to hire an hand. Employ only that much human capital that you can employ and use profitably. Human capital grows when organisation uses more of what people know and when more people know more stuff that is useful to the organisation. If everybody in the organisation can be involved the best ideas will rise to the top. To use more of what people know, companies need to create opportunities for private knowledge to be made public, tacit knowledge to be made explicit. Human capital is easily dissipated. It needs to be massed and concentrated. We have to develop leveraged skills and proprietary skills. We need to develop people that add high value to their job and are difficult to be replaced.

STRUCTURAL CAPITAL

Structural capital is the organisational capability including physical systems to transmit and store intellectual capital. Structural capital creates the environment by which smart people come to work here and stay here. The best structural capital is one that does not seem to exist: a transparent, super conducting connection between people and customers. The best structural capital is the least noticeable. The efficiency, the agility with which a company augments human capital is the true measure of the effectiveness of structural capital. The ultimate purpose of structural capital is to connect people to experts and information and customers to the company. Customer capital must configure itself so that innovations move to customers very fast. Structural capital takes from employees what they know and delivers it to the customers. It marshals the resources of the corporation to augment and support the ideas and work of employees. Structural capital provides the information that enables employees to do a better job. Patents, product, and process improvement, data bases, networks are components of structural capital. Creation, collection and dissemination of information are the most important function of structural capital. Those who learn to take advantage of this increasing amount of information economically become much more successful. But one should not be over concerned with information.

Structural capital should codify bodies of knowledge that can be transferred, to preserve the recipes that might otherwise be lost. It should connect people to data, experts and expertise-including bodies of knowledge on a just-in-time basis. Information should neither be pushed to employees; rather they must be free to pull the information they want instead of information being sent, it must be accessible, the ability to get it if an employee needs it.

Structural capital must provide knowledge that you know you do not have and knowledge that you do not know that you do not have. Value of structural capital can be raised by leveraging through specialization. Work Innovation Network (WIN) must be developed. Programs like WIN and knowledge links reflect a healthy balance between the human and technical sides of structural capital. Human capital begets structural intellectual capital, which begets human capital. Human capital is what builds structural capital, but the better your structural capital, the better your human capital is likely to be. Structural capital is the organisational capabilities of the organisation to meet market requirements.

CUSTOMER CAPITAL

Customer capital is the value of an organisation's relationship with the people with whom it does business. It is the depth (penetration), width (coverage) and attachment (loyalty) to the organisation-relationship capital. It is this relationship with customers that turns intellectual capital into revenue. Brand equity is a form of customer capital for which well-established valuation methods exist. It is done by calculating the premium customers are willing to pay for a branded one against a generic product. Shared knowledge is the ultimate form of customer capital.

Every company with customers has customer capital. Customer capital is the value of its franchise, its ongoing relationships with the people or organisation to which it sells. Of the three broad categories of intellectual assets-human, structural and customer capital – customers are the most obviously valuable. They pay the bills. And because they do, the footprints they leave on financial statements are easier to follow than those made by people, systems or capabilities. Though many companies' financial reporting systems are not set up to do so, it is relatively easy to track indicators of the customer capital, such as market share, customer retention and defection rates and per-customer profitability. However, customer capital is probably the worst managed of all intangible assets. Many companies do not know who their customers are but treat them as adversaries rather than assets, with take it or leave it arrogance. That customer capital is valuable may seem obvious, but it is startling to know just how valuable it is. Getting that kind of a return on customer capital requires more than acknowledging that customer relationships are assets, not just events. It demands understanding dynamics of managing this asset.

It is a principle of managing intellectual capital that when information is power, power flows downstream toward the customer. We have to try to empower the customer; because empowered customers enormously increase the amount of information a company has about its market and customers have about it. Turning this knowledge into customer capital requires the ability to respond flexibly to individual customers want. One-to-one dealings with customers depend on human and structural capital to develop the ability to do mass customization. Economists consider this as consumer surplus.

Profit margin is shrinking as competition increases. In such circumstances an organisation can sustain only if the buyer is loyal in purchasing from the same company again and again. That means, to create trust about our product and/or service is the role of customer capital. This trust cannot be held by just providing quality product and charging competitive price. Because, other companies also offer the same things, therefore, if the company has to survive it has to pay concerned attention to innovation, continuously upgrading the product and provision of service after sales to the customer. Loyal customers are created out of loyal behavior of satisfied employees. Performance and profits of the company depend upon following four factors related to employee behaviour and approach. These four factors are —

(1) Employees must realize that they are given opportunities to do the work that they can perform in best possible manner.

(2) Employees must feel and they must become aware that their views, their opinions are taken care of.

(3) Employees must realize that their colleagues value quality in their work.

(4) Employees must feel that the work that they do is in line with the mission of the organisation.

If we consider human aspect of customer capital, we feel that loyal employees alone can create loyal customer. Employees behave courteously and positively with the customers if they are satisfied with the work they do and they derive inducement out of their work. In todays competitive world competitive advantage of a company depends upon its relations with the customers. Knowledge-workers approach towards their work and feeling about organisation in which they work are the factors that decide the direction of company's relations with the customers. On the basis of their relationship a possibility of customer buying goods from the same company again and again and recommending it to others arises. Employees must feel that the values and mission of the organisation are their own values and mission and these things must mean the same to all. Knowledge-workers consider this organisation as their own, only if the values and mission of the organisation are depicted in its decisions and acts.

VALUE OF AN ORGANISATION

Value of a commodity is determined by its utility to the customer. Value of a commodity or service is created by co-operative efforts of the three constituents of an organisation — human capital, organisational capital and customer capital. Value of a product or service depends upon its utility. Value is comparative; value is not the price of the product. Value is the satisfaction derived from ownership of a product or service. Value of an organisation is determined by the knowledge created for its commercial use in future and capacity of the organisation to earn maximum profit in the present times from the use of this knowledge. Value of an organisation can be determined by discounting future cash flows. Organisation managing intellectual capital efficiently has to take into consideration short-term as well as long-term factors while calculating its value. Short-term factors in determining value of an organisation are, products produced by the organisation, their quality, uses, price charged for the product and the systems adopted to command loyalty of the customers. Long-term factors determining value of an organisation are the objectives that the organisation cherishes to achieve in future and ethical base on which its values are founded. Value of an organisation is enshrined out of the confidence and co-operation of all constituents of the organisation. Value creation is creation of new knowledge and turning it into innovations having commercial value. Extraction of value from intellectual capital is done by transforming it into something that is useful to the organisation.

Business organisation cannot alter its resources often. It cannot improve its competency suddenly. Development of business with a view to increase value of the organisation is a very complex matter. Organisation commanding sophisticated production systems and resources do reap competitive advantage over the other organisations because of lower cost of production and better quality of products. Organisation having non-immitable products and resources also derives competitive advantage.

An organisation can create value in many a different ways by utilizing its intellectual capital. There are four major methods of doing this. They can be multiplied by permutation and combination of these major methods. The four major methods are:

(1) Direct value creation: An organisation can increase its revenue and profits by selling goods and services that are developed by innovation done with the help of intellectual capital. Profits can be increased by improving quality of the product or service and reducing cost of production with the help of intellectual capital.

(2) Indirect value creation: Business organisation improves its status in the industry and commands loyalty of the customers on the basis of intellectual capital it has. Such organisation can bargain purchases at lower price by utilizing its status in the industry.

(3) Offensive value creation: Business organisation defeats rival organisations in the market by utilising its status and power in the industry. As a result its comparative value improves.

(4) Defensive value creation: An organisation implements measures to defeat the strategies of rival organisation that are introduced to belittle it. The organisation improves its value by implementing various policy measures.

Many a times the strategy of using intellectual capital may be offensive as well defensive at the same time. For example, measures introduced to reduce cost of production, strategies of buying or acquiring rival organisation with a view to reduce competition, strategies introduced to raise barriers to obstruct entry of an organisation, measures taken to command loyalty of buyers and efforts to defend our innovation by taking patents are simultaneously offensive and defensive measures of creating organisational value.

An organisation has to create value from its intellectual capital so as to achieve its objectives. The program beginning from conceptualization of an idea or innovation to the end of achieving objectives is a value chain. A full documentation is done when search for a new product is completed. If that search is important from the point of organisations mission, it is patented to prevent other organisations using and imitating it. Then the product is produced on commercial scale and revenue is earned by selling that product. This value chain is exhibited in figure 8.1.

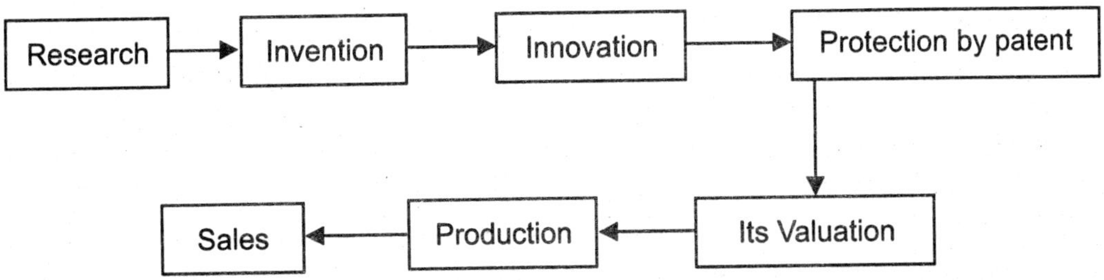

Figure 8.1
Chain Describing Creation of Value from Intellectual Capital

Value creation can be accentuated by using trade-marks extensively, by harvesting benefits of reputation and goodwill of the organisation and by reaping benefits of customer relations

In this process a review needs to be taken as a part of the broad system of managing intellectual capital. It should be seen, whether production of new goods or services based on new idea or innovation would be profitable or not. If this act is likely to be beneficial then only that product and/or process is patented and protected. Strategies are to be formulated to produce this product or provide this service. A comparative study is made as to whether the benefit from producing and selling this product and/or service would be greater or smaller than selling this patent to other organisation. It is also necessary to find out how maximum value can be created from the intellectual capital. Additional value can be created also by gaining customer recognition to the trade names from quality and advertising. Amul, Close-up, Brooke-bond are a few examples. Additional value can be created by establishing cordial relations with customers. Eureka Forbes is an illustration. However, customer relations, reputation and recognition of the name of industrial house, and names of goods do not carry any legal protection granted under trademarks and patents. That is why protection of customer relations, reputation of the name of industrial house depends upon customer loyalty and capacity of the company to create value for the customers.

METHOD OF MEASURING ORGANISATION VALUE

It becomes necessary for different reasons to assess the standard, the status of the organisation and its monetary value. When an organisation is being merged or is purchased/taken over by another firm then it becomes necessary to calculate money value of the former organisation. Patrick H. Salivan has developed a formula to calculate monetary value of an organisation.

Monetary value of an organisation = Market value or original value of tangible assets, which ever is less PLUS discounted present money value of future cash inflows.

VCO = V (TA)+DCF

Where VCO is Money value of the organisation

V is Money value

TA is Tangible assets,

DCF is discounted present money value of the future cash inflows

Let us discuss the method of calculating value of a company when it is being amalgamated or purchased by another organisation. Let us suppose that A and B are two business organisations. They have assets in the form of tangible, intellectual capital and complementary assets. Value of the three types of assets will have to be taken into account and the formula can be rewritten as below.

Money value of new organisation = Money value of tangible assets of company A + Money Value of tangible assets of company B + (Money value of intellectual capital of company A + Money Value of complementary business assets of the company A + money value of intellectual capital of company B + Money value of complementary business assets of company B + Money value of discount cash inflows of company A + Money value of discounted cash inflows of company B).

This can be represented in a formula as below

$V_{new\ co} = V_{TA} + V_{DCF}$

$= [V_{TAA} + V_{TAB}] + [V(CI)_A) + (BA_A) + V(IC_A)] + [V(CI_B) + V(BA)_B) + V(IC_B)]$

Let us take an Hypothetical numerical illustration –

Table 8.2
Values of Organisations

	Item	*Company A*	*Company B*
(1)	Value of tangible assets.	Rs.10 Cr.	Rs.15 Cr.
(2)	Cash inflows of intellectual capital for next five years (Net Present Value).	Rs.20 Cr.	Rs.35 Cr.
(3)	Complementary business assets.	Rs.30 Cr.	Rs.12 Cr.
(4)	Value of intellectual capital.	Rs.13 Cr.	Rs.15 Cr.

Value of new company = Rs. 10 Cr. + Rs. 15 Cr. + Rs. 20 Cr. + 30 Cr. + Rs. 13 Cr. + Rs. 12 Cr. + Rs. 15 Cr. + Rs. 35 Cr. = Rs. 150 Crores.

Money value of companies whose shares are traded on stock exchanges can be calculated from any of the three formulae given below:

(1) Money value of organisation in stock market = Money value of tangible assets of the company (V_{TA}) + Discounted present money value of cash in-flows that the company can generate in the future (D_{CF}).

$V_m = V_{TA} + D_{CF}$.

(2) Money value of organisation in stock market = Money value of structural capital (V_{SC})+Discounted present money value of innovations created by intellectual capital of the company in future (V_{dcfic}).

$V_m = V_{sc} + V_{dcfic}$.

(3) Money value of organisation in stock market = Net Present Money value of earnings of intellectual capital of the organisation (NPV_{eic})+Money value of tangible assets (V_{TA})+Net Present Money value of earnings complementary business assets (NPV_{ecba})+Net present money value earnings of general structural capital of the organisation (NPV_{esc})

$V_m = NPV_{eic} + V_{TA} + NPV_{ecba} + (NPV_{esc})$

Where,

V_m	=	Money value of organisation in stock market.
NPV	=	Net Present Money Value calculated by discounting method.
Eic	=	Earnings of intellectual capital.
Ecba	=	Earnings of complementary business assets.
Esc	=	Earnings of structural capital.

EXTRACTION OF THE VALUE OF INTELLECTUAL CAPITAL

Intellectual capital in an organisation is its intellectual assets. It can be given protection legally in five different ways. They are – Patents, Copy-rights, trademarks, business secrets and semiconductor masks. The assets created on the basis of ideas suggested by employees, inventions done on research and innovations made by them are the property of the organisation. Above mentioned five methods are used to enable the organisation to extract value from these assets by covering them under protection. Collection of information, its analysis, editing and innovation are the ways of creating knowledge. Value can be created by utilizing this knowledge in a right way at the right time. Value extraction is to take benefit by utilizing this knowledge in a right way at a right time. Value extraction is to take benefit by utilizing the knowledge so created. It is very necessary for an organisation to be successful in the present competitive situation to create intellectual property to the maximum extent and to extract maximum value out of it. An organisation can extract maximum value from its intellectual capital by developing efficient decision-making system, by creating broad information base and by introducing appropriate work culture. Relationship between value creation and value extraction is exhibited in Table 8.3.

Table 8.3
Relationship Between Value Creation and Value Extraction

	Items	*Value Creation*	*Value Extraction*
(1)	Objective	To increase knowledge of employees to innovate newly or by improving earlier innovation for commercialisation.	To leverage innovations of the organization to increase profits and enhance strategic status of the organisation.
(2)	Emphasis on intellectual capital.	To give emphasis on employee capital	To give emphasis on intellectual property.
(3)	Programs to be implemented for that	To create knowledge To share capital To learn and secure knowledge To make organization dynamic To use information technology.	To decide in which form do we need value and how to measure it To monitor process of innovation To create and store intellectual property To evaluate comparative value of extracted value To implement this program To transform extracted value into profits.

VALUE CREATION AND VALUE EXTRACTION

Creation of intellectual capital, its transformation into intellectual property and extraction of maximum value out of it is a chain process. It is necessary to achieve efficiency to maximum extent in each of the link of this chain to achieve maximum value extraction. It is like six-sigma achievement. Unless all units of all components achieve zero defect level it is not possible to reach six-sigma level in the final product. Even achieving six-sigma level of all units of all components makes the final product short of six-sigma level. Intellectual capital needs to be transformed into tangible form to extract value out of it. New products, new method of producing commodity, novel uses of the same product, innovative ways of reducing cost of production, economical use of capital, planning novel strategies of marketing, search of new markets and balanced as well as appropriate management. Of all factors in business of production are the methods of transforming intangible intellectual capital into tangible intellectual assets. Some of these intellectual assets can be legally protected from invasion of rival business organisations. Patents, copyright, trademark, trade secrets and semiconductor masks are the legal means available to protect our intellectual assets. Intellectual capital in tangible forms is intellectual property. Organisation can extract value by trading intellectual property. However, one needs to protect its products that are in the market. Organisation has to take, at the same time, measures to produce maximum from joint ventures floated by it. Value extraction can be done even from strategic co-operation. Decisions taken for extracting value from intellectual capital can be used at strategic level also.

Intellectual property can be used for value extraction in future only. Some thinkers opine that the best use of valuable asset like intellectual property is to protect our innovations from offensive stance of rival firms. Objectives of use of intellectual property should be limited to those four basic goals for which patents are obtained. These objectives are — (1) Innovations patented should be protected from others using them, (2) to construct the structure of organisation around the strategic business factors and keep this structure as decentralized as possible, (3) to earn maximum profits from sale of services and products that are produced by using strategic business factors, and (4) ownership of these innovations should be vested with business units and they should be authorised to decide which innovations should be patented. However, one danger arising out of such arrangement needs to be avoided. It is quite likely that business unit may begin to put more emphasis on commercialization of innovations and may begin to move away from objectives. Some thinkers argue that organisations intending to extract maximum value from intellectual property can use innovations to enhance the value of business organisation. While some thinkers opine that organisation can use intellectual property as business assets of the organisations. Organisations considering innovations as business assets of the company can think of earning profit by selling this technology to other companies rather than trying to earn profits by selling commodities produced on the basis of these innovations. Patented innovations can be gainfully utilized to reach markets where we cannot enter by launching joint ventures or by signing memorandum of understanding and thereby can earn maximum profits. Both the approaches, namely earning profits by selling commodities produced with the help of innovation and earning profits by commercial sale of technology based on innovations, must be welcome. Acceptance of such varied approaches opens up alternative opportunities for extraction of value from intellectual assets. However, while implementing such approaches it is necessary to harmonise technology used in the organisation with the method of value extraction. For example, If an organisation has introduced the system of outsourcing as a method of value extraction, it must be seen that the production method, quality assurance system, cost accounting practices must be aligned in outsourcing company and outsourced company. Then only value extraction can reach the peak point. That is why two wheelers and four wheeler auto vehicle producing foreign companies or MNCs insist on training of employees and tool rooms in outsourcing companies to be of our standard. They also make it imperative to follow just-in-time method of providing components as a method of materials management.

Value can be extracted by creation of intellectual capital in the business organisation, by nurturing and transmitting it as well by transforming intellectual capital into intellectual asset and intellectual property. Value can be extracted also by reducing cost on intellectual capital. Taxes and other expenditure on patents can be reduced by cancelling patents that are either out of date or that are not useful from the point of business. Revenue from intellectual property can be increased either by transferring patents from organisations paying less amount of royalty to the organisations ready to pay more amount of royalty or by gett'ng more amount of royalty agreed upon by the same organisation. Marval Comics Company (Estd. 1940) could earn better royalty by giving rights of using their core product Spiderman to Holleywood film makers. Value that can be extracted from intellectual capital can be increased to maximum level, even in short period, by following various methods. As against this, value extraction can be increased in medium term of about five years by developing innovations of better quality and by seeing that even though they are few in numbers are of greater commercial value. More emphasis must be laid on innovation division while doing commercial negotiations. More licenses should be granted for using patents. Goodwill of patents of innovations can be increased by floating joint ventures. Goodwill of patents of innovations can also be increased by signing memorandum of understanding with other organisations. Organisation having high quality innovations has always an upper hand in negotiations. In such a situation royalty on use of patents can be got increased. If all business is done in this way, business organisation can extract maximum value from intellectual capital even in medium term period.

Strategies of fundamental nature need to be framed and implemented for extracting value from intellectual capital. Patenting innovation secures protection from competition. Even if an organisation is not likely to make use of such patents, it can secure protection from the efforts of other rival organisations by producing the commodities with the help of different types of raw material or different production processes that the organisation has innovated. In this way an organisation can build up a protective wall of supplementary patents around main patent. Problems likely to arise in future can be avoided by patenting at present the products, production processes, production techniques and technologies that the organisation is likely to use in future. This gives the organisation freedom in preparing drawing of the product. Such patents enable the organisation to secure new cooperators. The organisation must silently and secretly concentrate its attention on developing innovations by undertaking research in areas of its core competence. Thus, the organisation on one hand should expand its core competence areas and on the other hand at the same time should shed off non-core competence areas. Raymond, on one hand, purchased colour plus Fashions Private Limited at a price of Rs. 58 crores and broadened its core competence in ready-mades and apparels. Prior to that Raymonds sold out its cement factory with annual capacity of 22 lakhs tonnes at a price of Rs. 3500 per tonne installed capacity to world renowned cement producers Lafarge. In this way Raymonds reduced its liability in non-core-competence area.

All the organisations around the world make utmost efforts to create value out of new knowledge and innovations. This emphasis on knowledge creation and value creation is very correct. However, while doing this the organisation should assess whether its capacity to absorb value extracted from innovation matches its capability to create value from intellectual capital. The organisation should ensure that it possesses requisite equipment, systems and employees to absorb value extraction done from intellectual capital. Then alone the organisation can carve for itself an important and respectable place in the industry and market.

Organisations, in the fervor of creating knowledge and creating value, should not side track its responsibility to compensate those who should risk in this endeavour of knowledge creation and value creation. This is more important to extract maximum value from business knowledge that the organisation has than to create innovations and new concepts. Probably this may be a point of debate. Conclusion of this debate is related to the situation in the organisation. Organisation having many innovations should rigorously examine such innovation and select best and attractive ones for investment. Having done this, the organisation should make adequate and appropriate investment to extract maximum value from such intellectual assets and enhance ones strength and power. Equally so, the organisations not having enough commercialisable concepts and innovations should make investment to become creative.

Knowledge company secures balanced situation in the work process spread over from value creation to value extraction. The method of creating balance between the speed of creating knowledge concepts and the speed of extracting value from knowledge concepts is the optimal situation for the organisation. Balanced approach to intellectual capital management strikes this balance. However, in reality many an organisations put more stress on one of these two factors and consider that even though doing so is not optimal it is adequately rewarding. Many an organisations spend more energy, time and resources on extracting value from intellectual capital than spent on developing intellectual capital. And they do not realize that their intellectual capital is wasted.

Figure 8.2 measures value creation on vertical axis and value extraction on horizontal axis. We can find out how does an organisation secure balanced position.

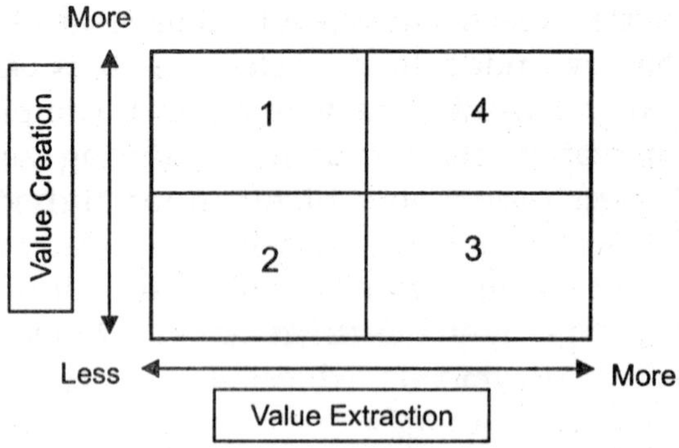

Figure 8.2
Value Creation and Value Extraction

An organisation situated in box 1 is at an imbalance because though it creates more value but it extracts very little of it. It means the process of knowledge creation and investments done in that process are not optimally utilised. Such organisation inspite of having piles of inventions and patents cannot extract adequate value for want of efficient intellectual capital management system, and it cannot reduce cost of it. Methods to remedy the situation are to install intellectual capital management system and develop processes for value extraction from intellectual capital.

As against this, the organisation situated in box 2 creates value and extracts value in limited quantity. It is necessary to educate employees in this organisation as to what is knowledge, how is knowledge created and how is this knowledge shared between employees. Such organisations are functioning on traditional models of management and they are unaware of the benefits of knowledge revolution.

The organisation situated in box 3 has developed well the process of value extraction; however, it is not able to create atmosphere conducive to continued creation of knowledge, is not able to develop evaluating methods required for commercialisation of knowledge and earning profits out of it. Such organisation needs to make much effort on creating and nurturing knowledge.

Organisation functioning in box 4 is on the vanguard in creating value from intellectual capital and efficiently extracting value out of it. It must be able to shoulder the challenge of maintaining continuity in it. It must develop, for that, a system of auditing intellectual capital. It must periodically examine comparative competitiveness in creating value out of intellectual capital and extracting value out of it. Such company can re-organise means of creating intellectual capital so as to become effectively supportive to business strategies and logistic arrangement.

Considering location of our organisation in figure 8.2 it can evaluate its intellectual capital effectively and can implement methods and measures to come out of that situation more effectively and efficiently.

The role of intellectual capital in an organisation becomes amply clear from the objectives that the company cherishes and the strategy it follows. The role of intellectual capital has remained to be offensive in organisation providing services. However, at least in earlier years, the role of intellectual capital in organisations based on technology has remained to be defensive. It is so because intellectual capital has to play the role of creating barriers for rival companies to prevent them from either coming into this market or from introducing new innovation. It has also to play role of creating protective wall for major and sensitive patents. As a result rival companies cannot copy, cannot imitate our innovations. In reality, organisations based on technology do use their intellectual capital for offensive strategy, either by selling patented innovations or by floating joint ventures or by signing memorandum of understanding. Thereby the organisation can set its own standards in the market and can establish its power and image in the market. On the basis of this power established in the market the organisation can make other organisation buy its technology, innovations at higher price. The organisation, in this way, exhibits its strength to the market and to the economy. In this way it can make stock market and the government to chalk out a policy, to take decisions that are in the interest of the organisation. Reliance Industries Ltd. is an illustration of this.

Once the role of intellectual capital in the organisation is fixed, the organisation has to develop internal capability to enable intellectual capital play its role effectively. This capability can be created and enhanced by implementing following nine-point program.

These nine points are –

(1) Organisation has to decide which type of intellectual capital it has to develop. Accordingly it has to create a portfolio of patents and patent rights.

(2) Organisation has to create an intellectual capital management system.

(3) It has to prepare a database, on computer system, related to patents, their detailed description and related information.

(4) It has to make a comparative review of our own patents and patents of rival organisations, their status in the market and capacity of the organisation to develop new innovations.

(5) Organisation has to establish a very strong, efficient and effective Research and Development wing. It has to assess commerciability of innovations developed by this wing and protect them by patenting. Such patents should be taken even for those innovations that may be used in future.

(6) Organisation should develop a permanent system of developing new patents, taking patents regularly and deleting patents that have become outdated or are of no commercial value any more.

(7) It has to develop a system of making qualitative and commercial evaluation of its intellectual capital.

(8) Organisation has to develop infrastructure facilities for extracting maximum value from its intellectual assets. It should undertake periodical analysis of value extraction system.

(9) Organisation must develop capability of establishing joint ventures with worthy partners or signing memorandum of understanding for effective and efficient utilisation of its intellectual capital.

Every organisation needs to measure intellectual capital that it possesses, so its role in the organisation can be fixed. If the organisation suffers from shortage of intellectual capital it can take measures to accentuate intellectual capital. I have developed a detailed comprehensive model for measuring intellectual capital. It is discussed in section IV.

METHODS FOR MEASURING INTELLECTUAL CAPITAL

Benefits associated with disclosing intellectual capital are significant enough that some companies have begun disclosing it voluntarily. Three methods of computing intellectual capital are envisioned. They are—

(1) Return on Assets

It uses average pretax earnings of a company for three to five years. These average earnings are then divided by the average tangible assets of the company over the same period of time. The resulting ROA is compared with the companys industry average to calculate the difference. If this difference is zero or negative, the company does not have an excess intellectual capital over its industry average. Thus, the value of intellectual is assumed to be zero. However, if the difference between the company's ROA and its industry average is positive, then the company is assumed to have excess intellectual capital over its industry. This excess ROA is then multiplied by the companys average tangible assets to calculate an average annual excess earning. Dividing this excess earning by the companys average cost of capital, one can derive an estimate of the value of intellectual capital. The formula is

$$\text{Value of intellectual capital of a company } \frac{AEBT_t5}{ATA_t5} = \frac{IEBT_t5}{IATA_t5}$$

Where, AEBT = Average earnings of the company before tax for five years.
ATA = Average Tangible Assets of the company for five years.
IEBT = Industrys earnings before tax for five years.
IATA = Industrys Average Tangible Assets for five years.

(2) Market Capitalisation Method

This method is based on the capital market premium. The excess of a companys market capitalization over its stockholders equity is its intellectual capital. To calculate market capitalization more accurately, the historical financial statements must be adjusted for the effects of inflation or replacement costs. Using historical data may distort the measurement, particularly, in industries with large balances of old capital assets.

The formula is –

Market capitalization = Average market value over last three years i.e., market value of share × number of shares subscribed – paid up capital discounted at the rate of inflation over three years.

$$= \text{Market value of shares} \times \text{number of shares subscribed} - \frac{\text{Paid up capital}}{(1+i)}$$

Where, "i" is rate inflation.

(3) Direct Intellectual Capital Method

In the first instance various components of intellectual capital are identified. They are – (a) Customer loyalty, (b) intangible assets such as patents, (c) technological assets such as know how, (d) human assets such as education and training, (e) structural assets such as the information systems. Once, these components are all measured, they can be aggregated to derive the total value of a companys intellectual capital. This method is the most complex, but also the most accurate means of measuring intellectual capital. This method is also expensive to implement because of the large number of components that have to be identified and individually measured.

(A) **Customer loyalty:** Number of customer who have been consistently buying from the company for last five years × monetary value of purchases over last five years, divided by five.

(B) **Patents:** Number of patents registered over last five years – number of orphan patents = number of live patents × market value of the products sold based on these patents over five years, divided by five.

(C) **Technology assets:** Royalty paid over last five years for the technology adopted from other companies + research and development expenditure on development of new technology over five years, divided by five.

(D) **Human assets:** Annual expenditure incurred by employees in acquiring University education + average expenditure incurred on training of employees over the last five years.

(E) **Structural assets:** Average investment in last five years on purchase and installation of computers, cost of terminals and their interconnection and cost of software like floppies etc.

Therefore:

Intellectual capital = Average value of purchases done by customers who consistently purchase from the company over five years.

+ Average sales value of products of live patents

+ Average royalty payments and average R and D expenditure on development of new technology.

+ Cost of acquiring University education by employees + Average cost of employee training.

However, these methods fall short in case of those companies and/or divisions using intellectual abilities and time as capital. They would prefer to compute Return on Investment on Time as a resource and time as capital. In such cases we would have to find a standardized method of valuing or quantifying intellectual capital and returns accrued by company from the use of intellectual capital and value of time spent on services provided by intellectual capital. As we will discuss in the fifth section, we will calculate value of intellectual capital in the form of monetary units. Return from such intellectual capital is the total of earnings after interest and tax but before depreciation minus value added by physical assets. This is labour productivity. Value of time as capital can be calculated by the time spent on contacting customers, maintaining customers minus time spent on customers lost to be multiplied by the salary of the personnel contracting the customers. This is also called as entrepreneurial return on investment.

One more way to evaluate the intellectual capital value is to measure the net market value of the company. James Tobin has developed a ratio commonly called as TOBIN's Q. It compares the market value of an asset with its replacement cost. He developed a ratio as a way to predict corporate investment decisions independent of macro economic factors such as interest rates. Tobin's Q is the market-to-book ratio. It can be calculated as –

Price per share × total numbers of shares outstanding = Market value of the company.

Paid up capital-debt = Book value of the company.

Therefore: Tobin's Q is $\dfrac{\text{Market value of the company}}{\text{Book value of the company}}$

It is in a way monopoly returns. It is the company's ability to get unusually high profits because it has got something no one else has. It is the manifestation of intellectual power. This ratio reflects the value of investment in technology and human capital.

Having discussed the meaning and characteristics of intellectual capital as well methods of measuring the intellectual capital, in the fourth section, we embark upon to discuss methods of measuring human capital, structural capital and customer capital in sections five, six and seven respectively. In the eighth section, we will discuss the model of measuring intellectual capital in totality. While developing this model, the fact that globalization of Indian economy is effected, is taken full care of. Equally so, a note has been taken of the fact that, with opening of Indian economy, enabling foreign companies to come to India, and Indian companies to spread their wings in foreign coutries, the very organisational structure of MNCs has undergone a fundamental change. This model has made a modest effort to evaluate intellectual capital in such a changing environment.

MEASURING HUMAN CAPITAL

Human capital is the abilities, the knowledge, skill and experience, competencies, creativity and innovativeness of individual. The frequency of generation of new ideas, frequency of implementation of these ideas in the organisation and their success ratio determine human capital. Thus, to measure value of human capital of an organisation a common model encompassing the various aspects of human resources is to be developed.

In what follows, I have first described how leadership index, motivation index and empowerment index are to be developed. Then I have discussed Adjusted Discounted Future Wages Method to account value of human resources. At the end of the discussion I have analysed values and weightages to be ascribed to these indices and other components that make the value of human capital.

LEADERSHIP INDEX

Below are given twenty-four statements for answers of which five-point scale is applied to evaluate the leadership qualities of individuals. Leadership scores of all, lower, middle and top management people are added up and an average is calculated by dividing number of members of each status of management. Weightage ONE is ascribed to average leadership index of lower management group, Weightage THREE is taken to calculate middle management group index and Weightage FIVE is allotted to evaluate leadership index of top management group. Lower management group comprises of supervisory level employees, Middle management tribe comprises of assistant heads and heads of divisions and top management enclave comprises of Chief Managers and members of the Board of Directors.

Statements:

(1) I know myself, my values and skills, my strengths and weaknesses.

(2) I am confident of meeting most challenges and emerging intact and feeling good about myself.

(3) I have a vision of where we ought to be going as group, community, society, people.

(4) I call my group, community, or organisation to act out of values that transcend the day-to-day, business, as usual, garden variety of norms of operation.

(5) I possess above-average intelligence, I have lived long and perceptively and use that intelligence to create wisdom and my actions are tempered by judgment.

(6) I am constantly excited by the learning process, which stretches out before me as far as I can see.

(7) I am constantly renewed by what I learn and my interaction with others.

(8) I am constantly amazed at how I pick out the very broadest implications of enterprises and projects which others see in narrow terms.

(9) I see events today along a continuum in time, with major trends and the sweep of history propelling change.

(10) I see the way to success is through steady coalition building.

(11) I see great wisdom in building the capabilities of others, empowering them, motivating them to do their best.

(12) I possess stamina, energy, tenacity and enthusiasm for my work.

(13) I have the courage to take on what I know is right, regardless of my critics and detractors.

(14) I possess high integrity and intellectual honesty.

(15) I have high moral character, I know what is right and wrong, and act accordingly.

(16) I am willing to take risks for something I believe in, whether for people or for ideals.

(17) I am an active, effective listener, people seek me out as listener.

(18) I present my ideals logically, forcefully, and effectively, my ideas are often adopted.

(19) I understand the nature for power, I exercise and respect power.

(20) I translate authority as responsibility and assume my share of it.

(21) I achieve results through concentrating on clear goals, over time, I build small success in to something larger.

(22) I have a healthy sense of humour, I laugh at myself and keep cynicism and sarcasm in rein.

(23) I keep perspective; I know where we are in a process, how far we have come, how far we have got to go, what is important in the short-run and in the long.

(24) I am known for my flexibility, responding to a variety of situations with appropriate skills, styles and perceptions.

Score of leadership index less than forty is supposed to be a poor quality of leadership; between forty and eighty is a fair performance; score between eighty and one hundred twenty is better leadership and greater than one hundred twenty is exemplenery leadership.

MOTIVATION INDEX

Performance of employee depends to a large extent upon self motivation and motivation of subordinates. Answers to the statement enlisted below are to be evaluated on five-point scale. Motivational score of all lower, middle and top management is added up to arrive at organisational motivational index. It is divided by the number of members of each status of management. Weightage ONE is ascribed to average motivation index of lower management, Weightage THREE is taken to calculate index of middle management and Weightage FIVE is allotted to evaluate motivation index of top management group. The status classification is as given for leadership index.

Statements:

(1) Describe yourself through the eyes of your main subordinates. Would he/she be irritated, frustrated or disappointed by any of your traits or actions and what would be seen as your strong points?

(2) Describe yourself as seen through the eyes of your boss. Are there any ways in which you could appear to better advantage or be understood more fully?

(3) List main likes motivating, dislikes-demotivating influences. Do you know them well enough to be reasonably sure you are right?

(4) List any main causes of frustration and job satisfaction (excluding 5 O'clock and pay day)

(5) Do you feel almost hungry for more information and personal growth?

(6) Are you happier/less happy at work than last year?

(7) Are you having difficulties because you cannot persuade someone to agree with you on a particular matter?

(8) What criteria or qualities did you use to judge competence? On finding deficiencies in your performance did you do anything to remove them?

(9) When did you last learn a major new task or procedure? Were you taught; did you teach yourself? Did you learn it satisfactorily or could it have been handled better? Would you want your subordinates trained by you?

(10) Identify the factors that give you results better than expected? Identify the factors that give you results worse than expected? Are there any occasions when you feel you cannot give your best?

Score of motivation index less than ten is supposed to be poor motivation; between ten and twenty is a fair performance and between twenty and thirty is better motivation. Score greater than thirty is excellent motivation.

EMPOWERMENT INDEX

Answers to the thirteen questions indicate how the organisation makes efforts to improve performance of its employees.

Statements:

(1) How frequently are you trained? Every three years/five years/as required/occasionally/never.

(2) How are you inducted to new technology? New scales? Through training programs/class lectures and work experiences/seminars/conferences /in house training program/Training institute.

(3) How much of your time you utilize in daily work? Forty per cent/Fifty per cent/Seventy five per cent/Eighty five per cent/Full time (utilization more than 80 per cent burns out expertise.)

(4) Do you get support from organisation to utilize new ideas, techniques, skills? Never/some problems/few problems/many problems/all problems.

(5) Is every problem put on the network, so that anybody in the organisation who has solution can provide one? Never/some problem/few problems/ many problems/all problems.

(6) Are you overloaded with information? No/Yes.

(7) Do you have corporate systems and culture that allows free flow of knowledge? No/In some cases/Yes.

(8) Does your company have work innovation network and knowledge links? No/In some matters/yes.

(9) Have you to pull information or is it pushed to you? Pulled/Pushed.

(10) Do you share brain in your organisation? Not at all/In a few matters/In some matters/In almost all matters/Always.

(11) Do you feel you have intellectual capital complimentary to your business? Two are completely unrelated/in some matters/In routine matters/In difficult matters/In all matters.

(12) Do you understand how your work benefits customer? This does not occur to me/in some cases I do/In few matters I understand/In almost all matters/Always.

(13) How much time did you take to become full- fledged contributor to the team? I have never felt myself a member of the team /Three months/Six months/Nine months/A year.

Answer to the questions excluding 6, 7, 8, and 9 are to be scored one to five in that order. In case of questions 7 and 8 ranks to be given are 3, 4 and 5 respectively. In case of questions 6 and 9 scores 4 and 5 are to be awarded.

HUMAN RESOURCE VALUE

I have suggested below two methods of human accounting based on adjusted discounted future wages method. Value, computed by these two methods will have to be compared. In my opinion there would not be much difference in computed values as per these two methods.

First Method

There are five stages, as explained below, to compute present value of human capital.

(1) Average rate of return on owned assets for all firms in the industry for the current period

$$ARR_{it}\ \frac{\text{Earnings after interest and tax but before depreciation}}{\text{Total Assets} \times \dfrac{\text{Networth}}{\text{Total capital employed}}}$$

$$\text{Total assets}\ \frac{X\text{———}}{\text{Total capital employed}}$$

Where ARR = average rate of return,
i = all firms in the industry
t = current period

(2) Weighted average rate of return for all firms in the industry for last five years.

$$WARR_{it} = \sum_{t_{1-5}}^{t=1} \text{Average weightage for year}_t\ X$$

$$= \frac{\dfrac{\text{EATT}}{\dfrac{\text{Total Assets} \times \text{Networth}}{\text{TCE}}}}{\sum_{t_{1-5}}^{t=1} \text{Average weightage}_t}$$

Where WARR = weighted average rate of return
i = all firms in the industry
t = 5 = for a period of five years.
EAIT = Earnings after interest and Tax.
TCE = total capital employed.

(3) Weighted average rate of return for the organisation.

$$WARR_O = \sum_{t=1-5}^{t=1} \frac{\dfrac{\text{EAIT}}{\dfrac{\text{Average wage}_t \times \text{Total assets} \times \text{Net worth}}{\text{TCE}}}}{\sum_{t=1}^{t=1} (\text{Averagewage})}$$

Where WARR = weighted average rate of return
O = for the organisation.

(4) Efficiency ratio of organisation.

$$ER_O = \frac{WARR_O}{WARR_i}$$

(5) Present value of estimated wages and salaries as human capital value of organisation.

$$PV_{HC} \sum_{n=1}^{5} \frac{\frac{t+n}{EWS}}{\frac{(1+ARRit)^n}{ER_o}}$$

PV_{HC}	=	Present value of human capital
EWS	=	Estimated wages and salaries
t+n	=	In next 5 years
ARR	=	Average rate of return
i	=	All firms in the industry
t	=	Currency period
ERo	=	Efficiency ratio of the organisation

Second Method

According to this method value of human capital of the organisation is the present value of future earnings of the employees. The employee force as a whole remains constantly associated with the firm. As long as the employees can be replaced, it may not matter for the purpose of the model whether the employee force always contains the same persons or a rapidly changing group. As such, premature termination is not relevant for the estimation of future earnings. We would consider the possibility of death prior to retirement to assess the expected value of the human capital.

To assess the annual earnings we use current data available on earnings we use current data available on earnings distribution by (a) age, education, race, geographic area of employment, and (b) different skill and transform the observed across employees earnings profit to over time earnings profile by transformation as practiced usually in the organisation.

The seven steps to calculate present value of human capital are –

(1) Find out the number of employees in each category of employees. For example – Executives, Managers, supervisors, non-supervisors, skilled workers, semi-skilled workers, supporting technical staff, clerical and office supporting staff.
This can be sub-divided by nationality – Indian, American, British, German, Indonesian etc.

(2) Find out the age profile of each category/sub-category of employees.

(3) Find out the probability of death at different age as available from general mortality table in different nations.

(4) Find out annual earnings of each category/each nationality of employees till the date of retirement/at the date of death.

(5) Find out cost of capital of organisation.

(6) Calculate present value of expected total earnings upto retirement/upto death of each type of employee at current age:-

PVETE	=	NECA Σ PDCA (x+1) ΣAE_{tn} (1 + CC_{ot})
Where,		
PVETE	=	Number of employees at current age
PDCA	=	Probability of death rate at current age
X	=	number of employees
AE	=	Annual earnings of employees in each category and sub-category
tn	=	over the period of time up to retirement/death
CCO	=	cost of capital to the organisation
t	=	at current time

(7) Present value of human capital

$$PV_{HC} = \sum_{t=1}^{n} PVTE$$

Where,

PV_{HC}	=	Present value of human capital
n	=	time span up to the age of retirement in years
Where,		
t = 1	=	year
PVETE	=	Present value of expected total earnings.

VALUE OF HUMAN CAPITAL

Thus, we have identified four components of human capital – (a) Leadership index, (b) Motivation index, (c) Empowerment index, and (d) Human resource value. Value of human resources is automatically calculated in monetary units. Financial data in annual reports is also expressed in monetary units. Therefore, we are obliged to convert values of above indices into monetary units. Moreover, most of the public sector units and a few private sector units, which calculate and publish human resource accounting and brand value data, do so in monetary units. Our data in monetary units will enable us to compare our position and status with that of other organisation.

Each index point in the above three indices is considered equal to 10,000 monetary units of the country in which the plant is located. Thus, the monetary value of the human capital of the plant is –

Value of human capital = Σ monetary value of leadership index + monetary value of Motivation index + monetary value of Empowerment Index + PV_{HC}.

There are many an organisations having headquarters and plant in one county and plants/subsidiaries/branches in other countries. We will have to convert monetary value of human capital of each plant/subsidiary/branch located in other countries to monetary value of parent country so as to enable us to present intellectual capital report of the organisation. This can be done by multiplying factor of coefficient of per-capita income of two countries. Authentic data are available in World Development Report of the World Bank.

As per the per capita income statistics given in World Development Report for 1999-2000, the per capita income of the U.S.A in 1998-99 was US $ 29340 and that of Canada was US $2002. If an American company has a plant/subsidiary/branch in Canada the human capital value of Canadian plant/subsidiary/branch will have to be multiplied by factor 1.47 so as to equate it with value of human capital in American plant. Likewise, if an American company has a branch in India, India's per capita income being US $ 430, and American value of human capital in the plants/subsidiary/branch in India will have to be multiplied by 68.23. On the contrary if an Indian company has a plant/subsidiary/branch in America, Indian value of American establishment can be arrived at by multiplying it by 0.015. Thus, the above formulae will be –

Value of the human capital of the company =

Monetary value of Leadership Index in HQ + monetary value of Motivation Index in HQ + monetary value of Empowerment Index in HQ + PV_{HC} in HQ + (monetary value of Leadership Index in branch + monetary value of Motivation Index in branch + monetary value of Empowerment Index in branch + PV_{HC} in branch) X $\frac{\text{percapita income of parent country}}{\text{per capita income of branch country}}$

OR

Value of the human capital of the company =

Monetary value of Leadership Index in HQ + Monetary Value of Motivation Index in HQ + monetary value of Empowerment Index in HQ + PV_{HC} in HQ + (monetary value of Leadership Index at branch + monetary value of Motivation Index at branch + monetary value of Empowerment Index at branch + PV_{HC} at branch) X $\frac{\text{Per capita income of parent country}}{\text{Per capita income of branch country}}$

MEASURING STRUCTURAL CAPITAL

Structural capital is the knowledge that is embodies in the company. It is the embodiment, empowerment and supportive infrastructure of human capital. Structural capital is the organisational capabilities to meet market requirements. It is the intangible assets that company owns outright. Human capital and structural reinforce each other when a company has a shared sense of purpose combined with an entrepreneurial spirit. It includes quality and reach of information technology systems, company images, proprietary databases, organisational concepts, intellectual properties like organisational, innovation and process. organisational capital is the company's investment in systems, tools and operating philosophy that speeds the flow of knowledge through the organisation. Innovation capital refers to the renewal capability and the results of innovation in the form of protected commercial rights, intellectual property, talents used to create and rapidly bring to the market new employee programs that augment and enhance the efficiency of manufacturing or the delivery of service.

Organisation Capital

	STATEMENT	*RESPONSE*	*SCORE*
(1)	Have you developed corporate 'Yellow pages'?	YES/NO	1/0
(2)	Have you developed 'knowledge highway' 'connecting existing lessons learnt' and repeated mistakes?	YES/NO	1/0
(3)	Have you organised knowledge about suppliers, customers and competitors?	YES/NO	1/0
(4)	Do you make information move fast?	YES/NO	1/0
(5)	Do you keep expertise of best people available to the organisation?	YES/NO	1/0
(6)	Have you adopted methods to share corporate knowledge?	YES/NO	1/0
(7)	Has your organisation changed survival techniques while transforming from 'information scarce' to 'information abundance'?	YES/NO	1/0
(8)	Does information overloading create a challenge to managing intellectual capital?	YES/NO	1/0
(9)	Do you feel you people are over-occupied with information?	YES/NO	1/0
(10)	Do you use the principle of 'just in time' or 'just in case' in collecting information?	YES/NO	1/0
(11)	Does you structural capital connect people to data, experts, expertise, on 'just in time' basis?	YES/NO	1/0
(12)	Have you created a living mechanism that continuously updates information?	YES/NO	1/0
(13)	What is the proportion of orphan I.T. inventory to total I.T. inventory?	20 p.c/30 p.c./50 p.c.	1/2/3
(14)	What is your I.T. expenses per employee?	Rs.40,000/- Rs.50,000	1/2
(15)	What is the proportion of I.T. development expenses total I.T. expenses?	10p.c./20p.c./ 30p.c	1/2/3
(16)	What is the proportion of I.T. training expenses total I.T. expenses?	5p.c/7p.c./ 10p.c.	1/2/3
(17)	What is the I.T. literacy rate in your organisation?	60/p.c./ 70p.c./80p.c.	1/2/3

INNOVATION CAPITAL

	STATEMENT	*RESPONSE*	*SCORE*
(1)	What is the investment done in last five years on development of new market?	Rs. 5 cr./Rs. 7 cr./Rs. 10 cr.	1/2/3
(2)	Give the number of new products in development.	4/5/6	1/2/3
(3)	What is the annual company historic rate of new products reaching market?	2/3/4	1/2/3

(4)	Give the ratio of new products (less than two years) to full product family.	2 p.c/2.5 p.c/3 p.c	1/2/3
(5)	Give the number of patents the company has.	50/60/70	1/2/3
(6)	What is the proportion of orphan patents to total patents?	2 p.c/2.5 p.c./10 p.c.	1/2/3
(7)	What is the proportion of the premium income resulting from new business operations to ordinary business?	5 p.c./7 p.c./10 p.c.	1/2/3
(8)	What is the premium from new launches?	25 p.c/30 p.c./45 p.c.	1/2/3
(9)	What is the proportion of the revenue resulting from new business operations?	10 p.c./15 p.c/20 p.c.	1/2/3
(10)	What are the profits resulting from new business operations?	2 p.c./3 p.c./4 p.c.	1/2/3
(11)	Give the number of patents pending.	5/6/7	1/2/3

PROCESS CAPITAL

	STATEMENT	*RESPONSE*	*SCORE*
(1)	How do you make structural intellectual capital offer greatest support to people?	By opening it to all/to few/to none.	3/2/1
(2)	How much structural capital do you use?	60 p.c/70 p.c/80 p.c.	1/2/3
(3)	What measures do you take for fuller utilization of structural capital?	Make people aware of it/give training/Give practice	3/2/1
(4)	Have you opened all information to all in the organisation?	YES/NO	1/0
(5)	Do information users have access to any data that would help them perform their jobs?	YES/NO	1/0
(6)	Do you send reports to people in the organisation or do you make them just accessible?	Send/just accessible	1/2
(7)	How do you collaborate information with creative work?	By having access to information/by giving due consideration.	2/1
(8)	How do you pu best people in the organisation on front line?	By job assignment/By availability	2/1
(9)	How do you integrate best practice into operation?	By making all know them/by making key people aware.	2/1
(10)	How fast a newcomer learns what the institution knows?	3 months/6 months	2/1
(11)	What is your retention ratio?	85 p.c/90 p.c/95 p.c.	1/2/3

(12)	What is the expert retention ratio?	90 p.c/95 p.c/97 p.c.	1/2/3
(13)	What are training expenses per employee?	Rs. 20 lakh/Rs. 22 lakh/Rs. 25 lakh	1/2/3
(14)	What are business developments expenses per employee?	Rs. 6 lakhs/Rs. 10 lakhs/Rs. 15 lakhs	1/2/3
(15)	What is the average age of people in your organisation?	30 years/35 years/40 years.	3/2/1
(16)	What is the proportion of employees under 40 years of age?	30 p.c./35 p.c./40 p.c.	1/2/3
(17)	Give proportion of full time permanent employees to total number of employees.	60 p.c./65 p.c./70 p.c.	1/2/3
(18)	Give proportion of full time temporary employees to total number of employees.	5 p.c./7 p.c./10 p.c.	3/2/1
(19)	What is the proportion of women managers to the total number of managers?	5 p.c./6 p.c./7 p.c.	1/2/3
(20)	What is the percentage of employees based in countries other than the country of origin?	5 p.c./6 p.c./7 p.c.	1/2/3
(21)	What is the proportion of managers of different nationality to the total number of managers?	5 p.c./6 p.c./7 p.c.	1/2/3
(22)	Have you developed in-house consultancy?	YES/NO	1/0
(23)	What is the corporate quality performance such as ISO 9000?	Very good/ good/satisfactory/Not so good.	4/3/2/1

We expect maximum score 95 (80 per cent of 118). Each score point is worth rupees three crores giving approximately value of structural capital to be Rs. 285 crores.

Valmatrix: The set of following sixteen questions gives us a matrix to measure value of structural capital.

(1) Give the pretax margins of the company for current year.

(2) Give the breadth of the product line.

(3) Describe the potential for line extension.

(4) State different barriers created for entry of new firm in the industry.

(5) What new licenses can you secure?

(6) Give the share of market commanded by your organisation in the current year.

(7) Give the amount of revenue resulting from new business.

(8) Give the percentage of profit resulting from new business.

(9) Give the loyalty rates for the new products (less than two years old).

(10) Amount of professional and consultant fees paid in the current year.

(11) Amount paid for drawings and documents taken.

(12) Amount of user license fee for supply of chain management software.

(13) Amount of price/royalty paid for database.

(14) Expenditure done on knowledge management architecture.

(15) Amount spent over last five years on knowledge integration.

(16) Amount spent over last five years on leveraging through specialization.

It is difficult to specify score value and its value in monetary units because the answers to these statements/questions would vary from organisation to organisation and industry to industry.

Thus monetary value of structural capital of an organisation is (Score or organisation capital + score of innovation capital + score of process capital) × Rs. 3 Crs. + monetary value of valmatrix.

MEASURING CUSTOMER CAPITAL

Customer capital is the most important of three categories of capital we are talking about. Customer capital of an organisation is based on its market share, customer retention and defection rate and per customer profitability. Knowledge is the chief ingredient of customer capital. The most important knowledge is what happens at customer end. Information about customers is always most valuable knowledge. Customers can be empowered by pursuing cost saving practices and by developing intimacy with them. This provides enormous information about the market. Blind pursuit of market share is much less rewarding than open eyed pursuit of increased share of business of your best customers. Most of the companies follow practices of mass customisation and flexible manufacturing. Customers should get most of the benefits from a companys productivity gains what economists call consumers surplus . The closer the relationship between producer/seller and buyer greater the consumers surplus. Companies should coordinate the information about buyers needs and their capabilities. That enables the company to gain from customers valuable expertise and retain him long.

Customer of any product or service can be viewed from three angles. Customer angle, company angle and market angle. Customer chooses a particular product, particular trademark, particular brand or services because of a number of psychological drives. A set of ten questions tries to measure the score of psychological phenomenon of purchases. Producer and/or seller tries to assess the behaviour of the consumer from the point of consumer loyalty, volume of purchases. A set of seven questions evaluates producers perception of this phenomenon. There are formulae to measure brand equity. They are presented below. A composite index of these three components of customer capital is negotiated at the end of the section.

CUSTOMER COMPONENT

Following ten questions measure the views of the customers about a particular product or a brand.

(1) **Why do you prefer this specific brand?**
Availability/ habit/liking/appealing/acquired-drive.

(2) **Does this brand satisfy your expectations?**
Not at all/to some extent/sometimes/frequently/always.

(3) **How frequently do you buy this brand?**
Once-in-a-while/sometimes/many times/usually/always.

(4) **Why do you prefer this brand to other brands?**
Satisfies demand/offer schemes like exchange/gives commission/gifts/better looking.

(5) **How much are you attracted to this product by advertisement?**
Not at all/once a while/sometimes/many a times/always.

(6) **Which brand comes first to your mind when you think of a particular want/demand?**
That satisfies me most/that satisfies my spouse most/that neighbors use/ that is offered by seller/that is advertised most.

(7) **How do you recollect the brand?**
By name/by trade mark/by carton/by smell/by colour.

(8) **Which factors do you give preference while buying the product?**
Liking/price/utility/availability/prestige.

(9) **Whose opinions do you consider while selecting a brand?**
Of friends/of reviews/of experts/of family/of spouse.

(10) **Would you consider any improvement in the product?**
In physical attractiveness/in composition of ingredients/in its effectiveness/in its packaging/in its standardization.

The answers to the above questions are so sequentially arranged that score one to five would be considered equivalent to Rs.5000/-

COMPANY COMPONENT

Following questions/statements try to evaluate importance of the customer in the books of the company.

(1) Annual sales per customer.

(2) Average duration of customer relationship in years.

(3) How many times does the customer visit in a year?

(4) How much time is spent on visiting customer?

(5) Service expenses per customer.

(6) Number of new customers acquired in the year.

(7) Number of customers lost in the year.

Monetary valuation of these seven questions would change from organisation to organisation and nature of business of the company.

Brand Equity – Market Component

Cognitivity evaluation process considers product attributes, importance weightage to attribute, importance and attribute salience, brand beliefs-brand image and utility function. A consumer forms an attitude towards each brand that is based on importance weights he assigns to the brand attributes times his brands beliefs. This expectancy-value model can be written in following form.

$$Ajk = \sum_{i=1}^{n} WjkBijk$$

Where, Ajk = consumer Ks attitude score for brand j
Wjk = the importance weight assigned by consumer K to attribute i
Bijk = consumer ks belief as to the amount of attributes i offered by brand j.
n = number of attributes important in the selection of a given brand. The consumer preters that product in case of which value of Ajk is maximum.

Brand equity of an organisation can be measured by a formula as given below:

Premium on price of company X – average price of the same type of product of the industry multiplied by premium on volume of the sales of the product of company X – average volume of the sales of the product of the industry.

Let us suppose there are eight companies in the industry. Company X sales the product at price Rs. 12 and average price of the same type of product of remaining seven companies is Rs. 8. then premium of price is (Rs. 12 – Rs. 8) Rs. 4.

Let us further suppose that total sales of the industry are one-lakh units. Share of the company X in the market is 30 per cent i.e. 30,000 units. Average share of remaining seven companies is 10,000 units (70,000-:-7). Thus, premium on volume is (30,000 units – 10,000 units) 20,000 units.

Thus, brand equity of the company X is Rs. 4 × 20,000 units = Rs. 80.000

However, this approach of averaging and volume of sales is not acceptable to many. They argue that the premium company X derives on price and volume is excess it has over next company i.e. company Y. Accordingly brand equity can be measured as —

Let us suppose that there are eight companies in the industry; X company being leader and Y next leader. Company X sales the product at price Rs. 12 and Y at Rs. 10. Therefore price premium is (Rs. 12 – Rs. 10) Rs. 2.

Let us further suppose that, total sales of the industry of the product are one-lakh units. Company X has a share of 30 per cent (i.e. 30,000 units) and company Y has a share of 25 per cent (i.e. 25,000 units), volume premium 5000 units.

Thus, brand equity of company X, is Rs. 2 × 5000 = Rs. 10,000

Value of customer capital is thus the sum total of customer component index plus company component index plus market component index: that is brand equity.

Value of customer capital = customer component index + company component index + market component index.

MEASURING INTELLECTUAL CAPITAL

On the basis of analysis presented in preceding sections V,VI and VII developing criteria to measure human, structural and customer capital, I put in this final discussion a structured format measuring intellectual capital in an organisation. There are so many possible, non-financial measurements creating a risk of using too many clouding the objective of measuring intellectual capital. Therefore, I have tried to be simple to pick as few measurements as possible and as essential. I have tried to include only those aspects that are strategically essential and important. Thirdly, I have concentrated on those activities that produce intellectual wealth. I have focused on terms that tell about intellectual capital.

I present below a sketch of a few methods that were introduced in earlier discussion.

(1) Return on Assets Method

On the basis of statistical data that could be extracted from annual report 1999-2000 of Asian Paints (India) Ltd., I have tried to calculate intellectual capital. However, industry data being not available I have taken a proxy figure.

(Rs. lakhs)

Year	*1995-96*	*1996-97*	*1997-98*	*1998-99*	*1999-2000*
Earning before tax	8035	8538	10050	10088	14309
Average earnings before tax: Rs.10204 lakhs.					(Rs. lakhs)
Tangible Assets	11979	17107	23146	30111	32934

Average tangible assets: Rs.230554 lakhs.

Therefore, $\frac{AEB_t5}{ATA_t5} = \frac{10204}{230554} = 0.044$

Industry average: 0.021

Value of intellectual capital of the company is 0.044 – 0.021 = 0.023 per cent higher than that of the industry. It means the company has excess of intellectual capital.

(2) Market Capitalisation Method

Annual report 1999-2000 gives data on – (a) average market value of shares of Asian Paints (India) Ltd., (b) number of shares subscribed, (c) paid up capital of the company, and (d) rate of inflation is available in economic journals, India reference book.

(1) Average market value of shares Rs. 380/-

(2) Number of shares subscribed 40116220

(3) Paid up capital Rs. 4012 lakhs.

(4) Rate of inflation 4.5 p.a.

Therefore,

Value of intellectual capital is $\text{Rs. } 380 \times 40116220 - \dfrac{\text{Rs. } 40.12 \text{ crs.}}{(1+0.045)} = \text{Rs. } 1486.02$ crs.

(3) Direct Intellectual Capital Method

This method requires huge data that can be collected by extensive in depth survey. No organisation publishes such data, even if any is collecting. Therefore, calculation of intellectual capital as per this method could not be shown.

(4) Tobin's Q

Data given in the annual report for 1999-2000 of Asian Paints (India) Ltd. can be gainfully used to calculate Tobin's Qmarket value of the company = Rs. 401 market price of share X number of shares 40116220.

Book value of the company = Rs. 89.09 book value per share X number of shares 40116220.

Therefore,

$$\text{Tobins Q} = \frac{\text{Rs. } 401 \times 40111 \times 6220 - \text{Rs. } 160866 \text{ lakhs}}{\text{Rs. } 89.09 \text{ time } 40116220 \text{ Rs. } 35739 \text{ lakhs}} = \text{Rs. } 4.5 \text{ lakhs}$$

So Asian Paints (India) Ltd. has Rs. 4.5 lakhs of excess intellectual capital.

MEASUREMENT INTELLECTUAL CAPITAL

Value of intellectual capital that an organisation possesses is the sum total of value of human, structural and customer capital. I have discussed and evolved comprehensive pragmatic formulae of computing values of components of the intellectual capital. The calculations will have to be done separately for an organisation having all activities in the country and in different countries. In the days of globalization changes that takes place in the value of human capital, in structural capital because of reorganisation, acquisition, merger, demerger and changes that take place in consumer psychology, attitude are taken into account. Having discussed this, I venture upon to project the formulae for valuation of intellectual capital of organisations having activities in one country (domestic organisation) and the organisation having activities in more than one country; the organisations commonly identified as Multinational Corporations (MNCs).

Domestic Organisation

We first measure value of human capital on the basis of formula developed in the fifth section.

Value of human capital = Σ monetary value of leadership index + monetary value of motivation index + monetary value of empowerment index + 5

$$PV_{HC} = \sum_{n-1}^{5} \frac{\frac{EWS_{t+n}}{(1 + ARR_{it})^n}}{ER_o}$$

OR

Value of human capital = Σ Monetary value of leadership index + monetary value of motivation index + monetary value of empowerment index + PV_{HC} =

$$_{P}VETE \sum_{t=1}^{N} NECA\ \Sigma\ PDCA\ X_{(x+1)}\ \Sigma\ AE_{tn}\ (1 + CCO_t)$$

We add to this score of human capital, the score of structural capital as developed in the sixth section.

(Score of organisation capital + score of innovation capital + score of process capital) x Rs. 3 crores + (score of Valmatrix index)

We add to this the score of customer capital as developed in the seventh section.

(Score of customer component + score of company component + score of market component i.e. the Brand equity).

We could not derive value of each score of customer component and company component because that depends upon the nature of product and/or service provided by the organisation, the segment of the market to which it is provided and the customer composition that is catered by the organisation. In case of many an organisations product as well as service will have to be valued.

Thus, formula is

IC = HC + SC + CC.

Where, IC is intellectual capital, HC is human capital, SC is structural capital and CC is customer capital.

Multinational Organisation

We calculate value of intellectual capital of a multinational organisation the same way we calculated the value of domestic organisation. However, we will add to it the value of franchises/branches/subsidiaries of the organisation in other countries.

We first consider value of human capital as discussed in fifth section.

Value of human capital = Σ monetary value of leadership index in HQ + monetary value of motivation index in HQ + monetary value of empowerment index in HQ + $PV_{HC} = \sum_{n=1}^{5} \frac{\frac{EWS_{t+n}}{(1+AARR_{it})}}{ER_O}$ at HQ + (monetary) value of leadership index in the currency of branch + monetary value of motivation index in the currency of branch + monetary value of empowerment index in the currency of branch + $PV_{HC} \sum_{n=1}^{5} \frac{\frac{\{EWS_{t+n}\}}{(1+AARR_{it})}}{ER_O} \times \frac{\text{per capita income of parent country}}{\text{per capita income of branch country}}$

OR

Value of human capital = Σ monetary value of leadership index in HQ + monetary value of motivation index in HQ + monetary value of empowerment index in HQ + $PV_{HC} = \sum_{t-1}^{n} NECA\ \Sigma\ PDCA \times (X + 1)\ \Sigma \frac{AE_{tn}}{(1+CCO_t)}$ at HP + (monetary value of leadership index in the currency of branch + monetary value of motivation index in the currency of branch + monetary value of empowerment index in the currency of branch + $PV_{HC} \sum_{t=1}^{n} NECA\ \Sigma\ PPCA \times (X + 1)\ \Sigma \frac{AE_{tn}}{(1+CCO_t)}$ of the branch

$\times \frac{\text{per capita income of parent country}}{\text{per capita income of branch country}}$

We add to this value of structural capital as discussed in sixth section.

(Score of organisation capital + score of innovation capital + score of process capital X value equivalent to Rs.3 crores in the currency of the branch + (score of Valmatrix index) X value in the currency of the branch

$X \frac{\text{per capita income of parent country}}{\text{per capita income of branch country}}$

We add to this score of customer capital as developed in the seventh section.

(Score of customer component + score of company component + score of market component i.e. brand equity) X value in the currency of branch country $X \frac{\text{per capita income of parent country}}{\text{per capita income of branch country}}$

Radar Chart

Figure 8.3 presents a coherent picture from several heterogeneous factors that go in to making intellectual capital. There is a circle like a radar screen. Three main lines radiate from the centre to earmark human, structural and customer capital. In each of these three pie are exhibited the components that make each type of capital. There are four segments in each of human and structural capital and three in customer capital. We have made relevant scale on each of these eleven axes. They may be representing absolute numbers, ratios, and percentages. We start from the centre marking zero and progressing towards circumference. We plot the score of each component on relevant axis and join these points. The shaded area is the intellectual capital navigator. The irregular polygon inside shows what you have got, what is outside it is what you want. It tells you where you are and where you have to go. It exhibits your strengths are weaknesses. The polygon in figure 8.3 of an imaginary company shows that the organisation has achieved well in structural capital; it is good in latter two components of customer capital and somewhat good in customer component of customer capital. However, its performance in leadership, brand equity is lacking much.

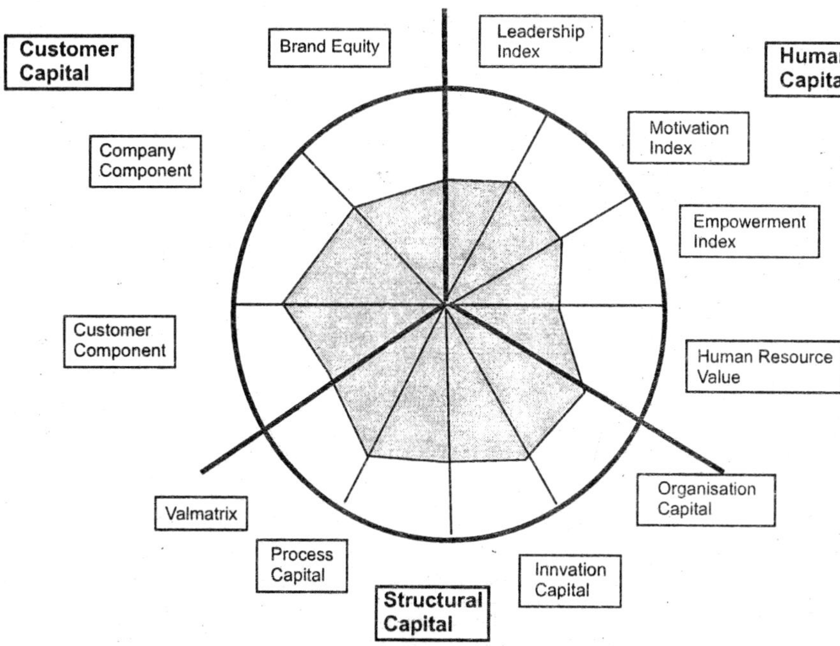

Figure 8.3
RADAR CHART

Such a radar chart has comparative quality as besides absolute quality. The radar chart of the company of a year can be compared with the radar chart of another year to see whether we have become stronger or weaker in our performance. The polygon of the company can be compared with that of the industry, which can be taken as benchmark. There from, strength and weakness of the company *vis-à-vis* industry can be gauged. The chart can bring out anomalies in particular areas.

For example, figure 8.3 indicates that company has difficult future because it is low on leadership that will create obstacles in future progress. It also indicates that the edge that company has over its competitors (brand equity) is progressively eroded. This can teach us a number of lessons.

The days of capital-intensive industries have gone; future is with knowledge capital-intensive industries. Earlier we take to measure the intellectual capital and build knowledge in our company better our future would be. In the changing scenario because of globalization and regulations of W.T.O, the need to fortify knowledge base of the company has increased many fold. Because of onslaught of MNCs in all sectors and areas it is necessary to identify core competencies; concentrate on them; remove weakness and strengthen further our strengths. With a view to win the confidence of the shareholders, investors, bankers and customers, it is imperative to build and develop intellectual capital on which, future of the company depends and make it known to all concerned. This is an effort to take us on that path.

❑ ❑ ❑

9 Core Competence

C. K. Prahalad and Gary Hamel on the basis of their study of production strategies and performance of many companies have put the concept of 'core competence' in the literature on management.[1] Indian corporations seem to have implemented this concept in their business activities from 1990. They had to do so because of the introduction of policies of liberalisation and privatisation in India. Prahalad and Hamel write, 'core competencies are the collective learning in the organisation, especially how to co-ordinate diverse production skills and integrate multiple streams of technologies. Core competence is communication, involvement and a deep commitment to working across organisational boundaries.' A core competence is a set of skills that have been integrated in a unique way by a firm in order to add value. Its utility increases with its use. Physical assets deteriorate with use while core competence enhances as it is used and shared.

In and around 1990s many a companies had begun to outsource almost any process that they were performing very well earlier. Thus, the management began to ponder as to which were the activities that they should not outsource on any account. Those were the activities that were core of their business. So, those activities that were basic to the existence of the company were known to be core activities. Those were the activities with which the company added maximum value to the product they produced or service they provided

Some companies, that had a very diversified business, introduced a product in markets and that was so much liked by the customers that they became world leaders. However, with political and economic happenings in the world, the market boundaries had been changing so quickly that the leader companies found that the superiority they had gained in the market was temporary. So, they began to discover new markets, enter into emerging markets and change the pattern of the product and the pattern of the customer choice in the established markets. Creation of such a corporation capable of entering into others markets and capable of infusing new products with new functionalities and better in all respects was a difficult task indeed. It was so because they had provided such products to the customers that the customers had not dreamt of.

Prahalad and Hamel state that there are three tests on the basis of which core competence of a company can be determined. These tests are— (1) Concentration on that activity enables the company to access new market. That activity is the core activity. (2) Such activity should provide significant benefit to the perceived customer. That activity is the core activity. (3) Competitors should find difficult to imitate such activity. Harmonisation of technology and production skills is so complex that competitor finds it difficult to imitate it. That harmonisation is the core competence.

Over the period of time companies realised that 'core competence' is not limited to an innovative product or unique production process but it can be any aspect of organisational activity. Therefore, the concept of 'core activity' was extended to 'core process' 'core skills, 'core market strategy' etc. It was realised that if the company wants to identify itself it must locate its 'core activity' and fully concentrate on it. Then only the company can identify its scores of strengths and weaknesses. The company can stand firmly in this constantly changing economy, only if it leverages its strengths and eliminates its weaknesses. Then only it can add value to its products and/or services, the factor that is necessary to acquire competitive advantage. A company can divert and make best use of its resources by identifying its 'core activity' and at the same time avoid misuse of these scarce resources on 'non- core activity.' Core competence developed in respect of a system, process or product should not be considered as a permanent achievement and hold it fast or stick to it. Core competence that way, is not a static phenomenon; it is a dynamic process. After having achieved competence in one aspect and reaped its fruits for enough time the organisation has to search for another competency of better order and of higher value. So the organisation can enjoy better returns, more sweet fruits of its toil of searching and acquiring new competencies. If the organisation is imprisoned in one core competency, as described by Burton D. Leonard, that may become core rigidity. Organisation will lose its social legitimacy. Philip Kotler argues that a company should enhance its 'core competence' by acquiring such core resources and by nourishing them. According to Kotler there are three characteristic features of 'core competence' - (1) A company can increase the expected benefits of the customer by utilising its core competence. In this way core competence is a means to acquire competitive advantage. (2) The concept of core competence holds capability to make use of its Innovativeness in different ways in different markets. (3) Core competence of a company cannot be imitated by rival company; because core competence is a concept that determines superiority in variety of business methods, skill in particular technical and technological production process. Management of a business organisation should identify activities of its 'core competence', nurture them so as to achieve development of the organisation. The management should take full advantage of such competence. However, it is necessary to completely restructure the organisation of the company.

RESTRUCTURING ORGANISATION

Organisation producing a variety of various goods used to direct their strategic business units towards particular markets and instruct them to achieve leadership in that market at global level. Market boundaries are disappearing, as a result of development in information technology, invention of new products, use of new production processes, collapse of boundaries between economies and globalisation. As a result the targets of production and marketing are becoming blurred and the competence acquired in market is becoming momentary. In such a situation, corporations are struggling to discover new markets and penetrate into them swiftly. They have become successful in dramatically changing the pattern of consumer choice even in established markets. This brings to our knowledge that the most important function of management is to introduce into the market multi-utility products and provide to the consumers, products that they need but they have not dreamt of. This change in mind-set is not as easy as it appears to be. In reality the pace of development of companies is slowed down because of slow change or no change in the mindset of the management. That is why, if we want to develop world economy, rather than introducing economic and political reforms at national level we should necessarily bring change, do improvement in the principles of management. Core competencies can vary among firms based on unique benefits they intend to provide to their customers. This capability to deliver benefits depends upon company's ability to achieve effective combination of human capital, intellectual and intangible assets, processes and technologies used. Thus, the core competency of one company cannot be replicated by another firm because its capability may not essentially be the same.[2]

Management should identify its objectives in clear terms and make them known to all in the business corporation. Management should constitute committees of knowledge workers with devotion and commitment to establish core competence and develop core products. The organisation should develop such flexible systems that these functional groups and members of the committees would mix up and converse with each other. Organisation should assemble all its resources and strengths and devote them to development of core products. Resources belonging to different strategic business units should be pooled together. This increases capability of resources at geometrical proportion, and enhances further the scope of core superiority. The corporation can establish 'core competence' in respect of many products and in many markets by giving stress on and importance of production of strategic components and constituents of end products. This enables the corporation to conclude memorandum of understanding (MoU) with various organisations. The MoU of such type enables the corporation to master management styles, products, product processes and marketing strategies of various organisations. However, for development of such co-operation and give and take the mental strength of the management must be of high order, of highest standard. The management must show mental strength of giving something to obtain something. As a result the organisation can save financial investment in R and D programs. This also saves time involved in development of new products, new concepts and varied ideas. These factors are very important in establishing one's strength in the market and therefore decisive. Change in the mindset of the organisation plays very important role in the concept of core competence.

Though top executive officials in the business organisation discuss the strategic goals and important structural changes required for developing core competence, they themselves are unaware and unable to agree in which products, in which product processes and skills their core competence resides. Thus, the concept of core competence is limited to discussion level. In many an organisations top management having not shown any interest in disseminating the idea of core competence to lower level, middle management people behave as usual as if they are running an independent business. As a result attention is not focussed on competence and the organisation has to depend upon outside people for strategic skills. In such a situation we pave the way for them to take over our company with the help of memorandum of understanding we have concluded.

The discussion in foregoing two paragraphs enables us to differentiate between two types of organisations. First type of organisations think about their core areas while second type of organisations think about their business.

FOUNDATIONS OF CORE COMPETENCE

Many organisations develop such characteristic features in their products that they become unique in the world market. However, prices of such products are less or in comparison to their characteristic features they are competitive. Quality and efficiency of these products is much higher in comparison to the price charged for them. The organisation derives competitive advantage out of such situation. If we take into account long period, the company that brings such unique products in the market in much less time than the competitive firm and at low price, derives competitive advantage. Core competence of a company depends upon the capability of the organisation to bring unexpected products, full of unexpected features at earliest time in the market. Core competence of a company depends upon the capability of the management to activate production skills and techniques that are collected from strategic business units with a view to take advantage as early as possible of the changing opportunities. Core competencies are a part of organisation's personality. C. K. Prahalad and Gary Hamel argue that business organisations, like trees, grow on the strengths of their roots. Core products are nurtured on core strengths of the organisation and these core strengths are foundations of core competence. The main four components of core competencies are business processes, strategic capabilities, and strategic investment in support infrastructure and chief officers who champion capability-based strategies. Core competency enables organisation to create its monopoly.

Some executives argue that we cannot develop core competence because the independence of strategic business units in our organisation is a sacred gospel and our hands are tied down by quarterly budgets. Such executives should rethink whether these factors are causes or excuses of not acquiring core competence. Other companies possess equal amount of reservoir of technological capabilities and have developed core competence. However, the management of such business organisation is so much devolved in the concept of being a corporation that it cannot reap adequate advantage of the reservoir of technological capabilities.

A corporation doing various functions is like a large tree. The roots represent the Values, the Vision and the Mission of the Corporation. The trunk represents the Core Competence of the Corporation. The big branches are like the Strategic Business Units (SBUs) of the corporation. The leaves, flowers and fruits represent the Core Products of the Corporation, which is the outcome of its Core Competence operating through its SBUs, and is based on the Core Values, Core Vision and Core Mission of the Corporation. This is evident from Figure 9.1. The Values, Vision and Mission of the business organisation are like roots of a tree that provide nourishment, sustenance and stability to the organisation. These roots support the 'core competence' of the organisation. The large and small branches representing the strategic business units (SBUs) give end products represented by leaves, flowers and fruits. We cannot assess the health of a tree only from its leaves, flowers and fruits. In the same way we cannot assess the competence of an organisation only from its final products.

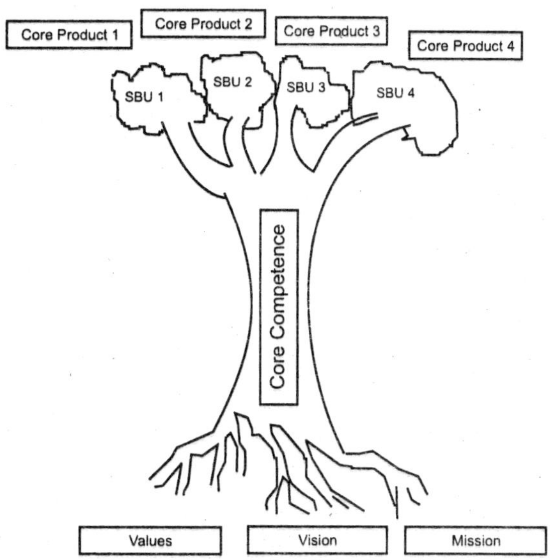

Figure 9.1
Corporation Tree

Capability to co-ordinate various branches of technologies, ability to co-ordinate diverse production skills and the urge to acquire knowledge from various branches of organisational structure create core competence. An organisation cannot develop a visiting card size radio just on the basis of theoretical knowledge of transforming electric circuit of a radio on a chip. It needs collaboration of various technologies. It would need to master miniaturisation technology, designing a microprocessor, knowledge of properties from physical sciences and preparing a very thin precision casing. However, once this knowledge is mastered, it can be gainfully used for fabricating cardboard thin calculators, pocket television sets, digital watches etc. A technology like nano-technology itself has become core competence of many an organisations. An organisation like LABINDIA INSTRUMENTS Pvt. Ltd. has acquired core competence in tools for nano-technology. They produce instruments like tribometer (wear tester), high temperature tribometer, scratch tester, nanonics imaging like Dual Microscope System, Multiview 1000 tm head, Laser Raman Spectrometer, Thin Film Metrology and Plasma Technology etc. However, it is a point of debate what would be the effects of spreading nanotechnology to unprecedented limits. We need not go into it.

Core competence is not limited to collaborating various branches of technology. It can be mastered in organising work or in successfully transforming the value created in products or services fully to the consumer. Technicians, engineers and marketing personnel working in organisations providing products or services must possess full knowledge of needs of customers. They must also know the technological possibilities required for producing such products or for providing such services. Importance of core competence is equally felt in activities providing services as in producing products. Organisations putting their foot-prints in service providing activities also become world-renowned.

Dialogues between different people, attitude to involvement and deep commitment to work even across the organisational boundaries are the three major aspects of core competence. This requires involvement of people from all levels and all functions. It is the skill of people who recognise opportunities of developing new products by blending functions of own organisation with those of others in novel and interesting ways. Core competence enables organisations to consolidate business. This opens up new opportunities in business. Core competence decides pattern of diversification and direction of entry into the market. Diversified divisions of business can be developed on the foundation of restricted core competence. The strength of core competence decides the extent of development of various divisions.

Many organisations could not develop in spite of having capability to develop core competence. This happened because top management presumed that their organisation is a conglomeration of unrelated strategic business units. Some organisations had to sell out strategic divisions just because they found difficult to maintain core competence of those divisions. And unfortunate matter is that the organisations had to sell out those sectors in productive activities of which they enjoyed dominating leadership. Bell Laboratories, the organisation that invented transistor, that revolutionised not only telephone industry but many others, gave it away being of very little use at a paltry sum of $ 25000. Bell Laboratories did not realise that transistor could be its most valuable core competent product.[3] Top management of many organisations feel that the future of the organisation is constrained in the success of strategic business units. As a result they fail to realise that outsourced products are not mearly spares of our final products but are core competencies enhancing competitiveness of our various products.

Many an organisations being in the race of capturing leadership at global level, fail to realise that they are a conglomeration of various business units producing different products. They emphasise on producing goods that apparently appear to be unrelated but having same core area. In other words, such unrelated goods are also inter-related. Honda has acquired core competence in producing machines and electric locomotives. This competence provides the organisation huge benefits in producing motor cars, motor cycles, moving machines, generators etc. Canon has acquired core competence in the technique of audio-visuals, images and control on micro-processors. As a result the corporation could not only penetrate but establish leadership in markets of copiers, laser printers, and image-scanners. These products apparently appear to be unrelated but have the same technology at their base. Philips has worked for long fifteen years on optical media-laser disc and has acquired core competence in mechantgronics- the ability to marry mechanical and electronic engineering. On the basis of this foundation it has taken a stride in producing goods for video recording, video display, bioengineering and microelectronics. Coca-Cola Company has different core products for different regions. In the U.S.A. it is carbonated coke, in France it is fruit juice and in Japan it is coffee. This discussion brings us to a conclusion that a company cannot acquire and maintain world leadership on the basis of core competence and mastery over technology. Along with this core competence, the management of the organisation has to chalk out and implement unidirectional competitive strategy at strategic business unit level and at the organisational level. It must also be realised that the battle of global leadership and core competence cannot be won by just spending more on research and development than the rival firm. Equally, using collective facilities of main strategic business units of the organisation effectively is not acquiring core competence. Effective use of such collective facilities of strategic business units does lead to economising cost of production. However, acquiring core competence requires co-ordination in the collective facilities of strategic business units. That is more difficult.

Building core competence is different and much more ambitious than vertically integrating production facilities. Organisations deciding to buy or make components of products will have to take into consideration efficiency of suppliers and of distribution channels so as to deliver maximum value to the customer. There are three tests of recognising 'core competence' of an organisation. They are— (1) Core competence provides potential access to the organisation in variety of markets, (2) Core competence provides considerable benefits to the user of the end products, and (3) Nature of core competence should be such that competitor firms should find it difficult to imitate. It is impossible to imitate if it is a complex harmonisation of various technologies and production skills. Rival firms may be able to acquire some technology comprising of core competence. However, it is not possible for such rival firm to acquire and master comprehensive pattern of internal co-ordination and of learning. Some organisations can acquire world leadership in five or six core competencies. However, even if an organisation owns rare capabilities in producing 20 or 25 products, it is doubtful whether it can build up core competence in producing one product. This organisation can sign memorandum of understanding on the basis of these rare capabilities with other organisations and can build up core competence by connecting missing links.

Many an organisations do not appear to be considering such competitive superiority from its all angles. They consider own company with rival company in respect of prices and performance only. As a result their core competence instead of increasing erodes. The 'intrinsic skill' of developing products that will stand in competition even in future cannot be created by establishing contacts with suppliers providing genuine components or from outside. Many an organisations lose their 'core competence' because they consider investment in products that will stand in competition in future as expenditure.

Honda Motor Company concentrated its full attention on developing car engine that is catalyst in motor car. On the basis of this it has established its 'core competence' in world market in respect of producing engines of various types of auto-vehicles. As against this Daimler Chrysler Motor Company considered car engine as a part like any other parts and got them outsourced from Mitsubishi and Hyundai. As a result its dependence on these firms increased and the core competence that it had built up was lost.

An organisation may not be able to develop core competence in respect of any product even though it might be producing competitive high standard various products. If an organisation wants to introduce a new product in the market, world-renowned companies may produce that product for some time for the former organisation. However, the former company will be cornered if the world-renowned company produces and introduces that product in the market with its own trademark. Suzuki Motor Company encouraged Maruti Udyog Limited to introduce its cars in Eastern European countries. However, when the market was developed for these cars Suzuki Motor Company stepped in this market and ousted Maruti Udyog Limited. The system of outsourcing spares and components is the shortest route to step into a competitive market. But this does not leave room for developing skills of our employees. Such company cannot maintain its leadership in the market for long time.

The policy of intelligent alliances and of outsourcing does not become successful unless the organisation has decided in which area it has to build up its core competence. Companies can be benefited from alliances if the partners are not committed to protect and preserve their core competence. World has witnessed many such incidences. Such strategic alliances include give and take of resources, pooling of dedicated employees, creating testing facilities at production sites. If the organisation is not careful in preserving its core competence then the partners will take full advantage to build up their own core competence.

C. K. Prahalad and Venkat Ramaswamy have recently discussed one more dimension to the concept of core competence. Organisations develop core competence in excellence in managing experience of the consumers. They state, people while buying a product or while availing a service do not buy the product or the service but acquire an experience of consuming the product or experience of using the service. Product or service is a part of experience environment. Organisations can look to such experience and enhancing it as an opportunity of developing core competence. Consumer while buying a product and in consuming it derives an experience and his satisfaction depends upon the intensity of the experience. Enhancing his experience and helping him to make right choice of right product, at right time and at right price is a core competence that the organisation must develop. Managing this type of customer relationship itself is core competence. Prahalad and Ramaswamy further argue that experience is co-created by the organisation and the consumer. Organisation's involvement in enabling the consumer to enjoy his experience can be made more intense by making goods and services available easily and in pleasant manner. Such co-creation of satisfaction transforms consumption into experience.

Organisation can acquire such 'core competence of experience' by developing prototype of product based on the concept of experience design rather than on the concept of product design. Such production activities necessarily require a whole new set of skills. The organisation has to think and acquire a whole bunch of new functional capabilities. This is a new dimension to core competence, experience in co-creation. In such an experience, the whole range of functional capabilities is to be reengineered.

One more aspect of core competence that Prahalad and Ramaswamy have highlighted is 'successfully managing capacity loads'. Each economic activity is built up with a capacity to carry a particular load. There are many an instances when customer demand outpaces the load that the capacity can carry. Religious festivals, vacation tours, popular opera or drama shows, entrance examinations and recruitment interviews in countries like India are examples of this. Prahalad has cited example of Tirupati and Ramaswamy of Disney Land. At Tirupati the inflow of devotees is so large that that it causes inconvenience to both the devotees and the temple administration. At Disney Land particular shows are overcrowded. Spectators wish to reach such popular shows on time without facing inconvenience of standing in long queues. Management of such capacity loads is itself a core competence. Devotees desire to have an experience of joy of the God's Darshan and Prasad without spending time in long queues. Spectators desire to have an experience of reaching particular show on time and enjoy it without waiting in long queues. While interviewees desire to have an experience of being interviewed without hustle and long waiting. Providing such experience to people without causing inconvenience is the 'core competence' of the administration. Organisations have found different methods of managing capacity loads. Tirupati administration issues armbands with microprocessors embedded in them to devotees in their towns specifying day, date and time of the God's Darshan. This is done with the help of centrally controlled distribution network. So it becomes easy to manage capacity loads. The administration knows the number of devotees visiting the temple every day, every time. This eases the pressure on queuing management, security arrangement and enhances the experience of Darshan of the devotees. Disney Land manages this by routing bus services on different roads. Organisation arranging central entrance test (CET) does it by holding examination at as many centres as possible. While interviewing committees do it by staggering interviewees in manageable batches. Thus, the capability of the organisation to enhance the experience is its 'core competence'. Authors suggest that, listening to responses of visiting devotees, spectators, examinees and interviewees can be used as an antenna for feedback. Implementation of workable and practical suggestions can improve management of capacity loads.

The information received in the form of feedback gives the organisation a new knowledge about customer experiences. The organisation can prepare itself, on the basis of this knowledge, to provide customers new experiences, compelling experiences by getting into their mood to have the God's Darshan or viewing particular show, facing entrance test or appearing for interview. Organisation needs to look at the whole incidence as an exercise of improving and maintaining quality of experiences. The traditional TQM thus becomes a subset of such exercise. Creating such new compelling experience can build up competitive advantage of the organisation. Consumers develop immediacy to the experience. They legitimatise such experiences and the such experiences become brands. Brands are not products, but legitimatised consumer experiences. We ascribe brands to products because our thinking of experience is based on and is related to products. No doubt, this creates a need to develop new skills where more than one organisation will have to be involved and co-competence will have to be evolved. Such skills will develop new revenue generating opportunities.

If an organisation presumes that the opportunities of developing new products and of creating new ideas in areas of its core competence are exhausted, the company will not take much time to lose its core competence. Motorola and Thorn, world renowned producers of television sets presumed that this business has matured and there being no further scope withdrew from coloured television business. They lost video based core competence and America was thrown out of this 200 crore-dollar business. As against this Sony Corporation, while reducing its emphasis on production of video-cassette recorders preserved its core competence in video related products.

This discussion leads us to two conclusions. We cannot calculate in advance the deficits that we will incur due to loss of core competence. An organisation is likely to lose everything in such divestment. Second conclusion is that, an organisation works year after year, decades after decade to produce and improve the product and build core competence. Once such core competence is lost the organisation will find it difficult, almost impossible to enter emerging markets. And even if enters it will be performing secondary function as a distribution channel.

Korean electronic business organisations began to produce chips containing miniature integrated circuits at very low cost of production. Then Motorola even though it had build up core competence in producing 256k random access memory chips, stopped its production. Motorola learnt a very painful lesson out of this, because it had to enter this market by sourcing chips of one- megabyte capacity from other American business companies.

PREPARING FOR CORE COMPETENCE

Every economic entity, may it be in the area of production, service or distribution has to choose a line of production or a group of lines in which it desires to operate. Management of such entity has a dream to acquire name and fame and be a model organisation. These are the seeds of the concept of core competence. In the endeavour to achieve this level of activity choice of right and appropriate product is the first step. Management, considering its business acumen, technological expertise, availability of resources, ethical and value base, market conditions, customer needs, and government policy, has to choose the group of products it wishes to produce. No doubt, there are many a factors besides these that need to be taken into consideration while choosing a line of activity. Some of them are capital market, availability of funds, policy of lending institutions, international market and currents and cross currents in it etc.

The organisation has to build up a knowledge base by identifying which knowledge does it need to march towards the objective of core competence. Then it has to make an inventory schedule as to which knowledge does its people possess either in implicit or in explicit form. It is very necessary for the organisation to know what knowledge does it have and what knowledge it does not have. The organisation must make concerted efforts to build up a reservoir of knowledge. It must develop a practice of sharing knowledge and best practices, instilling responsibility for sharing knowledge. It must make efforts to capture and reuse best practices and embed knowledge in products, processes and services. The organisation has to endeavour to produce knowledge as a product, drive knowledge generation for innovation. It has to undertake mapping network of experts, building and mining customer knowledge bases, understanding and measuring the value of knowledge and leveraging intellectual assets.

Core competencies are the real resource of the firm. The multi-business companies can leverage it by consolidating corporate wide technologies and production skills into competencies that empower individual businesses to adapt quickly to changing opportunities. The firm has to develop special skills or technologies that provide lasting competitive advantage to the firm. The firm should identify forthcoming opportunities and create new markets and expand its activities beyond traditional products and services. Core competencies are connective tissue that holds together seemingly diverse businesses.

Knowledge is the foundation of building core competence. Figure 9.2 explains the process.

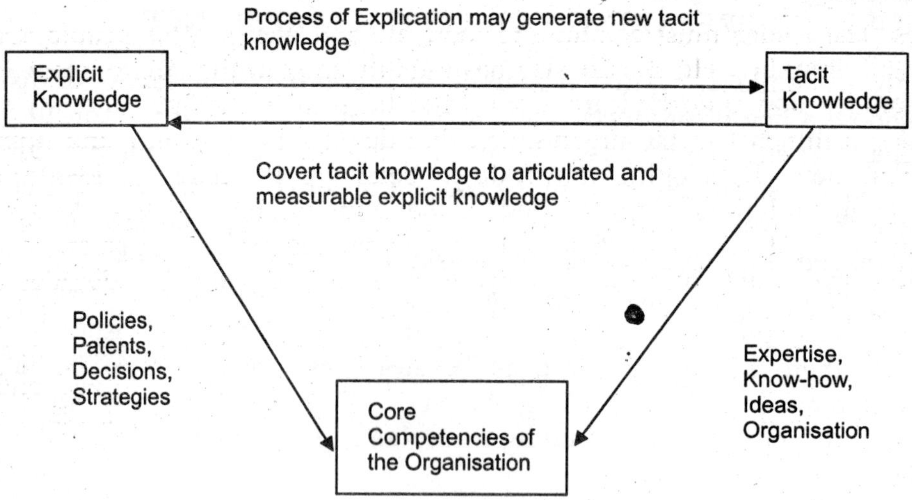

Figure 9.2
Linkages between Explicit and Tacit Knowledge and Core Competence

Explicit and tacit knowledge improves a range of organisational performance characteristics, and adds value by enabling the organisation to act more intelligently. The list of ten knowledge concepts that Alavi and Leinder[4] have articulated determine that the most important knowledge domains concern customer service, business partners, internal operations and marketing and sales. Knowledge base helps the organisation in activities like problem solving, dynamic learning, strategic planning and decision making. Knowledge is the foundation of ideas, research, invention and innovation. The goal of knowledge management as a process is to improve the organisation's ability to execute its core processes more efficiently.

Organisation trying to achieve core competence must build up its organisational structure. Structurally the organisation must be very lean, flexible and delayered. It must not have barriers of functional and departmental boundaries. Employees in the organisation must possess inter-functional, inter-departmental skill. So that, they are ready to commit to the development of the new product, new process and new market. The organisation must be very sensitive and responsive to the changes that take place in the business world, economy, polity, society, technology and market. Organisation that desires to build core competence must be an intelligent organisation capable of solving any and every problem and providing products to the consumers that they have not dreamt of. Organisational structure must be consumer centric, consumer focussed. It must be not only able to anticipate needs of the consumer and satisfy them; but it must be capable of creating new patterns of consumption; so that it can enjoy competitive advantage. Such an organisation must build groups and teams that can accept and shoulder any and every challenge that are posed in the polity.

As a part of the preparation for building core competence the top brass must build up strong leadership. No matter what the external climate, corporate leader must be able to find creative ways to restructure his business to accommodate new realities. The leader must continue to motivate and energize his people and inspire innovative thinking. He should also have ability to scan the environment for future opportunities and quickly learn from what he sees. He must build up a culture, an ethics, a mindset in the organisation that devotes to excellence and doing things right first time. Developing a workforce believing in character, identifying with organisation and remaining satisfied is the duty of the corporate leader. Such a work force must seek its satisfaction in the delight of the customer. Developing, spreading and maintaining core competence is a task that takes decades and it is a lifetime achievement. Corporate leader must develop a band of leaders, a team of leaders. He must develop a few best persons who would be capable of replacing him and continue the journey of the organisation in the same gust and enthusiasm. D.C. McClelland calls this process of creating able persons as, 'the leader must have capability to multiply himself.'

Thus, there are four stages that I have discussed for preparing the organisation for achieving core competence. The first step is to identify the product, product line, market, market segment for developing core competence. Second step is to build up knowledge base capable of taking up the task of developing product, product lines, services that would be rated as first class, best in the class by the world customer. The third step is to build up a lean, flexible, responsive, sensitive, intelligent organisation. The fourth step is to develop a world-class leadership capable of sensing every change that future may present. The corporate leader must develop people because they are the fountains where from core competence develops. However, it must be seen that core competencies do not become core rigiditties.[5]

SETTING TO CORE COMPETENCE

Core competence may be in products, product lines, and services or even in soft skills that the corporation has developed. Building up core competence and guarding it, protecting it from rivals, competitors are two different things. I will discuss the first, first and then the second.

In real life, companies, on the basis of decades of hard work, devotion and commitment develop core competence. Chain of transformation from core competence to core products is very important from the point of standing of the corporation in the market. Such end product is known as core product. Physical transformation of core competence into core product is very important from the point of view of protection of core competence. Engine is the core product of Honda Corporation. Development of designs, skills to develop and produce the end product 'engine' is a chain of transformation. All the links in the chain are of great importance. Core competence of the automobile or motorcycle on which this engine is fitted depends upon the quality of the engine that Honda has developed. Engine is the core component in the core product, namely, automobile or motorcycle. The company must be able to distinguish between its share in manufacturing the core product in the industry and the market share its core brand has achieved. Both factors have different significance. The former factor determines company's status in the industry while the latter determines market leadership. Both these factors are of equal importance; one without the other may erode its status in the other. Kirloskars have core competence in production of compressors and thus it has achieved good status in the industry. Equally so, it has captured sizeable share in the refrigeration market.

As the competition at global level is played with different rules and with different risks at various levels of production, it is necessary to differentiate between 'core competence', 'core production' and 'end product.' Corporation has to be winner at each level to build and defend leadership at national and global level. If a company has developed core competence at global level it must be able to build world leadership in the design and development of a particular class of product functionality. Philips has developed functional superiority in luminaries from simple electric bulb to electric decors. Philips could do it because it has developed competence in optical media- a leadership in design and development. These products are compact and user friendly. They are world-class products functionally. Gillette has developed world-class leadership in designing and developing shaving products, especially 'sensor blades', 'mark III blades', and 'victor plus shaving set'. Production of all shaving and allied health care products is the core competence of Gillette. Gillette has spread its core competence by acquiring Greenfield projects like 'Harbans Lal Malhotra and Sons Ltd.' In India. In this way Gillette has sustained leadership in chosen core competence areas. It has maximised its share in manufacturing world-class core products.

Considering the amendments in Monopolies and Restrictive Trade Practices Act (1969) Implemented from 27th September 1991, Brooke Bond Lipton India Ltd. acquired Kothari General Foods, Quality Frozen Foods, Milk Food Ice-cream, Kissan Food Products. Almost at the same time Hindustan Lever Ltd. acquired East Coast Fertilisers, Tata Oil Mills, Vashishti Detergents and finally acquired Brooke Bond Lipton India Ltd. This enabled Hindustan Lever Ltd. to establish its prominence in the 'fast moving consumer goods' (FMCGs) market. Strategies and policies implemented by Hindustan Lever Ltd. (HLL) in acquiring and strengthening core competence are worth discussing and analysing. When such an organisational restructuring in HLL was underway, the company conducted an intensive and extensive research survey of rural potential demand and created consumer awareness and confidence about packaged and branded consumer goods. HLL has developed capability of penetrating small sized large capacity markets. In this marketing strategy HLL introduced new products competing with its own products and deleted established products of acquired companies. (Tej-detergent, TOMCO-hair oil). This strategy was aiming at reducing company dependence on any one range of products. Even with all this, FMCGs have remained to be HLL's core production. This provided HLL a shield from cyclical ups and downs. However, weightage of core products in HLL changed. The share of HLL's core business, namely, soaps, detergents and household care products — in total production declined from 70 per cent in 1991 to 45 per cent in 2002; whereas that of food products rose from 2 per cent to 30 per cent and of personal products (tooth paste, shampoo, deodorants and skin care) from 5 per cent to 22 per cent in the same period. HLL has shed off its business in chemicals, agricultural products, fertilisers and animal feeds.[6] HLL's philosophy was to concentrate resources on potentially more valuable brands and migrate from non-core brands to power brands. Nirma, a competing product of rival company was encircled by variants of Lifebuoy and Breeze was fitted in between Nirma and Lifebuoy. Unfortunately, this strategy could not provide shield from increased competition and recession. Varied 110 products in 950 packagings of HLL began to defeat HLL itself. As a result, the company changed its strategy to concentrate on power brands. Thirty national power brands and ten regional power brands were selected. Emphasis was laid on bringing those power brands in limelight. Emphasis was shifted from 'Ala Bleach' to 'Rin' and from '501 soap bar' to 'Rin bar'. Certain trademarks were chosen as core brands and all efforts were concentrated on pushing them into market. Pepsodent in tooth paste, Surf Excell in detergent, Lux in toilet soaps, Rin Shakti in detergent cakes, Vim in utensil cleaner, Tajmahal in tea were the core brands chosen for implementing core development strategy. HLL has ten products under home and personal care category, while its competitor Proctor and Gamble has fourteen products in this category. In 2003 HLL launched new products for home care, kitchen care and laundry care. This was an important initiative to launch HLL's home range products.[7]

The discussion in foregoing paragraphs brings us to a conclusion that HLL has established core competence in respect of raw material, technique of production process, trade marks, packaging, quality of product, administrative management, financial management, dividend policy, advertising and marketing. As a result it has been able to build core competence at organisational level. This HLL could do because it distinguished between core products and core competence.

Sumitomo Corporation has established its' integrated corporate strength' at global level and then leveraged it further. As a result capability to use 'integrated corporate strength' effectively has itself become Sumitomo's core competence. Sumitomo meets varied needs of its customers by systematically and strategically integrating strong business foundation and capacity to perform varied functions. It gives emphasis on creating maximum value for customers by foreseeing changes in social system, economic environment and technology. Following four factors are the strong business founding pillars.

(1) Sumitomo Corporation has created a lasting confidence in the minds of customers about its functions by establishing and nurturing relationships for long period of time. This 'lasting confidence 'itself is the corporation's fundamental and valuable asset. Customers are sure of handing over their business to a secured business organisation.

(2) Sumitomo Corporation transmits quickly and securely commercial goods, financial funds and information through its 190 offices and 350 franchises spread over the entire world.

(3) Sumitomo Corporation has established varied and various types of relationships with more than one lakh business partners. It could do that

because of the confidence of customers and network of offices spread over the entire world.

(4) Sumitomo Corporation has developed a very strong foundation of intellectual capital. Knowledge accumulated by skilled employees working in various areas of technologies and having varied experience and information are the founding pillars of the Corporation.

Sumitomo Corporation provides expert services in respect of risk management, services in market surveys, and risks in marketing and project business. The Corporation undertakes following activities –

(1) It provides services in business creation that involves identifying promising new products, developing new markets and organising appropriate business operations.

(2) It provides expertise in developing logistics. It develops and deploys integrated logistic services to match demand and supply of cargoes, trucks, warehouse space etc.

(3) It has expertise in financial services. These services include provision of capital, project financing and advanced financing services such as securitisation of assets.

(4) With its expertise in information technology it builds supply chain management systems and support network.

(5) The Corporation can expertly manage diverse risks associated with credit standing and enterprise operations.

Sumitomo Corporation has developed core competence in providing services for creation of supply chain management systems in various fields. This service enables the customer companies to reduce the size of the company, to trim the workforce and thereby reduce direct operating costs. It helps them to reduce and optimise inventory through just-in-time delivery, This service relieves them from the core of managing lead time, helps them to increase efficiency through information sharing. Companies are able to eliminate redundant input and are able to improve their cash flow.

Discussion about core competence of Sumitomo Corporation teaches a number of lessons. The organisation should identify its aim, objectives and goals. It should develop appropriate work culture that will support the objectives. It should clearly identify what constitutes its core competence and it should establish world leadership in every activity and at every level. The organisation can develop core competence at corporate level only if its every activity becomes core activity. The concept of core competence in one product has become history and the concept of organisational core competence has come forth; this is a wider concept indeed. Reliance Industries has developed core competence in management style, team building and marketing strategy. As a result it automatically owns core competence in every activity that it undertakes from textiles to information technology.

C. K. Prahalad and Gary Hamel argue that organisations make all out efforts to raise share of their 'core products' in the world market to maximum level. This is done to maintain world leadership in their chosen 'core competence area.' The organisation earns good revenue by producing core products for internal and external customers. More important than that, the company can decide at what pace can it grow and spread its core competence. This forecasting is to be based on feedback information it receives from its internal and external customers. The case study discussed at length by C. K. Prahalad and Gary Hamel is very interesting and illuminating. I have discussed some part of it in following paragraphs. Victor Company of Japan made an agreement in 1970 to provide video-cassette recorders to American companies producing consumer electronics. The agreement was based on the thinking discussed above. Victor Company of Japan could acquire such deep and rich experience of various markets by providing video-cassette recorders to American partner business organisations like Thomson, Thorn, and Telefuncan. As a result it could beat world leader companies like Philips and Sony. Philips developed competency in producing videotapes but could not compete with Victor Company of Japan, because it had not developed worldwide relationship for supply of original equipment. LG, Samsung, Kia and Daewoo developed worldwide core competencies in production of diverse equipment like displays, semi-conductors, and automotive engines. This they could achieve through original equipment supply contracts they had signed with western companies. But they could not beat Victor Company of Japan. The goal of above mentioned Korean companies could 'hallow out' their competitors. They concentrated first on developing organisational competence; then they built core products. That means they first developed competence in component production and then they moved on the foundation of that competence to build up core product competence. So they could capture good brand share in the world market. After brand leadership they acquired price leadership also. That means, an organisation that wants to build up all round core competence leadership moves strategically from developing competence at component level, product level, price level and then at organisational level, the objective it had cherished long. It must be remembered that competence in one activity must be fortressed by competence in all complementary areas. Such unidirectional devoted strategic policy enables the company to build organisational core competence. These companies acquire all these competencies so fast that other companies do not have opportunity to build their own competence

Control on core products is important for other reasons also. It plays an important role in the development and deployment of various policies and strategies in respect of core products. It helps the organisation to mould the nature of the market. Godrej and Boycee Manufacturing Company made its name in India in respect of production of office furniture, steel cupboards, fire proof lockers, bank lockers, type writers etc. and created standards of drawing, nature, looks and quality of these products. The company developed new uses to which these products can be put to. As the company unveils new uses of the same products before customers, cost of production, time required to produce these goods and possibilities of entry of competitors are reduced. Now they have developed a new concept 'FORMULA' 'S' one stop shop catering to absolutely any furniture need, setting up offices from design to finish providing seatings, deskings, open plan office systems, storage units etc. That is how core competence is enhanced. Core products produced by focusing on consumer needs provide economies of scale to the organisation and enhances its scope.

NEW CONCEPT OF BUSINESS ORGANISATION

The philosophy of today's business organisation is basically and completely different from the philosophy of business organisation based on strategic business units. Earlier organisations used to compete in respect of producing existing goods while today's organisations compete on the concept of building 'competence.' As a result organisations of present days have to pay attention along with their business on developing 'core products' and building 'core competence'. New approach towards responsibilities of management changes attitude towards types of diversification, skillful deployment of resources, priorities of distribution of resources, agreement to be reached with other organisations and sourcing jobs from outside.

An organisation has to fight on all the three fronts of 'core products', 'core competence' and 'final product' to acquire world leadership and maintain it. More importantly organisation has to develop core competence of people. It has to analyse its success or otherwise in each of these four respects. Even if an organisation can acquire best technology on the strength of its investment, it does not mean that she can acquire leadership in 'core competence'. However if an organisation has become successful in building up 'core competence' it can surpass many organisations. If an organisation can win greater share in world market in respect of production of core products it can surpass many organisations in reforming the nature of the product and in improving price-performance ratio. It is however difficult to measure success or otherwise of an organisation in the market of final product, because share of an organisation in the market cannot gauge underlying capacity of an organisation to compete. Many an organisations, instead of investing in core competence area and building leadership in the core product market try to increase their share in the market by evaluating competitiveness of other organisations. Actually they are walking on slippery ground. Many an organisations have developed in large number world-renowned brands on the basis of the strength of core competence. This has helped them to build up their image, customer loyalty and utilise various channels of distribution.

One thing becomes clear from the foregoing discussion that the days of organising a company on basis of the group of strategic business units are gone. It was considered to be suicidal to succumb to the benefits of decentralisation when people had faith in the concept of strategic business units. Organisation having predominance of strategic business units considered it to be the only and major policy to fight to position their products in global market. Organisations trapped in this concept did not make adequate investment in developing their core competence and core products. That was a big loss. No strategic business unit in an organisation shoulders the responsibility of leveraging the position of core product. Because the company is considered to be a group of strategic business units. No strategic business unit in such an organisation considers it necessary to justify investment for acquiring global leadership in core competence. Many an organisations have realised that the concept of strategic business unit is likely to be a potential problem in the development of a business organisation. And to resolve this problem they are in search of new architectural pattern of business organisation.

Another important disadvantage, the organisations trapped in the concept of strategic business units have to face, is that, when strategic business units are evolving they develop unique competencies. Individuals who have build up competence while developing the strategic business units consider themselves to be sole proprietor of that unit. If another strategic business unit wishing to borrow services of such talented persons would be denied of that. Managers of such strategic business units are not only unwilling to lend services of such talented competent persons but actually hide their talent to prevent redeployment in pursuit of new opportunities. Development of Knowledge Corporation depends upon flow of knowledge and intelligence. The resources of an organisation are locked in the structure of business organisation based on strategic business units. Companies in the Western countries had large reservoir of talented people but they did not take advantage of utilising these talents for the betterment of the organisation. Asian companies, in spite of having comparative scarcity of such talent, utilised the skills of such talented persons by quickly redeploying them. As a result they could take full advantage of changing opportunities. Such persons were quickly moved from one strategic business unit to another. We cannot assess the strength of core competence of a company by looking to its research and development division. We cannot even have an idea how quickly and efficiently the organisation can redeploy persons holding core competence to derive benefits of existing opportunities.

People holding competencies when locked in one strategic business unit are not deputed to another strategic business unit to take advantage of existing opportunities. And then the skill and competency of these persons begin to become inactive and deteriorate. Small organisations by leveraging core competence of their people, can compete with large corporations and defeat them. Such incidences have occurred on global level. Managers of strategic business units competing for budgetary allocations to their units do not seem to be caring for allocating human skills embodying core competencies. Top management of orthodox organisations while implementing huge project of capital investment does not use any method to get maximum out of people holding core competencies. They do not seem to be making efforts to find out what competencies their subordinates have acquired.

Organisation should build core competence and top management must make its optimum use. Concept of this strategy was accepted much later. Prahalad and Hamel narrates an illustration of an American company. They state that the company enjoyed a world-wide position in power and motion controls and engineered plastics. A major division of this company transformed its existing business by applying electronic technology with its traditional technologies. This was done with an objective of not distancing the organisation from customers. Division of the company realised soon that it could not protect its present market and grab new opportunities of development unless it acquires new skills. Management of the division attempted to conceptualise the likely evolution of — (1) technologies relevant to the power and motion control business, (2) functions that would satisfy emerging consumer needs, and (3) new competencies that are needed to creatively manage the marriage of technology and customer needs.

While implementing long-term strategy, such company may find that its short-term profits have declined. However, without coming under pressure of declining profits the company, whose profile has been discussed by Prahalad and Hamel in the above paragraph, developed a map of core competencies that it would have to build up to bridge the gap between emerging customer needs and changing technologies. 'Towards 21st Century' was the slogan developed by the said organisation. Another case study discussed by C.K. Prahalad and Gary Hamel states that — Vickers is presently enjoying core competencies in fluid power components. It is building core competence in electric-power components and electronic controls. It is providing computer hardware, software and services related to that. Its present concern is to build core competence in integration of these three activities.

The strategic architecture discussed in preceding paragraphs is mapping of efforts to develop linkages between core competencies and customers' functional needs that may crop up in the future. This integration cannot be achieved by creating hierarchical structure embodying business organisation and strategic business units functioning under it. To achieve such effect an integrated structure responding positively and quickly to changing environment, and embodying modern mindset that synchronises the ability of utilising and need for creating core competence are required. That means, in today's scenario of cut-throat competition organisational structure needs to be so developed as to match the need of creating and protecting core competence. In such an organisation nobody is an owner and nobody is a worker or nobody is an officer and nobody is a worker; all are colleagues; all are associates.

Future products and systems cannot be described accurately; however, even if they can be conceived in blurred form; they can be helpful in building core competence. As a result markets can be developed much before rival firms come in. The company can rule over such a market. Such architectural mapping of the structure of business organisation becomes helpful in developing new core competencies within the organisation. This enables the organisation to identify and fill in the gaps in availability of technology and products and thereby build up core competencies. The organisation can integrate different technologies, disciplines and reach the benefits of this to the customers. The organisation must be competent to bring all persons, holding core competencies, together crossing the boundaries of strategic business units.

If the organisational structure is not reengineered in such a drastic way, the strategic business units will pursue only those innovations that can be achieved easily and may do marginal product-line extension or may do little geographic expansion. Hybrid products like lap-top, hand-held televisions or portable music key boards can be developed only if the managers of strategic business units think beyond the boundaries of their units and co-operate with each other. Conceiving the concept of corporate core competence widens the zenith of innovations.

DEVELOPMENT OF UNIFIED ORGANISATION

Core competence of the organisation is fragmented because many factors like diversified information system, methods of communication, career development, system of developing strategies do not cross the boundaries of strategic business units. Top management must counteract this phenomenon by devoting adequate time in developing a strategy that encompasses whole organisation. It must identify objectives for competence building. Such strategic map is a guiding principle for identifying core competencies to be built in future and their constituent technologies.

The organisation need not make substantial investment to secure market leadership in future. A strategic map needs to be prepared on the basis of new and newer methods learnt from alliances. Attention needs to be focused on development of internal systems prepared for securing market leadership. The organisation, then, will be able to reap full benefits of alliances. The organisation must be conscious of competence it is developing and must prevent other organisation from snatching it.

Organisation should control its competencies to preserve its competitive status in the market. Organisation can preserve its competitive position in the market only if core competence plays the major role in transforming benefits of competency to customers. It would have to forego many an opportunities in future if it cannot preserve this competency. That is why it is necessary to protect major core competencies by building a shield of complementary competencies around it. Out of such organisational structure flows the logic of diversification of products and diversification of markets. Organisational structure erected on this logic provides opportunity to become the best player in the market and this enshrines the competence further.

Strategic structuring of the organisation makes priorities of resource allocation very clear. Such structuring provide a template to top management to take decision regarding allocation of resources. It enables the middle management to maintain coherence in organisational objectives and allocation of resources. Such strategic restructuring helps lower management to understand the logic of allocation of priorities. And all people in the organisation get a feel of the organisation and of the market in which it provides services. Organisation, because of such strategic restructuring, can establish linkages between strategic business units in respect of technology and production. Consistency in resource allocation and creation of administrative infrastructure consistent to it puts life into the organisation. Such structure enables the organisation to develop management culture conducive to its aims and objectives. It induces employees to work in teams. Employees must have developed ability to adapt to the new set of circumstances. It develops attitude among strategic business units to share resources. Organisation learns to protect proprietary skills and to think long term. Organisational strategic structuring can be used as a means to communicate with external constituents and customers. It is important that such unique strategic structure is difficult to be copied by rival firms.

RESTRUCTURING TO UTILISE COMPETENCIES

Core competencies of an organisation are its critical assets. Therefore, top management must ensure that competence holders are not held hostages by a strategic business unit. Managers of strategic business unit must have freedom to bid for competencies as they have freedom to bid for capital. Once the top management has identified most important competencies it must direct the managers of strategic business units and divisional heads to prepare project reports for utilising such important competencies and identify people closely associated with such projects. Top management must take upon itself to identify places to locate such projects, their number and assess quality of people who embody such competencies. This discussion makes it very clear that the core competencies are corporate property even though a strategic business unit holds it. The organisation has right to allocate and reallocate them to ensure their maximum utilisation. A strategic business unit gets right to use that competency if it proves that it can utilise these competencies most efficiently and effectively. Managers of strategic business units must present at the time of annual strategic planning and budgeting process meeting proofs of maximum utilisation of such competencies and control over people holding these competencies. Ambitious organisation, desiring to exploit unprecedented opportunity in developing a product and capturing the market, should empower strategic business unit to pool competent people from all over the organisation.

Such organisations should felicitate persons by presenting award for developing a new innovation. They should honour the persons and teams developing new innovations by crossing the boundaries of strategic business units and unifying inter-organisational, inter-departmental and inter-functional activities. In many an organisations divisional managers discuss as to what can be and should be the competencies of next generation. They prepare an action plan as to how much investment and how many employees will be required to build up such competency. In achieving such competency the contribution of a division, in short period may be more or less, but in long-run such inequalities balance out. One important point needs to be made. It is very necessary to make the entire organisation know the positive contribution of the manager of the strategic business unit. Manager of the strategic business unit, whose employees have made positive contribution in building organisational competence, must be equally felicitated. Otherwise managers of strategic business units will not consent transfer of competent persons to collective projects on the pretext of obstruction to the work in their units. However, such problem would not crop up if the objectives and priorities of redeployment of employees are clear and transparent

Redeployment of employees for building core competence must be recorded and their contribution should be appreciated in corporate history. One thing must be taken care of; shortfall in the performance of a strategic business unit or division should be condoned if it is because of transfer of competent people to acquire organisational competence. It is necessary to wean the idea from the minds of key employees that they belong to a particular strategic business unit or division. It is important, that people, in their earlier career, should be rotated as per well-programmed plan and exposed to variety of business skills and functions. In the middle of their career they should be purposely nominated to cross-divisional and cross-functional teams. This would facilitate diffusion of core competencies and build up courage to break bonds with their own department in pursuit of opportunities for development. Persons who possess critical core competencies should be periodically brought together from across the organisation to discuss and exchange their ideas and notes. A feeling of belongingness must be rooted in their minds. This will develop loyalty towards the integrity of core competence rather than towards the division or the strategic business unit they belong to. They will have opportunities to discuss and discover new ideas when they travel and talk with peers and customers. They should be given an opportunity to be peripatetic. They may be able to discover new market opportunities. This helps building up a knowledge reservoir and facilitates dissemination of knowledge. Organisations holding core competencies are intelligent corporations; they are knowledge corporations. A small but significant advancement deserves mention. In a pharmaceutical company all persons belonging to managerial cadre were served coffee at their desks. The waiter would collect empty thermocol cups and throw them in the dustbin. Next day morning stray children would fight to collect these cups; which were, latter it was found, recycled in the kitchen that served the coffee. This was a great hazard to the health of the people. Thus, HR people proposed that managerial cadre people should assemble in a room and take coffee together. Besides avoiding health hazard this arrangement had a considerable trade-off. People, who seldom talked to each other ideas they had in mind, began to discuss their ideas with colleagues and exchange their thoughts. This developed into a concept of developing a new molecule. A team of representatives of these managers was formed; a research project was floated and in short spans of time a new molecule was developed. It is needless to state the HR man was felicitated by reward of an award and announcement of promotion.

In the preceding seven sections, we have discussed the concept of core competence, its scope, reconceptualisation of organisation in terms of core competence, foundation of competitive advantage and preparing organisation to develop core competencies. We have also discussed comparative views of core products and core areas and final products, new concept of core competent organisation. We have analaysed the process of redeployment of physical, human and intellectual resources for maximisation of exploitation of core competence. This discussion brings us to a conclusion that core competence is the foundation of organisational development. Core competence must be the centre of focus of corporate strategy. It should build world leadership in production of core products. They should acquire sizeable share in the global market by creating prestigious trademarks to reach the objective of maximum exploitation of market opportunities. The organisation can ride over waves of globalisation of present days by creating an insurmountable, implacable chain of strategic business units that focus attention on market, core products and core competencies. Management system that builds corporate strategies providing guidance and patronage for building corporate competencies can alone survive today. Organisations hypnotized with the fervor of building core competency under any circumstances would be the corporation of 21st century. This necessitates reconceptualisation of the very structure of corporate body.

References

(1) Prahalad C.K. and Hamel Gary- 'The Core Competence of the Corporation' *Harvard Business Review*, May-June, 1990, pp. 79-91.

(2) Turban Efraim and Aronson Jay E. –*Decision Support Systems and Intelligent Systems-Pearson Education*, Asia, 2001, p. 369.

(3) Drucker Peter F., *Management Challenges for the 21st Century*, Butterworth-Heinemann, 1999, p. 24.

(4) Alavi M. and Leidner D. –'Knowledge Management Systems – Issues, Challenges and Benefits' *Communications of the Association for Information System*, Vol. 1, February 1999, Art.7.

(5) Leonard –Burton D. –'Core Capabilities and Core Rigidities- A Paradox in Managing New Product Development' *Strategic Management Journal*, Vol. 13, 1992, pp. 111-125.

(6) Hindustan Lever Limited, *Report and Accounts*, 2002, p. 24.

(7) Business India – Cover Feature, March 18-31, 2002, pp. 53-57.

❑ ❑ ❑

10 Corporate Governance

R. M. Cyert and J. G. March have discussed the process of decision-making adopted by mulitiproduct firms in the environment of uncertainty experienced in imperfect market conditions. A business organisation is a conglomeration of shareholders, labourers, customers, owners, government, suppliers, financial institutions, administrative officers and ministers and tries to satisfy all these constituents. Business organisation should, with a view to satisfy all of them, take decisions on the basis of maximum information collected from all possible sources. Accordingly, financial provision should be made for all strategic business units. In doing so the past performance of strategic business units should be scrutinised. However, managers of such strategic business units provide that information to the organisation that is favourable to them; even sometimes the information is distorted. This created a paradigm known as managerial capitalism. It has been further strengthened by the method of granting stock options under the pretext of providing incentives (or perverse incentives) to attract and retain skilled and efficient managers in the business organisation. Such a system of linking executive compensation to equities has created a tendency to inflate the stock prices even by using unfair practices. Executives, many a times, cook the books of accounts by fudging the figures even by transgressing the rules of accounting and auditing standards. This is done with a view to inflate profits of the organisation by not showing cost of stock options as expenditure in annual accounts of the organisation. It is established that Enron did the same thing. Behaviour of Indian Tobacco Company in respect of avoiding Central Excise Duty and in respect of Foreign Exchange Regulation Act, Board of Directors of Shaw Wallace and Company turning deaf year to the fact that its shares were being wasted by middle class investors, not paying any heed by British Physical Laboratories, Sterlite Industries and Videocon International to the artificial price hike of shares by 'Big Bull' Harshad Mehta – all these events support the theory advocated by Cyert and March. They support the general belief that business organisations hide many facts from the government and the public and maintain no transparency in their business.

The same thing is experienced in respect of most of the business organisations all over the world. Directors of most of the corporations entail illegal activities and try to do all out efforts to put the organisation back on the track when it is derailed.

The results of the survey conducted by 'Business Week' in 1996 showed that business organisations scored from 9.9 points to 97.8 points out of 100 points. That is why, Cadbury Committee was appointed in England and National Association of Corporate Directors of the U.S. were organised in the United States to fully regenerate, to reengineer corporate governance practices. Corporate bodies have to institute quality and transparent governance practices so that they can stand in the competition to woo the customers, so that they can work in the interest of the customers and deliver maximum value to them. Corporate bodies have to install good governance because financial institutions begin demanding transparent behaviour and disclose all information as per international standards. Corporations have also realised that good governance pays them by enhancing their competitive advantage. As a result boards of directors have become active and responsible; they object to the autocracy of chief executive officer. South-East and East Asian crisis of 1997-98 brought it forth that witty-gritty of transactions between companies, banks, financial institutions and capital markets endanger the existence of world renowned companies and destroys the image of fast growing nations. In such a milieu there seemed to be an urgent need to impose concepts like better accounting practices, greater disclosure and independent board oversight.

Asian crisis barely touched India. However, 1992 stock market scam and onset of international competition consequent of liberalisation of economy that began in 1990 required a change in corporate practices in India. The movement to make small investors, partners in primary capital issues of private sector industries required maximisation of value of their investment, and protection of this value and their interests. Permission to collect deposits from public on certain conditions required greater importance to the rights and interests of depositors in the governance of corporate bodies in private sector. That is why since April 2001 a number of stringent guidelines have been imposed on governance practices in India. They rank among some of the best in the world. Even so, there is scope for improvement. Though India has instituted excellent rules and regulations, regulatory authorities are inadequately staffed and lack sufficient number of skilled people. This has led to less than credible enforcement. Delays in courts compound this problem. India has had its fair share of corporate scams and stock market scandals that has shaken investor confidence. This situation can be improved by making companies adopt practices of good, transparent governance and companies adopting practices of good governance on their own and in their own interest.

MEANING OF CORPORATE GOVERNANCE

It is very difficult to explain the concept of corporate governance. Researchers in management science and management professionals have defined corporate governance differently. It is generally agreed that the corporation must be so governed that customers, employees, financiers, investors, suppliers, government and society should feel it to be rational and honest. The concept of corporate governance is based on the principle of accountability. It must be accountable to minority shareholders, small shareholders, founder promoters, institutional shareholders, depositors, creditors, customers and employees. Complete involvement of employees towards quality and cost, empowering employees and accountability towards risk bearers are the constituents of corporate governance. Meaning of the framework of corporate governance is to respond to the risk bearers by owners and managers of corporate bodies.

Corporate governance creates a set of various processes and systems that will protect interests of stakeholders in best possible manner. The concept of corporate governance lays emphasis on maximising shareholders value, protect interests of employees, creditors and customers and make management accountable about corporate performance. However, it would be wrong to presume that this can be achieved by maximising returns to shareholders. Corporate governance considers that it is more important to resolve complex problems of environment, ethics, politics, religious understanding and society than to produce goods and earn profits.

Corporate governance is a means to secure benefits for all corporate stakeholders. Corporate governance is practised for furthering corporate objectives. Corporate governance invigilates daily business of the company by creating various constraints and balances. In a very broad sense corporate governance is trusteeship. Objective of corporate governance is to work for customer satisfaction, maximise shareholders' value, and protect interest of stakeholders and to create a corporate body performing better than expectation.

Corporate governance has been defined as —

(1) It is a systematic process by which companies are directed and controlled to enhance their wealth generating capacity. These processes should ensure that the resources are utilised in a manner that meets stakeholders' aspirations and societal expectations.

(2) Corporate governance deals with conducting affairs of a company to maximise shareholders' value, such that (a) trust is built around the enterprise which is managed adequately and efficiently in its chosen business, (b) there is openness, integrity and accountability in the dealings of the company, (c) there is fairness to its shareholders, and (d) there is adequate supervision of its business activities.

(3) Corporate governance is a code of conduct that requires maintenance and enhancement of the reputation of the company and wins trust and confidence of all those with whom it deals. The company should maintain ethical standards in its dealings with all those with whom it is concerned.

(4) Corporate governance is concerned with the process by which corporate entities, particularly limited liability companies, are governed. This is concerned with the exercise of power over the direction of the enterprise, the supervision of executive actions, the acceptance of a duty to be accountable and the regulation of the corporation within the jurisdiction of the states in which it operates. Corporate governance refers to the discipline and control of firms designed to ensure that they are efficiently managed and that economic welfare of society is maximised. Critical issues in governance include: standards of audit and financial control,

accountability, disclosure and transparency of company direction, the selection, quality and competence of directors and the weakness of self regulation and the efficacy of external regulation.

OBJECTIVES OF CORPORATE GOVERNANCE

Objective of corporate governance is to secure healthy growth of the company in a self-propagating manner in intense competitive conditions. That is why emphasis is laid on improving the quality of governance to enhance shareholders' value and make the business transparent as far as possible. Objective of corporate governance is to make the business honest, accountable and healthy. Otherwise people lose confidence and trust in the company. Corporate bodies have to have replicable behaviour so as to attract domestic and foreign capital. Financially corporate body must be sound enough to withstand any eventuality. Company must do business honestly and must treat all its employees honourably and satisfactorily. The distribution of work, wage system and reward pattern in the company should reduce labour turnover to the minimum.

FUNDAMENTAL PRINCIPLES OF CORPORATE GOVERNANCE

The principles of corporate governance accepted by all can be discussed as below—

(1) Company institutes a system of corporate governance considering the structural and organisational factors as to how the functions and businesses in the company should be carried out. These procedures and practices are evolved taking into account interests of all stakeholders of the company. Every corporate body is constituted artificially and legally; it is an independent entity. But it cannot function by itself. The board of directors depicts personality of corporate body. That is why; board of directors is the major and important arm of the corporate body. How best the business of a company is run is evident from the constitution and unity of the board of directors. Size of the board of directors, its constitution, role of directors, their individual competence, educational qualifications, frequency with which constitution of the board of directors is changed and proportion of representation of stakeholders on the board are important factors in corporate governance. Corporate governance is the management system developed to fully protect the interests of the stakeholders. Board of directors, various committees of the board and chairman of the board of directors must deliberately develop such practices that will enable the organisation to function effectively. These practices include system of managing performance, periodical review of the business, environmental audit, energy audit, security audit, secretarial practices, audit of legal matters, benchmarking and customer satisfaction.

(2) Bifurcation of ownership and management is an important part of corporate governance. Many have misconception that the board of directors have no role to play in management. Board of directors is fully responsible to decide strategy of the organisation considering the directives issued by it and to manage it. The board

of directors must be fully committed to achieve customer satisfaction to the highest level to increase shareholders' value to the highest limit.

(3) Philosophy of corporate governance rests on the factors that the board should not limit its role in discharging legal responsibility only; it should focus its attention on directing the activities of the organisation and manage it. Board of directors must see to it that the organisation is functioning honestly and fairly and obeys all standards of legal provisions and controls. The essence of corporate governance is in providing freedom to management to develop the organisation and at the same time limit it to discharge accountability effectively within the framework of values cherished by it.

(4) Freedom and independence granted to the managers is the foundation of accountability. Equally so, each corporation needs separate board of directors to implement the best practices of corporate governance. It is a point of debate whether it is advisable to have one person on two positions of chairman and chief executive officer of the organisation. The practice of appointing chairman of public sector undertaking in India limits their independence. Cadbury committee appointed to make recommendations about corporate governance in England opined that the distribution of work and responsibility among managers must be acceptable to all. The committee further recommended that power should not be unduly concentrated in the hands of any one person. The position of chairman and chief executive officer are, if at all, in the hands of one person must be counter-balanced by inclusion of respectable, experienced and principled persons on the board of directors. Their independence must be secured. This principle is highly honoured in the U.S.A. Most of the directors on the board must hold independent views.

Khan S.H., the former chairman of the Industrial Development Bank of India, argues that 'Roles of chairman and chief executive officer must be clear, independent and different. Then only we can counter concentration of power in one person and accept the role of chairman in establishing the best practices of corporate governance. Two different persons must be holding these two positions. Chairman of the corporate body should hold no executive authority.' However, in most of the public sector projects and enterprises in India both these posts are vested in one person. The functions are politically interfered but best governance is expected of them. This is paradoxical.

(5) Scope of corporate governance is much wider and beyond the rules and legal provisions. Corporate governance is related to unwritten rules, work procedures, processes, legal provisions that limit the ability of corporate body to take decisions on the basis of required information. Corporate governance is concerned with economic, legal and organisational environment that helps the management to develop the company. This provides the management an opportunity to achieve diversification, to reengineer the corporate structure and to compete with rival firms. The corporate governance may be carried out by minimal observation of controlling provisions; however, that is not ideal, that is not the best governance. Minimisation of controlling

provisions and development as well as strict implementation of voluntary constraints is the best way to achieve efficiency and effectiveness of corporate governance

(6) Self control is the key to best corporate governance. Business organisations realise the fact that best corporate governance practices are the major source of competitive advantage when they are honoured by suppliers, potential co-partners, investors and customers for following good corporate governance practices. This makes it amply clear that there is no need to enforce rules of good corporate governance on any organisation. Every organisation should develop and sincerely implement its own constitution of corporate governance for protecting own interests and that of stakeholders.

(7) The main pillars of corporate governance are to disclose the information and to make the business practices transparent. Financial institutions are closely and continuously related to all sectors of the economy; they are connected with all transactions. It is of paramount importance for financial institutions that business houses should disclose information and impart transparency in business. Both these matters are of greater help in supervising corporate bodies by financial institutions. Moreover, they voluntarily observe discipline of markets. The very existence of non-financial institutions in free market economy depends upon competitive advantage. Therefore, the pressure on improving corporate governance increases as the economy becomes freer.

THEORY OF CORPORATE GOVERNANCE

Most of the corporate bodies have large number of widely dispersed shareholders. They have specific objectives, which the corporate bodies should endeavour to achieve. Fair and good rate of return on their investment, fair and equal treatment of all shareholders, honest and rational system of doing business, paying due share to the exchequer, disclosure of maximum information, presenting fair and true picture of financial position of the company, creating wealth, maximising and distributing value to the shareholders and customers can be listed as some of the major objectives that shareholders would want their companies to achieve. As all shareholders cannot directly or indirectly participate in the business of the company, this responsibility is transferred to the members of the board of directors who are expected to vigilantly guard the interests of stakeholders.

However, such large multi-product, multi-divisional, multi-segmental, multi-national corporations though supervised are not managed by the board of directors. Managers of such corporate bodies pay a lip service to the objectives, because their interests lie somewhere else than the interests of the stakeholders. J. H. Williamson[1] has made this amply clear in his model. Managers derive utility from discretionary policy. R. M. Cyert and J. G. March[2] have argued that managers provide only that information to the decision-making top management that secures their position. In other words objectives of managers are quite different from those of the shareholders. This misalignment in the objectives of shareholders and managers results into governance of lesser quality. The misalignment in objectives is called the agency problem. The cost inflicted by such dissonance is the agency cost. The fundamental theoretical basis of corporate governance is agency costs.

Corporate history suggests that there are two types of agency costs and both relate to the basic concept of separation. The first is the separation of ownership and management. With vast and dispersed shareholding, managers enjoyed wide playing fields. Such huge de-facto uncontrolled managerial playing fields led to wrong investment decisions, unconnected diversification and taking of excessive risks with shareholders' funds. This deteriorated efficiency and declined long-term corporate value. This is the first type of agency cost. This agency cost was visualised by Adam Smith. He wrote—

'The directors (managers) of such companies, however being managers of other people's money than their own, it cannot well be expected that they should watch over it with the same anxious vigilance with which the partners in a private co-partnery frequently watch over their own. Negligence and profusion, therefore, must always prevail more or less in the management of the affairs of such a company'.[3]

Separation of ownership and management causes second type of agency cost which affects rights of minority shareholders. Companies having small equity base can take decisions that promoters find to their advantage. Promoters find it relatively cheap to own majority shares; they can takeover other companies very easily which also have a small equity base. Promoter directors have considerable complex cross-holdings. This enables promoter directors to do fixing of the election of board members, crowding the boards with crony directors, ensuring that key shareholders' resolutions are vaguely worded and in-adequately discussed at shareholders' meeting, fobbing off minority shareholders' complaints, issuing preferential equity allotments to the promoters and their allies at discount, transferring shares through private bought out deals at prices well below those in secondary market. All these agency costs of second type lead to improper corporate governances.

In India a number of incidences of second type of agency costs can be sighted. However, their nature is basically different than discussed above. Many a companies, after having raised money in primary market have just disappeared and shareholders have lost all their investment. Many a corporate bodies have bought loss making small private companies belonging to allies of managers and/or directors or having beneficial interest in such companies at exorbitantly high prices using shareholders' money. Prices of shares of companies are artificially raised to make existing shareholders to invest more and new investors to invest anew. In many companies opportunities for maximising stakeholders value are diverted to increase promoter's value.

Diversions between shareholder's objectives and manager's objectives, which are named as agency costs, deteriorate the quality of corporate governance. Two broad instruments to reduce agency costs and hence to improve corporate governance are *financial and non-financial disclosures* and *independent oversight of management*. The company has to disclose, its financial position, production activities, environment friendly measures, intellectual capital, equal treatment to all, through its annual reports. The company should get its accounts audited from independent auditors and ensure that the company practises only world standard accounting methods. These annual reports should be published and circulated to all shareholders. Quarterly financial reports and segment reports should be published to improve the quality and frequency of disclosures.

Companies should provide along with this financial information, non-financial information also. Companies should provide information about constitution of board of directors, proportion of independent directors, formation of committees to invigilate various activities of the company, educational status of the board, meetings of the board and attendance at the meetings. Method adopted for computing intellectual capital and its monetary value should be included in the report in clear and factual terms.

Independent oversight of management comprises two aspects. The first relates to the roll of independent statutory auditors. They are appointed by shareholders at annual general meeting, to audit a company's accounts and present a 'true and fair' view of the financial health of the corporation. The quality and independence of the statutory auditors are fundamental to corporate oversight. These auditors must posses the skills to scrutinise complex accounts of today's multi-divisional, multi-product, multi-segmental, multi-national corporations. They must be conversant with international accounting practices and auditing standards.

The second aspect of oversight of management is the board of directors of the company. They must supervise management and ensure that it does all that is necessary by legal and ethical means to make the business grow and maximise long-term corporate value. The board, being nominated/elected by shareholders, is accountable to them. If the objectives of management differ from those of the shareholders, non-executive independent directors must speak in the interest of the shareholders, discharge their fiduciary oversight functions and stand up and be counted. That is why 'independence' has become such a critical issue to determining the composition of the board of directors. Poor quality of boards usually lacks acumen for independent oversight. The non-executive independent directors must ask for all relevant and important information from management, scrutinize it for its fairness and correctness and see that it is made public to the shareholders. They must insist on detailed debate on every issue that interests stakeholders, employees, suppliers and society.

There are two distinct models of corporate governance. One is market-based outsider model and the other is representation-based insider model.

Market-based corporate governance: Members of the board of directors and managers of the company are closely allied with each other. Capital market exercises control and discipline. If shareholders feel that the company is not managed properly or their interests are neglected they begin to sell shares held by them exhibiting their disapproval of corporate governance. Naturally, the company is exposed to hostile takeovers. The shareholders base their decision on the information that is disclosed by the company and consider that it is true and fair.

Representation-based corporate governance: Members of the board of directors play a strong monitoring role on managers of the company. Diverse groups of stakeholders, like employees, banks, other companies, development banks, influential persons in the society, represent on the board of directors. Most of them are loyal investors and they hold considerable cross-shareholding. Naturally, stock market control and discipline on the corporate governance is not possible, as discussed in market-based model. In countries like Japan even suppliers and contractors associating with bank or financial institution take active part in corporate governance. Naturally, managers being free from external supervision and monitoring, they tend to work on the basis of their internal consensus.

In the United States structure of board of directors is unitary in which management dominates. A reform was introduced to induct non-executive directors that have strengthened the value of the company. However, they have not been successful in discharging oversight function. This model of corporate governance has dynamic market orientation; it provides fluid capital to the company and enables the company to extend globally. But it suffers from volatile instability, "short-term"ism and inadequate governance structure.

As against in the United States, in the United Kingdom the board of directors dominates the management. Naturally, they were hardly accountable to the stakeholders for their deeds. As per the recommendations of the Cadbury Committee a balance of power is to be established by including non-executive directors who carry significant weight in the board decisions. An audit committee of the board of directors composed entirely of non-executive directors is constituted to go into all financial transactions of the company. A remuneration committee would fix the remunerations of directors and senior managers. This model suffers from the same shortcomings of the U.S. model.

In Germany small and medium sized enterprises are in large number. Therefore, ownership is strongly concentrated in the hands of individuals. Naturally, there is a close correspondence between owners and managers. That means governance of enterprises is in the hands of inside people. Therefore, interested stakeholders like managers, employees, creditors, suppliers and customers monitor the performance of the company. Thus, the company is able to plan long-term strategy, it has very stable base of capital and therefore robust governance procedures have been established. But this model suffers from a few weaknesses. It is a rigid organisational structure that lacks flexibility. Most of the enterprises being small or medium sized, cannot reach global platform. As ownership of capital is concentrated in the hands of few individuals adequate investible funds are not available.

The Japanese system of corporate governance relies on trust and implicit contracting and a relationship oriented approach. Companies are closely linked with banks and there is considerable cross shareholding. This makes hostile takeover almost impossible. Board of directors has not much say in the governance. Boards are far too large, composed mainly of company executives. They are highly secretive, totally loyal and exclusively appointed by the president of the company. Statutory auditors are ineffective; therefore their warnings of future debacle are not taken seriously. Companies have been able to plan very long-term industrial strategy; they enjoy a stable foundation of capital and can make major overseas investments. However, secrecy of management leads to corrupt governance procedures. Financial speculations mar performance. There is hardly any accountability towards stakeholders.

Government of Mauritius had appointed a committee on corporate governance in September 2001 under the chairmanship of Tim Taylor. The committee made extensive recommendations on (a) board of directors, (b) auditing and accounting, (c) internal audit control and risk management, (d) compliance and enforcement, and (e) non-financial aspects. The committee stated that good corporate governance is a means to achieve sustainable economic and social objectives and it feels that the fundamental principles of good corporate governance are accountability, transparency, responsibility, fair treatment, mentocracy, and management discipline and fight against corruption.

Studies done by various researchers in diverse disciplines like Economics and Finance, Organisational Theory, Sociology, Politics and Law have outlined theoretical perspectives on Corporate Governance. They are exhibited in Table 10.1.

Table 10.1
Theoretical Perspectives of Board Role on Corporate Governance

Authority	*Management of Assets*	*Theoretical Perspective*			
		Resource Utilisation	*Stakeholders Stay*	*Managerial Influence*	*Class Influence*
Ensure Association and Collaboration between Managers and shareholders	Ensure safely Rational use of Corporate Assets	Reduce Uncertainty And external Limitations of Corporate body	To further the Interests of the stakeholders	Consider Board of Directors as Least Influential	To increase The power of masses and elite Class for long Period

PRINCIPALITIES OF CORPORATE GOVERNANCE

Corporate governance is a factor in the organisation that resides in the macro-factor like national economic policy, product market and factor market. The legal, procedural and organisational environment in the country conditions the framework of corporate governance. It also depends upon business ethics, organisational awareness about environment and the importance given by society to social problems. Corporate governance and decision process as well the image and success in the long-term of business organisation depend upon such a host of factors. Even then the principalities of corporate governance depend upon division between ownership and management of business organisation.

The sincerity, with which business organisation follows these principalities, plays an important role in its decision-making process. The relationship between investment decisions and good governance has acquired immense importance since the nature of investment has become international. Business organisations have entered into a wider financial market since the source of international investment has opened up. Corporate governance of business organisations must be reliable, trustworthy and of international standard so as to enable the nation to reap the benefits of global capital market and to attract foreign capital permanently. It is accepted that many an organisations have not to depend primarily upon foreign capital market, even then the best corporate governance system is useful in enhancing the confidence of domestic investors, in reducing cost of capital and in developing insatiable source of capital.

Interrelationship between different factors in the process of governance does affect corporate governance. Shareholders, may they be individuals, undivided families or contracting groups or promoter organisations, do affect the behaviour of corporate body. Institutional investors as shareholders are demanding for greater involvement in the process of corporate governance of business organisations. Individual investors, though not demanding participation in the process of corporate governance, do expect rational treatment from shareholders controlling management of organisation and from the management itself. Creditors of business organisations do play important role in some systems of corporate governance. These creditors do play the role of observing the performance of the business organisation from outside. Government creates the institutional and legal framework that assists and at the same time controls corporate governance. All the above-mentioned factors do participate in determining the nature, system and effectiveness of corporate governance. The interaction between these factors also affects the process of corporate governance.

There is no authentic model of corporate governance. Business organisations must constantly innovate new systems of corporate governance. It enables them to maintain their competitiveness in the changing circumstances and in dynamic world. So that they can satisfy the new demands of circumstances and grab new opportunities. They must implement sincerely, efficiently and effectively systems of corporate governance so innovated. It is the responsibility of government to create institutional and legal structure to enable corporate bodies to function effectively. Every business organisation must develop its own model of corporate governance by calculating cost and benefits while observing the rules made by the government. It must make improvements in the model as demanded by needs and expectations of changing circumstances.

Principalities of corporate governance are discussed in five parts, namely — (1) Shareholders' rights, (2) Equal treatment to shareholders, (3) Role of risk bearers, (4) Disclosure of information and transparency in business, and (5) Responsibilities of the board of directors. They are discussed in following paragraphs. This discussion is based on the recommendations made by the Committee on Corporate Audit and Governance appointed by the Government of India on 21st August 2002 under the chairmanship of Naresh Chandra.

(1) Shareholders' Rights

Share is an asset and to buy, hold, sell, transfer the shares are the rights of the shareholders. Liability of shareholder is limited to the money value of the shares that he holds. He has a right to share the profits of the organisation in proportion of the shares held by him. Shareholder has the right to receive information of the organisation and put ethical pressure on the business organisation. He can exercise this right by remaining present at the time of shareholders' meeting and by casting votes.

However, shareholder cannot conduct the business of the company through the medium of public opinion. Shareholders consist of individuals and organisations whose interests, objectives and capabilities and limitations of investment are different. Managers must be able to take business decisions quickly. Considering this fact and quickly changing market situations and happenings, shareholders cannot bear the responsibilities of managing business of the organisation. Responsibility of architecturing organisation strategy and of running business is explicitly handed over to the board of directors. This function is got done from work induced management team. Management team can be altered as per requirements. Shareholders can pressurise the functioning of corporate body by electing representatives on the board of directors, by following the method of determining constitution of board of directors as per the provisions of the company law and rules and regulations of the business organisation. Shareholders can pressurise the functioning of the company also by nominating auditors and granting consent to their appointment, by nominating persons on the board of directors, by mortgaging shares and by consenting declaration of dividend. These rights can be capsulated as below—

(A) Shareholders' fundamental rights: (1) to get acquainted with the system of registering ownership of shares, (2) to transfer shares or giving shares to somebody, (3) to receive information periodically and regularly about the business of the company, (4) to participate in the general body meeting of the shareholders and to cast vote, (5) to nominate members on the board of directors, and (6) to claim dividend as a part of profit of the company.

(B) Shareholders' rights to participate in corporate decisions: (1) to receive information regarding changes made in the constitution of the company, changes in the rules and procedures as well changes made in the managerial procedures, (2) to give rights to the management to allot additional shares, (3) to express opinion regarding important business like sale of the company or its assets.

(C) Shareholders' rights to participate in general body meeting are discussed below: (1) Shareholders have to have equal opportunity to participate spontaneously in the general body meeting and cast vote. They should receive full information regarding rules of businesses transacted in such meetings and method of casting votes, (2) They should receive well in advance the information regarding date, time and place of general body meeting, its agenda and subjects coming for discussion before the meeting, (3) Shareholders should have an opportunity to get subjects of their desire to be included in the agenda of the meeting, and ask questions, make queries in the meeting. Corporate bodies should make very easy and simple, the system of placing resolution and proposals for improvement before the meeting. However, every care should be taken to prohibit people from wasting time of the general body by asking inappropriate questions. Resolutions to be placed before the general body must be seconded by requisite number of shareholders, (4) to have the right to cast vote in person or through proxy, and both these votes must carry equal weight. Allowing them to vote through telephone or through an electronic media can increase participation of shareholders in the meeting of the general body. Non-resident shareholders also can participate in the general body meeting. Such votes should be counted immediately and results should be declared on the spot. This will bring transparency in the business of the general body. Shareholders should be allowed to confer and discuss through electronic media.

(D) Shareholders' right to know capital structure of the company: Shareholders have right to know the capital structure of the company and have right to know names of persons or institutions that hold sizeable share of shares. With a view to reduce their control on the company pyramedic structure of capital should be created and the system of cross share holding should be implemented. Some shareholders use the method of grouping shareholders to establish control over the company. Such groups agree not to sell individual shares for particular period of time or to sell shares to the persons in the group only. Shareholders in such groups can derive the advantage of collective voting. Such groups can include in their agreement a clause to do collective voting on appointment of members of the board of directors or election of the chairman of the board of directors.

These oligopolistic systems are countered in some companies by limiting the number of votes a shareholder can cast in spite of the number of shares he holds. This method redistributes the authority of establishing control over the company and does affect the attitude to be present and participate in the business of the general body. Such by-laws affect the authority to plan the policy of the company and therefore these by-laws should be published widely.

(E) Shareholders' right to work freely, effectively and transparently to establish control on the company: (1) All activities trying to gain control on the company, either by way of purchasing shares in the stock market or by amalgamation should be carefully planned and should be published in transparent manner. These transactions must be done at reasonable value and on appropriate conditions to protect interests of the shareholders totally, (2) however, these provisions against acquisition should not provide protection to management against accountability. In some organisations these provisions are used as shield against supervision of shareholders. Both these facts are detrimental to the best practices of corporate governance.

(F) Shareholders' voting methods: Returns received in the form of dividend can become much attractive if shareholders vote consciously on the basis of performance of the organisation. However, such method should not be extended beyond limit to turn profit into loss.

(2) Equal Treatment to Shareholders

It is necessary from the point of working of the corporate governance that all groups of shareholders receive equitable treatment. Every person should be given complete information regarding shareholders' right to vote, benefits and losses of this method, before he decides to purchase shares. Any changes made in the rights of voting and other matters must be communicated immediately to all concerned.

(a) Board of directors decide the optimal pattern of capital and shareholders have to consent that. Some are preference shares; in this capital pattern persons holding preference shares receive dividend at higher rate and on priority but they do not have voting right. Some corporations issue non-voting equity shares. However, they are entitled to higher rate of dividend for having sacrificed voting rights. These shares are traded on secondary market at different price. Equity shares with voting rights are also issued. Such a pattern of share capital balances risks and benefits. Good corporate governance adopts the principle of 'one share one vote.' People have right to receive information regarding voting rights before they invest in the organisation. They should hold opportunity to express views and participate in the decision of making any changes in their voting rights. Proposal for any such change must be placed before the general body and consent of shareholders of that class must be obtained.

(b) Beneficiary owners of equity shares themselves or their proxies must have voted for or against such change. There is a system of financial institutions, safekeeping shares of other shareholders and voting on behalf of these shareholders. The shareholders can issue instructions to such financial institutions about voting in favour or against particular resolution. But in absence of such guidelines holder financial institutions and banks vote in favour of management.

However, there is an increasing tendency to close the system of automatic granting of voting rights to holder banks and financial institutions. Every holder bank or stock-broker must provide full information to the investor about all alternatives of voting. Many national governments have made legal provisions to that effect. Equity shareholders communicate their voting alternative choice to the banks and stock-brokers. Investors have right to receive information from holder banks or brokers regarding the intention of shareholders. The holder banks or brokers should not pressurise shareholders in this respect. The holder bank or broker is free to vote as it pleases if no communication is received from shareholders to that effect.

(c) All processes and systems in the general body must treat all shareholders as equal. Shareholders should not find casting vote difficult or costly because of peculiar and unique method adopted by the organisation. It is not proper on the part of the management and controlling investors to deprive foreign investors and some shareholders from deciding the direction of organisational policy. Some organisations charge fees for casting votes. Some companies do not grant permission to proxies to vote and make by-laws that shareholders should be present personally in the meeting and cast vote. Some organisations despatch relevant papers, voting literature, proxy forms to the shareholder so late that he cannot communicate with other shareholders, consult them and nominate his proxy. It is a welcome matter that many an organisations, establish contact with shareholders through electronic media and remove all artificial obstacles in the way of exercising franchise. Section 293-(I)(a) of Indian Companies Act 1956 requires the management to obtain approval of the shareholders through postal ballot on all-important matters of the business of the company.

(d) Insider trading and allusive self-trading of shares must be stopped. Some people, taking disadvantage of their contacts with top officials in business organisations, bring lower the prices of stocks and buy shares for the benefit of self. In a way they cause loss to the business organisation and investors. Some people take disadvantage of lacunae in capital market, lower prices of shares artificially and derive benefits. Securities control authorities have declared this as illegal. However, in stock markets where rules and procedures are not strictly followed, such things happen and directors of business organisations are involved in them for self-interest. These things hamper the functioning of good corporate governance, as they are contrary to equal treatment to equity holders. Government of India have amended Company Law to that effect and Securities and Exchange Board of India is making all out efforts to avoid their recurrence. This is discussed in detail in the next section.

(e) Managers and members of the board of directors should disclose matters of their interest in the company and publicise for the information of the shareholders and general public matters that affect the image and working of the business organisation. Many a times managers and members of the board of directors have business interests of their organisations in this company and those interests do affect provisions of business to be done with those organisations. That is why such interests must be disclosed.

(3) Role of Stakeholders in the Corporate Governance

Stakeholders should educate themselves about the rights given to them by law and they should enhance their co-operation with business organisation so as to increase the wealth and employment in the organisation. They should also see that the organisation achieves financial stability and stands on sound footing. It is the major responsibility of corporate governance to see that the organisation always enjoys continuous flow of external capital. It is also the responsibility of corporate governance to induce the stakeholders to participate in socially efficient physical and intellectual capital of the organisation. Corporate governance should realise that the contribution of stakeholders plays strategic role in developing competitive and beneficial organisation. It is necessary to develop co-operation with stakeholders for generating corporate wealth over a long period of time. That is why the framework of corporate governance must be such as to protect interests of the stakeholders The Company must address, in its annual reports, the concerns of a wider group of stakeholders than simply of shareholders. Following four principles are important from that point of view — (a) Corporate governance must respect the protected rights of the stakeholders. Commercial laws, Contract Act, Insolvency Act, all these legal instruments have protected the rights of the stakeholders. Corporate bodies try to improve their image, increase their reputation so as to protect the stakeholders in matter where stakeholders are not legally protected. (b) There must be provision of adequate opportunity to resolve and compensate stakeholders in matters where their legal rights are overridden. That is why such legal provisions must be clear and transparent. So that the business organisation will not venture to take disadvantage of such ambiguity. (c) Framework of corporate governance must ensure increasing co-operation of the stakeholders in improving performance of the company. Naturally, participation of different categories of stakeholders will be different and will depend upon nature of legal provisions in the country, traditions and work procedure; it will also be related to the corporate body. A number of measures can be taken to increase active and effective participation of stakeholders in the working of the organisation. Some of these measures are — nomination of employee representatives on the board of directors, stock options, employee profit sharing, value addition bonus to employees on increase in corporate value in the market, development of a process of corporate governance of taking note of the advice of stakeholders after consulting them in matters of important decisions. (d) Business organisation must provide adequate information to those participating in corporate governance and bearing risks. The business organisation should provide information about characteristic features of various products, new products to be launched, sales revenue, segmental revenue, market share of the company, export revenue, incidence of taxes on the organisation and dispersal of shareholding.

(4) Disclosure of Information and Transparency

Business organisation, as a part of corporate governance must publish accurate information indicating physical position of the company in respect of management systems, ownership of the company and its financial status. Many an organisations voluntarily collect much more information than statutorily required, publish and circulate on large scale. We can read all this information on Internet even while at home and use it. This information is aptly available in annual report, however quarterly and half yearly information is collected and published with comparable earlier statistics. People are given information about merger of other organisations, purchase or sale of brands and their value etc.

Publication of information in this way is an important part in determining market value of the organisation and it is the principal basis of good corporate governance. As a result of publication of this information shareholders can exercise knowledgeably their voting right. Economies in which capital market is well developed the system of publishing such information brings discipline in the corporate administrative mechanism and protects interests of investors. Confidence of investors and of general public in the business organisation increases. The organisation can attract more capital. Prospective investors, if made available adequate and reliable information, can draw inferences about the quality of corporate management and valuation of the organisation. If people are provided inadequate information they develop misunderstanding about the organisation; that increases cost of raising capital; reduces possibility of requisite and optimum allocation of resources.

If the organisation publishes its information, people understand the nature of working of the organisation, its policy in respect of ethics, values and environment. Organisation has not to incur much cost and bear administrative burden in disclosing its information. The organisation is not expected to disclose information that is sensitive and necessary for secrecy of its business. Organisation is expected to disclose following information.

(a) It should publicise financial and managerial results. Audited balance sheets exhibiting corporate financial performance, profit and loss account, trading account, funds flow statement should be published. Such financial results are prepared and published so as to enable adequate supervision and provide base for valuation of the bonds. Managerial remarks on financial results are also included in annual reports. As a result investors can foresee future progress of the company. Results of all strategic business units belonging to an organisation need to be published. There from the reader can grasp the position of the entire group.

(b) Business organisations are expected to declare along with their business objectives, their policy regarding business ethics, environment and policy regarding discharging its social responsibility. This provides information to investors and readers about relationship between organisation and the society in which it is functioning.

(c) People must be provided information regarding the structure and nature of equity capital, ownership rights and owners' rights and responsibilities. It is necessary to publish information regarding the individuals and institutions owning sizeable portion of capital of the organisation, their unique voting rights agreement of equity holders and nature and relationship of cross shareholding. Related people should be provided information about agreement signed with relevant persons and institutions.

(d) Information regarding directors of the organisation, terms of their service, honorarium and commission payable to them on profits and information in respect of educational qualifications, length of service, designation, salary, perquisites of employees must be provided to the investors.

(e) Information in respect of foreseeable risks should be provided in all possible details to the investors. It is important to provide information regarding risks about particular industry or particular organisation. Respective persons should be made known if any system or any method is developed by the organisation to foresee such risks.

(f) Organisation should deliver information to the stakeholders regarding effect of employee activities on organisational performance. Information should be published about labour relations, relations of the organisation with creditors, suppliers and local society. Information should be made available regarding human relations policy, programs undertaken for employee empowerment and development, stock options and competitive situation of the organisation in the market.

(g) People should know the structure and the policy regarding objectives of corporate governance as outlined by the organisation, policy planned for implementing and measures taken for achieving these objectives of corporate governance. People should be made known of the distribution of responsibilities and functions between board of directors and managers as well as between chairman of the board of directors and executive officers.

(h) Organisation should get its financial transactions audited with highest standards of auditing and publish the same. This should be done to make people known of the financial facilities of the organisation. It should collect and publish non-financial information also. Publication of financial transactions audited with highest standards of inspection increases credibility of the organisation. This information can be compared with that of other organisations and reader can have detailed understanding about the performance of the company. This comparison can be done on international level also.

(i) Organisations should publish in their annual report information regarding stock options granted to employees. The cost of stock options should be calculated as per the method developed by Fischer Black, Robert Merton and Myron Scoles and rules prepared by International Accounting Standards Board. This will exhibit the actual and realistic financial position of the business organisation.

(j) Financial transactions of the organisation should be got inspected from renowned outside auditors employing universally accepted methods and should be published. This creates confidence in the minds of the public about fair and impartial treatment of financial transactions. Many a countries have made legal provisions to safeguard the independence of auditors and their accountability towards shareholders. In addition to this an auditing committee of the directors is functionalised. Its constitution, functions, procedures and conclusions drawn by the said committee are published. In many countries remuneration paid to the auditors, other than audit fees are restricted. Organisations are required to publish the information regarding such extra remuneration. There is a system prevalent in some countries of reviewing auditors' work by other auditors. Law in some countries limits tenure of auditors. Tradition of appointing and selecting auditors directly by shareholders is honoured in many countries. This means, all out efforts are made to improve trustworthiness and transparency of the working and of financial transactions of the organisation.

(k) All this information must reach all the persons in the organisation, stakeholders and to persons who want to use it. This information must be available without much cost and time. Channels of distributing information must be reliable, because they are as important as the details of the information. Many a times this information is provided reluctantly and just to satisfy legal provisions. Naturally, people have to make efforts, spend much time and money to collect such information. This is improper. Provision of this information through electronic media is authorised. This has made it easy for the people to acquire information. Internet and other media of information technology have made this task easier.

I have discussed in preceding eleven points, the means available to corporate bodies to institute clean administration and make it society oriented. This improves the quality of corporate governance.

(5) Responsibilities of Board of Directors

Board of directors through the system of corporate governance should direct the organisation in matters of strategic policy and supervise management effectively. This should develop such an arrangement that will create accountability of board of directors towards the organisation and shareholders. In some countries two tier board of directors is constituted; one part supervising and other part managing the organisation. Various committees of the board of directors are constituted for the purpose. Supervisory wing of the board consists of directors having no executive responsibilities. Managerial wing has directors with executive rights. In many countries there are uni-layered boards of directors consisting of executive and non-executive officers. Principles of corporate governance are so architectured that the organisation is efficiently managed and management is effectively supervised.

Important functions of the board of directors are to direct the corporate strategy, to supervise the performance of management, to provide adequate returns to shareholders, to avoid conflict between different divisions of the organisation and to strike balance between the competitive demands on the organisation. Board of directors must enjoy freedom, independence from management so that it can discharge its responsibilities effectively. Board of directors must develop and implement such procedure that the business organisation will obey fully all the legal provisions applicable to it. The organisation will discharge tax liabilities and obey all rules regarding competition, labour, environment, equal opportunities to all, health care and security. Board of directors must treat rationally all stakeholders. Points discussed below aptly make clear the responsibilities of the board of directors.

(1) Members of the board of directors should act only after collecting all information. This act must be in the interests of the people. Directors should act diligently and cautiously and bear in mind the interests of the organisation.

(2) When any decision of the board of directors is likely to affect different shareholders differently the board must take care that the effect will be uniform.

(3) Board of directors must discharge following functions—

(a) The board must direct corporate strategy and review it periodically. It must pay attention to all important action plans. It must chart policy regarding all risks that the organisation has to face. It must overlook that annual budget is prepared, business plans are charted, targets of performance are fixed, and see to it that they are implemented and achieved. It has to supervise large capital expenditure. It has to look into the matters of acquiring firms and disinvestments.

(b) The board of directors will select officers, decide their salary scales, review and evaluate their performance. The board may change the chief executive officer if required. The board has to prepare a succession plan to replace existing officers.

(c) The board should review salary scales of executive officers and directors. It should observe that the members of the board of directors are formally elected and the procedure is adequately transparent.

(d) The board must see that the assets and property of the organisation are not misused and no disadvantage is taken of relationship with requisite persons. The board must take precaution that no conflict is developed between different sections of the business organisation.

(e) The directors should supervise that the corporate governance is effectively used to the advantage of the organisation, employees and the society.

(f) They should supervise system of providing information to the people and communicating with them.

(g) The board of directors must take decisions independently and objectively regarding working of the organisation. Directors capable of taking decisions independently and objectively should be nominated in adequate number to handle the situation where conflict is likely to develop and these directors must be non-executive.

(h) Directors must spare adequate time required to discharge their responsibility. Directors should not work on boards of very many organisations. They should accept only those many positions that equity holders will have confidence in their honesty and integrity.

(i) Organisation must provide all required information to the directors to enable them to discharge their responsibility.

In this section on principalities of corporate governance a review is taken about (1) shareholder's rights, (2) equal treatment to shareholders, (3) role of stakeholders, (4) disclosure of information and transparency, and (5) responsibilities of board of directors.

PREPARING ORGANISATION FOR GOOD CORPORATE GOVERNANCE

Corporate governance is a concept embracing the entire organisation. It is not limited to top management or middle layer of the organisation. Therefore, every effort has to be made to develop and spread the theory, principles, principalities and practices of good corporate governance from board room to shop floor. This is a Herculean task because making people submerge personal interests in the broader interest of the organisation, society and humanity is difficult like swimming against the current. That is why, the corporate body has to cautiously, deliberately, diligently, efficiently and effectively introduce the concept of good corporate governance and create unanimous approval, acceptance and adoption in the organisation.

The first step towards good corporate governance is to develop a board of directors consisting of people of reputed and recognised standing having extraordinary diligence, honesty, integrity and devotion. They must involve and commit wholeheartedly to the all-round prosperity of the organisation. Such persons must possess cross-functional, cross-disciplinary skills. They must have business acumen and urge to fight. They must possess high need for power, high need for achievement and low need for affiliation. They should have a broader outlook and wider zenith of understanding. They must be professionals in and out. They must be good Janusian leaders.

The board of directors must institute systems and practices to make all people know rights and duties of shareholders, investors and depositors. Shareholders must be able to exercise their rights without difficulty, inconvenience and cost. All the information in respect of organisation; business and activities of the company should be fully and promptly made available to all the people concerned. All shareholders must be treated equal. The board of directors must protect all rights of the stakeholders and solicit co-operation of all the stakeholders and sections of the society. The board must collect, assimilate and publish all information regarding its decisions, plans, activities and business. This information must be so published that everybody interested in acquiring the information must be able to get it easily and fully. Board must discharge all its responsibilities fully and oversight the management so as to achieve the objectives of the organisation.

The second step towards good corporate governance is to develop a delayered, lean organisation capable of sensing any change in the economic, social and political environment. Such organisation must be sensitive and responsive to any demand made on it. It must foresee the needs of the customers and provide today the products that they would otherwise dream tomorrow. It should be innovative, expermentative and proactive. It must be an intelligent corporation.

The board of directors should select such persons to work in the organisation that are conversant with the modern principles and practices of management, are possessing leadership qualities, have mastered communication skills, can organise, lead and participate in teams. They must have such a royal as well as Fabian outlook to care the employees as co-partners in the organisation; as associates in the company. Management of the organisation should develop ethical, value ridden, open and transparent practices of management. It should see that the same practices are honestly followed to the lowest level in the organisation. Management should develop practices of receiving suggestions for improvement in administration, quality of product, reduction in cycle time, better practices of observing delivery time, better relations with suppliers, reducing links in the supply chain and doing every job right first time. All these are the ingredients of good corporate governance.

Management should constitute teams of persons belonging to different divisions, different functions, and different departments and innovate new products, new processes of producing products, new ways of serving customers and achieving their critical criteria. Management should pool the physical, financial and human resources from any and every strategic business unit as and when required so as achieving their maximum and optimal utilisation. Achieving six-sigma level of final product must be the objective of every activity in the organisation. Every employee should be encouraged to give best of his life to the organisation.

The third step towards attaining good corporate governance is to develop the knowledge base of the organisation. Management should create a knowledge map, determining which knowledge does the organisation need to achieve total quality product level, to achieve that approach, and attitude to make the organisation known for its best practices. Then it should assess the knowledge that it possesses, implicit and explicit. This will give the organisation an idea of the knowledge gap. Then every effort should be made to acquire that knowledge by hiring knowledgeable persons. The management should do everything to educate and train inside people by deputing them to attend and participate in symposia, seminars, conferences, action learning courses, experimental learning, refresher courses and executive coaching. They should be trained in black belt philosophy, modality and techniques. If required this knowledge should be preserved by recording on audio-video-cassettes, VCDs etc. so that it becomes a depository of knowledge. Company should be developed as a learning organisation.

Fourth step in attaining good corporate governance is to develop intellectual capital of the organisation, Management must have the ability to attract and hold the best of the knowledge workers. It is the first and most fundamental test of good corporate governance.[4] Structure of the organisation should be so developed as to provide all infrastructural facilities for the intellect, knowledge, of the organisation to function efficiently and effectively. It must develop organisational capital, meaning that the barriers, walls between different sections, departments and functions are pulled down. This will make the organisation a unitary flexible body. Management should make concerted efforts to develop customer capital by creating long-term total marketing relationship. Not the physical or financial capital determines the future of the organisation but the intellectual capital. Therefore, every effort should be made to leverage, empower intellectual capital, human capital in the organisation. The management should develop such a system that these knowledge persons, intellectual persons do not leave the organisation to join any other company. Otherwise, that organisation will become an educational institution rather than a production organisation.

Fifth and last step in the creation of practices of good corporate governance is to develop the organisation as a unified, unidirectional unit. All employees in the company must feel proud to be associated with the company. Creation of that sense of belonging to one family is the success of good corporate governance. Discharging one's duty diligently, dutifully, honestly and observe one's rights honourably must be the attitude of every employee in the organisation. They must develop an attitude to listen to others carefully, so carefully that the speaker develops a sense that he is being heard. Caring the employee is not just paying good salary, granting bonuses, felicitating by declaring awards; it is much beyond that. If suppliers, employees, customers feel that they are cared then the organisation has achieved the long cherished objective of good corporate governance.

CORPORATE GOVERNANCE IN INDIA

Directors of business organisations, managers and executive directors while governing an organisation, may misuse financial resources, disclose information that is beneficial to them and fatten their performance. They take care of their salaries and rights even when the organisation is incurring losses and is about to become bankrupt. With a view to defeat all these wrong doings and to enable corporate governance to function efficiently and effectively efforts are made and are being made in all countries in the world. Cadbury Committee constituted in England in May 1991, made nineteen recommendations to improve the level of corporate governance, to enhance people's confidence in the financial accounting and reporting, to set standards for peoples' expectations about the organisation and the things actually happening. Blue Ribbon Committee constituted by the Securities and Exchange Commission in America made recommendations to improve corporate accountability and set standards for the audit committee to safeguard interests of the investors. Blue Ribbon Committee further recommended that an arrangement should be evolved by improving provisions in the listing agreement of the stock market to enable the audit committee to work more effectively on the support of legal provisions. In India, even though law does not introduce these provisions, business organisations like Infosys implement these provisions voluntarily to enhance their credibility at global level. They draft their annual reports accordingly and discuss these matters.

The Securities and Exchange Board of India in November 1999 constituted a committee under the chairmanship of Shri Kumar Mangalam Birla to recommend how should good corporate governance be. Accordingly the Institute of Chartered Accountants of India have made it mandatory to report and give segmental information of the company, consolidation of audit reports, earnings per share and publish it. Such publication is made compulsory from April 2001. Besides organisations have to compulsorily publish process and procedure of corporate governance of the company. Companies are required to give information regarding constitution of board of directors, information regarding working of the audit committee, compensation committee, and investors' grievance redressal committee of the board of directors. They are required to implement provisions published in Europe in the year 2000 in respect of corporate governance about equity holders.

Company Law (1956) was amended to improve corporate governance in India. Sub-section 2 of Section 146, Section 192A and Section 293 (1)(a) of The Company Law as well Company Regulation 2001 require the organisation to obtain opinion of the shareholders, on every important matter, by post, so as to make the decisions as transparent as possible. This enables the organisation to maintain healthy atmosphere. It has put many a restrictions regarding the size and constitution of the board of directors, proportion of independent directors in the board and their tenure. It has restricted honorarium payable to independent directors to half a per cent of net profits of the organisation. Amended Company Law holds managing directors, managers, whole-time directors, company secretaries and persons under whose instructions corporate boards function, responsible as officers in default. They are liable to punishments, penalties and imprisonment for default committed by the corporation. An amendment to the Company Law is proposed to include specific non-executive directors in the above list who are suspected and found to be directly or indirectly involved with default. If the liability for an offence cannot be attached to any other employee, the entire board of directors including the non-executive members are proposed to be held liable. Such a provision will definitely make the corporate body govern its business more responsibly and professionally. Amended Company Law has made explicit provision that the posts of company chairman and executive director should not be vested in one person. Even then many organisations seem to be violating this provision. Even the government vests both these positions in public sector undertakings in one person. Chairmanship and managing directorship of Shipping Corporation of India were awarded to one person in October 2002. As in May 2004 chairmanship and managing directorship of Canara Bank were vested in one person. Company is required to prepare and publish balance sheet, profit and loss account, trading account and segment accounts as per generally accepted accounting principles and Indian accounting principles. However,

Company Law amendment makes no provision for inclusion of the cost of stock options granted to executives in financial statements of the organisation. Cross investment done by various companies in a group must be declared as per Section 217 of the Company Law.

Financial sector was the first to be freed after the introduction of economic reforms in India in 1991. Private sector was permitted to establish banking companies. A committee was constituted under the chairmanship of Narsinham to recommend measures to reform corporate governance of banks. As per the recommendations of the said committee, capital adequacy ratio has been raised to nine per cent and this has subsequently made applicable to co-operative banks. A system of classifying banking assets was introduced. A system of managing asset liquidity proportion was introduced in April 1999. Repayment of loan instalment delayed for more than ninety days is regarded as asset of lower status. Ratio of non-performing assets to total assets is to be brought below five percent. Risk weighted asset ratio to paid up capital is to be brought below nine percent. Banks are authorised to acquire and sell assets and property of defaulting borrowers as per the Securitisation and Reconstruction of Financial Assets and Enforcement of Security Interest Act (2002) and Rules 6,7,8 and 9 of Security Interest (Enforcement) Rules 2002. Structure and pattern of the balance sheets of banks are changed so as to disclose more information to the public. The committee constituted by the Reserve Bank of India under the chairmanship of Y. V. Reddy have recommended that advisory committee of the bank should review the performance of the board of directors of the banks and they should be asked to improve the same if found below expectations. A committee appointed by the Reserve Bank of India under the chairmanship of Rashid Jhilani has recommended constitution of internal inspection and internal audit departments in every bank and any overlapping in their jurisdictions should be removed.

The Securities and Exchange Board of India has directed all corporate bodies (inclusive of banks) registered with stock exchange to observe from April 2001 accounting standards coming under Sections AS-17 to AS-22. As per Section AS-17, every corporate body, including banks, should reorganise its financial reports and publish the same as per segments and geographical areas. As directed in Section AS-18 they should crystallise their relationships with co-operative organisation and publish the same. AS-19 requires companies to publish information regarding assets leased out. Earning per share of the company must be made known to the people as per AS-20. AS-21 expects firms to publish the balance sheet as per provisions of the Reserve Bank of India rules. Companies are required to publish details of income tax payable by them. All these systems have brought discipline and transparency in the business and transactions of the banking and non-banking companies. Recommendations of the Ganguli Committee (April 2002) have placed much additional responsibility on the board of directors of banks. Recommendations of the Naresh Chandra Committee appointed by the Government of India on 21st August 2002 have already been discussed in earlier section.

Discussion in this section makes it amply clear that many efforts have been made during the period of economic reforms to improve corporate governance. Indian companies and banks have to improve quality of their governance to stand in the competition that has come forth because of globalisation. Even then episodes like that of Unit Trust of India take place which indicate that India has still much to do to fully make good corporate governance functional in India.

References

(1) Williamson J.H., (1966) *'Profit, Growth and Sales Maximisation'* Economica.

(2) Cyert R.M. and March J.G., (1967), *A Behavioural Theory of Firm*, Prentice Hall.

(3) Smith Adam, *An Enquiry into the Nature and Cause of the Wealth of Nations*, p. 31.

(4) Drucker Peter F., *Management Challenges for the 21st Century*, Butterworth-Heinemann, 1999, p. 159.

❑ ❑ ❑

11 We Will Manage This Way

Management of an organisation is a social act; it has to change as changes take place in the milieu around the organisation in which it functions. In the 21st century, management involves three processes, namely — Nurturing, Leading and Path making. Nurturing is a complete and continuous process of preparing, building, guiding and ensuring progress. Leading is a process of interacting with colleagues and teams through anticipating, relating, supporting and assuring to fulfil the mission of the organisation. Path making is a process of visualizing, facilitating, backing and trusting for the journey of the course towards the vision of the organisation. Many a discontinuous changes have taken place in every aspect of life in which the organisation functions. Politically on one hand Communist block of Eastern Europe has broken down, South and North Korea have begun discussion on ending enmity; while on the other hand European countries, including some countries of the erstwhile communist block have united. On economic front formation of trading blocks like NAFTA, COMECON, ASEAN have changed the rules of competition. Creation of World Trade Organization has changed the ethos of rules and procedures of manufacturing, transport and trading. Creation of Euro has created an effective threat to the supremacy of the U.S. dollar. Socially humanity has become more unified, mobile and converged on many a concepts and thoughts that affect the people. Psychologically, people have become more concerned about environment; have become more cautious about their health and user friendly nature of products and services they consume. They have become more aware about choice of product they want and value they derive for the price they pay. Technology has changed very fast, revolutionizing the whole pattern of productive activity. Convergence of technologies has given birth to new technologies like mechantronics, bioengineering, biotechnology, bioinformatics, medical electronics, genetic. This has made, products of unprecedented characteristic features and qualities, possible. Information technology has brought revolution in not only production, distribution and services but in our day to day life. It has changed our way of thinking; it has changed our approach to life; it has changed our life style. Organisational structure has also undergone a change in-and-out and made it more responsible, responsive, active, sensible, sensitive and stimulating. Management has changed so much that it has broken its legacy with earlier practices. Now not products but people are managed. Management is now concerned with customer values and customer decisions on the distribution of their disposable income.[1]

Managers possess new skills, cross-functional ideas and fundamentally different approach to their roles. Employees being fully or partially knowledge workers, demand greater say in the decision-making process and expect closer interactions with customers. They want to be more creative than productive. Many more, evolutionary and revolutionary changes are to come in the coming years of the 21st century. We cannot predict them fully and therefore cannot foresee and plan our path. The only thing that is in our hands is to make our polity, economy, society and organisation so flexible, absorptive and adoptive that we are prepared to face every challenge posed by such changes and ready to take full advantage of the opportunities that are opened before us. With more and more companies having access to new technology, better machines, better methods of production, segmented-niche marketing methods and variety of channels of distribution, the competitive environment has fundamentally changed. Disparity between these factors being reduced, strategic management of talent has become critical to win competitive advantage.

I propose to discuss in this chapter, leadership — individual as well as organisational, organisation and management that need to personify to respond to the challenges that coming years of the 21st century are going to pose. This discussion is done on the backdrop of changes that are described in the preceding paragraph and various aspects of productive activities that were discussed in nine chapters — two through ten. It is very difficult to foresee the political, economic, social, organisational and technological changes that may take shape in the future; but change is inevitable; that is sure. However, it can be safely presumed that politically and economically situation is likely to be more liberal, socially more health and environment conscious, psychologically more rational, choosy and pragmatic. As argued by Peter F. Drucker, change leader should build into enterprise a systematic policy of innovation so that a new mindset is produced to make the organisation a change leader.[2] Organisations will place more emphasis on delivering greater value to the customers at reasonable prices. Competition leadership in organisation and in teams, organisational leadership in market and managerial leadership in industry are going to be more intense and complex. All these individualities will have to strive hard to live, to survive. Organisational objectives, structures, strategies and policies are going to be peoplelistic. Product is likely to be consumer centered.

INDIVIDUAL LEADERSHIP

Leadership is the catalyst functionary in achieving competency in every aspect of life. It is defined as — Leadership is the capacity of a human being to shape future of humanity and to sustain significant development. Leadership is the relationship between those who aspire to bring dreams into reality and those who choose to follow. Leader must be able to create a sense of citizenship—may it be national or corporate, in an organisation with a mature appreciation of its rights and responsibilities.[3] Every entity trying to achieve competency must have leader to guide it. A nation desiring to achieve world level competency must have strong political leadership; an industry desiring to achieve pride of place in an economy must exhibit organisational leadership and a company that fights to conquer market must possess effective functional managerial leadership. Jim Collins on the basis of his study has explained in his book 'Good to Great' that companies that had polite, frugal and industrious leadership came to achieve place of pride, while companies that had leadership who neglected these qualities became bankrupt. Leaders at all these levels have to face the same four types of challenges. These are—

(1) **They face the challenge of initiating** — National, industrial and company leaders have to introduce new ideas, concepts, thoughts, approaches and new ways of working.

(2) **They face the challenge of sustaining** — All these leaders have to keep the growth going, development progressing, and achieving higher and higher standards of ethical values, ethnic co-operation and positive approach towards world of work.

(3) **These leaders face the challenges of redesigning and rethinking** — Leaders have to develop a new approach towards living a common peaceful life, new approach towards problems. They must encourage development of new products and new processes of production.

(4) **They have to face the challenge of leading change** — In present days change is a norm. Change is painful and risky and it needs good deal of hard work on the part of the leaders to ride a change. In a period of rapid structural change the only who survive are the change leaders.[4] Leaders of tomorrow are bound to be different than those of today. Their nature will depend upon transforming changes into certainties.

We need local leaders, adult leaders and executive leaders to carry out all these activities. Local leaders are those who initiate new idea, concepts and approaches at firm level as at national level. Local leader is not a spatial character; it is a premier character introducing new things. This requires diligence, confidence and courage to be correct. Adult leaders are the personalities who have capabilities of making, compromising, trusting and committing. They are the individuals having vision and capability to convey this vision to others and convince them. Executive leaders play a transformational role. They lead the team in a fruitful way and achieve insurmountable goals. These three types of leaders play complementary roles. Leadership in 21st century will rest with those who maximize productivity of knowledge workers. Leaders have to bring out the best that is in all the knowledge workers.

At organisational level, the theory chracterising these three types of leaders and emphasising their complementary roles is the 'Systems Theory of leadership'. Organisational leader must be trustworthy and credible. He becomes trustworthy when he cares for people, listens them patiently, develops relationship with all, shares openly thoughts and feelings of others, sets peoples' spirits free and inspires them. In all business operations three things are important. They are-people, product and profits. People come first. The leader must know people side of business. He becomes credible if he is honest, forward looking, inspiring and competent. His values and beliefs must be core to his thinking; he does as he says; he must show capacity to bring change. His leadership, his personal quality and total quality control make quality a way of life. Stuart R. Levine argues that leader is a person driven by core values, who builds trusting relationships through effective communication. He focuses on moving people and organisation forward by teaching and increasing competency of employee-associates. Stuart R. Levine names such person as 'Edu-leader.'[5] He must search dreams. And as soon as one dream is achieved he should seek another. Leader must be 'next mentality breed'. Leader in an organisation should look backward and take stock of his achievements and failures. He should assess the factors that enabled him to achieve his objective and analyse the factors that caused his defeat. He should take a lesson not to repeat the mistakes that brought him failure and strengthen the thoughts, decisions and activities that brought him success. Every person in the 21st century intelligent corporation must exhibit these leadership traits.

The most important function of a leader is to identify qualities and character, values and beliefs of people and to develop them. He has to search for new talents, bring in talented individuals, satisfy their needs, invest in them by providing opportunities to sharpen their talents, create challenging environment for them to work and use them effectively. The key metrics of success of the 21st century organisation is not to maximise ROI or ROA only but to maximise return on talent. Subir Chowdhury gives a formula to measure return on talent in his book "Management 21C' as —

$$\text{Return on Talent} = \frac{\text{knowledge generated}}{\text{Investment in talents}}$$

Monetary value of knowledge generated can be roughly calculated by measuring the value of new products introduced plus the difference between the value of improved product and old product. Investment in talents can be calculated by measuring difference in the compensation paid to such persons and other persons; that is the excess compensation disbursed to retain these people plus investment done on training facilities provided to them. Return on talent measures the pay back from investment in people. The leader has to deploy talented people in such a way that they become creative and innovative so that opportunities can be capitalised. Leader has to build competitive environment so that an initiative culture develops in the organisation. He must develop the culture of making decisions quickly and develop entrepreneurial spirit in the staff. In the 21st century business cannot afford luxury of slow decision making.

Another function leader has to perform is to get closer to the people so that they open up, share their thoughts and feelings. He should express affection, warmth and fondness. People can be motivated by communicating with them. A leader must be proficient in conveying his listener what he exactly wants to communicate and he must be a good listener too, to understand what other persons wants to convey him. Real communication goes in both directions. In corporate life leader has to encourage people to make contribution to the common good and come up with better ways of doing things. Listening people are a good way to motivate them. Leader must speak in the language of the listeners, let be alone or group. They accept him as a leader because he is speaking what they have in their mind, because he is following them. Leader should speak as direct and straight forward as possible to let the audience know goals, plans of the organisation. Leader must reach out to the people trying to help them to do their jobs better. Leader must know how to delegate and how to motivate. Leader must look for pressure points and how to set priorities. People work cheerfully with leaders, who care about them, encourage them. Leader should appreciate, acknowledge and praise their small small successes. 'Thank yous' conveyed by them are the feedback received by the leader. This two-way communication shows people that they are on the right track. As a result their spirits are set free; their self-esteem goes up. All this makes colleagues, associates, subordinates go beyond the performance they ever thought possible. Leader should bring people forth rather than beat them. He should make others feel powerful. Feeling powerful literally means feeling 'able'. Encouraging the heart is the most important leadership practices because it is most personal. This way leader creates corporate culture bit-by-bit, brick-by-brick.[6] 'Organisation can achieve high performance by developing leaders at all levels in the organisation; they make extra-ordinary things happen.

Leader has to exhibit skill of forming cohesive, co-operative teams, comprising of individuals coming from different nations, regions, and localities; speaking different languages but having good cultural match.[7] People with good cultural match can be developed by seeing people, hearing them, smelling, testing and feeling them. Good cultural match of the members of the team makes their talent fruitful. People in the team must have congenial temperament. They must be spirited men; men of character and mettle. They must be taught to work as a team, not as a bunch of individuals. Team members have to care for one another. Every member of the team has to do his job well so other members can equally do their jobs well. This is a team spirit. Working well with colleagues is a way to success. Leader must have some ego drive, strong but not large. Leader's responsibility is to balance their career aspirations and developmental needs with the organisational performance objectives. Team formation is to be done carefully by putting key people at right place. This can be done with the help of intensive human capital budgeting or people budgeting. Not only teams but leaders have to re-equip themselves still more to use tools of new technology effectively.

Leader of the team must be proficient in transferring skills to the members of the team. He must possess the skill of transferring personal effectiveness to team effectiveness. Team members have maximal contacts with suppliers and customers; therefore, it is necessary that they possess high levels of communication abilities.

Team leader can sharpen their communication skills and turn them effective, if he is an effective coach. Team leader has maximum contact with team members; that gives him the best opportunity to develop communication skills of the team members. He can do it best if he is an effective coach. Team leader can perform these functions of transferring skills and developing communication capabilities if he thinks purposefully and bases his actions on thinking. Thinking is the most important skill gifted to the team leader. Thinking is a unique human ability to guide and sharpen skills for better performance. The leader must possess ability of lateral thinking that enables him to find different approaches to solve the problems that the team faces or the tasks that the team has to perform. He should have developed the capacity of parallel thinking also; that enables him to think about solutions from different angles and find most appropriate solution by focusing on one thing at a time. However, such approach does not provide the leader as well to the team holistic approach of the problem or to the task that the team has to perform. Edward D. Bono advocates that the team leader can have better experience to transfer skills if he practices multiple thinking. Multiple thinking comprises of – (A) Controlled thinking that enables the leader to seek additional information in a neutral way. (B) With the help of emotive thinking the leader can express his feelings and intuitions clearly and powerfully. (C) On the basis factual thinking the leader can express his thoughts objectively and make his judgement acceptable to all. (D) The leader can look at and analyse data in a logical and positive way if he has capacity of speculative thinking. (E) The leader can offer alternative solutions to the problem or alternative methods of performing tasks on the basis of his power of creative thinking. (F) The team leader can, on the basis of careful thinking, control the process of solving the problems or control the method of performing tasks assigned to the team. Multiple thinking, consisting of these six types of thinking, presents a holistic view of the problem that the team has to resolve or of the task that the team has to perform. An appropriate solution can be reached at, even beating conventional wisdom.

In the flat and lean corporation, of 21st century, in which boundaries of hierarchy, functions and geography have disappeared it is the responsibility of the leader to make these corporations 'one big happy family'.[8] Leader of a company must become 'brand ambassador' of the company embodying values of the firm and ensuring delivery of the results that the firm and society can expect. Impact of leadership process can be assessed and measured by addition to the revenue of the company, reduction in turnover of the employees and client satisfaction. Impact of leadership development effort can be assessed by evaluating participant reaction, knowledge acquired by leaders, by associates and by partners of the company, behavioral change and business results. These leaders are company ambassadors, many a times they are industry leaders too. G.D. Birla, J.R.D. Tata, Jamnalal Bajaj, Azim Premaji, N.R, Narayana Murthy, John Hoppkins, Cecil Rhodes, R.W. Johnson, Andrew Carneji, Levin Zu, Bill Gates are just a few to name. Persons in every organisation cannot become leaders of such a status, of such a stature, but that should be the aim to be cherished for. One important aspect of leader's life to which Peter F. Drucker has drawn attention is managing second half of life.[9] Leaders must in their first part of life prepare for equally successful second half of life by electing new career or parallel career or volunteering for some social activity. Success in earlier half-life depends upon planning for second half of life.

LEADER ORGANISATION

Individual leaders in the organisation discussed in preceding paragraphs are the persons who can run an intelligent business organisation of 21st century. Individual leader has his own individuality, identity; equally so an organisation has its personality. Peter Drucker states,' each organisation has distinct strengths, distinct limitations and specific applications.'[10] Therefore, organisation must be leader of its own so as to establish its identity, entity and social legitimacy. Leader organisation is one having de-layered, lean, flexible structure, catering for present and future needs of the customers to their utmost satisfaction. This it can do by producing quality goods or by providing quality services with the help of skilled, knowledgeable, devoted, committed and satisfied employees constituted in teams. Associate employees seek knowledge from all sources so as to enrich product contents and their self-esteem. Such organisation is responsive to every change that takes place in the environment. It cultivates and maintains cordial relations with all constituents of extended organisation. Leader organisation has to perform various roles and functions.

Firstly, it has to have its own culture based on sound ethical values and proven accepted business practices. Business organisation has to develop its value system based on the turbulent conditions of the 21st century. The value system for 21st century business organisation is exhibited in Table 11.1. The business organisation inherits its values from the past, nurtures them in the present times and develops for the future.

Table 11.1
Value System for Business Organisation

Space Description	*From Past*	*For Present*	*For Future*
Physical Space	Learn and Record	Work and Contribute	Prepare and Equip
Mind Space	Forgive and forget	Give and Take	Intend and Extend
Thought Space	Review and Evaluate	Think and Innovate	Predict and Plan

Secondly, it has to have a well-defined business mission, well laid down strategy and business policy that are known to everybody in the organisation. Thirdly, it should very well know who are its customers, what their needs are, their psychological makeup and ways to satisfy their demands with goods and services they have in mind. Further more, it adopts pleasing and satisfying manners and caring attitude in delivering goods and in providing services. Fourthly, the organisation should develop a cadre of associates, encourage them to acquire skills and knowledge, provide them every avenue to make full use of their skills and knowledge. This will make them feel that the organisation provides them very good opportunities to develop in every possible way. Thus, they will be able to reach out of their expectations and capabilities. Knowledge workers become valued, self-respected assets. One important thing must be taken note of; present organisations are multi-product, multi-divisional and multi-national. Organisation needs to have structure to accommodate its activities in such differentiated environment. Therefore, it is likely that in the same organisation there may exist different structures to match different activities; and these structures co-exist. Organisation may need centralisation in certain areas of activity and complete decentralization in other areas of activity. Thus, an individual employee has to work under different organisational structures at a time He has to work in a team to perform one task. In such a team he enjoys much freedom in choosing the way, the method of doing the work. At the same time he has to work under command and control structure while performing another task. Leader organisation has to develop organisational attitude to accommodate different structures to fit the task and make employees comfortable to work under different conditions. Fifthly, the organisation maintains cordial and friendly business relations with all partners in extended organisation and establishes two-way communication so as to develop trust. The organisation should put small amount as investment in supplier firm as a gesture of commitment so that supplier puts the relations between the two on business terms. The organisation and supplier should maintain a balance of power so that neither the buyer organisation nor the supplier firm takes undue advantage of unwritten part of the contract. The buyer organisation should provide, by a clause in contract agreement, freedom to the supplier firm to sell fifty per cent of his output to competitor firms. This will ensure quality of the components supplied by the supplier firm. Sixthly, the organisation has to take into consideration demographic pattern in market locality while deciding proportion of various products. It should also pay attention to the decisions of customers to spend their disposable income on various products. Finally, the organisation should develop social legitimacy. Business organisation is a conglomeration of many constituents and it has to satisfy all of them. Organisations in 21st century do not achieve their objectives to the 'maximum level' but to 'satisfying level' that makes the organisation a leader organisation. There are a number of illustrations of leader organisations that are looked as models by other firms not only in the same industry but in other industries also. Tata Iron and Steel Company, Infosys Technologies Limited, Larsen & Toubro are to name a few. The way through which the organisation achieves leadership is exhibited in Table 11.2.

Table 11.2
Organisation Leadership

Work Ethics		*Leadership Ethics*	
Attitude	Work	Leadership	Energy
Dedication	Endeavour	Nurturing	Love
Sincerity	Work	Managing	Delegation
Honesty	Contribution	Leading	Empowerment
Nobility	Excellence	Path making	Trust

Not that all individuals in the organisation and all organisations in the country can reach leadership status. However, it should be an earnest effort to achieve that position. That is very necessary to manage the organisation in 21st century. Leadership of an individual and leadership of the organisation are complementary and supportive to each other. In many a cases individual leaders have set their organisations to the status of leader organisation. However, it is not imperative that individual leader alone can develop leader organisation or leader organisation alone can nest individual leader.

Society requires an organisation, a firm, a company to introduce innovations because market by itself cannot introduce any innovation. Organisation must realise that product development is moving up on the value chain. Organisation of the 21st century has to invent, discover new organisational practices that involve self-reinforcing process, develop new approaches to reach new results. Organisations, in the present century, are people centered, knowledge focused and customer oriented. In that sense, behaviour of the organisation is to be such that it becomes 'community of independent entrepreneurs.' In the present century organisations have to be intelligent, visionary and sustainable. They need to stress the ability to keep on going; the ability to sustain something for long period of time; they stress sustainability of renewal. They have to aim for a purpose beyond profit. As J.C. Collins and J.I. Porras argue, that such organisations should exercise ideological control but should grant operational autonomy to managers. They have strict and intense commitment to organisational culture but at the same time they have ability to change, move and adopt.[11] Organisation must balance change and stability. De Geus A. states that 21st century organisations are knowledge companies. They possess ingenuity, innovative ability and knowledge that add value to the company through the optimisation of people as a source of creativity that develop the consistent knowledge base of the enterprise.[12] Such organisations make knowledge more productive.

Success of an organisation depends upon effective use of talented people; 21st century organisation must be talent centered. People are most valuable assets of the organisation. Peter Drucker argues 'the productivity of knowledge is determining factors in the competitive position of the organisation. The only thing matters is management performance in making knowledge productive and introduce organized improvement.'[13] Thus, organisations have to make deliberate effort to collect data, transform it into information and develop it into knowledge. Organisations must realise that information and knowledge are powerful weapons. This knowledge should be preserved by recording it, disseminating it and making it available to employees generating ideas and knowledge. Knowledge must be available at a flip of finger-tip of those, who can make best use of it. That creates competent people.

From 1991 almost all economic activities are globalised. Organisations have to collect resources globally, produce goods in very many countries and market them all over the world. 'Globalisation of industry refers to an evolving pattern of cross border activities of firms, involving international investment, production, sourcing and marketing. These international activities enable firms to enter new markets, exploit their technologies and organisational advantages and reduce business costs and risks. Underlying the international expansion of firms and in part driven by it, are technological advances, the liberalisation of markets and increased mobility of factors of production. These complex patterns of cross border activities increasingly characterise the international economic system and distinguish it from the earlier predominance of arms-length trade in finished goods.'[14] This is how Thomas Clarke and Stewart Clegg define globalisation. Twenty first century corporations have world resources available to them. They raise finance from world capital market and transfer to any location they desire; they can tap ideas from any institution and apply them to any place of production. They can hire people in very many countries and utilise their skill, knowledge, and competence and experience anywhere any time. They are present everywhere at once. Naturally, they have to produce goods and services that are universal in nature but local in use. They have to perform upto world standards, standards of world leaders. Credit/debit cards are an excellent illustration of integration of whole cluster of technologies adopted at global level and used at local sphere. These factors do provide a number of opportunities and challenges and the firm that wins in this competitive war take all markets. Organisations should be conscious of their market standing and they should try to find out changes in the share of income of customers spent on products marketed by them. They should try to measure change in trend and change within the trend.

Organisations functioning at global level have to face grave risks. They employ people coming from different ethnic, cultural, religious, tradition and linguistic background. They are required to be grouped into cohesive, co-operating teams. Making them rise above their differences and unite them in the cause of organisation is rather a difficult task. These people come from different curricula, they have mastered different technologies, and their approaches are different. To bind them into one team motivated to configerate their independent technologies into one new technology and develop new product is an Herculean task. And none of these secrets are to be allowed to be leaked. Global organisations work across boundaries of nations that are governed by different political ideologies, different national laws and rules and complex production and marketing practices. They have to abide by, at a time, by laws and rules of all those countries in which they operate and through which they pass. They have to face and surmount problems arising from fluctuations in currencies. Naturally, impact of globalisation is different on different industries. For example, in respect of science based industries like pharmaceuticals globalisation is based on the criteria of firm-specific advantage and foreign affiliates have a large share of sales in host markets. Naturally, therefore, international trade is largely intra-firm. Collaborations are technology based. As against this, in respect of, scale-intensive industries like motor vehicles and electronics and labour intensive industries like textiles and clothing most of globalisation is restricted to trade, in components in respect of former category of industries and in finished clothing in respect of later.

With globalisation, organisations have come to acquire different structures; newest of them being mother-daughter structure[15] and Keiretsu[16] (the firm is an arm of an industrial group). Many an organisations have become heteraechy[17] an organisation having multiple centers. Most of these structures are temporary in nature. Organisations change their structural architecture with a view to strategically focussing on pre-empting competition. The organisation makes and breaks alliances so as to succeed in fast moving markets. It happens that in such a volatile scenario the organisation may lose its identity temporarily. The fact is that, the organisation has to simultaneously rely on collaboration and competition. This helps the organisation to build partnership with customers that strengthens customers' competitive position and leverages competitiveness of the organisation. As a result, interactions develop between individual leadership and organisation leadership.

In the process of globalisation organisation has to learn to welcome new techniques of production, information technology and new approaches to manage employees. The organisation has to learn many a processes of configuration in each aspect of its structure and functioning. The organisation has to develop intelligent infrastructure and intelligent manufacturing structure such as Manufacturing Resource Planning II. This will allow managers to view and manage production activities of all divisions spread over to many locations in many countries from a single centralised point. This will enable the organisation to optimise efficiency of operations and satisfy all the stakeholders. The organisation will have to produce goods or provide services to customers all over the world considering the tastes, likings and needs of consumers in each of the market segment; in other words, the organisation has to customise its production. Equally so, the organisation has to plan and manage productive activity, alliances, supply partners, considering the regional, lingual, ethnic, traditional practices and work culture; in other word, it has to workmise its workplace also.

CUSTOMISED PRODUCTION WORKMISED WORKPLACE

People no longer want to be unidentified part of the mass. They exhibit their identity with subsets of a homogenous society. Now people have plural, multiple and niche-based foundations of identity. They distinguish themselves on the basis ethnicity, gender, culture, tradition etc. They have individually particular ideas, concepts, and expectations about products that they want to buy with particular satisfaction they desire to derive in satisfying their specific needs. Customers want maximum value to derive from the product at a reasonable price. As they are particular about the quality, characteristic features, ingredients of the product they are also insistent the way the ingenuity, the intensity the hospitality with which the service is rendered to them. In other words, they want individuality in product or service and individuality in the process of marketing the product or the service. As customers they would like to be taken care of by the providers. At many a places they would be interested in participating in designing and processing the product. They would appreciate receiving much more information about the decisions that the organisation makes about the products it produces and the status of the orders they have booked. Customers insist that the products should be user as well as environment friendly. Organisation has to do this observing laws, rules, and practices in each of the countries in which it functions. Customisation of production has gone a long way in the journey of globalisation. Niche-based global markets require flexible production systems. So the firm has to produce products with different features suitable for niches in different markets. Customers want products to be delivered quickly and appreciate new models. This has obliged organisations to reduce design to delivery time to less than twelve months. Organisation has to develop a very complex, fast responding supply chain global logistics to reach this goal. The organisation has to take help of Advanced Planning and Scheduling Packages with Enterprise Resource Planning.

In developing customised models of various products, companies have been introducing new, improved and quality models so fast that many a markets have acquired characteristic features of fashion markets. To cope up with this scenario companies have configurated different technologies so closely and intensely that they have produced maximum number of interchangeable components so that advantages of both the mass production and customised production can be reaped. Multinational corporations follow a strategy of producing one or two key components in one or two of its global centers and supply them to the plants spread over in number of countries all over the world. Thus, each center becomes a cost center. For example, Unilever Global Research Center develops a product that is then produced at all centers of the company. Peter Drucker has given an illustration of Customisation of production from a very interesting perspective. In different countries different products behave differently, they are appreciated differently. Coca-Cola Company though basically a manufacturer and marketer of carbonated cokes, sells fruit juices in France, in Japan one of its major products is coffee dispensed in vending machines and coke in the U.S.A. Though physically these products are different, as business strategy they are the same.[18] Use of interchangeable components is much more in electronic and automobile industries. The company that succeeds in developing maximum number of interchangeable parts can produce a variety of models, a variety of products and reach every niche of segmented world market. Satisfaction of maximum number of customers satisfies the company.

Increasingly organisations have to invite and make supply chain partners co-operate and involve in developing new products, new models, improved models and interchangeable parts. Many a companies have developed partnership with research institutes and universities to take up the work of research and development so that this task can be completed in less time and in less investment. In India agricultural universities and research institutes have provided improved seeds of cereals that ripe in time and are pest resistant; they have also developed new varieties of vegetables and fruits that provide larger yield in less time and are more nutritious. Organisations, in the 21st century have to search out new and newer avenues to spread their domain in every possible direction so as to reach the customers with new novel products before any other organisation thinks of.

It must be realised that in the 21st century, individual employee is no more an object but is subject of management. Individual as an employee has changed so much that he would like to participate in formulation and execution of managerial policies rather than to receive them as commands. Employees as individuals are educated, trained and empowered. They acquire sense of market and they visualise what the customer does not want and what does he desire; employee is also an customer in the market. As educated individuals, employees have acquired opinions about the way of life they should have; their families should have; education their sons and daughters should receive so as to live better life than they have. Many an educated industrial as well as agricultural workers have instituted democratic practices in their families of providing freedom to wives and children. They have given freedom to sons and daughters to choose their educational and career path as well their life partners. New social forms and norms are emerging. They create need for more democratic corporations that will reflect and support increasingly democratised, reciprocal interpersonal relationship.[19] It is natural that employees expect the same democratic atmosphere at their workplace. While accepting employment their commitment is to discharge so much work with quality in the time frame prescribed, in return of remuneration agreed upon. In present century the employees are to be trained in latest technology, state of art, computer operations and practices of zero defect production. They need to be given professional education during their entire working life. The culture of doing the job right first time is to be imbibed in the approach, attitude and behaviour of these employees. These employees want content of the work rich, creative, challenging and satisfying. They wish that they should derive joy out of work. They want good things happen in the organisation. They want some control over the fundamental aspects of the work. Organisations should encourage employees to make suggestions in respect of decisions regarding location of facilities, acquisition of machinery etc. These employees commit to a continuous process of learning to support best in class performance. In response to this, the organisation has to provide freedom to improve their employability by making available opportunities of continuous updating.[20] These employees have a passion to do something new, to innovate and have courage, confidence to make that innovation successful. These employees are a link in the relationship between change and continuity. Hassan, an employee in the paint shop of Honda Motor Cycles and Scooters India Limited at Aurangabad (Maharashtra-India) developed an instrument to reduce the pollution caused by particles of paint spreading in the atmosphere. His innovation was appreciated by the management and he was selected to present his innovation in a convention held in Malaysia. Employees, engineers, managers of Honda plants from all over the world attended the convention. Hassan presented a slide-show to explain his innovation. He was deputed twice to undergo training in paint technology. He knows what are the strengths of Hero-Honda motor cycle and shortfalls of motorcycles of other producers. He has proved his employability. Such employees are assets for the company and therefore not disposable. These employees have developed confidence of abandoning the stability of lifetime employment. In their opinion security of employment comes from performance; and that security is more durable and more satisfying. Such skill advancement improves competitive performance of the organisation. These employees prefer to stay in the company. Many such employees develop intellectual diversity of converging technologies into a new hybrid technology.

Peter Drucker argues that, people working in workmised workplaces must have trust in one another even if they have different opinions. Trusting one another means understanding one another; trusting one another means making relationship responsibility.[21]

As a requirement of smooth functioning of workmised workplace, organisation must share information with employees as much as possible. This will require employees to take the responsibility of organisation's present status and situation. This will establish trust between employees and management and will become core of the employment relationship. Uniformity of trust will bring uniformity in organisational structure. Trust will make organisation and employees mutually accountable. For long time our society has accommodated free enterprise, now time has come to accommodate free persons. This is basic to the concept of 'Quality Circles'.

Organisation, management, workmised workplace, especially knowledge workers must educate associates to prepare for second half of their life. As discussed by Peter Drucker in his book "Management Challenges for the 21st Century', one has to prepare for second half of his life before he 'retires on the job'. However, many a times these thoughts do not occur to many employees, even to knowledge workers. And they rust, get bored and lose charm in life and in work. They lose challenge in their work after 40 plus and their productivity reduces considerably. This makes the organisation suffer. Therefore, to keep interest in his job alive, the organisation has to educate knowledge worker to develop interests somewhere else; something like volunteering in some NGO, social institution, religious or educational institution.

MANAGING THE TWENTY FIRST CENTURY ORGANISATION

Integration of international forces offers many opportunities and poses new challenges before management of organisations. Management has to function in an altogether new, complex and unfamiliar environment of globalised economy. Management has to perform fundamentally different roles and functions in the 21st century ethos as compared to those in 20th century. Foundations of management policy are going to be customer value and decisions of customers regarding distribution of their disposable income between different expenditure avenues. The most important mission of management is creation of value and wealth. Management has to face great risks in achieving these objectives in this turbulent period. At the same time it has to strike a balance between short period profitability and long period share in the market. Management has to mould a lean, delayered, flexible, responsive, intelligent and function oriented world class organisation. The organisation may be local, regional, national or international in character; it has to achieve international standard of performance. Management has to develop an unified organisation where functional, departmental and skill barriers do not exist. Management must become a part of the workforce of the organisation. Thus, development of multi-national, unidirectional, democratic, open organisation is the first function of the 21st century management. An organisation in this century functions in three overlapping spheres of global, national and local character. It has to make decisions and take actions that suit these three overlapping spheres.

Management has to develop healthy, credible and trustworthy practices of governance. This is to be done just not to obey the laws and rules of the country but to observe the laws and rules of the 21st century. The board of directors of the organisation must comprise of persons of long and varied experience, persons of expert knowledge, independent opinion and trustworthy and credible character. The board of directors must have at least one Master Black Belt or at least a Black Belt on it, so as to keep organisation quality conscious by introducing Six Sigma projects. Representation of one chartered accountant is required to keep financial practices fair and transparent and of one cost accountant to introduce total quality management. The board must consider its responsibility and accountability to people who make the organisation and the society. The apex body of the organisation must treat all constituents of the organisation equally and maintain integrity. Every act, every business of the board must be beyond doubt and suspicion.

Organisation of the present century is people oriented, people centered. This has made the job of the management more demanding and complex than before but more creative and exciting. Management has to develop a cadre of associates, who prefer challenging and difficult tasks. Management has to make the organisation, learning organisation, knowledge organisation, and an intelligent organisation. It should develop a culture of long term relationship with all the stake-holders. That enables the organisation to show superior performance. It is a proven fact that people centered organisation earns more profits and lives a long life. T. Donaldson and L.E. Preston argue that' the manager's role is to satisfy a wider set of relationships, not simply the share-holders.[22]

Present century is dawned with a host of new technologies that has touched every aspect, every sphere of our life. Organisations as production units are no exception to that. Adoption of new technology, configurations of different technologies give competitive advantage to the organisation. Therefore, management has to constantly look out for new technology within the industry and outside the industry. Management would have to think of adopting a technology that may be remotely related. Now a days technologies crisscross. Knowledge and adoption of technologies never heard of can revolutionise production process in the organisation and make it a world class producer. There is no one technology that pertains to any industry. Search for new technology, state-of-art is a continuous process that the management has to exercise.

Management must be always in search for 'rising products'. It should also look for novel distribution channels. Management should introduce systematic 'abandonment policy' to write off old, absolete and dead products. Every product has a particular life span. On completion of its role, utility, it should be substituted by a new product. Spirits division of United Breweries group announced on 21st June 2004 its intention to drop production of 12 slow moving liquor brands because some of them have outlived their usefulness and others are superceded with new products like 'ready to drink' category segment brands that are still nascent in India but are very popular and fast growing in western and eastern parts of the hemisphere.

Management should develop new products on the basis of earlier successful products. It is the way to exploit success. Abandonment policy gives new products to the organisation. Companies should develop products with aesthetic qualities.[23] That improves performance and customer satisfaction. Management should seek opportunities for developing new products, list them as per their expected contribution to the organisation. Along with that it should identify people capable of developing these products and allocate most performing and ablest people to tap opportunities. Such experiments require multi-skilled, multi-functional individuals to be organised in a team to develop a hybrid technology by configurating apparently distant, unrelated technologies but fundamentally complementary to one another. In doing so, management should concentrate on non-routine aspects of quality controls, advanced statistical measurement and work redesign. This is the total quality approach called as TQM.

In many a countries, especially in many a states in India, there is a competition among state governments to attract, to invite industrial organisations, information technology companies to establish their plants in respective states. They offer many a concessions, remissions and subsidies. State governments grant tax holidays, provide land, water, and electricity at cheaper price. However, it is not wise to locate a plant in a state or a country because it offers concessions and subsidies unless the management is sure that the economy presents a viable atmosphere for the plant to work without such supports. Management decision to locate a plant at a particular place must be motivated by economic reality rather than by such concessions.

Management should study carefully country-risk analysis report prepared by Economic Intelligence unit of the Economist Group (June 2004) before locating plant. The report has ranked countries on the basis of political and economic risks. Experts maintain that country-risk report comes in handy as a decision-making tool for MNCs to enter or expand in new markets. Report considers security, political stability, government effectiveness, legal and regulatory framework as political factors and macro-economic conditions, financial and tax policy, labour market and infrastructure as economic factors while ranking countries as business destinations. Rapid growth, highly skilled labour and new opportunities in outsourcing are the factors that go in favour of India as safe global business location.

Peter Drucker argues that, if the plant can be established as a part of business strategy it should be wise to deny such concessions and subsidies. The same strategy should be followed by management while merging and acquiring a company. It should be acquisitioned only if it fits into overall strategy of the management. It is not advisable to acquire a loss-making unit just because it gives tax relief. Management has to see that such opportunity advances strategic goal.

Every decision, specially, key decision taken by management should be put on paper, results expected from such action along with the time in which results must fructify should be documented. If possible the expected results should be divided into parts and the time required to achieve that part should be specified. At the end of every span of time, achieved part of the result should be compared with expected performance during that segment of time. Such comparison will serve two purposes. It will provide management an idea as to where does it want to go and where it is going. Management will be able to discover its strengths and weaknesses. Management can put itself where its strengths can produce performance and results. It would have to further fortify its strengths and eliminate weaknesses. This feedback system enables management to pin point the necessity to improve skills and knowledge. A detailed information infrastructure can be developed to bring accuracy in this exercise.

Management should build up relational contracts with suppliers, contracts on the understanding of continuous improvement. These partners should be involved in design decisions also, based on price led costing. Consortium of mother organisation and daughter supplier organisations can help in developing happy marriage of skills of large and small companies. This arrangement facilitates partnership to extend to other activities. An exercise of product development undertaken in partnership with supplier small companies makes both to move up the value chain. Product development itself can become core activity. Supplier companies become responsible for all aspects of components including testing, usability, performance and development of next generation of product. This will enable the mother organisation to create new layer of competitive advantage because it is capable of integrating wider variety of skills and technologies.

Suppliers should establish their production facilities in the vicinity of the organisation so that just-in-time (JIT) delivery schedule can be strictly adhered to and close relationship can be developed. JIT ensures defect free production. This can be furthered by adopting JIKODA principle in designing machine with built in inspection facilities. Routine work can be robotised. Naturally, management of the organisation and of the supplier partners would have to train smart workers to work on these smart machines so that better products satisfying six sigma principle can be produced. This will enable the organisation to be world class organisation — better in its class and better than the competitors at least in producing strategic components.[24]

Information is an important input on the basis of which almost all decisions need to be taken and the health of the organisation can be diagnosed. Information is the basis of knowledge that helps the organisation to build its competence. Information is a commodity that has very many uses. End user requires various kinds of information. Decision-maker requires information about product, cost, sales, technology, life cycle, competitors moves etc. Information is a distinct commodity;

even after selling it owner retains its ownership. As information spreads and is used its value increases. That is why management has to build information network. Information enables the management to know whether it is creating adequate wealth or not. It tells management whether the organisation is prospering or not and if prospering is that rate enough to maintain competitive position in the market. Economic value added analysis, bench marking, measuring performance of core competencies, preparing and analysing capital appropriate budget are a few exercises that are based on information. Conclusions drawn from these exercises tell the management about productivity of knowledge workers.

Management should collect as much information as possible from inside the organisation and from outside the organisation. Both these information should be integrated. Inside information tells the management the facts about the products produced in all their respects. Outside information gives the management an understanding of taxes it has to pay, social legislation, market preferences, intellectual property rights etc. Integration of these two information forms sound basis on which decisions can be taken. Decisions like, what to produce, where to produce, how much to produce and where to sell, needs latest and accurate information.

Information is needed to communicate with colleagues so as to help them in arriving at decisions. Every executive has his own style of work and as such he requires different kind of information. Management should make that information available to the executive. Information provides to the executive perception of things happening in the organisation — this perception is called threshold perception. Information brings to the knowledge of management frequency of unusual and exceptional things happening in the organisation. Management has to take serious note of such unusual and exceptional things if their frequency crosses threshold frequency and should limit their occurrences.

Information makes knowledge worker more productive, creative and innovative. Information regarding various technologies enables knowledge worker to develop a new hybrid technology; it enables him to innovate new product or new way of producing a thing. Peter Drucker states,' knowledge worker's productivity is the biggest of the 21st century management challenges.'[25] Information technology has increased inward focus of management. It enables the management to develop contact with all the partners of extended supply chain. Information provides knowledge to the supplier regarding quantity and quality of components to be produced, order position, delivery time schedule and payment position. As a result supplier partners and the organisation are closely knit so as to further co-operation. The entire decision support system is based on information network. Naturally, quality of decision does depend upon quality of information available to the decision-makers. Entire worldwide logistics enabling management to regulate inventory is based on information system. Information enables the customer to find out the status of his order. That is why management invests huge amounts in developing information network.

Management should introduce activity costing in the organisation. It enables the management to assess the costs incurred on entire product cycle, entire economic chain. Activity costing makes all partners in the supply chain to follow the same accounting practices and share maximum information. This unifies the supply chain. Activity costing enables the management to cover all costs from the point of resource procurement to delivery and follow up processes. Activity costing enables the organisation to undertake price-led costing. That tells the management the price the customer is willing to pay for the product. This determines the cost that the organisation should incur on producing the commodity and accordingly design the product. On the basis of this analysis management can decide the least cost location for production of the commodity and high price segment to market the commodity. Activity costing tells much about the cost centers and profit centers. Management can make efforts to reduce the cost and maximise profits.

Management has to take into consideration exchange rate fluctuations, even if it is a domestic or local company. Rupee has been made fully convertible on current account if not on capital account. Indian farmers, who never cared to know foreign currencies, have to carefully watch rupee-dollar, rupee-pound, and rupee-Euro rates as inputs come from foreign markets and they sell in overseas markets. Every organisation has to manage its foreign exchange exposure.

Employees are comparatively better educated and trained. They are knowledge workers; this is so even if they do manual work. They operate computer-controlled machines and thus they have to be computer literate. They inculcate business values, ethics and professional attitude. Employees show acumen in their task and as far as knowledge of their task is concerned they are in a position to educate their superiors. Naturally they expect courteous treatment at the hands of their superiors; democratic atmosphere in the organisation and creative, challenging and satisfying job at the workplace. Management has to work with such enlightened employees. Employees expect that the management should provide them facilities for learning and training, opportunities for exposure and avenues for employment so that they can become highly skilled workers. This benefits both, the organisations as well as employees. Organisations are benefited because their competitive advantage is improved as better quality products are produced at comparatively lower cost. Employees are benefited because their core competencies are strengthened that improve their employability.

Management has to manage performance of the people more than the people themselves. Management has to understand that different people are to be managed differently and the same people are to be managed differently at different times. People are to be managed in a different way as members of the team and as individuals. Management has to find out methods of getting things done from employees allowing them to work in their own way. Management should, as far as possible let the employees perform the task in which they are good and in the way they can do it best. Management has to inculcate firm ethical values, strong beliefs in the employees. It is not always possible for management to have employees who have values identical to that of the organisation. However, people in the organisation should have developed values that can co-exist with organisational values. That enables employees to give best performance and management best results. Management, instead of trying to provide employment to persons misfit in these days of technological shifts, should improve their employability by providing them opportunity to acquire various skills. Management should try to change their attitude to work individually as well in multi-cultured, multi-functional and multi-skilled teams. Management should analyse multifunctional skills of employees in terms of standard skills. This enables management to make precise analysis of competencies of teams. Management should exhibit graphical displays of these competencies at shop floor so that management can focus attention on areas of relative scarcity. It should be known to teams as a rule that quality is the whole responsibility of the team along with the team leader This nurtures proactive attitude to quality. This trust in quality develops total marketing relationship contacts with customers and buyers. Such arrangement has one advantage, management would not find multi-functional skilled workers redundant in the day of slowdown and scarce in the days of progression. Most successful businesses in the 21st century will be those that best exploit the skills and talents of their employees. The most successful of those businesses will see themselves as creating the conditions in which their employees can make best use of their talents.

Management should introduce flexible employment conditions especially for women employees. They can take off for a period of two to three years during the period of child rearing and join back their job on the same terms and conditions of employment. This arrangement will benefit the organisation as well as women employees. Management should also provide flexible work schedules to employees in their post-retirement age. They can be given less strenuous and less complex jobs. This will be a great social service.

Management would have to follow threefold strategy in respect of workers in India. Many a workers in India are less educated and sparsely trained. Management has to concentrate on improving productivity of these manual labourers by following Fredrick Winslow Taylor's principle of 'task management'. Management's task is to eliminate or at least reduce to the minimum the production that falls below the minimum standard level as prescribed in six sigma principle and total quality management.

There are many knowledge workers employed in Indian industries. It is necessary to improve their productivity. That is the biggest challenge of the 21st century. This can be done by entrusting to knowledge worker the responsibility of fixing his task and giving him freedom to complete the task in scheduled time frame. He has to achieve as many breakthroughs as possible. Knowledge worker should be provided every opportunity to learn and to teach new things to members of his team. So that he can derive satisfaction and improve his competence. Improving productivity of knowledge worker is a task more difficult than the task of improving productivity of manual worker. Peter Drucker argues,' manual worker is a cost and success of management is in reducing it; while knowledge worker is an asset and achievement of management is in maximising its value.

Equally, there are a number of employees in each organisation or establishment whose work contains knowledge work as well manual work. Peter Drucker calls them 'technologists'. As knowledge worker they need to be given full theoretical knowledge of the system of which their job is a part and manual expertise to carry out the task. They should be given autonomy to decide the method, the way of doing the task to the satisfaction of the customer.[26]

Management should implement green technology in all productive activity the organisation undertakes. This is what management owes to the humanity. It is important that management implements environmental strategy. The fact that industrial activity is bound to harm environment is no more acceptable. Therefore, management should in the first instance, adopt measures for pollution control by cleaning up all types of wastes. Secondly, it has to implement pollution prevention measures and improve these measures continuously as it improves total quality. Customers insist that the products they buy, they use should be natural and Eco-friendly. Management must create industrial Eco-systems in which the waste from one process is used as raw material in the next process. Thirdly, it must minimise pollution not only in manufacturing process but from the full life cycle of the product. The organisation should develop design of the product, of the production process and layout of the plant for the environment. So that it can recover, reuse and recycle the products and wastes easily. This will reduce all effects the production process has on the environment. The organisation has to ensure that the consumers while using and disposing of the remains of the product do not harm the environment. Such design for environment must economise the use of materials and energy. This is not a dream; these are not Utopian ideas. The exchange schemes announced by companies for refrigerators, washing machines, television sets have this concept at its base. Reusable components are fitted into fresh products and non-reusable parts are converted into raw material.

Peter Drucker mentions an illustration of Xerox Corporation. It reuses components of leased Xerox machines in manufacturing new machines and saves about $ 300 million a year. As a fourth step, management should develop clean technology. In agriculture this is being done by using bio-fertilisers, manuers and green pesticides like Neem. Development of super concentrated detergents using recycled material and advertising these attributes has improved customer relationship. Improved detergents that require less water for washing off the detergent from clothes has improved acceptability of detergents. Industries in India, specially, engineering and polymer industries need do much in this direction. Sugar factories need install purification plants before releasing their effluents. Management should emphatically include practices of pollution control and environmental protection in their annual reports.

Discussion of management practices that need to be implemented in running intelligent corporation in 21st century contains three aspects, namely —

...ip-individual as well as organisational, customised production and workmised workplace and management in 21st century organisation. The last section includes management task in moulding lean, delayered responsive and intelligent corporation. It should undertake technology development; product development and improvement. It should decide location of organisation plant. The management should do performance appraisal and review relationship with partners. It should maximise use of information and information technology. Management should follow prudent pricing and costing system. Management should introduce and implement pollution free system spread over the entire product cycle from raw material to disposal of the product after use. Management of the 21st century organisation is really an exacting and complex task. The various aspects of management discussed in nine chapters-two through ten- are the basis of discussion done in this chapter. Management to be successful, if not to lead, at least to survive and prosper has to implement all these aspects genuinely and sincerely.

CONCLUSION

The theme of the book, as stated in the first chapter, is to outline and discuss managing the 21st century intelligent corporation. In present days of close and complex business world, management has to plan and execute its own activities. Management has to, at the same time, search what other organisations, other industries desire to do. Management has to make its own organisation intelligent by becoming 'the stochastic competitor' and at the same time employ business intelligence agents to know what others are doing. Management has to develop, in collaboration with supply chain partners, products so simple in design but complex in technology that rival organisation cannot copy and cannot imitate. It has to continuously develop new products, new models of earlier products with the help of homogeneous teams, so fast and display on shelves before competitors can copy earlier version of the product. The management has to benchmark world class practices and implement through total quality management program based on six-sigma philosophy. Management must develop long term relationship with all constituents because it gives neat footing inside the customer's business. It enables the organisation to project the inputs it will require and finance it has to arrange. All this can be done if the organisation possesses firm information and knowledge base. Management should make every effort to learn from every bit of information and experience and build its success step-by-step, brick-by-brick.

An organisation to be successful, in the present century, has to make good amount of home- work and take steps, arrive at decisions, on the conclusions drawn from that rigorous exercise of home-work. Management of such organisation has to dedicate, devote itself to the cause of business to make all in the organisation to plunge into the task of creating successful organisation.

Many a concepts discussed in this book, though apparently seem to be addressed to large organisations; they are equally applicable to small and medium sized organisations. Management is scale neutral except for its scope and spread. Our effort is to develop, build an organisation that not only survives in 21st century but moulds the present century to the cause and welfare of the humanity, peace to the polity and green to the environment.

References

(1) Drucker Peter F., *Management Challenges for the 21st Century Corporation*, Butter-worth-Heinemann, 1999, p. 29.

(2) Drucker Peter F., *Ibid.* p. 84.

(3) Chowdhury Subir, *Management* 21 C.

(4) Drucker Peter F., *Op. cit.* p. 73.

(5) Levin Stuart R., *The Value-based Edu-leader, in Management 21C*-Ed. Chowdhury Subir.

(6) Hill Linda A., *Leadership as a Collective Genius in Management 21C.*

(7) Hill Linda A., *Ibid.*

(8) Fulmer Robert M. and Goldsmith Marshall, *Future Leadership Development in Management 21C*, Ed. Chowdhury Subir.

(9) Drucker Peter F., *Op. cit.*, pp. 188-195.

(10) Drucker Peter F., *Op. cit.*, p.11.

(11) Collins J.C. and Porras J.I., Successful Habits of Visionary Companies, London, Century, 1996, p. 44.

(12) de Geus A., *The Living Company*, London, Nicolas Brealy,1997.

(13) Drucker Peter F., *Post Capitalist Society*, Butterworth-Heinemann, 1993/ New York, Harper Collins, 1993.

(14) Clarke Thomas and Clegg Stewart, *Changing Paradigms- The Transformation of Management Knowledge for 21 the Century*, Harper Collins Business, 2000, p. 61.

(15) Clarke Thomas and Clegg Stewart *Ibid.* p. 101.

(16) Clarke Thomas and Clegg Stewart *Ibid.* p. 101.

(17) Hedlund G. The Hyper-modern MNG: A Hierarchy? *Human Resource Management*, Spring 1986, pp. 9-35.

(18) Drucker Peter F., *Op. cit.*, p. 66.

(19) Bouchikhini Hamid and Kimberley John R., *The Customised Workplace in Management 21C* Ed. Chowdhury Subir.

(20) Kanter R.M., 'The New Management World', *Harvard Business Review*, Nov.-Dec. 1989, pp. 85-92.

(21) Drucker Peter F., *Op. cit.* p.187.

(22) Donaldson T. and Preston L. E., 'The Stakeholder Theory of the Corporation: Concepts, Evidence and Implications', *Academy of Management Review*, Vol. 20, Issue 1, 1995, p. 75.

(23) Schmitt B.H. and Simonson, *Marketing Aesthetics*, New York, Free Press, 1997.

(24) Hodgetts R.M., Luthans F. and Lee S.M. 'New Paradigm Organisations: From Total Quality to Learning to World Class', *Organisation Dynamics*, Vol. 22, Issue 3, Winter, 1994, p. 14.

(25) Drucker Peter F., *Op. cit.* p. 157.

(26) Drucker Peter F., *Ibid.* pp. 149-154.

❑ ❑ ❑

31